Praise for C

"Beckman and Long provide the reader with a wide range of case studies that demonstrate how community-based research [CBR] can impact the community for good. They distill useful lessons and principles to guide the development of partnerships that organize collaborative research work in ways that demonstrably impact the community to bring about changes that promote social justice. This book fills a gap in the development of the CBR field while simultaneously equipping CBR partners to engage in meaningful, transformative work."—*Sam Marullo, Professor of Sociology and Director of Wesley Theological Seminary's Institute for Community Engagement; former Professor and Chair of Sociology and Senior Research Fellow at Georgetown University Center for Social Justice*

"This volume is an outcome of a federal grant designed to support and expand the practice of high-quality community-based research in colleges and universities across the United States. This book shows how it is possible to emphasize both student learning and community impact. The principles of community-based research are grounded in practical examples from a variety of disciplines; the range of models and disciplines should spark new ideas for courses and long-term community collaborations."—*Trisha Thorme, Director, Community-Based Learning Initiative (CBLI), Princeton University; and Coleader of the Corporation for National and Community Service Grant "National Community-Based Research Networking Initiative"*

"Never before have the opportunities for campus-community research partnerships been so abundant and diverse. Hospitals, social service agencies, juvenile corrections, education, and health services are just a few of the community-based organizations wanting to measure the validity of their work through outputs, outcomes, and impact. However, these organizations do not usually have staff with the skill-set to develop meaningful research. For years, community-benefit investment was measured by process indicators, such as program attendance, or satisfaction surveys. Speaking from the community, we did not know how to begin, nor have the scientific discipline to reach decision-making indicators, which would lead to change and ultimately, to constructive change over-time.

Community-Based Research: Teaching for Community Impact is like an operation manual for moving from the publish-or-perish doctrine to conducting real-world research, which can make significant differences to where you work, live, and play. CBR can be a powerful conduit to improving the well-being of the community, while simultaneously educating all the various individuals engaged in the resolution of an issue or problem. Collaboration, communication, synergism, innovation, respect, and transparency are identified as key components for transformative change on a large scale. The authors drill to the epicenter of identifying targets for change, decisions being made, and moves outward to the valid measurement for long-term, sustainable change within the community."—*Margo DeMont, PhD, Executive Director, Community Health Enhancement, Memorial Hospital of South Bend, Indiana*

"Community-based research changes lives. This book can transform the way you teach and do research and the impact your work has on students and communities near and far."—*Daniel Lende, Associate Professor of Anthropology, University of South Florida*

"Bringing the university and the community into effective learning and mutual contribution is one of our country's greatest needs. This book provides both breadth and depth in CBR and gives insights into the future direction of moving service-learning into community enhancement."—*Rev. Dr. Carmen Porco, CEO, Housing Ministries of American Baptists in Wisconsin; and President, Porco Consulting*

COMMUNITY-BASED RESEARCH

COMMUNITY-BASED RESEARCH

Teaching for Community Impact

Edited by Mary Beckman and
Joyce F. Long

Foreword by Timothy K. Eatman

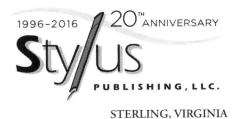

1996-2016 20ᵀᴴ ANNIVERSARY

Stylus
PUBLISHING, LLC.

STERLING, VIRGINIA

Published by Stylus Publishing, LLC.
22883 Quicksilver Drive
Sterling, Virginia 20166-2102

Library of Congress Cataloging-in-Publication Data
Names: Beckman, Mary, editor. | Long, Joyce F., editor.
Title: Community-based research : teaching for community
impact / edited by Mary Beckman and Joyce F. Long ; foreword by
Timothy K. Eatman. Description: First edition. |
Sterling, Virginia : Stylus Publishing, LLC, 2016. |
Includes bibliographical references and index.
Identifiers: LCCN 2015028425|
    ISBN 9781620363553 (cloth : alk. paper) |
    ISBN 9781620363560 (pbk. : alk. paper) |
    ISBN 9781620363577 (library networkable e-edition) |
    ISBN 9781620363584 (consumer e-edition)
Subjects: LCSH: Community and college. | Service learning. |
Education, Higher--Social aspects.
Classification: LCC LC237 .C614 2016 | DDC 378.1/03--dc23
LC record available at http://lccn.loc.gov/2015028425

13-digit ISBN: 978-1-62036-355-3 (cloth)
13-digit ISBN: 978-1-62036-356-0 (paperback)
13-digit ISBN: 978-1-62036-357-7 (library networkable e-edition)
13-digit ISBN: 978-1-62036-358-4 (consumer e-edition)

Printed in the United States of America

All first editions printed on acid-free paper
that meets the American National Standards Institute
Z39-48 Standard.

First Edition, 2016

10   9   8   7   6   5   4   3   2   1

To Ken Briggs and Robert Long

CONTENTS

vii

FIGURES AND TABLES

Figures

Tables

FOREWORD

In an era of dynamic communication conventions enabled by our interactions through the Internet, I relish this, my first opportunity to use a hashtag for a piece of writing in a physical book. I am compelled to do so in this instance after being struck by the intentionality of this volume and its cut-to-the-chase design and energy. Hashtags, succinctly chosen words preceded by a number sign commonly used in social media, help us bring concentrated attention to an idea or aspect of contemporary life. In most cases this involves technologically enabled engagement among people from a range of demographic backgrounds, disciplines, and corners of society. Similarly, Beckman and Long have edited a robust collection of scholarly insights and gleanings on the importance and power of community-based research (CBR) with a very clear and unapologetic purpose. Their bottom line is that the purpose of CBR has a positive and powerful impact on communities. Likewise, this volume strengthens a variety of fields in many ways, especially by homing in on the signature elements of CBR and providing lucid examples of how to activate CBR as a pedagogical tool.

As a resource to assist scholars and practitioners who wish to effectively conduct CBR, this volume provides useful suggestions for facilitating the process and substantive examples of research projects within a range of disciplines and at different stages of development. Equally important is its potential to serve as an instrument to facilitate strategic thinking and a design for research undertakings that lead to ameliorative outcomes and impact in the communities where the work is done. As such, this book advances the field significantly and helps move us toward these purposes in a focused manner.

The aims of this volume are needed to strengthen the field, but the focus on CBR impact helps us to attend to critical but often overlooked ethical issues of engagement research. Some scholars have argued that the myriad issues of ethical verity may be the area of greatest vulnerability for community-engaged scholarship and work (Newman & Glass, 2015; Stoecker, 2005).

As faculty codirector of Imagining America: Artists and Scholars in Public Life (IA), a national consortium of more than 100 colleges, I have the good fortune to come in contact with a wide range of publicly engaged scholars who work at the nexus of the cultural disciplines—humanities, arts, and design—and community engagement and social justice. Colleagues in the IA network celebrate the power of creating knowledge through methodological approaches such as CBR, action research, community-based participatory research, and participatory action research, to name a few. Similarly, readers from any discipline will find in this book thoughtful links to disciplinary practice with interdisciplinary and transdisciplinary inflections.

In a keynote address titled "Engagement Across the Faculty Roles: Mission, Method and Momentum" (Eatman, 2015), I urged colleagues to appreciate the fullness of engaged learning by keeping its mission in clear focus: to strengthen our democracy. To be sure, when effectively and skillfully conducted, CBR supports the mission of engaged learning, and institutions of higher education represent a ripe milieu for this work. Yet this *mission* has no teeth without *methods*. This book likewise presents a powerful set of methodological choices to advance the mission and to provoke the kind of momentum needed to sustain the field. As the reader delves into this treasure of thoughtful, carefully designed and grounded scholarship, I urge you to actually use #CBR4Impact to punctuate the findings and gleanings documented herein. By doing so, you can contribute to the momentum of the movement for publicly engaged scholarship.

Timothy K. Eatman
#CBR4Impact

References

Eatman, T. K. (2015). *Engaged scholarship across the faculty roles: Mission, method and momentum.* Retrieved from leccap.engin.umich.edu/leccap/viewer/r/99R6Ln

Newman, A., & Glass, R. D. (2015). Ethical and epistemic dilemmas in empirically-engaged philosophy of education. *Studies in Philosophy and Education, 34*(2), 217–228.

Stoecker, R. (2005). *Research methods for community change: A project-based approach.* Thousand Oaks, CA: Sage.

ACKNOWLEDGMENTS

From Mary Beckman

This book was conceived through conversations (around 2005) with my colleague Naomi Penney over how to better evaluate our community-based research (CBR) grant program at the University of Notre Dame. We were largely motivated by two questions: What contributions resulted in our geographic community from research funded through the CBR grant program we ran? How could we design the grant-funding program to have an even bigger impact? I am grateful to Naomi Penney, who was the catalyst in helping me shape this book project.

Our search for others with the same interest in community impact was enhanced when Trisha Thorme invited us to participate as subgrantees in a Corporation for National and Community Service (CNCS) grant for developing a network of CBR initiatives on U.S. campuses. Through participation in the work funded by this grant, I met colleagues with similar concerns, and a number of them became contributors to this book. I am appreciative to Trisha for opening this door.

The first of those grant colleagues I talked with about the book was Jennifer Pigza, the initial coeditor of this volume. When she bowed out because of other commitments, she continued to urge me on.

My thinking developed significantly while I was coauthoring a book chapter with Randy Stoecker. His perspectives were formative, and I am enduringly grateful.

I'm also grateful to my Center for Social Concerns colleagues, who were receptive and patient as my ideas developed. Angela Miller McGraw (now at Georgetown University), Andrea Smith Shappell, Rachel Tomas Morgan, Annie Cahill Kelly, Jay Brandenberger, and Connie Mick were each willing to incorporate the fledgling ideas into their work in some fashion and added insight to my own evolving thoughts. I am also grateful to Jay Brandenberger and Fr. Paul Kollman for their support.

Thanks also go to my CBR colleagues in South Bend, Indiana. I thank Debra Stanley, Jay Caponigro, Daniel Lende (now at the University of South Florida), Dennis Jacobs (now at Santa Clara University), Stuart Greene, and Jim Frabutt, whose innovative applications of CBR helped me refine my ideas about how to attain community impact. Daniel was instrumental in the creation of a university CBR learning community that I facilitated. Felicia LeClere helped me give form to the grant program that Naomi and I subsequently ran. John Borkowski prodded me to articulate more fully the value of CBR.

I would also like to acknowledge my coeditor, Joyce F. Long. Our joint work with the Education Collaborative Group in South Bend helped me clarify the community impact framework described in this book. I was grateful when she agreed to coedit because she was the perfect person for it. She is a devoted, capable university teacher, a highly valued community partner, and an excellent editor. It is to my great benefit that she dove in and made the project her own.

Finally, I would like to thank Rod Ganey, who has funded most of the work in CBR that I've had the privilege of guiding since I arrived at Notre Dame in 2001. I remain indebted to him for his commitment to the local South Bend area, for the force of his belief that this privileged university should share its research resources in the community, and for placing confidence in me to carry on this effort.

From Joyce F. Long

My first excursion into CBR began with a small gathering of campus faculty and public school principals, who met for three years over dinner, to design and implement research that could transform instruction and learning. I am grateful for every person who was committed to that Educational Collaborative Group (ECG). Our projects shaped my belief that CBR can empower student learning, collegial relationships, and community problem solving.

I initially met Mary Beckman in that group, and this book is just one example of the fruit that continues to emerge from our original camaraderie. Mary is a diligent advocate in refining and expanding the reach and effectiveness of CBR in our community and other nations. It is an honor to be her partner on this project. She is a capable leader under fire and knows exactly how to challenge my understanding of what is possible. She is dedicated to being inclusive, so this book is actually an invitation to join CBR's ever expanding merry band of provocateurs.

I am especially thankful for Stuart Greene, former codirector of the Educational, Schooling, and Society program at Notre Dame, and Darice Austin-Phillips, a local primary school principal. We worked together on an ECG parent involvement project that lasted for multiple years and various iterations. We became different people because we allowed our work to transform us. Darice introduced me to a host of local educators and potential collaborators, including John Ritzler and other local school district personnel, who invited me to collaborate with them. Stuart provided numerous opportunities to freely design new classes and build engagement in CBR. Both inspire and model true collaboration, passion for educational equity, and creative freedom.

I want to honor the board members of No Parent Left Behind (NPLB) and the Latino Task Force for Education for their practical help and steadfast hearts. I also applaud all my undergraduate student partners, who participated in CBR courses and faithfully labored with NPLB. They generously served the community, tackled difficult research questions, and enthusiastically searched for deeper meaning in nuanced words and survey trends. Each of those scholars in training invested dedication, labor, and insight toward our pursuits.

The participants in our CBR projects blew me away with their intense levels of vulnerability and honesty. Whether school dropouts or parents, they had solid dreams for themselves and their children. They possessed vital wisdom for improving learning and generously shared their ideas when we assured them of their value. I still treasure their ideas and friendships today.

Finally, I extend a bouquet of thanks to my colleagues at the Community Health Enhancement Department of Memorial Hospital-South Bend. For the past two years, I have benefitted from Margo DeMont's visionary leadership and Patty Willaert's remarkable management of details. We enjoy creating an atmosphere where people can ask hard questions and become inspired to obtain positive community outcomes and impact.

From Mary Beckman and Joyce F. Long

We want to thank Patrena Kedik, who has been a stalwart, good-humored assistant through the final part of the process, and Christina McDonnell for assistance with editing. We also thank our editor at Stylus, Sarah Burrows, for her suggestions for synthesizing the content, as well as her colleagues in the production department. We are particularly grateful to Alexandra Hartnett for her efforts to move this project forward. Special appreciation goes out to Tim Eatman as well as to our colleagues in the field who took the time to read our draft and offer comments for the cover. We are grateful to Center for Social Concerns colleagues John Guimond, JP Shortall and Nathalia Casiano for their assitance with design issues. Appreciation goes out as well to our colleagues in the field who took the time to read our draft and offer comments for the cover, and especially to Tim Eatman. Huge gratitude especially goes to the contributors to this volume, which has been in progress for a long time. We have been demanding editors, asking for many revisions, but they have cooperated and also challenged us. They were incredible allies, patient and diligent at every phase of development. We hope they are proud and happy with the results of their effort. We are honored to highlight their important work.

INTRODUCTION

Mary Beckman and Joyce F. Long

This book is about the use of participatory research to create beneficial change—change in us as teachers, scholars, practitioners, students—and perhaps most strikingly, change in the communities in which we, our families, and our neighbors reside, work, and desire to thrive. What we describe can be messy, because research is not always a neat and tidy process. Like other empirical projects, community-based research (CBR) can tackle an issue that is complex and resistant to one-dimensional solutions. Nonetheless, we believe these pages will encourage you to engage in the type of investigative work that can maintain and expand the vitality and growth of your family, neighborhoods, and community. If you are already doing CBR, we hope your commitment to its potential will be strengthened as you read the chapters that follow.

Let's start with some definitions and background. *CBR* is a form of investigation in which the question to be studied arises from the needs of a group of individuals, such as undocumented workers or people who are homeless; from a concern of a nonprofit organization; or from the interwoven social challenges a geographic or other type of community faces. CBR aims to assist in empowering individuals, building organizational capacity, and ultimately fostering positive social change—and many would say social justice—on a local level (Marullo et al., 2003).

The term *CBR* came into use in the 1990s as an extension of the well-known teaching and learning pedagogy called service-learning, in which students make contributions in off-campus communities as part of their course work (e.g., Eyler & Giles, 1999). The field has produced many publications that help guide faculty members to understand and facilitate service-learning, such as the American Association for Higher Education's Series on Service-Learning in the Disciplines (2015), guidelines for course construction (Heffernan, 2001), and *Partnerships for Service-Learning: Impacts on Communities and Students* (Kelshaw, Lazarus, & Minier, 2009). Work continues to expand upon the extant literature by conceptualizing service-learning in modern university and community settings (e.g., Bringle, Hatcher, &

Jones, 2012; Kronick & Cunningham, 2013; Vogelgesang, Drummond, & Gilmartin, 2012).

While some of the lessons from service-learning translate to the work of CBR, the particularities of building and sustaining course-based CBR require specific attention. Until now, however, there has been no elaborated collection of experiences on incorporating CBR into student academic learning. This book presents innovative ways of integrating and implementing CBR across curricula and higher education institutions, as well as in single academic endeavors.

The book has another focus as well; it pertains to what happens in communities when CBR is used. While anecdotal evidence suggests that students frequently praise the courses in which they learn and apply this approach to doing research as outstanding learning experiences (see Chapter 4), it is not enough to practice this form of research simply because it is an excellent pedagogical method. Even if CBR always achieved superb student learning, its findings can also ultimately have an effect on some community organization, a community process or issue, or even a community as a whole, if guided to do so. And we believe CBR should be directed in this way.

Although contributing to social improvement is an element of the definition of *CBR* (Strand, Marullo, Cutforth, Stoecker, & Donohue, 2003), related literature shows scant documentation of such success (e.g., Currie et al., 2005) despite recent public calls to consider impact and engagement at the community level (Beckman, Penney, & Cockburn, 2011; Kania & Kramer, 2011). Furthermore, examination of links between CBR and actual broad community development results, such as reductions in crime or improvements in high school graduation rates, are strikingly missing. With so little tracking of community results linked to CBR, it is not surprising that the focus on ways CBR projects might be designed to actually enhance the possibility of real-world improvement is lacking. This book has been written to address this deficit by providing guidance for those engaged in CBR to design and conduct research that targets community change.

Emphasis on Teaching

We conceived this book while working as subgrantees in a project funded by the Corporation for National and Community Service (CNCS) called the National Community-Based Research Networking Initiative. The University of Notre Dame, where we were both working at the time, participated with more than 30 other higher education institutions in the United States to develop an infrastructure for CBR in colleges and universities across the country over a four-year period from August 2006 to August 2010. One pressing issue that concerned the CNCS grant leaders and many of the subgrantees was the lack of guidance for faculty members on how to develop and teach classes involving CBR. For example, one of the signature volumes describing CBR includes only two chapters about CBR as a teaching strategy (Strand et al., 2003), and *Research Methods for Community Change: A Project-Based Approach* (Stoecker, 2005) serves as a research methods text rather than a guide for faculty members who may wish to integrate CBR into nonmethods courses.

To begin addressing this need, the CNCS-funded network published a collection of several white papers (e.g., Pigza & Beckman, 2010) and compiled a number of case studies (National Community-Based Research Networking Initiative, 2010). This book goes further, presenting a collection of examples on the use of CBR in student learning. The content in the chapters in Part Two provides specific guidance for effectively incorporating CBR into classes, shows ways to integrate CBR into entire curricula, explains how individual student research can be supported, and highlights cross-campus academic endeavors. Additionally, Chapters 10 and 14 focus on using CBR in graduate studies courses, and Chapters 11 and 17 describe international experiences. This content gives readers the knowledge needed to implement CBR into a variety of venues.

Assisting Community Improvement

Another concern that emerged from the four-year CNCS grant initiative was related to the contributions of CBR in local communities. Some of the questions subgrantees posed were: Is CBR effective in contributing to social improvement or attaining social justice goals? How could it be designed to be more useful? The grant resources for assessment supported, primarily, the evaluation of student learning and student development (Lichtenstein, Thorme, Cutforth, & Tombari, 2011) and not the effects of the research in and on communities. Therefore, questions relative to community and societal effects could not be answered.

This need for linking research to observable, measurable, positive social change has been widely and increasingly recognized in recent years across a number of academic fields. In the "fields of health promotion, education, community development, science and technology, and research utilization," it has been noted that there have been "no generic, comprehensive models of types of impacts that reveal the real-world relevance of research partnerships" (Currie et al., 2005, p. 401). At the same time that members of disciplines were noting this absence, a strong and definitive call was coming from multiple directions for a greater focus of national attention toward community outcomes. In 2010, for the first time, the CNCS asked applicants seeking recognition on its honor roll of community-engaged campuses to identify community outcomes associated with the engagement they were describing. Likewise, conferences that heretofore have given modest notice to the effects in communities of academic community engagement are calling more and more for presentation proposals that describe such work and are even centering their national gatherings on the subject. For example, the title of the annual conference of the International Association of Research in Service Learning and Community Engagement in Chicago in November 2011 was Research for Impact: Scholarship Advancing Social Change.

To support the exploration of connections between CBR and community outcomes, the CNCS grant leaders invited Randy Stoecker and Mary Beckman to lead a session on the subject at the group's third annual meeting. Subsequently, Stoecker and Beckman (2010) led a small learning community on the same topic during the summer of 2009 for Campus Compact, an organization of over 1,000 member campuses designed to support academic community engagement. Stoecker, Beckman, and Min (2012) went on to describe the lack of attention on the part of higher education institutions to their effects in their local environs and outlined the causes behind this inattention, suggesting changes that would have to occur for higher education to become a better citizen. Following this, Beckman, Penney, and Cockburn (2011) published a framework they had been developing to enhance CBR's contribution to long-term positive social change in their local community (see also Beckman & Long, 2013). This framework is laid out in a further developed form in Chapter 2, providing a context for much of the work described in Part Three of this volume.

The potential always exists for research efforts to assist community change. It is important for any practitioner of CBR to be equipped to provide students not only with authentically motivating learning experiences but also with ones that are aimed at creating transformative changes in communities. This book assists with this challenge.

Overview

Each of the three parts of this book begins with a general description of its contents and its purpose.

Part One: Definitions, Orienting Frameworks, and Partners

Part One contains four chapters, which lay the foundation for the rest of the book. Chapter 1 contextualizes CBR in the realm of engaged and applied scholarship, providing definitions of various terms and methods used in CBR. Chapter 2 provides guidance for developing and carrying out CBR projects that contribute to community improvement over time. Chapters 3 and 4 offer perspectives from CBR collaborators: the community and campus partners.

In Chapter 1, "The Language and Methods of Community Research," James M. Frabutt and Kelly N. Graves introduce terms and definitions that describe research in the community, including *community-based participatory research*, *action research*, and *participatory action research*, which are variations on the concept of CBR used in this book. The authors also describe the signature elements of the CBR approach and how CBR is used in conjunction with methods employed across disciplines.

In Chapter 2, "The Role of Community-Based Research in Achieving Community Impact," Mary Beckman and Danielle Wood present an approach for conceiving and conducting CBR in such a way that it will contribute to community improvement over time. This involves situating CBR initiatives in community-wide ongoing efforts, such as coalitions focusing on long-term impacts.

Jessica Quaranto and Debra Stanley bring community partner voices to this volume in an explicit way in Chapter 3, "Community-Based Research From the Perspective of the Community Partners." By reflecting on their own experiences with CBR and citing other community collaborators whose projects are discussed in this book, they share the importance of addressing issues such as power differentials, historical factors, and stereotypes that might get in the way of productive CBR. They offer strategies for addressing partnership challenges, including the use of storytelling, and end their chapter with a summary of the do's and don'ts of CBR for students and faculty.

Chapter 4, "Why Teach Community-Based Research? A Story of Developing Faculty Interest," by Joyce F. Long, Paul Schadewald, and Brooke Kiener, presents the findings from interviews of 16 faculty members at five institutions to determine their motivation for using CBR in their courses. Their findings reveal how an interest in teaching with CBR can develop over time and is strengthened through positive community outcomes.

Part Two: Guiding Community-Based Research Toward Community Outcomes and Student Learning

Part Two has two primary goals: to introduce fundamental concepts and principles associated with the effective teaching and practicing of CBR and to provide faculty with a number of perspectives on how these concepts and principles can be used in various academic disciplines and curricular arrangements toward attaining community outcomes. The discussion introducing

Part Two includes a description of effective higher education pedagogy and its authentic application in teaching CBR courses. This creates a general context for the experiences of the contributors who facilitated specific initiatives that achieved varying levels of campus and community effects. Although most faculty members are already extensively trained on how to conduct academic research, this section provides guidance on how to integrate and use research expertise in ways that can benefit local neighbors and communities.

Chapter 5, "The POWER Model: Five Core Elements for Teaching Community-Based Research," provides a shorthand method for faculty, community partners, and students to learn about outcome-oriented CBR. Using the acronym of POWER, Jennifer M. Pigza discusses how implementing the following elements creates the structure for an effective CBR course: cultivating partnerships (on and off campus), determining objectives (for faculty, course, and community), working (i.e., the actual process of the research activity, the partnerships, students learning), evaluating (the research, course, and partnerships), and reflecting (with faculty, students, and community partners to strengthen the learning outcomes for all). This chapter is useful for beginners as well as more experienced CBR practitioners who desire to expand the effects of their research projects on communities, providing a good template with numerous examples.

In Chapter 6, "Applying the POWER Model in a Second-Language Class," Rachel Parroquin discusses her experience of introducing a CBR unit into an advanced Spanish class. Using Pigza's POWER model and contributions from Emily Geiger-Medina, an undergraduate student in the class, she describes the class's analysis of a parent involvement program that offers workshops to Spanish-speaking parents.

Christopher S. Ruebeck describes his CBR course in Chapter 7, "Multicampus Partnerships Studying the Feasibility of Buying Local," as part of a multiuniversity research collaboration on buying local foods. While students from two other campuses focused on other aspects of the wide-scale project, Ruebeck's students conducted market research using regression and qualitative research methods. In addition to describing how the CBR work at his college was integrated into the larger partnership, Ruebeck elaborates on how these efforts aligned with Pigza's POWER model. This chapter is intended to not only help faculty identify and anticipate the requirements, challenges, and benefits associated with participating in a larger cross-campus network but also provide a relevant example of a multilayered productive relationship with a community partner.

In Chapter 8, "Meeting the Objectives of Faculty Engagement in Undergraduate Community-Based Research Projects," Anna Sims Bartel and Georgia Nigro describe how an interdisciplinary, cocurricular CBR Fellows

Program at a college with a strong commitment to CBR offers distinct ways to advance community outcomes along with student learning. With broad institutional support in place, undergraduate students are encouraged and given the freedom to pursue individual projects, which leads to a broad range of complex partnerships and outcomes. They also discuss how a campus civic engagement center can help form peer learning communities that foster best practices in CBR and shepherd departments and students toward projects that are useful, reciprocal, and sustainable. This chapter should be useful to readers as they consider ways disciplines enhance and constrain undergraduates' capacity for CBR.

Ethan Berkove in Chapter 9, "Mathematical Modeling + a Community Partner = the Fulfillment of Student Learning Objectives," focuses on one particular CBR project with Rising Tide, an organization that provides microloans at an affordable rate to small businesses in Lehigh Valley, Pennsylvania. His students participated in CBR to assist the organization in becoming more financially self-sufficient.

In Chapter 10, "Strategic Training Goals: Preparing Graduate Students to Conduct School-Based Action Research," Anthony C. Holter and James M. Frabutt describe a series of action research courses for master of arts students in educational administration who work in Catholic schools across the United States. This graduate four-course sequence equips teachers and principals to investigate needs in their own schools that when addressed, result not only in strengthened local communities but also in broadly improved Catholic education. They also offers insight on how to handle the challenge of working with students who are at remote locations across the United States and only meet for a limited number of weeks during two consecutive summers.

Elizabeth Tryon and Norbert Steinhaus present CBR in a global context in Chapter 11, "Working Through the Challenges of Globally Engaged Research," by providing the reader with a sense for the CBR networks that have formed in recent years across the globe. Although student and faculty experiences in Ecuador and Kenya are featured, the chapter also includes a European perspective as Steinhaus works with the Science Shop model, an approach analogous to this country's CBR. In addition, they highlight a three-country European Union partnership and an example of what might be called *reverse CBR*, in which lessons learned in Germany were tried in Wisconsin. Practical challenges and solutions for conducting CBR outside the United States are described to appropriately equip faculty for such explorations.

In Chapter 12, "Deepening Levels of Engagement: What Works, What Doesn't, and the Important Role of a Community-Based Research Center," Judith Owens-Manley describes the role of a community research director in facilitating and negotiating CBR projects at Hamilton College. Four course projects are evaluated in terms of how well they fulfill three basic principles for good CBR. The chapter also includes a description of the varied roles a CBR center director can perform in supporting community-engaged education. These variations help faculty reflect upon what works well in different circumstances and realize the importance of building continuity into relationships with the community, whether they are upheld and maintained by faculty themselves or campus center coordinators. The projects represent a variety of disciplines including public policy, computer science, government, women's studies, and art.

Chapter 13, "Engagement With the Common Good: Curriculum and Evaluation of a Long-Term Commitment," describes CBR conducted in a long-standing partnership through a regularly offered course that is part of an innovative four-year curriculum at Cabrini College called Engagement in the Common Good. Amy Lee Persichetti and Beth Sturman explain how their years of collaborating in this effort have achieved outcomes that benefit campus and community partners alike. The third contributor, Jeff Gingerich, helps the reader understand the curricular structure for the course and how the philosophical underpinnings of the course theory can be articulated through its design and learning outcomes. The chapter also grapples with the complexity of assessing the transformative learning claimed to be achieved through the curriculum.

Jody Nicholson describes her CBR experience in Chapter 14, "Reflections on a Graduate Student's Dissertation Experience Using Community Data for Research and Mentoring." For three years as a doctoral student, she created and then directed a CBR initiative aimed at mitigating the high prevalence of subthreshold exposure to lead poisoning among children in a neighborhood in South Bend, Indiana. The chapter details how the project fostered undergraduate learning and her own professional development in addition to contributing to the well-being of children in the community.

The CBR initiatives in Part Two reflect a number of academic disciplines and address a variety of issues through the work of undergraduates, faculty, staff, graduate students, and community partners in and outside the United States. While some of the research occurs over time, much of it focuses on one issue for the short term. Community results are considered in each case, and the course or student learning is a priority. Ultimately, our purpose in Part Two is to focus on the many ways students can be involved in CBR to help ourselves and our readers understand how to do it well.

Part Three: Community-Based Research in Community-Wide Long-Term Efforts

Although community outcomes are highlighted in Part Two, they take a back seat to student learning to a large degree. In Part Three the emphasis shifts to prioritizing community change and suggests that situating CBR projects in broad endeavors—alliances, collaboratives, coalitions—that represent a variety of interests and stakeholders who are in it for the long haul is more likely to achieve community improvement, and ultimately community development, than individual projects or individual organization-based efforts. This section of the book presents four examples of how this type of arrangement can work.

Chapter 15, "The Poverty Initiative in Rockbridge County, Virginia," emerges from a coalition of campus and community partners coming together to address poverty-related issues in the Appalachia region. The effort was supported by Washington and Lee University's Shepherd Program for the Interdisciplinary Study of Poverty and Human Capability and a multitude of organizations in Rockbridge County, Virginia. Don E. Dailey and David Dax provide readers with a sense of the process needed to develop an ongoing endeavor intent on addressing complex issues such as poverty. They also explain the role CBR can play in such a broad initiative and describe some of the challenges faculty and students may encounter when participating in such an effort as community-based researchers.

In Chapter 16, leaders of an initiative begun by a coalition of community partners, the Neighborhoods@Work Initiative, sought assistance from academics at the University of Southern California (USC). In "Learning to Co-construct Solutions to Urban School Challenges in Los Angeles," Adrianna Kezar and Sylvia Rousseau describe the development of the coalition and the CBR project that graduate students in the USC Rossier School of Education undertook. Opportunities and challenges in developing the CBR efforts in such a partnership are described. This chapter should be of special interest to those working with graduate students in nontraditional ways or to students in CBR who already have substantial research skills.

Chapter 17 describes an initiative that was deeply collaborative between campus and community from the start. "Community-Based Research and Development in Haiti: Leveraging Multiple Resources for Maximum Impact" addresses the question of how faculty from any discipline who are interested in international CBR can organize their work to optimize academic student learning and community impact. In addition to providing a second international CBR context for this book, Anthony Vinciquerra describes the St. Thomas University/Port-de-Paix, Haiti, Global Solidarity Partnership. Readers will learn how a variety of student and faculty efforts—not just CBR—can contribute to student learning and community change.

Chapter 18, "Progressive Projects on Parent Involvement," is the final chapter in Part Three and describes an effort begun in 2006 in an education collaborative in South Bend composed of university faculty and staff and local public school administrators. At the initial meeting, low parent involvement emerged as a challenge each administrator faced. Addressing the issue began with an undergraduate student CBR project but soon led to the formation of parent workshops as part of a CBR-based program called No Parent Left Behind (NPLB). Joyce F. Long helped design and lead the research and workshops and later shifted to full-time director of NPLB. The program achieved consistently remarkable parent outcomes regardless of ethnicity in many of the city's poorest public schools for several years. Sustaining systemic progress has been difficult, however, after funding priorities abruptly shifted in the public school system despite an ongoing need. The chapter concludes with a discussion on using CBR to build a culture of support for long-term solutions.

Conclusion

In the book's concluding chapter, Mary Beckman summarizes the themes presented in and across all three parts, point out the challenges, and recommend suggestions for further empowering CBR's positive influence in communities. This includes pedagogical and partnering strategies that can equip faculty to effectively involve their students in collaborative research efforts aimed toward social improvement. Furthermore, the conclusion envisions how our future CBR work will explicitly support system change in communities.

We Are Writing for Us

First and foremost, this book serves faculty who want to not only know how to incorporate CBR into their teaching but also do it in a way that attends to student learning aims while attaining positive effects in communities. As several of the chapters focus on graduate education, they are likely to be of interest not only to those who teach graduate students but also to graduate students themselves as they ponder their futures as researchers and educators. Similarly, anyone working in a college or university center or responsible for supporting academic community engagement initiatives in other ways will find valuable information in our content. This is also true for individuals employed in nonprofit organizations that partner with academic entities and self-identified groups experiencing social challenges. Finally, this book is also for those taking students overseas or are interested in doing so for the purpose of conducting CBR.

We are part of the audience for which we are writing, and between the two of us, we have at one time or another belonged to all the groups of potential readers we named in the preceding paragraph. Having seen the need for this kind of material to assist our own work over the years, we decided to coalesce a collection of writing that would help us. We believe others like ourselves await this type of publication that reveals the power of CBR. CBR has the potential to transform our students and the communities where we live. It can also inspire us as academics and scholars, as community leaders and citizens. After reading this book, we think you will agree that the effort and time spent in CBR is a valuable investment.

References

American Association for Higher Education series on service-learning in the disciplines. (2015). Retrieved from bonnernetwork.pbworks.com/w/page/33663540/AAHE%20Series%20on%20Service-Learning%20in%20the%20Disciplines

Beckman, M., & Long, J. (2013). Beyond tomorrow: Charting a long term course toward community impact in local public education. In H. E. Fitzgerald & J. Primavera (Eds.), *Going public: Civic and community engagement, the scholarship of practice* (pp. 221–236). East Lansing: Michigan State University Press.

Beckman, M., Penney, N., & Cockburn, B. (2011). Maximizing the impact of community-based research. *Journal of Higher Education Outreach and Engagement, 15*(2), 83–105.

Bringle, R. G., Hatcher, J. A., & Jones, S. G. (Eds.). (2012). *International service learning: Conceptual frameworks and research.* Sterling, VA: Stylus.

Currie, M., King, G., Rosenbaum, P., Law, M., Kertoy, M., & Specht, J. (2005). A model of impacts of research partnerships in health and social services. *Evaluation and Program Planning, 28,* 400–412.

Eyler, J., & Giles, D. (1999). *Where's the learning in service-learning?* San Francisco, CA: Jossey-Bass.

Heffernan, K. (2001). *Fundamentals of service-learning course construction.* Boston, MA: Campus Compact.

Kania, J., & Kramer, M. (2011). Collective impact. *Stanford Social Innovation Review, 9*(1), 36–41.

Kelshaw, T. S., Lazarus, F., & Minier, J. (2009). *Partnerships for service-learning: Impacts on communities and students.* San Francisco, CA: Jossey-Bass.

Kronick, R. F., & Cunningham, R. B. (2013). Service-learning: Some academic and community recommendations. *Journal of Higher Education Outreach and Engagement, 17*(3), 139–152.

Lichtenstein, G., Thorme, T., Cutforth, N., & Tombari, M. (2011). Development of a national survey to assess student learning outcomes of community-based research. *Journal of Higher Education Outreach and Engagement, 15*(2), 7–33.

Marullo, S., Cooke, D., Willis, J., Rollins, A., Burke, J., Bonilla, P., & Waldref, V. (2003). Community-based research assessments: Some principles and practices. *Michigan Journal of Community Service-Learning, 9*(3), 57–68.

National Community-Based Research Networking Initiative. (2010). *Community based research case studies: 2006–2010*. Retrieved from cbrnet.pbworks.com/f/CBR+Case+Studies+FINAL.pdf

Pigza, J. M., & Beckman, M. (Eds.). (2010). *New directions in community-based research*. Princeton, NJ: National Community-Based Research Network Initiative. Retrieved from cbrnet.pbworks.com/f/New+Directions+in+CBR+FINAL+6.30.pdf

Stoecker, R. (2005). *Research methods for community change: A project-based approach*. Thousand Oaks, CA: Sage.

Stoecker, R., & Beckman, M. (2010). *Making higher education civic engagement matter in the community*. Retrieved from compact.org/news/making-higher-education-civic-engagement-matter-in-the-community/9748

Stoecker, R., Beckman, M., & Min, B. H. (2012). Evaluating the community impact of higher education community engagement. In H. E. Fitzgerald, C. Burack, & S. Seifer (Eds.), *Handbook of engaged scholarship: The contemporary landscape: Vol. 2. Community-campus partnerships* (pp. 177–198). East Lansing: Michigan State University.

Strand, K., Marullo, S., Cutforth, N., Stoecker, R., & Donohue, P. (2003). *Principles and practices: Community-based research and higher education*. San Francisco, CA: Jossey-Bass.

Vogelgesang, L., Drummond, M., & Gilmartin, S. K. (2012). *How higher education is integrating diversity and service learning: Findings from four case studies*. Palo Alto, CA: California Campus Compact.

PART ONE

DEFINITIONS, ORIENTING FRAMEWORKS, AND PARTNERS

Mary Beckman

This book is addressed to higher education teachers and scholars as well as to those who are not formally affiliated with colleges and universities but who are their partners. Its aim is to assist such readers in teaching and scholarship that will contribute to positive community change. For some, that community change will take the form of policy improvements; for others, the focus will be on community or economic development. Many may use the language of social justice and the common good to orient their work. Whatever the focus for action, our hope is that this book will provide inspiration and concrete guidance.

Before going any further, we want to say that although we refer to *campus* and *community* as if there were some clear demarcation between them, we know that a campus is made up of communities, and some of those communities and certainly the individuals who make up those communities are also part of off-campus communities; indeed, the divide is in itself an artificial one. Nonetheless, we will adhere to the usual language as it is currently widely used and understood.

We begin the book with a chapter that orients the reader on the breadth and depth of research in campus and off-campus individual and community collaborations. Chapter 1 offers definitions, provides historical contexts for the terms defined, and explains related geographical influences. It helps the reader understand the etymological development of *community-based research* (CBR) and defines precisely what we mean by the term in this book.

The chapter also addresses questions of method: Is CBR a method? What research methods are associated with CBR?

Every chapter in this book explicitly considers the role CBR can play in supporting positive community change. Toward this end, Chapter 2 helps the reader think about ways to orient specific CBR projects toward improving the situation of individuals and groups experiencing social challenges, and enhancing the capacity of nonprofit and other organizations to address those challenges. Additionally, the conceptual framework presented provides guidance for using CBR to contribute to collective efforts toward long-term community development. The chapter also helps the reader understand the meaning of the terms *outputs, outcomes,* and *impact,* which funders are increasingly expecting community organizations to use when evaluating and justifying the effectiveness of their programs in promoting community improvement. Moreover, these terms are sprinkled liberally throughout the examples of CBR in Part Two of this book. Finally, the content of Chapter 2, in particular, its *community impact framework,* is foundational for an understanding of what we have intended in our selection of the chapters in Part Three.

Chapters 3 and 4 describe the motivations, challenges, and benefits that community partners and faculty bring to and discover in CBR work. Chapter 3 offers the perspectives of a number of community partners on what faculty and others involved in CBR ought to consider and understand before bringing in their students as research partners with community collaborators. Chapter 4 reports on findings from a qualitative research project that explored why faculty become interested in CBR and how they maintain or expand that interest. In sharing their reasons for being enthusiastic about CBR, the chapter contributors also offer cautions that can help campus colleagues navigate through some of the challenges they may face when practicing CBR.

THE LANGUAGE AND METHODS OF COMMUNITY RESEARCH

James M. Frabutt and Kelly N. Graves

Forming civic-minded students, empowering local citizens, rejuvenating blighted neighborhoods, maximizing families' health and wellness, and strengthening the workforce for a twenty-first-century economy are but a few of the lofty ends for which community-engaged scholarship aims. This chapter is arranged in three sections to provide the essential foundation for achieving those ends. The first section presents the growing institutional movement toward engagement, highlighting some key touchstones. It also reacquaints the reader with Ernest Boyer's (1990) helpful recasting of scholarly work in the academy. The second section outlines the various terminology used and the key animating principles of community-based research (CBR) orienting the reader to a continuum of applied and engaged scholarship with varying levels of participation and social action. The third section turns to methodological approaches to CBR, exploring the panoply of research techniques that have been applied across a variety of fields and disciplines.

The Rise of Civic Engagement and Its Home in the Scholarship of the Academy

As civic engagement and democratic involvement are critical cornerstones for a vibrant and active citizenry, the National Task Force on Civic Learning and Democratic Engagement (2012) underscored the fact that our nation, indeed our world, needs global citizens who are "informed, engaged, open-minded, and socially responsible people committed to the common good" (p. 13). This formative work of shaping citizens unfolds with students each and every day in our institutions of higher education and is a leverage point for ensuring communities' future vitality and well-being. In short, this volume testifies to the utter centrality of community in a growing movement toward engaged scholarship.

Investments in community-engaged and civically oriented work for the common good are not a wholly new endeavor, however. Historical precedents such as the Morill Land Grant Acts, which gave rise to the formation of land-grant colleges, and the Hatch Act of the late nineteenth century staked out the importance of linking the best of science, technology, and agriculture with expressed community needs. More than a century later, university know-how continues to be an engine for economic, social, and human capital development. Even more critically, there are more and more examples of partnerships that move beyond unidirectional outreach toward positioning communities and universities as cocreators of knowledge and as coequal experts.

A few examples suffice to illustrate the new instantiations of community-university partnerships today. Consider the growth and entrenchment of national organizations such as Campus Compact, which since the mid-1980s has championed the civic and community engagement of higher education institutions. More recently, the national conversation on community engagement has been piqued by the Carnegie Foundation's establishment of a community engagement classification, an accolade awarded to more than 300 institutions so far. One field-specific example of community-engaged research is drawn from an appendix to *Community-Based Participatory Research for Health*, which lists more than 50 CBR centers and networks in North America alone (Minkler, Wallerstein, Ni, & Tran, 2008). Another prominent and related movement is *translational science* (or *translational research*), which, although rooted mostly in medicine, has appeared in the social and behavioral sciences as a term to capture the seamless transition of basic inquiry into the realm of practical, usable application. This approach answers the question of how findings from a laboratory can be quickly accelerated for use in the field. Some translational research explicitly invokes the participation of community members or other relevant stakeholders as part of the strategy for efficient movement from basic science to application/extension. Finally, community-engaged projects also receive investments of federal dollars from the National Institutes of Health, the Centers for Disease Control and Prevention, and the National Science Foundation (Mercer & Green, 2008) as well as from private philanthropic sources such as the W. K. Kellogg Foundation and the Wellesley Institute (Minkler & Wallerstein, 2008).

To make this type of engaged work possible in the academy, new frameworks were sorely needed. Boyer (1990) offered a conceptualization of scholarship that was broader and more expansive than traditional notions of what counted as the scholarly work of the professoriate. Prior to this time, the typical systematic construction of new knowledge through research that held pride of place at a university was a mode of inquiry Boyer dubbed the *scholarship of discovery*. To move beyond this traditional focus on developing the stock of human knowledge, Boyer highlighted three other core types of legitimate scholarship: teaching, integration, and application. He defined the *scholarship of teaching* as an examination of teaching models and practices with the aim of optimizing student performance and learning. When faculty carefully and systematically examined their pedagogical techniques to assess impact on student knowledge acquisition, they engaged in the scholarship of teaching. According to Boyer, a third realm of scholarship, the *scholarship of application*, represented professors channeling content-specific expertise and skills toward problem solving in the public sphere. Faculty embrace this mode of theory-into-practice scholarship when they form partnerships with business, industry, education, government, or community nonprofits to address pressing social issues. Fourth, the *scholarship of integration* involved building transdisciplinary connections or synthesizing disciplinary knowledge in novel ways, each of which places "discoveries in a larger context" (Boyer, 1996, p. 17). This was made evident, for example, by a group of scholars conducting research on a timely educational issue but working at the confluence of several fields, such as economics, education, psychology, and public policy.

Boyer's (1996) view of scholarship continued to deepen in important ways and eventually developed a cross-cutting type of scholarship that gets at the very heart of CBR. Boyer conceptualized the *scholarship of engagement*, which had an explicit end: "connecting the rich resources of the university to our most pressing social, civic, and ethical problems, to our children, to our schools, to our teachers and to our cities" (p. 21). He envisioned engaged scholarship emerging across any of the aforementioned types of scholarship and drawing heavily upon reciprocity and collaborative civic engagement and into the production of knowledge. Later, the term "tend[ed] to be used inclusively to describe a host of practices cutting across disciplinary boundaries and teaching, research, and outreach functions in which scholars communicate to and work both for and with communities" (D. Barker, 2004, p. 124). These seminal writings of Boyer set forth a framework that defined the characteristics of engaged scholarship and fostered a burgeoning national dialogue about it that continues to this day. The scholarship of engagement, in particular, has the national spotlight as a thriving approach for connecting universities to communities in a way that ensures that communities, and all the richness they bring to research, will matter.

Language of CBR

Wading more deeply into nuances of applied and engaged scholarship requires some language acquisition or fluency development. Thus, this section introduces the wide array of terminology in the domain of applied and engaged scholarship.

Navigating Terms

Situated in the realm of applied and engaged scholarship, Figure 1.1 illustrates a panoply of terms that can be classified under the overarching construct of participatory or CBR. Appreciating the semantic complexity clearly evident in Figure 1.1, Wallerstein and Duran (2008) commented that making

Figure 1.1 Overarching Framework of Terms

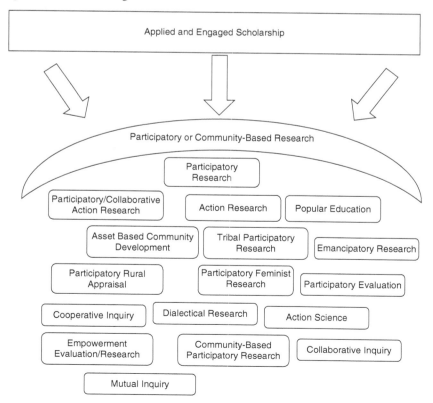

sense of such terms "has been fairly daunting, and the nuanced differences between them are often difficult to decipher" (p. 26). While the scope of this chapter does not allow for an in-depth treatment of each of these particular research approaches, the following schemas are presented to better orient the landscape: (a) identifying root descriptors, (b) cataloging by field or family, and (c) positioning types of CBR along a continuum of participation and activism.

Identifying root descriptors. The broadest and perhaps most common umbrella terms use the two basic descriptors *community* or *participatory/ collaborative* in combination with the word *research* (Jason, Keys, Suarez-Balcazar, Taylor, & Davis, 2004; McNall, Doberneck, & Van Egeren, 2010). As a case in point, Wallerstein and Duran (2008) used *participatory research* as their umbrella term, connoting a linkage of applied social science and social activism. Since community, participatory, and collaborative describe research, defining *research* is a key starting point of departure.

Attempts to define *research* may call to mind the steps of the scientific method, but a simple view captures the research cycle just as aptly: Pose a question, collect relevant data, and answer the question. Frequently used definitions of *research* describe it as systematic investigation or inquiry, but it is typically characterized by the formal gathering of information through planned, intentional, and thoughtful inquiry. The words *community* and *participatory* add to this basic definition, shaping it in meaningful ways by suggesting where, by whom, and how the research will unfold.

To press this point, consider the four definitions of *community-based participatory research* (CBPR) presented in Table 1.1. Despite deriving from varying authors and origins, certain commonalities are apparent. Chief among them is that research in this modality has its origin and unfolding practice in a community setting, whether the community is conceived according to geography, practice, race, or other descriptors. Strand, Marullo, Cutforth, Stoecker, and Donohue (2003a) offered a comprehensive definition of *community* as (a) educational institutions, (b) community-based organizations, (c) agencies that provide services or otherwise work on behalf of area residents, and (d) groups that do not share a geographical association but share an interest in cultural, social, political, health, or economic issues. In community research, issues, concerns, and topics of study arise from the community because the community itself has determined they are important, interesting, relevant, or timely. Thus, the community plays a major role in the first step of the scientific process: developing and refining the primary research question. In addition, community wisdom and experiential knowledge are valued on par with the scientific or technical expertise of university partners. In fact, the potential of synergistic colearning between the

TABLE 1.1
Cross-Cutting and Common Descriptors of CBR: Four Exemplars

Three Central Principles of CBR[a]	CBR *Defined[b]*
• A collaborative enterprise between researchers and community or members • Validates multiple sources of knowledge and promotes the use of multiple methods of discovery and dissemination of the knowledge produced • Aims for social action and social change for the purpose of achieving social justice	• Community situated: Begins with a research topic of practical relevance to the community (as opposed to individual scholars) and is carried out in community settings. • Collaborative: Community members and researchers equitably share control of the research agenda through active and reciprocal involvement in research design, implementation, and dissemination. • Action oriented: The process and results are useful to community members in making positive social change and promoting social equity.
The Nine Principles of CBPR[c]	CBPR *Defined[d]*
• Recognizes community as a unit of identity • Builds on strengths and resources within the community • Facilitates collaborative, equitable partnership in all research phases and involves an empowering and power-sharing process that attends to social inequalities • Promotes colearning and capacity building among all partners • Integrates and achieves a balance between research and action for the mutual benefit of all partners • Emphasizes public health problems of local relevance and also ecological perspectives that recognize and attend to the multiple determinants of health and disease • Involves systems development through a cyclical and iterative process • Disseminates findings and knowledge gained to all partners and involves all partners in the dissemination process • Requires a long-term process and commitment to sustainability	• Collaborative research approach that is designed to ensure and establish structures for participation by communities affected by the issue being studied, representatives of organizations, and researchers in all aspects of the research process to improve health and well-being through taking action, including social change • Colearning and reciprocal transfer of expertise, by all research partners, with particular emphasis on the issues that can be studied with CPBR methods • Shared decision-making power • Mutual ownership of the processes and products of the research enterprise

Note. [a]From *Community-Based Research in Higher Education: Methods, Models and Practice,* by K. Strand, S. Marullo, N. Cutforth, R. Stoecker, & P. Donohue, 2003a, San Francisco, CA: Jossey-Bass; "Principles of Best Practice for Community-Based Research," by K. Strand, S. Marullo, N. Cutforth, R. Stoecker, & P. Donohue, 2003a, *Michigan Journal of Community Service Learning, 9*(3), 5–15.

[b]"What Is Community Based Research?" by Centre for Community Research, 2015, communitybased research.ca

[c]"Critical Issues in Developing and Following CBPR Principles," pp. 47–66, by B. A. Israel, A. J. Schultz, E. A. Parker, A. B. Becker, A. J. Allen, & J. R. Guzman, in M. Minkler & N. Wallerstein (Eds.), *Community-Based Participatory Research for Health: From Process to Outcomes,* 2008, San Francisco, CA: Jossey-Bass.

[d]*Community-Based Participatory Research: Assessing the Evidence* (Evidence Report/Technology Assessment No. 99), p. 3, by M. Viswanathan, A. Ammerman, E. Eng, G. Gartlehner, K. N. Lohr, D. Griffith, . . . L. Whitener, 2004, Rockville, MD: Agency for Healthcare Research and Quality.

community and its university partners leads this type of inquiry to a deeper and fuller understanding of the topic.

CBR is also undeniably about action. In contrast to the pure scholarship of discovery mentioned earlier, community-based research often seeks transformative ends. The goals and products of CBR are aimed toward immediate social application rather than building a detached fund of human knowledge. While CBR in general is change oriented, one of the variants in Figure 1.1, *action research*, drives home this point (McNiff & Whitehead, 2006). This research orientation is often focused on solutions, perhaps either seeking to upend the status quo or bringing about social change. Much community research, action research included, explicitly bridges the chasm between theory and practice.

Moving from its root definitions, Table 1.2 presents CBR and its many variants by their more expansive definitions. At its core, however, community research focuses on a systematic research process and deep community participation with an orientation toward social action. In summary,

> Although there are differences among these approaches, they all involve a commitment to conducting research that to some degree shares power with and engages community partners in the research process and that benefits the communities involved, either through direct intervention or by translating research findings into interventions and policy change. (Israel, Eng, Schulz, & Parker, 2013, p. 6)

Cataloging by field or family. Beyond the core meanings just delineated, a second method of categorization builds on Wallerstein and Duran (2008) by grouping various terms according to the academic field with which they are most associated (Table 1.2). This strategy for understanding the nuanced meanings of these various terms grasps how they cluster in various academic fields. As an example, in the field of educational action research, terms such as *teacher research, practitioner research,* and *collaborative action research* are commonly used. In fact, the primary educational research body, the American Educational Research Association, has two special interest groups that focus on action research and teacher research. Thus, even within a single field one can find variants of community research that focus on the teacher's own professional practice or development as an educator (e.g., teacher professionalism through practitioner research; Burton & Bartlett, 2005), principals' use of action research to lead schools (e.g., action research for educational administration; Frabutt, Holter, & Nuzzi, 2008), or teams of teachers working collaboratively to improve educational practice (e.g., collaborative action research; Gordon, 2008). Table 1.2 also depicts how highly specified variations of community research emerge and can be applied in various areas of practice. In the field of evaluation, which often by its very mission and goals

TABLE 1.2

Clustering of CBR Approaches by Disciplinary or Practice Families

Disciplinary Families of CBR and CBPR	Specific Types	Description and Distinguishing Characteristics of the Family
Community development and social action	Collaborative action research Dialectical inquiry Emancipatory research Liberatory research Participatory research Participatory feminist research Popular education Tribal participatory research	These approaches have in common an expressed focus on the dynamics of power and that awareness, research, and action are instruments for fostering empowerment. These approaches bring a critical lens to power imbalances, structural inequalities, and unequal access to resources. They are acutely sensitive to community needs, illustrated, for example, by tribal participatory research, a collaborative and community-sensitive approach to scientific inquiry drawing upon tribal oversight, use of a facilitator, training and employing community members as staff, and using culturally specific intervention and assessment.
Education	Classroom action research Collaborative action research Critical action research Practitioner research Teacher research	This family of research approaches centers on practitioner-driven inquiry focused on enhancing all aspects of teaching, learning, and education. It features reflective, recursive cycles of inquiry and action targeted to improving educational practice. Projects can be conducted at the classroom, school, or district level and typically involve key stakeholders such as teachers, administrators, school support staff, students, and families.
Evaluation	Constructivist inquiry Empowerment evaluation Fourth-generation inquiry Participatory evaluation	This group of approaches to evaluation seeks program improvement as well as self-determination among program stakeholders. Core values of these types of evaluation seek to give power and responsibility to program stakeholders, increasing their own capacity and underscoring a cyclical and ongoing process of program improvement.

Nursing	Emancipatory inquiry CBPR Participatory action research	Participatory, collaborative, and often advocacy-oriented research approaches centered in the fields of nursing and medicine focus broadly on health outcomes. Emblematic projects cover topics such as disease prevention, service access and delivery, health promotion, and elimination of health disparities.
Organizational psychology and organizational development	Action learning Action science Action inquiry Industrial action research	These approaches are anchored in program and process improvement through systematic and reflective analysis of practice. Goals include refinement of practice, increased efficiency of operations, and improvement of outcomes.
Psychology, community psychology, and human relations	Cooperative inquiry Mutual inquiry Participatory action research Participatory research Reflective practitioner inquiry	Building upon collective action and egalitarian relationships, community members themselves shape questions, methods, and measures of effectiveness. There is a drive toward social action via increased sociopolitical awareness and heightened citizen power and voice. Research partnerships are highly self-reflective, involve colearning, and draw upon strength-based as opposed to deficit-oriented approaches.

has a posture of community engagement and collaboration, individual projects are cast as *empowerment evaluation, participatory evaluation*, or *fourth-generation inquiry*.

Positioning along a continuum of activism. A third approach to help understand the language of CBR is heuristic, anchored in the historical origins of community research that depicts a continuum of community-based research traditions. The plethora of terms reviewed in Figure 1.1 and Table 1.2 can largely be traced to two distinct origins, a northern tradition and a southern tradition (Wallerstein & Duran, 2008). Although McNall and colleagues (2010) use *collaborative inquiry* as an umbrella term, they state that all types of collaborative inquiry derive from either pragmatic (i.e., northern) or emancipatory (i.e., southern) traditions (see Figure 1.2). Defining the poles of this schematic provides a better sense of where a specific research orientation might be placed along this hypothetical continuum.

The northern tradition is firmly anchored in the pragmatic, action-oriented bent of applied social research. Work of this genre builds on the groundbreaking efforts of Kurt Lewin, often referred to as the grandfather of action research, and his championing of action research as a way to leverage social science for the improvement of practice. "Lewin challenged the gap between theory and practice and sought to solve practical problems through a research cycle involving planning, action, and investigating the results of the action" (Wallerstein & Duran, 2008, p. 27). Most characteristically, research in this vein is about technical problem solving, improving practice, and making processes more efficient. It has a decidedly practical orientation aimed

Figure 1.2 Conceptualizing Community and Participatory Research Approaches Along a Northern-Southern Continuum

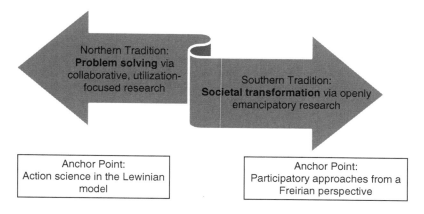

at systemic improvements, largely through an iterative cycle of "applying ever-increasing scientific knowledge to real-word problems" (Wallerstein & Duran, 2008, p. 27). Utilitarian in nature, the foundations of the northern tradition are postpositivism and pragmatism.

The southern tradition, in contrast, is more explicitly focused on action for transformative social change and empowerment. Emphasizing democratic participation, the southern tradition is emancipatory in nature, and it embraces notions of social justice. It is unabashedly political, acknowledging that research is value laden and deeply embedded in a given social context. The efforts of educational reformer and literacy worker Paulo Freire are frequently cited as emblematic of the southern tradition. His work in South America merged activism, solidarity, and scientific methods toward the larger goal of emancipation and empowerment. Thus, with a foundation in critical and emancipatory theories, the southern tradition embraces community research as a vehicle for community transformation by empowering disenfranchised groups through social justice advocacy.

CBR Approaches and Methods

This section turns to the *how* of CBR, for, ultimately, how the research is conducted determines whether it can legitimately bear the moniker of CBR. At the outset, however, it must be stressed that CBR or CBPR is best described as an approach rather than implying a particular suite of methods or research designs. "Because PR [participatory research] is an approach, orientation, or way of working, it can employ a diverse range of study designs, methodologies, and methods" (Cargo & Mercer, 2008, p. 327). This section (a) describes two ways to outline approaches to community-participatory research, (b) provides a glimpse of the myriad methodologies and designs that have been employed in community research projects, and (c) outlines the notion of mixed methods and methodological pluralism.

CBR: Approaches and Orientations

Practitioners and scholars of CBR have articulated a few broad brushstroke approaches to conducting community research. One is Strand and colleagues' (2003a) straightforward outline of the major steps and stages of CBR: (a) identify a research question, (b) choose a research design and method, (c) collect the data, (d) analyze the data, and (e) report the results. While these steps are familiar to researchers of all kinds, it's *how* they are executed that matters for CBR, so they "shape the way we approach the design and conduct of this kind of research" (p. 71). Only when these steps are taken for the purposes of mutual benefit, deepening a partnership, colearning, and collaborative social action can the process fairly be called *community/participatory research*.

In concrete terms, rather than pursuing a research question derived from the next steps and future directions section of a journal article, a CBR project might emanate from a neighborhood coalition's concern about a recent spate of armed robberies involving juveniles. Rather than having a faculty member conduct focus groups at a local community center, area residents are trained not only to conduct these groups but to assist with their design and planning. At the stage of dissemination, community research looks beyond the peer-reviewed journal article—often the coin of the realm in academic circles—to novel, accessible, and user-friendly ways to present study findings, ensuring that those community members closest to the project are integrally involved in discerning conclusions and implications.

Another orientation in CBR derives from Israel and colleagues (2013), who organized their text, *Methods for Community-Based Participatory Research for Health*, into the following domains specified for their generic approach to community research: (a) form a CBPR partnership, (b) assess community strengths and dynamics, (c) identify priority health concerns and research questions, (d) design and conduct etiologic intervention or policy research, (e) get feedback and interpret research findings, (f) disseminate and translate research findings, and (g) form and maintain a partnership. Although listed linearly here, these steps actually occur in an iterative and cyclical process. Furthermore, depending upon the unique contextual element of that community (e.g., politics, leadership changes, agency restructuring, etc.), these steps can vary greatly in the time needed to adequately complete them. Although "similar phases apply to the application of any approach to research" (Israel et al., 2013, p. 13) we also acknowledge there must be a dedicated effort to maintaining, sustaining, and evaluating the CBPR partnership throughout community-based work. Indeed, "what is unique to CBPR is its emphasis on the diverse partners involved, and on striving for equal participation and ownership, reciprocity, colearning, and change" (p. 13).

It is important to note that an essential element to forming the CBPR partnership is the establishment of trust among partners. The speed and ease at which that occurs can depend on a myriad of factors, but one factor that is particularly important to mention is the degree to which the research is culturally informed and appropriate to the target population. Researchers must be cognizant of the potential distrust of research in general among various subgroups. This distrust may stem from factors such as historically unethical research such as the "Tuskegee Study of Untreated Syphilis in the Negro Male" (Centers for Disease Control and Prevention, 2013), which went on for 40 years before it was deemed "unethically justifiable" (Heintzelman, 2003, p. 2) in 1972. Fears can also emerge that confidentiality may be breached even when the researcher has taken all steps necessary to ensure confidentiality, as in the case of a research study conducted in a small town in which participation is limited to those with a particular health condition or disorder (Fisher et al., 2002). Similarly, some ethnic groups may be skeptical when introduced to informed consent in which they are required to provide legal signatures and information, as in the case of undocumented immigrants (Fisher et al., 2002).

Because of these factors and the essential focus on *community* in the CBPR model, the research team should be composed of individuals from the populations of interest whenever possible and integrate culturally informed approaches to the CBPR process. This aspect of CBPR has been referred to as "community and participant consultation," or "an ongoing reciprocal and respectful dialogue among scientists, prospective participants, their families, and other community stakeholders . . . aimed at strengthening scientific merit and responsibility during research design, implementation, and dissemination" (Fisher et al., 2002, p. 1034). In this way, CBPR promotes the communities' respect of the research process and, thus, increases the likelihood of engagement and participation in the research and its findings.

An Overview of Methods and Designs

Since there is no methodological blueprint for executing CBR or CBPR, an eclectic array of methodologies is evident, reinforcing the notion that diverse questions from diverse communities require methods that are best suited to the project at hand. The questions and imperatives at play for the community partnership should determine the appropriate methodology rather than the other way around. To provide a glimpse of the variety of methods employed in CBR efforts, three touchstones provide a cogent overview.

First, Israel and colleagues (2013) present a broad exposure to CBPR methods from a public health perspective. For example, they include chapters dedicated to survey methodology (featuring deep involvement of community in survey design and administration), ethnography, key informant interviews, focus groups, and analysis of secondary data. Because mapping and understanding local contextual details is so important to community research, other featured methods include geographic mapping techniques, food audits, the use of neighborhood observational checklists, and home environmental assessments.

Second, anchored in community psychology, Jason and Glenwick (2012) organized their work around three methodological families: methods involving grouping of data (e.g., cluster analysis, person-oriented analysis, meta-analysis), methods involving change over time (e.g., time-series analysis, survival analysis), and methods involving contextual factors (e.g., multilevel modeling, epidemiologic approaches, geographic information systems, and economic cost analysis). They also foreground how advances in quantitative sophistication can bring more precision and depth to CBR, especially for the simultaneous analysis of "community-level and individual-level phenomena and their mutual impact" (Jason & Glenwick, 2012, p. 3). In sum, even this brief profile of methods makes clear that "for participatory research there are no methodological orthodoxies, no cookbook approaches to follow. The principle is that both issues and ways of working should flow from those involved and their context" (Hall, 1992, p. 20).

Although the first two descriptions of methods emanated from public health and community psychology perspectives, a third area sometimes referred to as *public scholarship*, draws from the humanities, arts, and design disciplines. One example is a well-known national movement launched in 1999, the Imagining America initiative, which uplifts civically engaged work in higher education (Goettel & Haft, 2010). In that vein of work, scholars and community partners use tools and methods such as exhibition and collections development, historical preservation, oral history, archival research, curricular development, documentary filmmaking, and educational programming. "The final products of this activity also can take a variety of forms, such as books intended for broad audiences, community dialogues, art installations, and collectively conceived performances" (Goettel & Haft, 2010, p. 363).

Methodological Pluralism and Mixed Methods

A coda to the notion that methods may be extremely diverse yet should be appropriate to the community issue is that multiple methods and unique combinations of methods are often the most optimal strategy. This idea, referred to as *methodological pluralism*, is described fully by C. Barker and Pistrang (2012) as "the valuing, within a field of science or scholarship, of a variety of different research approaches" (p. 35). Furthermore, methodological pluralism embodies the belief that:

> No single approach to research is best overall; rather, what is important is
> that the methods be appropriate for the questions under investigation. No

single research method is inherently superior to any other; all methods have their relative advantages and disadvantages. (C. Barker, Pistrang, & Elliott, 2002, p. 245)

To capture the complexity and context of community research, researchers and community members need not be wed to solely quantitative or qualitative approaches; instead "the research should be question driven, rather than method driven" (C. Barker & Pistrang, 2012, p. 36).

Another term frequently invoked, similarly intoning that diverse methods can bring about the fullest inquiry, is *mixed methods*. Campbell, Gregory, Patterson, and Bybee (2012) clarified that mixed methods represents more than simply adding qualitative data to a quantitative community project or vice versa; rather, mixed methods is a "third paradigm" with its own history, epistemology, and ontological assumptions (p. 52). They further pointed out that mixed-method designs can unfold in a variety of ways. For example, simultaneous/parallel mixed methods can be used in the same study or across a series of studies on a particular community topic (i.e., sequential).

McNall and colleagues (2010) likewise explored the use of mixed methods in collaborative, participatory research, noting that the end of the paradigm wars contributed to an explosion of interest in and the increasing legitimacy of mixed-method research. They reviewed a case for the utility of mixed methods, drawing on five purposes for mixing methods: triangulation, a variety of data sources and strategies has a greater likelihood of a convergence of findings; complementarity, overlapping methods offer distinct insights that when combined provide a fuller, richer picture of the phenomenon under study; development, similar to the sequential notion mentioned previously, mixed methods can be used in serial fashion so that one approach greatly informs the subsequent method; initiation, by exploring different aspects of a research problem using multiple methods, initiation intentionally seeks out contradictions among the findings to prompt a new round of research questions; and expansion, adding a distinctly new methodological approach is often the necessary next step to move beyond the initial inquiry and explore a new set of research questions. These five purposes for mixing methods highlight exactly why and how methodological eclecticism can make community research richer and more textured.

Conclusion

Many are convinced that some of the most relevant, compelling, and mission-critical projects emanating from institutions of higher education today are those that involve deep engagement with community stakeholders. Such applied and engaged work features the unique talents and perspectives of community members, students, and university faculty and staff. This chapter has shown that the academy recognizes the deep civic import of such work and that there is an evolving dialogue about how to frame, highlight, and support it. Also, although nuances abound in the terms and descriptions to explain community research, it is possible to define root constructs and see elements of commonality and distinction among the various extant terms. The various terminology describing participatory and community research is matched only by the wide array of methodologies that can be brought to bear on issues of community concern. The intricate and multilayered contexts of community projects often demand that research teams draw on a broad repertoire of tools and methods. And while methods are important and instrumental to the execution of community research, it is the *how* of their implementation—in partnership, toward colearning, in reciprocal and mutually beneficial ways—that truly characterizes CBR. The following chapters in this volume exemplify just a few of the novel ways CBR is used as a powerful lever for student learning, faculty development, citizen enrichment, and community revitalization.

References

Barker, C., & Pistrang, N. (2012). Methodological pluralism: Implications for consumer and producers of research. In L. Jason & D. Glenwick (Eds.), *Methodological approaches to community-based research* (pp. 33–50). Washington, DC: American Psychological Association.

Barker, C., Pistrang, N., & Elliott, R. (2002). *Research methods in clinical psychology: An introduction for students and practitioners* (2nd ed.). Chichester, United Kingdom: Wiley.

Barker, D. (2004). The scholarship of engagement: A taxonomy of five emerging practices. *Journal of Higher Education Outreach and Engagement, 9*(2), 123–137.

Boyer, E. (1990). *Scholarship reconsidered.* Menlo Park, CA: Carnegie Foundation for the Advancement of Teaching.

Boyer, E. (1996). The scholarship of engagement. *Journal of Public Outreach, 1*(1), 11–21.

Burton, D., & Bartlett, S. (2005). *Practitioner research for teachers.* Thousand Oaks, CA: Sage.

Campbell, R., Gregory, K. A., Patterson, D., & Bybee, D. (2012). Integrating qualitative and quantitative approaches: An example of mixed methods research. In L. Jason, & D. Glenwick, (Eds.), *Methodological approaches to community-based research* (pp. 51–68). Washington, DC: American Psychological Association.

Cargo, M., & Mercer, S. L. (2008). The value and challenges of participatory research: Strengthening its practice. *Annual Review of Public Health, 29,* 325–350. doi:10.1146/annurev.publhealth.29.091307.083824

Centers for Disease Control and Prevention. (2013). *U.S. Public Health Service syphilis study at Tuskegee.* Retrieved from www.cdc.gov/tuskegee/timeline.htm

Centre for Community Research. (2015). *What is community based research?* Retrieved from http://www.communitybasedresearch.ca

Fisher, C. B., Hoagwood, K., Boyce, C., Duster, T., Frank, D. A., Grisso, T., . . . Trimble, J. E. (2002). Research ethics for mental health science involving ethnic minority children and youths. *American Psychologist, 57,* 1024–1040. doi:10.1037/0003-066X.57.12.1024

Frabutt, J. M., Holter, A. C., & Nuzzi, R. J. (2008). *Research, action, and change: Leaders reshaping Catholic schools.* Notre Dame, IN: Alliance for Catholic Education Press.

Goettel, R., & Haft, J. (2010). Imagining America: Engaged scholarship for the arts, humanities, and design. In H. E. Fitzgerald, C. Burack, & S. D. Seifer (Eds.), *Handbook of engaged scholarship: Contemporary landscapes, future directions: Vol. 2. Community-campus partnerships* (pp. 361–372). East Lansing: Michigan State University Press.

Gordon, S. P. (2008). *Collaborative action research: Developing professional learning communities.* New York, NY: Teachers College Press.

Hall, B. L. (1992). From margins to center? The development and purpose of participatory research. *American Sociologist, 23*(4), 15–28.

Hatch Act, 7 U.S.C. § 361a et seq., (1887).

Heintzelman, C. A. (2003). The Tuskegee syphilis study and its implications for the 21st century. *New Social Work Magazine, 10,* 1–5.

Israel, B. A., Eng, E., Schulz, A. J., & Parker, E. A. (2013). *Methods for community-based participatory research for health* (2nd ed.). San Francisco, CA: Jossey-Bass.

Israel, B. A., Schultz, A. J., Parker, E. A., Becker, A. B., Allen, A. J., & Guzman, J. R. (2008). Critical issues in developing and following CBPR principles. In M. Minkler & N. Wallerstein (Eds.), *Community-based participatory research for health: From process to outcomes* (pp. 47–66). San Francisco, CA: Jossey-Bass.

Jason, L., & Glenwick, D. (2012). *Methodological approaches to community-based research* (1st ed.). Washington, DC: American Psychological Association.

Jason, L. A., Keys, C. B., Suarez-Balcazar, Y., Taylor, R. R., & Davis, M. I. (2004). *Participatory community research: Theories and methods in action.* Washington, DC: American Psychological Association.

McNall, M., Doberneck, D. M., & Van Egeren, L. (2010). Mixed methods in collaborative inquiry. In H. E. Fitzgerald, C. Burack, & S. D. Seifer (Eds.), *Handbook of engaged scholarship: Contemporary landscapes, future directions: Vol. 2. Community-campus partnerships* (pp. 257–273). East Lansing: Michigan State University Press.

McNiff, J., & Whitehead, J. (2006). *All you need to know about action research.* Thousand Oaks, CA: Sage.

Mercer, S. L., & Green, L. W. (2008). Federal funding and support for participatory research in public health and health care. In M. Minkler, & N. Wallerstein (Eds.), *Community-based participatory research for health: From process to outcomes* (2nd ed., pp. 465–479). San Francisco, CA: Jossey-Bass.

Minkler, M., & Wallerstein, N. (2008). *Community-based participatory research for health: From process to outcomes* (2nd ed.). San Francisco, CA: Jossey-Bass.

Minkler, M., Wallerstein, N., Ni, A., & Tran, R. (2008). Selected centers and other resources for participatory research in North America. In M. Minkler & N. Wallerstein (Eds.), *Community-based participatory research for health: From process to outcomes* (2nd ed., pp. 465–479). San Francisco, CA: Jossey-Bass.

Morrill Act, 7 U.S.C. § 301 et seq. (1862).

Morrill Act, 7 U.S.C. § 321 et seq. (1890).

National Task Force on Civic Learning and Democratic Engagement. (2012). *A crucible moment: College learning and democracy's future*. Washington, DC: Association of American Colleges and Universities.

Strand, K., Marullo, S., Cutforth, N., Stoecker, R., & Donohue, P. (2003a). *Community-based research in higher education: Methods, models and practice*. San Francisco, CA: Jossey-Bass.

Strand, K., Marullo, S., Cutforth, N., Stoecker, R., & Donohue, P. (2003b). Principles of best practice for community-based research. *Michigan Journal of Community Service Learning, 9*(3), 5–15.

Viswanathan, M., Ammerman, A., Eng, E., Gartlehner, G., Lohr, K. N., Griffith, D., . . . Whitener, L. (2004). *Community-based participatory research: Assessing the evidence* (Evidence Report/Technology Assessment No. 99). Rockville, MD: Agency for Healthcare Research and Quality.

Wallerstein, N., & Duran, B. (2008). The theoretical, historical, and practice roots of CBPR. In M. Minkler & N. Wallerstein (Eds.), *Community-based participatory research for health: From process to outcomes* (2nd ed., pp. 25–46). San Francisco, CA: Jossey-Bass.

2

THE ROLE OF COMMUNITY-BASED RESEARCH IN ACHIEVING COMMUNITY IMPACT

Mary Beckman and Danielle Wood

A key principle of community-based research (CBR) is to contribute to positive social change (Strand, Marullo, Cutforth, Stoecker, & Donohue, 2003). While there are various constraints at play in the use of CBR toward this end (Stoecker, Beckman, & Min, 2010), in this chapter we address a lack of understanding on *how* CBR might be used to create and sustain community improvement. The purpose of this chapter is to demonstrate that faculty, academic staff, graduate students, and undergraduates alike can engage in CBR with community collaborators in ways that foster long-term positive social change, as long as they understand certain critical elements and seek out opportunities to practice them.

We suggest that those who undertake CBR begin with this simple question: What result in the community should CBR help to achieve? If this question is asked at the start, then the research effort can be developed to achieve an outcome aligned with the desired result. Furthermore, we suggest situating CBR within existing broad community-wide or issue-oriented coalitions or partnerships whose purpose is to address social challenges. Faculty may even choose to help initiate and lead such long-term endeavors. The content of this chapter will help guide readers toward understanding and implementing CBR as a tool for shaping these possibilities.

Thinking About the Long Run

Although it seems clear that many who practice CBR are eager to use it to contribute to communities (e.g., Chupp & Joseph, 2010; Kubisch, Auspos, Brown, Buck, & Dewar, 2011), there are few published investigations of ways CBR or academic community engagement more generally can be used to attain community improvement. In a literature review, Beckman, Penney, and Cockburn (2011) found that the majority of service-learning and CBR research tended to consider the effects of academic community engagement only on student development. This extensive body of research has focused on student commitment to civic engagement (Knapp, Fisher, & Levesque-Bristol, 2010), attitudes toward community service (Bach & Weinzimmer, 2011), cultural competence (Amerson, 2010), political voice (Seider, Gillmor, & Rabinowics, 2012), awareness of social issues (Buch & Harden, 2011), appreciation of diversity (Levesque-Bristol, Knapp, & Fisher, 2010), and broader intellectual and personal development (Deeley, 2010; Felten & Clayton, 2011). While these factors affecting students are important, the approach presented in this chapter proposes ways of conceptualizing and engaging in CBR that can also achieve effects in communities.

It is important to acknowledge that the research results emerging from the CBR effort are not likely, in themselves, to attain the desired community improvement. Instead, the research provides only a piece of the puzzle. It is also important to recognize that community improvement is reached over time, because changes in communities generally happen slowly. Therefore, this chapter aims to provide some guidance for identifying the role CBR can play in the trajectory of change over time.

Output, Outcome, and Impact Over Time

When considering the role of CBR in reaching community improvement, it is helpful to separate effects into three general stages: output, outcome, and impact (Figure 2.1).

We clarify our terms because they are used inconsistently across a number of fields and even within fields (e.g., Currie et al., 2005; McLaughlin & Jordan, 2010; Wholey, 1987). *Output* is the term we use for the most immediate effect of some community action. In CBR specifically, the research findings would be the output. Outputs occur in the immediate or short term and could be considered the first stage in moving toward community improvement. We also refer to *outcome*, which is the result of putting the knowledge gained from the research to use. Outcomes can be thought of

Figure 2.1 Progressive CBR Influence

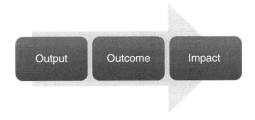

as the second stage, for they result in medium-term changes that develop from related outputs. Multiple outcomes can arise from an output, and outcomes can themselves lead to further outcomes. For example, a CBR project might investigate causes of low participation rates in educational opportunities among residents of a center for homeless people. If the research findings, which we are referring to as the output, are used to improve the center's classes so they attract a larger enrollment, then the revised educational offerings can be considered an outcome. It would also be possible to call higher attendance at the newly improved classes an outcome. This outcome might likewise lead to or be associated with other outcomes as well.

Finally, we define *impact* as the effect of the medium-term action or actions on the bigger issue or community as a whole, which represents the third stage and long-term goal of community improvement. Ultimately, an impact refers to a community's improved well-being or community development (Hendricks, Plantz, & Pritchard, 2008). To continue with the preceding example, if homelessness declined after putting the new educational programs into place, one might say impact has occurred. In speaking of impact, we are thus considering effects farther in the future than outcomes, but impact can result from an accumulation of outcomes over time.

It is important to note that it may not be easy to determine whether outcomes are in fact because of the application of the research findings (Currie et al., 2005; Walter, Helgenberger, Wiek, & Scholz, 2007). In the preceding hypothetical example involving educational opportunities for the homeless, how would we know if the CBR output that inspired the change in the educational offering actually led to the increased enrollment in the learning opportunities? Some sociologists conclude that impact is an even more elusive condition to measure than outcomes (Boothroyd, Fawcett, & Foster-Fishman, 2004; Matarrita-Cascante & Brennan, 2012) because it can be essentially impossible to disentangle the effects of the efforts of different collaborators (Currie et al., 2005).

There are methods, however, that can provide meaningful measurement to collaborative efforts. For example, contribution analysis focuses on identifying the impacts of the overall initiative and then attempts to examine the role and contribution of a particular programmatic effort (Mayne, 2008). Such a context-sensitive approach is rare; generally, the dynamic background into which the research is introduced is insufficiently considered when an effort is being assessed (Hawe, Bond, & Butler, 2009).

Documenting and Tracking

A critical and pivotal notion throughout this chapter is that CBR has a role to play in achieving community impact and that such change unfolds over time. To enhance the possibility that CBR will in fact contribute to the aims of community development, outputs and outcomes should be documented and tracked, which will provide information to analyze regarding the results of programmatic changes and research to date. This facilitates collective learning among those involved and the ability to identify new research needs and adjustments to programming.

In the CBR literature, Marullo and colleagues (2003) lay out a possible approach for such documentation in their conceptual framework for CBR assessments, which entails looking at three levels of effect: individual, organizational, and community. We might say that CBR contributed at the individual level if use of the results of a study on people who were incarcerated could be shown to have led to an improvement in their prison conditions. At the organizational level, CBR findings might increase the capacity of a nonprofit in some obvious way, such as through improved programming. Marullo and colleagues' third level of effect is at the scale of community impact. At this level, identifying outcomes becomes more complicated. While documenting and tracking are still needed, reaching such community-wide change, such as a reduction of obesity or decrease in the local unemployment rate, requires more than an individual project.

Situating CBR for Long-Term Change

Thus far, we have suggested that those engaging in CBR should begin by considering the community change that the research is designed to help achieve. Next, a CBR endeavor should establish the level at which the desired change is intended. Will the effect be at the individual level or at organizational level? Once this is determined, academic researchers can clarify with community partners how the output will be used to reach the desired outcome and ensure that all parties are clear regarding what they are working toward; then, corresponding documentation and tracking can ensue.

For community-level impact, however, more is necessary. Effective community development generally addresses issues with a multifaceted approach. Alleviating poverty, for example, requires that challenges in a variety of issues, such as housing, education, jobs, and health care, are all addressed (see Chapter 15). Focusing on a single issue, such as improving education, can in itself enhance community development. But even this single issue, seemingly narrower than tackling poverty as a whole, is packed with complexity; it must be addressed from multiple angles. No single research project can bring about such a significant change. Evidence suggests that such work requires more than one individual, and even more than one organization (Currie et al., 2005). To be successful, the commitment of a broader group is needed.

Kania and Kramer (2011) make this point in discussing the need for what they call *collective impact*. They criticize the current approach that many funders reinforce.

> Most funders, faced with the task of choosing a few grantees from many applicants, try to ascertain which organizations make the greatest contributions toward solving a social problem. . . . Each organization is judged on its own potential to achieve impact, independent of the numerous other organizations that may also influence the issue. (p. 38)

They call this tendency the *isolated impact approach* because it focuses on a solution that a single organization can bring about. Far from facilitating improvement in big issues, such as reducing violence in a community, they argue that the result of this isolated approach is that "nearly 14 million nonprofits try to invent independent solutions to major social problems, often working at odds with each other" (p. 38). According to these same authors, there is little evidence that such isolated efforts can address the increasingly complicated challenges of today.

Although the isolated impact approach has dominated community action, it has become evident that major social problems generally require a collective effort. Collective impact theory thus suggests that large-scale improvement and social change require coordination, collaboration, and cooperation among organizations and across sectors (Hanley-Brown, Kania, & Kramer, 2012; Kania & Kramer, 2011). In the collaboration literature, Innes and Booher (2010) further note that

> the rational decider utilizing research in an instrumental way to make policy choices from a position of power in government is gradually being replaced by the idea of an array of public and private players out there, linked together by networks in an evolving governance process, continuously learning and acting. (p. 143)

Thus, some theoretical models argue for the need to place the conceptualization of community change within a system's framework (Foster-Fishman, Nowell, & Yang, 2007; Tseng & Seidman, 2007). To help researchers think pragmatically about situating scholarship in long-term positive change, we have developed a framework that identifies some of the leverage points for CBR.

The Community Impact Framework

Our experience over years of working with campus and community projects and partnerships suggests that an evolving community impact framework can help those engaging in CBR to attain meaningful impact in the community. This framework, described next, consists of four components: a well-designed group with a commitment to a long-term collaborative endeavor, goal setting and other planning by the group toward the attainment of the goal, diverse participation in the group that is appropriate to the goal, and regular monitoring and revision of action and direction by the group.

The group and its design for long-term collective action. The first and most critical component for success in attaining positive social change is that a group of residents or organizations commits to a long-term endeavor. A variety of terms have been used to describe such groups: a *collaborative* or a *coalition* (Rowe, 1997); an *alliance* (Bibeau, Howell, Rife, & Taylor, 1996); or a *partnership*, *interdisciplinary community collaboration*, *collaborative research partnership*, or *consortia* (Caplan, Lefkowitz, & Spector, 1992). The vision and mission of the group may focus on a continuum of outcomes (Roussos & Fawcett, 2000), including (a) categorical issues (e.g., immunization or violence), (b) broader interrelated concerns (e.g., education and jobs), or (c) more fundamental social determinants of health and development (e.g., income disparities and trusting relationships).

The performance of these groups can be enhanced if their decisions are governed by principles of institutional design that address the chosen sphere(s) of influence of the group, membership in the collaborative effort, whether the collaborative effort is intended to be temporary or permanent, the decision-making process, and how formally or informally efforts of members of the group are aligned with one another. Adhering to a well-considered institutional design for collaborative action will heighten the effectiveness of such a group.

Perhaps most important, the use of an institutional design should suit the type of work to be accomplished. Margerum (2011) notes that the institutional design for collaboration should vary according to whether the group hopes to effect change at the level of action, organization, or policy. Promoting change at the level of action means that the group will be involved in direct on-the-ground activities, such as education or service delivery. If the chosen level for work is the organization, emphasis will be placed on priorities and programs of the organizations involved. Influencing governmental legislation is an example of how the policy level might be addressed. The level or focus for the work will determine other features of the group, for example, group membership. For instance, the service provision group will want members who are more effective in furthering service provision than policy change. It is also the case, though, that efforts do not have to fall neatly within one of these levels; some efforts can be nested within or traverse two or three levels.

One of the challenges presented by a collective approach to impact is simply sustaining the collaboration to fulfill the commitment to the kind of long-term involvement that will be required to reach a substantive, meaningful community goal. A variety of factors have been identified as important in sustaining a collaborative approach, including issues related to leadership, staffing, and information capacity (Margerum, 2011). Collaborative approaches require substantial time and energy, which highlights the importance and role of staff (Margerum, 2011) or a committed facilitator whether paid or not (Beckman & Caponigro, 2006). Although the form and purpose of collaborative efforts vary considerably and make generalizing difficult, considering and attending to known pitfalls during development will make the collaboration more sustainable.

Faculty and others interested in using CBR to reach community impact might take one of two approaches to such a group. First, they could find existing ongoing efforts aimed at reaching a long-term community impact and ensure that their own and their students' CBR are aligned with the effort. A second more labor-intensive and time-consuming approach is for academic teachers and researchers to help create a long-term effort to contextualize their CBR and that of others toward social improvement over time.

Goal setting and other planning. Creating a long-term goal is the second defining component of successful collaborative groups. After establishing a goal, perhaps through a concept mapping (Trochim, 1989) or logic modeling (Fielden, Rusch, & Sands, 2007; Kaplan & Garrett, 2005) process, the group may set objectives, and then initiate, guide, and monitor, through documenting and tracking, any number of endeavors that might emerge or be developed to move the community toward the goal.

In our experience, members of a collaborative group often staff and guide their own separate organizations that have their own individual goals and objectives. One of the aims for participants of the large coalition is to see where one or more of the activities of their own organizations could already be addressing the goal of the coalition or alliance. Coalition members can also come together to plan and take joint action toward the goal.

Once this group and a goal are in place, all kinds of academic efforts can be aligned with it. Clearly, CBR could make contributions to the aims of the alliance, whether led by undergraduates, graduate students, faculty, and academic or other staff. Other student efforts could likewise help, including direct service through service-learning classes, service as extracurricular activity through student organizations, senior theses, independent projects, and so on. Faculty service could also be part of such a large effort. The possibilities are many for ways members of an academic community might be involved.

Diverse participation. The third component is the involvement of a variety of people in the different aspects of such an effort; this is important for enhancing the possibility that long-term change will actually occur. Diverse participation can bring many perspectives to the work over time. For on-the-ground change, the group should represent a range of community perspectives; at the organizational change level, it should represent a range of management organizations; and at the policy change level, diverse participation would mean representation of a range of policy interests on the issue (Margerum, 2011).

An effort may involve individuals who are experiencing the challenge being addressed by the coalition. For example, in a health-oriented community effort, teens dealing with obesity or seniors struggling with diabetes might be members of the coalition. Media, politicians, and others can also be quite helpful when it comes to developing and carrying out strategies to address social challenges. Such diversity not only helps to ensure that information is adequately shared but also facilitates progress in reaching the goal. Expertise obtained from multiple types of community stakeholders, including community residents as well as professionals, is usually required to create community change that improves the quality of life in marginalized communities (Bayne-Smith, Mizrahi, & Garcia, 2008). Others have similarly noted that for such groups to be successful, "participants should include a diversity of individuals and groups who represent the concern and/or geographic area or population" (Roussos & Fawcett, 2000, p. 370–371).

It is worth saying why this diversity is so important. In many cases, a researcher is not likely to know the best way to get needed information from affected or relevant individuals. For example, if a researcher wants to talk with people who are HIV positive, he or she may not know how to find them or gain their trust. The researcher may also not know the best approach to collect information from them. However, if the researcher can collaborate with a person in the community who works directly with HIV-positive individuals, those directly affected, or those connected to others who are, the information acquired can be more accurate and detailed. Such a community contact person is sometimes referred to as the *critical bridge person*, who can play a crucial role in constructing an interactive dialogue between researchers and the community (Kezar, 2007).

Collaboration of diverse groups and individuals may be the most difficult aspect of CBR work aimed toward long-term impact. "Historical factors, different uses of geographic space by groups of different races and ethnicities, and other conditions of the specific context of the work must be considered and negotiated in this process" (Beckman et al., 2011, p. 86). However, if the aim is to enhance the chances of actually attaining a long-term goal, then an effort toward such broad involvement is invaluable (Baker, Homan, Schonoff, & Kreuter, 1999; Lynn, 2000).

Regular monitoring and revision. The fourth component of the community impact framework is that the partnership engages in regular review and revising of its outcomes and strategies to ensure that actions are moving toward the desired community impact. Ensuring alignment with the established long-term goal requires an oversight body to review and revise activities regularly; this review and revision process increases the likelihood that learning will occur not just at the task level but also at the level of strategies/goals, referred to as *double-loop learning* (Argyris & Schön, 1995). Indeed, the literature emphasizes the need for this rigorous evaluation over time, as well as for the integration of assessments into ongoing initiatives (Granner & Sharpe, 2004; Marullo et al., 2003; Sandoval et al., 2012).

The monitoring and revision element of the community impact framework could be thought of as a part of planning and thus included in the second element of the community impact framework described earlier. However, because of the difficulty we have found in getting groups to be attentive to this process, we are separating it explicitly as a fourth element. From our experience, it is much easier for groups to set goals and plan activities than to examine implementation strategies and make appropriate revisions. These steps are too easily put aside. Thus, if the effort is to move beyond simply producing outputs, we intentionally stress the critical role of this aspect of planning.

A Diagnostic Tool

To assist faculty and others in applying this framework, we have designed the CBR diagnostic table (Table 2.1), which provides a short description of each element of the framework as well as some guidance about timing. It includes questions to help researchers think through the strengths and weaknesses of their collaborative initiative.

TABLE 2.1
CBR Diagnostic Table

	Participation	The Group and Its Institutional Design	Goals and Planning	Monitoring and Revision
Time Frame	Prior to creation of group, attention should be given by initiators to the types of participants needed and regularly reconsidered in light of group aims.	This should be considered prior to formation of group and then clarified early by initial member stakeholders. It may change in light of monitoring information.	A goal is formalized as membership solidifies. Planning is ongoing and revisited in light of monitoring information obtained.	Once the group has formed, monitoring information is collected and reviewed regularly at predetermined times and used to improve action toward the goal annually at a minimum.
Characteristics	The group engages a broad range of stakeholders/citizens in development and ongoing review of research results and action toward the goal. Participants may include affected populations, service or issue organizations, funders, academic entities, elected officials, public staff, and media.	This depends on the aims of the effort and the level where change is to be effected. Aim(s) can organize along a continuum of action, organization, and policy. The level of influence (one or multiple) will determine who is involved, formality, alignment of efforts, decision making, and permanence of structures.	The group has a long-term goal. It either coalesces around that goal or addresses already occurring efforts toward that goal or addresses an issue at a new level or in a new way. Group activities are planned, or the group ensures that at least some member activities are aligned toward the goal.	The effort has routinized mechanisms for monitoring processes, actions, and results achieved; ensuring that reflective dialogue on monitoring information is obtained; and revising actions and processes accordingly. All should be accomplished with timing sufficient to allow outcomes or impacts to manifest themselves.

Questions				
Do participants reflect an appropriate mix to effect change at the desired level? How much time will each participant devote? Is participation voluntary or required, for example, by one's workplace? Are there appropriate organizational commitments? Are participation barriers (e.g. transportation, location, language) attended to?	Is there an existing effort on the issue? Is the group designed to manifest change at the desired level? What resources are needed for its function? Are they procured? Is the group formal or informal? Is there a method to address conflict, a leadership team or facilitator, and an appropriate alignment of the activities of member organizations?	Does group have clarity on the goal? Do individual stakeholder groups have clarity on their related contributions toward the goal? How will objectives be monitored and reported? Do action steps have deadlines? Is there a plan for review of appropriateness of stakeholders and recruiting new members as needed?	Are outputs and outcomes tracked? By whom? Is there a learning forum for review of monitoring information? Is there a plan for revising actions and processes to move the goal forward? Is the goal still appropriate? If not, do plans exist to revise the goal itself? Are these considerations routinized?

A Case in Progress

To aid in understanding how this framework is applied to CBR projects, we present the following case (see Stoecker & Beckman, 2014, for an abbreviated version). This case provides practical examples of the four elements of the community impact framework.

In 2011 the Center for Social Concerns (CSC) at the University of Notre Dame (ND) offered a small grant to an emerging neighborhood food co-op to assist in forming a food-related coalition in the area. In light of the number of disparate efforts over food throughout the county, the hope was that a coalition might focus energies and resources around one long-term goal and, in keeping with the community impact framework, monitor activities to help ensure the goal would be reached over time. The CSC also offered to provide some staff time to help the co-op leadership form the coalition and then facilitate it. At that time, no formal attention was given to the specific level of action (Margerum, 2011), but it was anticipated that the work would address more than one level. Over the course of a year, key leaders of the co-op, including an ND faculty member and a CSC staff person, selected invitees to ensure that the group would be appropriately diverse in its membership. Representatives from about 30 local organizations addressing food concerns including farms, food banks, community gardens, and related offices from other area universities came together to join in the effort. In addition, a number of neighborhood residents living in the area surrounding the developing food co-op joined the coalition.

It took the group about a year to come up with a goal, using a concept mapping process. The goal was very broad: to improve food security in the county by 2015. In addition to the goal, the concept mapping led to three related objectives: increase awareness locally about food-related challenges, foster connections among people and organizations dealing with food-related concerns; and enhance the infrastructure aimed at getting food where it could be most beneficial. All the organizational representatives involved saw their current jobs or other work as furthering one or more of these objectives, although there was no other discussion in coalition meetings about formulating measurable objectives or action strategies.

In the early part of year two, coalition members decided to work on a project together. They planned and held a conference that was attended by about 70 individuals from the county and areas beyond. By design, the event addressed two of the coalition's objectives: increase awareness in the area about food-related challenges and foster connections across the geographic area on food needs. Although the actions that followed from the conference have not been tracked formally, anecdotal evidence suggests that various groups and individuals took further action as a result of what they learned there or from the connections they made.

Two related undergraduate CBR projects are important to highlight. The first project was developed as part of an academic course, offered by ND theology professor Margie Pfeil before the formation of the coalition. It gathered information about the concerns of residents in the neighborhood. The output of this course informed the creation of the co-op. The second project was led by David Blouin, a faculty member from Indiana University of South Bend (IUSB), as part of a research methods course. The student research was conducted after the co-op was in existence for some time. The co-op used the results of the project to improve the types of products offered and address price concerns. In both cases, output from the research was used and led to outcomes.

The coalition leadership is attempting to track and document actions, outputs, and outcomes that are emerging from the coalition's efforts. In addition to the time-consuming nature of collecting such information, most outcomes are difficult to measure; it is even more difficult to assign causality, as noted earlier. The co-op has increased its hours, membership, and sales. Can the coalition be credited with this? That is not clear. It is possible this would have occurred without the larger body affiliating with the emerging co-op project. This lack of evidence to support what some clearly saw as outcomes underscores the importance of identifying clear approaches for obtaining monitoring information for various stages of the initiative. Doing so also provides a clear road map that allows for adjustment of strategies should the stakeholders find they are going in a direction they did not intend.

Informal conversations at a coalition meeting led coalition members to contact local farmers to request that they supply fresh produce to local food banks. These previously uninvolved farmers agreed to the request. This outcome directly relates to two of the coalition's objectives: Increase useful connections among parties across the geographic area and improve the infrastructure for food allocation. Although there was no direct connection made at any coalition meeting between these objectives and the informal conversations about the food bank needs, the facilitator of the coalition, who knows the local terrain of action on food issues, firmly believes this outcome would not have occurred without the coalition.

The CSC staff person who facilitated the coalition, Naomi Penney, has since moved away from the county. Our previous experience and that of others suggests that the facilitator is key in the work of such groups (Beckman & Caponigro, 2006). Whether because of the facilitator's departure or the inherent difficulty in bringing coalition members together, the fourth element of the community impact framework, monitoring and revision, has not been fulfilled to date.

This case provides examples of the two approaches noted earlier that a faculty member or other CBR facilitator might take when seeking to incorporate CBR into a class: (a) join an existing collaboration or (b) help start or lead a coalition and facilitate CBR as part of that role. IUSB professor David Blouin took the first approach. He brought his students into the work of the food coalition for one reason only: to help the co-op better focus its efforts. He aligned the CBR initiative with a broad, ongoing effort on food security, which is in accordance with the first option. In contrast, ND professor Margie Pfeil's student project is an example of the second option. She engaged her students in the identification of food concerns in the neighborhood the co-op now serves. Information provided from this CBR course jump-started a variety of food-related activities, including the development of the coalition itself. Pfeil remains a leader in the coalition and continues to involve her students in CBR projects related to its work.

Community-Based Research Toward Happier, Healthier Communities

This chapter urges readers to think about the role that CBR can play in community improvement as they design research. Whether the research is a one-shot effort or ongoing, designing research so that its intended output will address the information needs for a desired community outcome is an important step.

However, if researchers want to contribute to *impact* as defined in this chapter, we suggest they consider integrating their work with broader collaborative efforts. Such efforts, we have claimed, would do well to be guided by a group, made up of diverse actors, that has an agreed-upon long-term goal, and whose members regularly weigh in on successes and challenges in reaching the goal. These elements can ensure that needed perspectives and expertise are drawn upon and that appropriate adjustments can be made to activities to further progress toward the goal. It is our belief that alignment of CBR with such long-term efforts will enhance its contribution to community development.

References

Amerson, R. (2010). The impact of service-learning on cultural competence. *Nursing Education Perspectives, 31*(1), 18–22.

Argyris, C., & Schön, D. (1995). *Organizational learning II: Theory, method, and practice*. Boston, MA: Addison-Wesley.

Bach, R., & Weinzimmer, J. (2011). Exploring the benefits of community-based research in a sociology of sexualities course. *Teaching Sociology*, *39*(1), 57–72.

Baker, E. A., Homan, S., Schonoff, R., & Kreuter, M. (1999). Principles of practice for academic/practice/community research partnerships. *American Journal of Preventive Medicine*, *16*(3), 86–93.

Bayne-Smith, M., Mizrahi, T. & Garcia, M. (2008). Interdisciplinary community collaboration: Perspectives of community practitioners on successful strategies. *Journal of Community Practice*, *16*(3), 249–269.

Beckman, M., & Caponigro, J. (2006). The creation of a university community alliance to address lead hazards. *Journal of Higher Education Outreach and Engagement*, *10*(3), 95–108.

Beckman, M., Penney, N., & Cockburn, B. (2011). Maximizing the impact of community-based research. *Journal of Higher Education Outreach and Engagement*, *15*(2), 83–104.

Bibeau, D. L., Howell, K. A., Rife, J. C., & Taylor, M. L. (1996). The role of a community coalition in the development of health services for the poor and uninsured. *International Journal of Health Services*, *26*(1), 93–110.

Boothroyd, R. I., Fawcett, S. B., & Foster-Fishman, P. (2004). *Community development: Enhancing the knowledge base through participatory action research.* Washington, DC: American Psychological Association.

Buch, K., & Harden, S. (2011). The impact of a service-learning project on student awareness of homelessness, civic attitudes, and stereotypes toward the homeless. *Journal of Higher Education Outreach and Engagement*, *15*(3), 45–61.

Caplan, P. A., Lefkowitz, B., & Spector, L. (1992). Health care consortia: A mechanism for increasing access for the medically indigent. *Henry Ford Hospital Medical Journal*, *40*(1/2), 50–55.

Chupp, M. G., & Joseph, M. L. (2010). Getting the most out of service learning: Maximizing student, university and community impact. *Journal of Community Practice*, *18*(2/3), 190–212.

Currie, M., King, G., Rosenbaum, P., Law, M., Kertoy, M., & Specht, J. (2005). A model of impacts of research partnerships in health and social services. *Evaluation and Program Planning*, *28*(4), 400–412.

Deeley, S. J. (2010). Service-learning: Thinking outside the box. *Active Learning in Higher Education*, *11*(1), 43–53.

Felten, P., & Clayton, P. H. (2011). Service learning. *New Directions for Teaching and Learning*, *2011*(128), 75–84.

Fielden, S. J., Rusch, M. T., & Sands, J. (2007). Evaluation and program planning. Key consideration for logic model development to research partnership: A Canadian case study. *Science Direct*, *30*(2), 115–124.

Foster-Fishman, P., Nowell, B., & Yang, H. (2007). Putting the system back into systems change: A framework for understanding and changing organizational and community systems. *American Journal of Community Psychology*, *39*(3–4), 197–215.

Granner, M. L., & Sharpe, P. A. (2004). Evaluating community coalition characteristics and functioning: A summary of measurement tools. *Health Education Research, 19*(5), 514–532.

Hanley-Brown, F., Kania, J., & Kramer, M. (2012). *Channeling change: Making collective impact work.* Retrieved from ssir.org/pdf/Channeling_Change_PDF.pdf

Hawe, P., Bond, L., & Butler, H. (2009). Knowledge theories can inform evaluation practice: What can a complexity lens add? *New Directions for Evaluation, 2009*(124), 89–100.

Hendricks, M., Plantz, M., & Pritchard, K. (2008). Measuring outcomes of United Way–funded programs: Expectations and reality. *New Directions for Evaluation, 2010*(119), 13–35.

Innes, J. E., & Booher, D. E. (2010). *Planning with complexity: An introduction to collaborative rationality for public policy.* London, UK: Routledge.

Kania, J., & Kramer, M. (2011). Collective impact. *Stanford Social Innovation Review, 9*(1), 36–41.

Kaplan, S. A., & Garrett, K. E. (2005). The use of logic models by community-based initiatives. *Evaluation and Program Planning, 28*(2), 167–172.

Kezar, A. (2007). A tale of two cultures: Schools and universities in partnership for school reform and student success. *Metropolitan Universities, 18*(4), 28–47.

Knapp, T., Fisher, B., & Levesque-Bristol, C. (2010). Service-learning's impact on college students' commitment to future civic engagement, self-efficacy, and social empowerment. *Journal of Community Practice, 18*(2/3), 233–251.

Kubisch, A., Auspos, P., Brown, P., Buck, E., & Dewar, T. (2011). Voices from the field III: Lessons and challenges for foundations based on two decades of community change efforts. *Foundation Review, 3*(1/2), 1–2.

Levesque-Bristol, C., Knapp, T. D., & Fisher, B. J. (2010). The effectiveness of service-learning: It's not always what you think. *Journal of Experiential Education, 33*(3), 208–224.

Lynn, F. (2000). Community-scientist collaboration in environmental research. *American Behavioral Scientist, 44*, 649–663.

Margerum, R. D. (2011). *Beyond consensus: Improving collaborative planning and management.* Cambridge, MA: MIT Press.

Marullo, S., Cooke, D., Willis, J., Rollins, A., Burke, J., Bonilla, P., & Waldref, V. (2003). Community-based research assessments: Some principles and practices. *Michigan Journal of Community Service-Learning, 9*(3), 57–68.

Matarrita-Cascante, D., & Brennan, M. A. (2012). Conceptualizing community development in the twenty-first century. *Community Development, 43*(3), 293–305.

Mayne, J. (2008). *Contribution analysis: An approach to exploring cause and effect.* Retrieved from www.cgiar-ilac.org/files/ILAC_Brief16_Contribution_Analysis_0.pdf

McLaughlin, J. A., & Jordon, G. B. (2010). Using logic models, In H. Wholey, H. Harty, & K. Newcomb (Eds.), *A handbook of practical program evaluation.* San Francisco, CA: Jossey-Bass.

Roussos, S. T., & Fawcett, S. B. (2000). A review of collaborative partnerships as a strategy for improving community health. *Annual Review of Public Health, 21,* 369–402.

Rowe, W. (1997). Changing ATOD norms and behaviors: A Native American community commitment to wellness. *Evaluation and Program Planning, 20*(3), 323–333.

Sandoval, J. A., Lucero, J., Oetzel, J., Avila, M., Belone, L., Mau, M., . . . Wallerstein, N. (2012). Process and outcome constructs for evaluating community-based participatory research projects: A matrix of existing measures. *Health Education Research, 27*(4), 680–690.

Seider, S. C., Gillmor, S., & Rabinowicz, S. (2012). The impact of community service learning upon the expected political voice of participating college students. *Journal of Adolescent Research, 27*(1), 44–77.

Stoecker, R., & Beckman, M. (2014). Making higher education community engagement matter in the community. In J. Laker, C. Naval, & K. Mrnjaus (Eds.), *Citizenship, democracy and higher education in Europe, Canada and the U.S.* (pp. 123–146). London, UK: Palgrave Macmillan.

Stoecker, R., Beckman, M., & Min, B. H. (2010). Evaluating the community impact of higher education community engagement. In H. E. Fitzgerald, C. Burac & S. Seifer (Eds.), *Handbook of engaged scholarship: The contemporary landscape. Volume 2: Community-campus partnerships* (pp. 177–198). East Lansing: Michigan State University Press.

Strand, K., Marullo, S., Cutforth, N., Stoecker, R., & Donohue, P. (2003). *Community-based research and higher education: Principles and practices.* San Francisco, CA: Jossey-Bass.

Trochim, W. M. (1989). *An introduction to concept mapping for planning and evaluation.* Retrieved from www.socialresearchmethods.net/research/epp89/Trochim1.pdf

Tseng, V., & Seidman, E. (2007). A systems framework for understanding social settings. *American Journal of Community Psychology, 39*(3/4), 217–228.

Walter, A., Helgenberger, S., Wiek, A., & Scholz, R. W. (2007). Measuring societal effects of transdisciplinary research projects: Design and application of an evaluation method. *Evaluation and Program Planning, 30*(4), 325–338.

Wholey, J. S. (1987). Evaluability assessment: Developing program theory. *New Directions for Program Evaluation, 1987*(33), 77–92.

3

COMMUNITY-BASED RESEARCH FROM THE PERSPECTIVE OF THE COMMUNITY PARTNERS

Jessica Quaranto and Debra Stanley

When we started to write this chapter, we were struck by our mixed emotions. Stanley's long career in the South Bend, Indiana, community and decades of experience in forming partnerships with the University of Notre Dame left her questioning the overall dynamics of the community-university relationship. Similarly, Quaranto's experiences with community-university partnerships across several cities and communities left her feeling generally frustrated and searching for a better understanding of what ultimately makes these partnerships successful and worthwhile. Both of us have witnessed community-based research (CBR) done well and CBR that went so terribly wrong it should not have been called CBR. Those experiences have left us cautious about how we engage with faculty in this valuable work, yet still hopeful about the potential for CBR to help bring lasting community change.

To reach this potential, we believe the perspectives of community partners need to be incorporated into the work of CBR to a much greater degree than they are currently. In 2002 the Campus Community Partnership for Health (CCPH), in collaboration with nine other organizations including the Centers for Disease Control, undertook a four-year study to examine community-institutional partnerships focused on prevention research. Based on its findings, the partnership produced a curriculum for developing and sustaining CBR partnerships and published its report (Seifer, 2006). Similarly, discussions on a community-based participatory research (CBPR) electronic mailing list, cosponsored by CCPH and the Wellesley Institute, inspired a series of journal articles in the November 2006 issue of the *Journal of Urban Health* that addressed the nature of the challenges to CBPR partnerships and potential solutions. Despite these and other published reports, little has been written directly from the perspective of community partners (Stoecker & Tryon, 2009). Throughout this chapter, we address this deficit by highlighting concerns and recommendations of community partners in making the CBR process successful for all involved.

The chapter begins with two questions that frame the remaining content. We then examine two major obstacles that hinder successful CBR partnerships working toward long-term social change: the social-historical context of community–higher education partnerships and the often conflicting motivations for engaging in CBR. These obstacles stem from larger systemic challenges that academic and community partners each face relative to the lack of a culture of collaboration or structural incentives (e.g., peer encouragement, financial resources, job security etc.). To overcome these obstacles, we discuss three concepts that have been useful in our own projects and the work of other community members: bridge builders, narrative, and synergy. The chapter concludes with specific recommendations for ensuring that CBR work will be more likely to lead to long-term change in the community.

Key Questions to Consider

Before delving into the bigger picture of the community's perceptions of CBR challenges and potential solutions, we would like to raise two key questions. First, who is the *community*? Are we referring to specific populations within a city or area? Are we talking about people affected by a specific social problem, or simply those less fortunate than the folks on the academic side? Do we include just community organizations and nonprofits or other institutions, such as businesses and public associations that also comprise and support communities? For that matter, is the university not part of the community we speak of? Why do we so often refer to community-academic partnerships as if the two are distinct?

Using the term *community-based research* implies that research is located in the community, but it does not necessarily connote community-owned or community-generated research. In practice, community partners rarely play a direct role in shaping the discussion about the broader field of CBR or the semantics used. They seldom attend conferences on CBR or participate in presentations. Instead, the community voice is often peripheral or supplemental in academic discussions about CBR. Although the intent of CBR is to value equally the knowledge and experience of the academic and community partners (Strand, Cutforth, Stoecker, Marullo, & Donohue, 2003), regardless of how we define *community*, higher education is often the more powerful and amplified voice at the table.

The second question we urge those contemplating CBR to ask is what specific change do they hope to achieve through CBR? It is important to consider from the onset of the research whether the goal is simply seeking to obtain a short-term academic or educational effect or achieving a larger institutional or community impact. If the partners seek a dramatic shift in public policy or the alleviation of a broader social problem, they will likely need to consider how changing power and privilege dynamics plays into long-term social change and incorporate those components into their CBR project design.

We pose these questions not because we intend to provide all the answers but to introduce the complexity of the CBR process, its intent, and even the semantic disparity that exists from the community perspective. For our purposes, we propose that for those working in CBR, community should be broadly construed and inclusive and that the activity of CBR itself should always originate in partnership with community and ultimately be oriented toward long-term social change.

Challenges

Terms such as *community* are loaded with assumptions and implications, so addressing these two questions personally in the classroom and in the context of a research partnership is a good place to start. Wrestling with the answers to these questions may uncover some of the larger tensions inherent in most community-university partnerships. We now focus on two of those challenges.

Social-Historical Context of Community and Higher Education Partnerships

Is it contradictory to think that colleges and universities can be unencumbered agents of long-term social change when in and of themselves they frequently perpetuate structural injustices and inequities? Town-gown relationships are often characterized by disparities of power and privilege, but if unaddressed, these dynamics pose an inherent challenge and limitation to the role of CBR in long-term social change. To be effective, it is critical that CBR projects take into account the damaging effect these dynamics can have on the self-esteem and self-efficacy of would-be community partners.

In our experience, faculty and students often do not live in the neighborhoods with which they desire to form partnerships for research and change. When this geographical separation is added to larger sociocultural and historical inequities, the result is that students and faculty of service-learning or CBR rarely reflect the social demographics of the communities they serve (Stoecker & Tryon, 2009). This incongruity creates an often unspoken dynamic that academic partners with more perceived knowledge and skills are providing charity for those who have less perceived knowledge or skills. Fundamental social changes require addressing the underlying causes of these inequities, and partners operating in this context must acknowledge the reality of these problematic perspectives in viewing the community versus higher education. Partners need to name and attempt to dispel any resulting stereotypes they may have of one another (Freeman, Brugge, Bennett-Bradley, Levy, & Carrasco, 2006).

CBR partners must also work to undo preconceptions about the meaning of research and service. Both of us have witnessed the quick, self-entitled, and sometimes aggressive way institutions swoop into communities to conduct research. Community members have experienced thoughtless or poorly conducted student and faculty service and research projects. It is not uncommon to hear that a community has been "surveyed to death by students." Overcoming these tensions in a community's long-term collective memory can be quite difficult, particularly if a specific institution has a poor reputation in a community because of a project or survey conducted even a decade ago. Painful memories can remain after a perceived lack of sensitivity to community well-being based on geographical boundaries between the institution and the community, scarce sharing of campus resources, or even just bad off-campus housing policies. Communities can likewise grow weary of serving as a constant learning experience for students who are quick to adopt a savior or self-righteous attitude about their community service work rather than an attitude of partnership. This is not to say that all previous research or service-learning was poorly conducted or ineffective. It is simply important to be aware of this problem and if necessary make a distinct break from prior research and community-based learning when aiming for true collaboration in CBR.

Conflicting Motivations

We recognize that CBR is just one piece of the mosaic of most partners' lives. Students are engaged in multiple classes and activities, in addition to maintaining grades, studying for exams, and eventually graduating. Faculty members teach, chair departments, publish, and seek tenure, among other commitments. It is also no secret that most staff in community organizations can be similarly overwhelmed by the immediate needs of the communities they serve, coupled with the pressures of sustaining a nonprofit with perpetual funding uncertainty. Therefore, we find that most partnerships are formed by motivations for short-term gains. For example, a community partner needs a program evaluation required by a grantor, faculty seek to supplement a one-semester classroom experience, and students are required to take an applied research course. Even projects that begin with these short-term goals in mind can foster partnerships that eventually use CBR to focus on long-term social change. We highlight a few of those projects later.

At the same time, however, there is often an imbalance in investments on the part of each partner, which in itself is an obstacle to long-term social change. Our experience suggests that unnamed personal or short-term motivations and investments can inadvertently cause power struggles in which partners feel compelled to demonstrate and defend their own knowledge and values related to an issue. This can escalate into a conflict that could be avoided if motivations are clearly examined at the beginning of the partnership.

Unfortunately, even when partners prioritize community change over these other personal or short-term motivations, the institutional cultures they belong to may intentionally (or unintentionally) place the interests of the institution first. Colleges and universities can limit the degree to which individual faculty can prioritize community change given their position at the university; this poses significant complications for faculty partners as they attempt to balance intentional CBR with earning tenure or being published in a peer-reviewed journal.

Community organizations and even local government offices must regularly compete with each other for resources; consequently, collaboration can often be disincentivized in the short term. Community-based organizations (CBOs) that do not have the long-term support of their funders must prioritize their own short-term sustainability for the CBR and overall work to continue. Involving other community partners (e.g., local government, businesses, or long-time community residents) can help to mitigate these effects and anchor the work further in the community perspective. Yet many community organization staff do not recognize that without ongoing qualitative and quantitative research, they may only be perpetuating a cycle that serves the community organization and its employees rather than their target populations. Engaging in CBR can help staff situate their work in a larger context and help them understand the importance and need to involve their clients or participants in the planning, design, and implementation of CBR and its outcomes. Within this context, faculty (especially those in the social sciences) can offer wisdom from the broader field and the literature available to support the community workers' understanding of how their work compares with or may benefit from similar research.

For CBR to truly be effective at transforming communities, each partner must carefully examine its motives. Despite larger contextual challenges, collaborative partnerships are maintained for reasons other than the individual needs of each partner, but motivation influences the overall goal or tone of the research and partnership.

Strategies to Achieve Sustainable Community Impact

Three broad individual-level strategies can potentially prevent and mitigate these and other obstacles. They pertain to the kinds of people involved and the quality and intentionality of time and space allotted for the research.

Find or Forge a Bridge Builder

Successful partnerships are characterized by working relationships that are based on respect and transparency from the start. We have found that partnerships that are successful over the long term often involve an individual or group of individuals who have experience working in the academic and community spheres. Individuals with well-established relationships in community and academic settings can leverage those relationships to sustain projects and orient both groups to the needs of each individual partner. Initially, these bridge builders act to empower all partners and balance power among them, which can include managing expectations. They can support everyone at the table in recognizing the value of their voice, experience, and knowledge. Most of the current literature suggests that successful CBR partnerships are predicated on this equality of power and valuing of knowledge (Seifer, 2006; Strand et al., 2003), but it is often difficult to achieve if partners do not know each other well or do not share the same language.

Some CBR guides delegate this role to a formal campus center that coordinates CBR (Strand et al., 2003). While we agree that these university-hosted centers have the potential to bridge the gap between partners, they are not always successful in doing so because they are anchored in the university setting. One potential way to alleviate this anchor challenge is for universities (or for that matter larger community partner organizations) to create joint community-university positions or centers in the community.

Quaranto's experience as a bridge builder was forged at two locations: a university center on campus and a university-supported but community-placed nonprofit outreach center. Working concurrently at both locations allowed her to build relationships as a community partner and yet have access to the unique resources and networks of the university. In addition to leading a specific CBR project that evaluated a local program, she also used her role by linking other community partners to faculty and students at the university. It was critical to split her time between the two physical sites to best facilitate this work. Having access to space at the university and community tables allowed her to communicate on behalf of each partner, regardless of the context, and provide a safe space for meeting members of both groups.

Our experiences further suggest that some community partners find it useful to share space off campus with student or faculty partners while working on CBR. This shared space increases communication between partners and grounds the academic partner in the realities of the community organization and the community itself. Colocations can create a natural bridge in the partnership (L. Prior, personal communication, November 3, 2011) and help community partners feel equal ownership over the project's development and implementation. When larger coordinating or membership organizations have roots in the community and regularly work with multiple community partners on the ground, they may have similar access to community and larger institutional resources.

It is also not uncommon for recent graduates of postgraduate or undergraduate programs to be hired by local nonprofits, governments, or businesses. If they maintain links to their colleges while working in the community, they can serve as natural bridges for CBR projects. Similarly, paraprofessionals who have spent decades in community work may return to school later in life. These individuals are also uniquely positioned to build bridges between the campus and community.

Unlike those with dual-membership experience, not all individuals or organizations have the capacity to build bridges related to CBR. Those who do have a keen understanding of community-university relations, are able to facilitate and interpret conversations, and most important, earn the respect of community and institutional members. However, identifying or helping to develop bridge builders requires creatively understanding and taking advantage of the fluid nature of community and institutional membership. It is the responsibility of community and university partners to cultivate these individuals and institutions.

Bridging the Gap Between Market Research and Food Delivery

Lynn Prior, director of Buy Fresh Buy Local (BFBL) in the Lehigh Valley of Pennsylvania, works regularly with faculty and students from surrounding colleges and universities (see Chapter 7). The Lehigh Valley chapter of BFBL is one of 80 small local chapters throughout the United States. Each is an individually run nonprofit that promotes and educates farmers and consumers about locally grown food.

Through the Lehigh Valley Research Consortium, Prior connected with professors from nearby Lehigh University, Lafayette College, and Muhlenberg College in 2009 to research the food economy in the Lehigh Valley. Initially, Prior presented her ideas and questions regarding food production and consumer demand to a Lafayette professor's undergraduate market research class. She attended another session at the end of the semester where students presented their findings. (The academic partner's experience is described in Chapter 7.)

Prior notes that strong partnerships set clearly shared goals and expectations at the outset of a project, establish regular communication and feedback loops, narrow or simplify the initial focus of a project or partnership, and jointly determine not only the research questions but also the funding sources. She recognized a need for the academic partners, especially students, to better understand the reality of the community before embarking on CBR to comprehend the context and offer practical solutions. She also realized that she and other community partners needed to recognize their own power and voice.

Two years later, the faculty member overseeing the market research class began to serve with Prior on an advisory board that is writing a fresh food access plan for the region. Currently, BFBL hosts an on-site graduate student fellow and an undergraduate student who are both conducting research at the organization. The students are helping BFBL and its partners better understand food access in low-income areas of the region. BFBL serves as an intermediary between the colleges and universities (and other larger institutions) and the community partners that provide direct service to the community.

Prior takes BFBL's liaison role seriously, underscoring the importance of amplifying the voice of the consumer and the on-the-ground nonprofit partners. Based on CBR results and relying on broader institutional partnerships with universities, hospitals, and economic developers, BFBL and its partners were able to set up a farm share program to increase access to fresh foods in three local low-income communities (L. Prior, personal communication, November 3, 2011; February 13, 2013)

Prior's work in building bridges between BFBL and campus partners was successful because of the following:

1. She facilitated and maintained a network of connections among local community organizations, local farms, and larger institutional partners, including a hospital. The participation of all the organizations was critical in getting individual residents to take part in the newest initiative.
2. She helped her staff form cognitive connections between their prior knowledge and experience and the initial CBR work with the marketing research class, which affected their future projects and partnerships.

Cultivating Moral Imagination Through Narrative

Another concept we embrace as necessary for successfully achieving long-term social change and simultaneously addressing the complexities and contexts in which CBR is situated is the notion of creating space for a narrative that can help all partners develop a *moral imagination*, which is vital because it enables one to envision positive and negative consequences that may result from an imagined possibility (Johnson, 1993). With this skill, an individual can create the future but ground his or her work in the moral realities of the present (Lederach, 2005). People with a moral imagination understand how different actions might affect the current and future situations or be felt and interpreted by others. Lederach, a peace scholar and practitioner, writes:

> [The moral imagination] requires the capacity to imagine ourselves in a web of relationships that includes our enemies; the ability to sustain a paradoxical curiosity that embraces complexity without reliance on dualistic polarity; the fundamental belief in and pursuit of the creative act; and the acceptance of the inherent risk of stepping into the mystery of the unknown that lies beyond the far too familiar landscape of violence. (p. 5)

While institutions of higher education and communities are not at war with each other (at least we hope not), their relationships are complex and long-standing, with histories of often conflicting or at least differing cultures and motivations. Approaching these issues with a moral imagination can help overcome differences and acquaint CBR practitioners with the complexities that exist in their partners' environment. CBR, like peace building, is a technical exercise and a creative act.

Lederach (2005) identifies storytelling as a fundamental tenet to developing a moral imagination and relates it to a principle learned from a Tajik warlord: "You have to circle into the truth through stories" (p. 18). We too have come to better understand each other and how different decisions and actions might affect our partners by sharing the stories that shape our truths or realities. Other CBR partnerships with committed academic partners can likewise create sustainable spaces for communities to tell stories and think beyond immediate needs, to consider actions or drive policy for long-term change. Academic and community partners benefit from having space to discuss short- and long-term goals such as developing a program or instituting a policy change in the context of wider community change such as eradicating poverty (C. Collins, personal communication, November 6, 2011). When faculty possess this capacity, they can support communities' development and maintenance of long-term vision.

Sometimes the goal of CBR may not be to produce a paper for a peer-reviewed journal but rather actionable, accessible tools that can be applied to an issue. This can include using diverse kinds of dissemination to help extend the reach of the CBR project and the potential for social change. Storyboards, comic books, radio broadcasts, fact sheets, public forums, and intentional one-on-one conversations with key stakeholders or policy makers are all creative examples of how to disseminate results beyond traditional reports and to reach broad, nonacademic audiences.

The storytelling medium can likewise be used to organize, implement, and disseminate research. For instance, Quaranto coordinated a community-university partnership to develop a comic book about nonviolent conflict-resolution skills. Partners discussed the research design through storyboard planning, implemented youth focus groups to better understand skills that could be highlighted in the comic book, worked with youth authors and illustrators to tell the actual story, and used the finished product to disseminate the results. If the context is appropriate, partners can describe not only the results of the research but also the journey of the partnership. It is no accident that this chapter presents details and stories of different kinds of CBR projects to intentionally circle in on the truth of the community perspective.

We have found that creating the space for people to share their stories not only supports good research methodology but also amplifies the voice of the community members being served and benefits long-term sustainable partnerships and social change. Before embarking on CBR projects, creating a safe space for partners to share their own stories and listen to one another can likewise help alleviate misunderstandings and preconceptions resulting from social-historical contexts and seemingly conflicting motivations. For example, partners in a collaborative seeking to investigate the complexities of racism in health care went through an intensive training session before beginning their research (Yonas et al., 2006). Specifically, they all participated in a structured storytelling session designed to help them delve into their personal and collective experiences of racism in the health-care system. Participating in this intentional process helped humanize all the partners and eventually build trust. In the same way, interviews and focus groups that allow true space for storytelling encourage a richer understanding of the partners, research questions, and context in any community, and help explain the story behind numbers presented through quantitative data.

The Power of Stories in Health Care

Debra Stanley leads Imani Unidad, a nonprofit community-based organization that began in 2003 to provide HIV and substance abuse (SA) prevention education and advocacy through community efforts in South Bend. One of the initial outreach programs of Imani Unidad was a live, call-in program about HIV on a local faith-based radio channel. Later, Imani Unidad sought to generate a similar radio resource about SA. Before doing so, however, Stanley wanted to learn precisely what families needed and how best to support faith leadership in this area. She connected with an anthropology professor with a sincere commitment to CBR who had done extensive research in SA.

After listening to the concerns, goals, and expected outcomes of the project according to community partners (for three entire meetings), the professor supported the team in formulating potential research questions such as, "What additional knowledge did the faith community need to better serve members of their congregations?" The partners then presented the research opportunity to students who elected to join the team as part of their class credits. All of the partners then discussed and decided on methodology, landing on two targets: key informant interviews with individuals struggling with SA issues and several focus groups in the faith community. The community partners identified sites, recruited participants, and facilitated focus groups and interviews. Under the professor's guidance, the students conducted literature reviews, created research tools, recorded written and verbal responses, and analyzed data.

The team concluded there was a serious lack of adequate and effective treatment options for SA, and there was a substantial opportunity for the faith community to contribute to supplementing the available treatment centers. They also found that the existing community organizations' perceptions of what SA patients needed varied greatly from what the patients felt they needed or received.

To keep the conversation going, Imani Unidad ran two years of SSA radio programming based on the information collected and invited a variety of guests including recovering addicts, staff from local SA treatment facilities, and people providing support for family members with SA problems to tell their stories. The research thus informed the programming and made it more sustainable while solidifying Imani's essential partnership with members of the faith community, a critical component in disseminating the information. The partnership is now in its ninth year and has a new youth component. Many churches are now affiliated with a local chapter of Access to Recovery, a national initiative that provides vouchers to clients for the purchase of SA recovery outpatient support services (e.g., counseling) and receive technical assistance and training from Imani Unidad.

This successful community-campus partnership blossomed into a second project in which women with HIV were asked to talk about why they did not use local services. Students again helped collect these stories through interviews and focus groups, which established the need for support services as well as exactly what, when, where, and how women would prefer to receive these services from providers. These results allowed Imani Unidad to establish a weekly support group program that provides transportation and child care. The women share a meal, but education and socialization are the primary focus of the gatherings, not HIV. The group has been meeting for four years, and several of the first-generation survivors now serve as mentors for younger women in the group and assist with educational efforts to women's groups throughout the community. Imani Unidad has also received funding to hire a part-time case manager and an HIV-positive group facilitator.

Stanley's projects demonstrate the important role of facilitating storytelling and a moral imagination through CBR. They were successful because of the following:

1. Stanley and her academic partner heard each other's stories and used them to establish clear working roles and responsibilities as well as trust. This process broke down potential barriers between campus and community.
2. As the team created space for many facets of the HIV and SA stories to be collected through interviews and focus groups, they disseminated the results in diverse ways (e.g., storyboards, print materials, and intentional

one-on-one conversations), thereby reaching people who might not have paid attention to one particular format.

3. As members of community organizations listened to the stories, they became more understanding of obstacles community members faced in accessing their services and learned how to better meet residents' needs. Armed with this new knowledge, community organization members edited their own story lines and created new programmatic changes that provided community members with more effective services.

4. This storytelling process also expanded to include additional community members (recovering addicts, treatment facility staff, women with HIV), who publicly shared their stories in different formats (e.g., on the radio, in support groups). This created an inherent mechanism for long-term change by expanding the community's ability to tell, hear, respond, and learn from stories.

Orientation Toward Synergy

Successful partnerships are often characterized by a tone of mutual respect, unspoken shared values, and understanding. A strong sense of teamwork puts people at ease when saying what they think or aspire to without fear of hurting anyone's ego or feelings. The partners are committed not only to the partnership goals but also to each other. We suggest that this often intangible quality of relationships is actually an orientation toward synergy, an acknowledgment that together we are greater than simply the sum of our individual efforts and skills. This orientation requires a level of humility and interdependence that not every academic or community partner is comfortable with. Stoecker (2012) suggests the value of this synergistic quality in his example about flying geese.

> By flying in V formation the whole flock adds at least 71% greater flying range than if each bird flew on its own. People who share a common direction and sense of community can get where they are going more quickly and easily because they are traveling on the thrust of one another. (p. 24)

Synergy is often the result of a long-term investment in a community partnership and in social change. As partnership development is an inherently nonlinear process (Seifer, 2006) similar to a community organizing model or process, achieving initial shared small successes or rebounding from shared failures may help bring a partnership together in the long term. Over time, partners can develop a shared vision and commitment to community change. When this occurs, they take more risks and invite more people to the table to consider the implications of a research agenda or its results, including government officials and other potential agents of long-term social change.

Such developing partnerships stick (Palermo, McGranaghan, & Travers, 2006) because when trust is established and maintained, it keeps partners glued together (Greene-Moton, Palermo, Flicker, & Travers, 2006).

Synergy requires the self-awareness of each individual partner; that is, the ability to acknowledge one's strengths and potential weaknesses in the partnering process. It asks: How do you handle conflict? How flexible are you at communicating in diverse settings? Some helpful characteristics and orientations in CBR partners that help facilitate synergy are summarized in Table 3.1.

TABLE 3.1
Synergistic Tendencies: What Each Partner Can Bring to the Table

Faculty/Staff	*Community Partner*	*Students*
A sincere desire to use their expertise/skills/knowledge to assist community in answering community-developed questions	A desire to participate in CBR to transform their communities, amplify marginalized or underrepresented voices, and better serve community members	An understanding that CBR is a valuable component of the academic experience
A willingness to meet over time, beyond a single semester or academic year, listening and learning	A commitment to trusting the results even if they are not what were expected, and a commitment to act on those results	A respect for and valuing of what will be learned by engaging with people of different experiences
Reflective listening skills: the ability to hear what the community partner is saying and reflect it to formulate the question to arrive at the community partner's end goal	A willingness to provide honest feedback on how the project or its results are being implemented	An appreciation for the value of the contributions of those not formally a part of the academy
The ability to put unhealthy egos in one's pockets but maintain enough ego to want to do a good job	A courage and self-assurance about one's wisdom and knowledge of the community	A respect and appreciation for different kinds of knowledge and experience
An understanding that CBR is not consistently or even typically good for tenure, big grants, or status but can be in the long run if done well	A sense of activism and commitment to long-term community development	Humility to enter the project as an equal partner

Right People, Right Place, Right Time

In 2009 two undergraduate students from Washington and Lee University produced a CBR report about poverty in Lexington, Virginia. As the national economic collapse was profoundly affecting the area, the findings produced a strong emotional reaction in their community partners. The partnership decided to present the report at a larger community forum to solicit greater feedback and give futher community voice to the issues the partners felt were the most pressing.

The forum was a great success, producing a set of recommendations, picking up local press attention, and creating energy for action in the community and local government. Some suggested finding an organization in the community to own the project and move forward with the next steps, but community and faculty leaders recognized they needed a firm commitment from multiple partners who were already involved to maintain momentum. One such partner was David Dax, director of the United Way in Lexington and one of the original community members responding to the students' report to develop the forum. Dax and Don Dailey (then a faculty member at Washington and Lee), eventually co-led the Commission on Poverty, which emerged in response to the recommendations of the forum. Although no funding was available for this project, these two partners (and many others) pushed ahead by inviting a range of agencies to the table to see where the energy of the group would take them.

Claire Collins, former chief operating officer of Rockbridge County Government Services, attended the original forum and became a key partner in the commission. The report and forum had prioritized public transportation as a regular challenge for poor people in Lexington. The public transportation working group included stakeholders from local government, the community, and the university. As a result of the group's research and planning, a fixed bus route was established in March 2011 to better meet the community's transportation needs. Six months later, Collins reported the group was exploring further transportation issues in outlying areas because the initial bus route was a huge success in connecting those in need with access to food shopping and other resources.

Though many of the original partners moved on to other work and projects, overall the commission generated energy and momentum that continues to spin off into the community and university, creating lasting social change at many different levels (D. Dailey, D. Dax, & C. Collins, personal communications, October 6, 2011; October 13, 2011).

We believe the research partnership described in the text box was successful at achieving long-term social change because of synergy. Synergy and momentum emerged naturally as a result of the timing of the report and the willingness of the organizers to invite so many others to the table immediately after understanding the scope of the potential change that was needed. The partners continued to view the commission as the joint responsibility of all those at the table rather than a burden on any one organization. This further encouraged the process of building synergy.

All three partners we interviewed (and certainly many others) demonstrated a substantive community orientation by being patient and intentional about the process, waiting until the right people were engaged to move the work forward. All partners interviewed reported learning a great deal from one another, which indicates humility and self-reflection. Dax and Dailey's strong partnership and coleadership allowed them to apply their experiences across the community and academic worlds and made them excellent bridge builders.

CBR for Long-Term Social Change: A Journey, Not a Project

Strand and colleagues (2003) have identified three ways CBR affects long-term social change: helps develop and shape students who will be the leaders and community members of tomorrow, balances power between universities and communities, and provides society at large with a model of participatory democracy. We agree that done well, CBR can not only balance power but also transform the partners themselves, promote more just and collaborative community-university relationships, and create more just and equitable communities.

In this chapter, we try to identify core challenges and propose strategies for partners to undertake CBR that can lead to lasting community change. We summarize some key ideas and other practical dos and don'ts of CBR partnerships from the community's perspective in Table 3.2.

None of the strategies we offer here are guaranteed to be simple or comfortable to implement. Effective CBR requires a significant long-term investment of time and resources as well as sacrifice. Ultimately, however, faculty, staff, and students must come to an understanding that their university or college is indeed an inherent part of the fabric of their communities, and their own well-being is tied to those others in the community whom they are seeking to help change. They must also recognize and grapple with their own roles and responsibilities in the underlying social disparities that are so often at the heart of the challenges that communities face.

TABLE 3.2
A List of Recommended Dos and Don'ts for CBR Partnerships

Do	*Don't*
Be aware of power imbalances, recruiting facilitators to help name and discuss these contexts	Ignore power dynamics related to race, class, culture, or other differences
Integrate partners that are well versed in the campus and community contexts	Limit the number or kinds of people at the table based on discipline or perceived expertise
Cultivate a moral imagination and a willingness to be interdependent	Make assumptions about what others do or do not know, connections they may or may not have, or biases they may or may not hold
Spend time getting to know one another, identifying the strengths and special knowledge each partner brings to the table	Fear complexity in the process or messiness in the relationship
Plan far in advance, build the partnership before the project, and set learning goals based on community needs	Create the syllabus and then approach the community partner or plan a project and then approach the university partner
Make efficient use of everyone's time by establishing methods of communication and decision making	Rush decisions, processes, or research to meet deadlines at the expense of the long-term partnership
Create flexible tools that can be appropriately modified to fit ever-changing services	Prioritize the perfection of scales, surveys, interviews, and other tools over community participation
Plan and disseminate results widely in multiple formats for different audiences (especially clearer, less academic formats for less academic audiences)	Publish books or articles, apply for grants, produce or share reports without the express consent (and ideally involvement) of all partners
Make a plan to build on the results of the research before the research even begins	Act on assumptions of what the results will be before the research process is complete
Identify needs not found in initial group and bring in others with needed skill sets	Pretend you have knowledge about something or access to something you do not
Prioritize the partnership and the community transformation over your individual needs	Prioritize your grade (if you are a student), your publication, or your immediate organizational need over those of the group

This perspective shift requires a parallel change on the part of community members and the nonprofit and local government staff that serve and often represent them. They must recognize the value of their own knowledge and power to be part of learning processes that can improve their communities. As we become more aware of our interconnectivity and power, we can all become informed agents of lasting social change.

In the long run, it is the journey of collaboration in CBR, not the individual projects, that has the most potential for true long-term social change. Participants from communities and institutions of higher education must be open to changing themselves to be better partners in the CBR process, coming to the table thoughtfully and humbly, with a willingness to listen deeply and learn from one another.

That being said, we end with a reminder about the voices still missing in the discussion. Although we are people who have lived in communities, worked for community organizations, and listened to the reactions of many of those involved in CBR, we are not the subjects of research or people trying to access the services of the partnering organizations. The absence of these voices remains a major gap in our collective understanding about how to achieve community impact through CBR.

References

Freeman, E. R., Brugge, D., Bennett-Bradley, W. M., Levy, J. I., & Carrasco, E. R. (2006). Challenges of conducting community-based participatory research in Boston's neighborhoods to reduce disparities in asthma. *Journal of Urban Health*, *83*(6), 1013–1021.

Greene-Moton, E., Palermo, A., Flicker, S., & Travers, R. (2006). *Unit 4: Trust and communication in a CBPR partnership—spreading the "glue" and having it stick.* Retrieved from www.cbprcurriculum.info

Johnson, M. (1993). *Moral imagination.* Chicago, IL: University of Chicago Press.

Lederach, J. P. (2005). *The moral imagination: The art and soul of building peace.* New York, NY: Oxford University Press.

Palermo, A., McGranaghan, R., & Travers, R. (2006). *Unit 3: Developing a CBPR partnership—creating the "glue."* Retrieved from www.cbprcurriculum .info

Seifer, S. D. (2006). Building and sustaining community-institutional partnerships for prevention research: Findings from a national collaborative. *Journal of Urban Health*, *83*(6), 989–1003.

Stoecker, R. (2012). *Research methods for community change: A project-based approach.* Thousand Oaks, CA: Sage.

Stoecker, R., & Tryon, E. A. (2009). *The unheard voices: Community organizations and service learning.* Philadelphia, PA: Temple University Press.

Strand, K. J., Cutforth, N., Stoecker, R., Marullo, S., & Donohue, P. (2003). *Community-based research and higher education: Principles and practices.* San Francisco, CA: Jossey-Bass.

Yonas, M. A., Jones, N., Eng, E., Vines, A. I., Aronson, R., Griffith, D. M., . . . & DuBose, M. (2006). The art and science of integrating undoing racism with CBPR: Challenges of pursuing NIH funding to investigate cancer care and racial equity. *Journal of Urban Health, 83*(6), 1004–1012.

4

WHY TEACH COMMUNITY-BASED RESEARCH?

A Story of Developing Faculty Interest

Joyce F. Long, Paul Schadewald, and Brooke Kiener

Although university and college faculty regularly perform rigorous research, their results and best practices are not always applied in the community. Community-based research (CBR), however, is intentionally designed to involve the community throughout the research process and provide an application that will benefit the community (Strand, Cutforth, Stoecker, Marullo, & Donahue, 2003). Despite an upsurge in CBR publications, research on what motivates faculty to engage in the community is emerging (O'Meara, 2008; 2012) and needs to differentiate between service-learning and CBR (O'Meara, Sandmann, Saltmarsh, & Giles, 2011). As motivation explains "why people think and behave as they do" (Graham & Weiner, 1996, p. 63) and vigorously and persistently directs our behaviors (Bergin, Ford, & Hess, 1993), we decided to interview recognized leaders in the CBR field as well as other faculty with CBR experience on our three campuses to discover how their interest in CBR began and what supported its growth and development over time.

Interest is a particularly valuable form of motivation in educational settings because it empowers the learning process (Murphy & Alexander, 2000) and helps develop, expand, and transform personal capacities (Ryan & Deci, 2000). Not surprisingly, students can readily tell when they are not interested in a subject (Vispoel & Austin, 1995) and report that teachers are the most important factor in producing their interest in schoolwork

(Sjoberg, 1984). One study even suggests the strength of students' subject matter interest is integrally linked with their teacher's personal interest in the content (Long & Woolfolk Hoy, 2006). Teacher interest is a complex concept (Eren, 2012) that can exert more influence on student interest than the relevance of the subject matter or the quality of instruction (Prenzel, Kramer, & Drechsel, 1998). However, our understanding of how interest develops in teachers is very limited.

We chose several qualifiers to guide our convenient selection of participants (*n* = 16). We wanted to interview teachers with a range of academic experience, so we selected recent PhD recipients just beginning their careers and tenured full professors. Some had no CBR publications, others had written preeminent textbooks on the subject. Of the five private college campuses represented by the participants, most had been affiliated with programs developed by the Corella and Bertram F. Bonner Foundation. Our sample also included novice and experienced CBR teachers from highly structured (e.g., science, economics) and less structured academic disciplines (e.g., history, theater). Overall, the academic disciplines represented by our participants include American studies, anthropology, biological science, economics, educational psychology, educational leadership, environmental studies, geography, political science, public policy and poverty studies, research methods and statistics, sociology and social work, theater, and dance.

Participants were interviewed using a semistructured protocol of 18 open-ended questions and informal probes. Topics for formal questions included why they began, challenges they faced, and areas of professional or personal transformation. Interviews (60–90 minutes) were conducted in person or by phone, digitally recorded, transcribed, and then member checked.

We analyzed about 105 single-spaced pages of rich discourse in three sequences. First, we segmented the data into phrases and labeled the content according to codes associated with affective interest (e.g., emotion, value) and cognitive interest (e.g., understanding, knowledge, problem solving). Second, we identified conceptual terms and principles associated with interest development (Hidi & Renninger, 2006) and teacher disposition research (e.g., Splitter, 2010). Third, we noted trends and conceptual overlaps across each body of literature as well as emergent categories (Glesne, 2006). All the researchers read every transcript and engaged in weekly peer debriefing meetings to establish high levels of inter-rater reliability and identify any research bias (Creswell, 2009). These findings are presented in the remainder of this chapter after a brief overview of the literature on the development of interest.

Interest Theory

According to a classic theory of interest (Dewey, 1899), having an interest indicates that a relationship is forming between a person and a specific activity, subject, or topic. This relationship can grow stronger with every interaction, and the potential exists for a person to so identify with the topic or subject that the interest becomes integrated into his or her identity. As such, interest can increase one's personal significance and consciousness of worth, even as it simultaneously furnishes motives for investing more attention into the next interested effort.

Like a two-sided coin, interest has two highly integrated components that appear in every phase of its development (Hidi & Renninger, 2006). The first component, affective interest, consists of value or importance (Renninger, 2000) and positive emotions (Ainley, 2006), expressed as pleasure (Todt & Schreiber, 1998), excitement (Izard, 1977), fondness (Tobias, 1995), or liking (Gehlbach, 2006). When teachers describe their subjects as relevant or speak of loving the content (Turner et al., 1998), they are expressing affective interest.

Interest's second component, intellectual content or cognitive interest, is demonstrated when the interested person acquires more knowledge (Schiefele, Krapp, & Winteler, 1992) or skills in a subject (Shen, Chen, & Guan, 2007), expresses curiosity questions (Renninger, 2000), recalls more facts relative to the content (Shirey & Reynolds, 1988), or attains deeper levels of understanding (Schiefele, 1998). For teachers, other forms of cognitive interest can include pedagogical content knowledge and knowledge about students (Long & Woolfolk Hoy, 2006).

After synthesizing extensive student research on interest, Hidi and Renninger (2006) created a model of interest development that suggests its affective and cognitive changes occur across four phases. They portrayed initial levels of interest as situational or temporary responses "elicited by certain aspects of the environment" (Ainley, Hidi, & Berndorff, 2002, p. 545). As interest continues to mature, however, they theorize it is more typical of an individual interest, defined as a personal identification "with the content" (Renninger, 2000, p. 375). In this more robust and mature form, interest is linked to enduring levels of alertness or attentiveness (Renninger, 1992), and periods of intense cognitive involvement and creativity where individuals lose track of time as they engage with the object of interest (Schiefele & Csikszentmihalyi, 1994).

Initial Interest in CBR

Data analysis indicated that faculty interest in CBR developed across three phases, but the birth of interest emerged within two different contexts. Some faculty described their motives for pursuing CBR as extrinsically originating in students, community groups, campus initiatives, or external funding opportunities. When students asked for practical opportunities to apply theory in natural settings in the community, faculty interest was triggered as they searched for potential research sites and problems. Similarly, a faculty member's initial interest could be hooked by a community group's request for research expertise in solving issues in their organizations. Likewise, some faculty stepped into CBR because of funding opportunities or pressure associated with campuswide engaged scholarship initiatives. All of these situational nudges could provoke faculty to begin practicing CBR.

Others ventured into CBR for affective reasons linked with preexisting intrinsic interests (e.g., lifelong learning, teaching in general, interdisciplinary approaches to understanding, and research). Several from this group became interested in CBR after experiencing frustration with colleagues' instructional method of using community opportunities in a mediocre fashion or service-learning, as one put it, in a "very Mickey Mouse way" to replace lecture preparation. Others indicated their dislike of seeing peers use research methods as nothing but "busy work," and became motivated to design CBR experiences that students would be "more likely to put more into it and . . . get more out of it" so research could be moved "to the level it should be." After experiencing strong negative emotional responses as the result of colleagues' ineffective pedagogy, they imagined that an interest (Tin, 2013) in CBR could produce stronger student results.

Love for research also provoked other faculty to ask themselves, How can research be used to improve the well-being of groups? These teachers described their emotions in positive language (e.g., really interesting, love, exciting, fun) and often expressed values relative to social justice, civic engagement, and faith. Whether their values originated while they were undergraduates in service-learning courses or emerged from religious commitments and other intrinsic desires to alleviate marginalized community members' suffering, they undergirded decisions throughout their careers and became a natural springboard for venturing into CBR and, as one participant said, a "world outside of myself."

One individual with preexisting values for service took six years to make the transition into CBR. She waited until she felt rooted enough to approach people on her campus and request assistance with getting started. "I'm interested not just as someone who wants to make a career—which is really a distasteful reason for anyone to help me—but because I'm also invested now as someone who lives here."

Cognitively speaking, the practice of CBR also appealed to faculty with content knowledge across disparate disciplines. Theology undergraduates with doctoral degrees in economics could use both areas in CBR projects.

This was also true for individuals with interests in economics, sociology and American studies, or political science; South Asian studies; and environmental studies. CBR was likewise a good fit for faculty whose courses were cross-listed, drew students from multiple disciplines, or featured interdisciplinary reading assignments (e.g., arts, business, psychology, and education). Whether these individuals possessed an inherent interdisciplinary gene or simply loved learning, CBR offered stimulating opportunities to apply diverse areas of knowledge and understanding. Faculty with prior experience managing centers linked to civic engagement or multiple departments and content areas similarly gravitated toward CBR, and they tended to draw on campus and community knowledge throughout their subsequent teaching or administrative work.

Many cited the fact that CBR provided them with a structure for engaging in the whole process. They also liked the way CBR intertwined scholarship, service, and application across traditional disciplinary boundaries. Several individuals even began integrating it into the structural framework of all their courses.

In sum, whether interest in researching the community was sparked by external nudges from the environment or an existing intrinsic affective or cognitive framework within the individual, each person began developing an interest in CBR. Sometimes progress was slow; other times it grew with accelerated speed and intensity. Regardless of how they started and the pace of development, faculty interest in CBR was inevitably challenged along the way. How they responded to those challenges tended to expedite interest's growth and development.

As Interest Develops

If interest is to become more than a passing fancy, an individual's commitment to acquire deeper levels of understanding and passion for the designated topic will be tested. The two specific challenges our faculty members learned to overcome were related to CBR's unique workload and increased need for greater flexibility. As they conquered these obstacles, faculty became invigorated and inspired to choose even more challenging tasks (Inoue, 2007).

Work is required. Nearly all the teachers repeated the refrain—"CBR is a lot of work!" They found it required more communication time with the community partner and more designing or planning efforts in balancing the community partner's practical needs with students' learning needs. CBR could also demand accelerated learning of new and unfamiliar content, such as when a theater professor helped students create a stage performance about abuse of police power and had to educate herself about a myriad of law enforcement and public safety issues, theories, and practices.

Because the problems communities face tend to be intricately complex, researching these multilayered issues does not necessarily become easier with each succeeding project. As one CBR veteran related,

> I'm surprised that as I do more of it, it gets harder. . . . When you first start doing CBR, you don't know the potential it has and things go along pretty well. . . . But as your relationships develop with the community, and you learn more about what CBR could be and strive to be democratic and participatory, you realize it's more complicated.

Even a faculty member's personality or performance standards could complicate the scope of a challenge. As one remarked, "I really should stick with the same topic. . . . but I'm just so interested in moving on to other things." Another commented that it would be less work if he let what "was good" be enough. Some even suggested CBR's intensive labor was related to their need for overcoming personal tendencies toward introversion. Noting that it would be easier and more comfortable to work on their own research, or "just sit in [their] office and write," these teachers were willing to engage in the extroverted activities typical of CBR because they witnessed such valuable results in student learning and were convinced that this was "research that mattered." For these individuals, choosing a more difficult option helped maintain interest and avoid diminishing interest.

More flexibility is necessary. In addition to the taxing work that CBR projects could generate, the nature of the work also challenged faculty. Nearly all the teachers agreed that CBR was "messy," requiring flexibility and on-the-go problem solving, which was frustrating and invigorating (e.g., scary, fun, "I never know how the project will turn out"). Adapting to a constantly moving landscape required "knowing that things are going to change, being ready for it, and not being surprised by it. You have to make decisions rather quickly because you can't lose the momentum." Others echoed these sentiments: "Each and every project reveals some factor you didn't think of ahead of time. . . . You have to deal with realities. [The students will] have to switch gears in some cases, and that means as instructors, we have to, too."

CBR could require frequent adjustments to the course calendar and working with projects that lacked "a definite ending." In comparison to many more traditional courses where students could expect assignments to be delivered in a neatly wrapped package with clearly defined start and finish lines, even when students finished the research in one semester, the final presentation to a community group might not be scheduled until after the semester ended, when no students were present for the event. One described the fluctuating changes as "the ability to drop this ball and pick up another ball. And that's frustrating for students and me, but it's a real learning experience."

One scientist spoke of the emotional pressure of "working on the fly. It's scary. Because we're working with the community, we expect a lot of ourselves too. We don't want to disappoint them at all." Overcoming those negative emotions required learning to negotiate choices, becoming comfortable with flexibility, and demonstrating the ability to "juggle many balls," which many believed were important skills to develop in themselves and their students. One remarked, "I don't think I'd be very good in teaching or responding to the things that people run into—all these curve balls and all the frustrations that cause them to throw up their hands—if I hadn't run into those things myself."

A few faculty had to develop strategies to help their students become skilled in negotiating unpredictability. "Probably half of the students are much more structured, and they really want to know very specific dates and assignments ahead of time," so the struggle, as one teacher said, could become taking "my own real willingness to be completely flexible to re-work and re-think, and whipping that into something that enables me to be sensitive to students, who really do need more structure." Another responded to the challenge to students by broadcasting "truth in advertising" and regularly warning students, "If you can't go with the flow, if you can't roll with the dice—if you need to know what we're doing every class day so you can put it on your calendar—this is not the class for you." Over time, some tried to help students "re-channel that [frustration] into asking some good questions, not just giving up."

Overall, some faculty spoke of "being ready for anything" or always "thinking forward." They also described their classroom learning environments as places where boredom was not an option and where students and teachers alike were actively learning. As faculty exerted more effort in this intermediary phase of interest development, they built more content knowledge, strengthened affection and value for CBR, and sharpened their problem-solving abilities. They also became more persistent and tenacious, which researchers have found is essential for increasing interest (Dewey, 1913; Renninger & Wozniak, 1985; Schiefele & Csikszentmihalyi, 1994). Navigating new terrain likewise helped faculty strengthen their affection and value for CBR as well as their problem-solving abilities and content knowledge (i.e., both indicators of cognitive interest).

Mature Interest

Throughout their interviews, faculty members elaborated on why CBR remained a meaningful and memorable experience to them. Over time, faculty continued to teach CBR despite its concomitant challenges because the experience was professionally meaningful and personally significant, especially in three areas: student outcomes, campus/community responses, and personal transformation. The most frequently cited catalyst they attributed to their maturing interest was student outcomes.

Student outcomes. As students engaged in "research that makes a difference with folks in the community" or "research with a heart," faculty noted that students achieved higher levels of cognitive and affective interest, which often elicited reciprocal responses from their instructors. "Knowing that other people were dependent on them taught [students] a lot of things they couldn't have learned from just reading the book," and they became "excited" about their work. One faculty member likewise expressed incredible pleasure in watching students do wonderful things and bloom and develop skills.

CBR was likewise associated with more gratifyingly significant student-faculty relationships. Many echoed variations on the following statement: "My most long-lasting relationships with students have come from CBR or working with seniors on their thesis. I'm still visited by students from my first [CBR] group. . . . It's amazing the number of students who come back and say, 'thanks.'"

Often students expressed their appreciation for CBR with very positive course reviews. Comments like "This was the best course I've ever taken," validated faculty's hard work. Occasionally, however, students could be unaware of the full "meaningfulness of CBR . . . until three or four years later," and this delayed gratification was sometimes preceded by initially critical comments on course evaluations. Faculty had to learn to weather these storms, and according to one teacher, even when students were

> uniformly ticked off and felt like their time had been wasted, and they had not achieved anything. But within three months, . . . every single one of them . . . contacted me and said "I just want you to know I've been thinking about it. [CBR] had a big impact on me, and I'm sorry I said all those mean things." It was a powerful experience. It wasn't a good experience, but it was a powerful experience.

Because of students' delayed expressions of value for CBR, faculty suggested that evaluations of courses with CBR should include time, for example, to "reflect, not just to check a box, but to actually answer, 'Did this course have any impact on you?'" One remarked, "When I think in my own life about the things that have had an impact on me, hardly any of them have been fun or easy." Instead, they could be "difficult experiences."

Students also positively influenced faculty interest when their future course work, career decisions, or personal actions specifically related to their

CBR work. As one teacher said, "This past year I had a couple students who are continuing to work with refugees." When students developed a sense of citizenship, continued class work independently after courses ended, or attended graduate school to gain professional credentials in public policy or educational law, their actions positively influenced faculty interest. Faculty noticed CBR's effect on students' personal growth too, as one described a student from a small town who conquered her fear of taking the bus to her urban community theater site. In general, faculty seemed to appreciate the versatility of CBR in helping students "access their own voice and their own power." One concluded that when "any of them succeed, it's good, and you know you've had some impact on that."

Campus and community responses. Another factor that sustained interest came from outcomes and movement toward impact witnessed by faculty in two locations: campus and the community. On campus, positive responses from departments, disciplines, and institutions contributed to continuing interest. For example, when the political scientist heard enthusiastic remarks from her department about generally "embracing CBR more," her interest grew. Support from campuswide centers for civic engagement and "that kind of scholarship" similarly boosted faculty interest in CBR. These centers could create climate changes across campus and in departments, which enabled a faculty member to no longer be "the strange one doing the strange teaching thing. . . . It doesn't look weird."

In the community, several outcomes from their CBR work likewise strengthened faculty interest. For example, public dialogues on climate change's complex issues emerged from the research of the environmental studies professor. Similarly, the political scientist's project led to additional research and policy proposals, and the dance and theater faculty's work helped give voice to a range of residents who might not otherwise have had access to the public sphere.

Indicators of movement toward impact similarly supported interest. Examples include the geographer's research yielding data and visualizations of data for neighborhood groups (output). They used the information to draw attention to the potential for redeveloping commercial corridors (outcome), and over time, one particular corridor was transformed from a street with a lot of vacancies to one of the most thriving commercial districts in St. Paul, Minnesota (impact). The street literally reinvented itself and reversed urban blight, crime, and decay (Young & Lanegram, 1995). Obviously, the geographer's CBR contribution was only one of the many factors that caused this extensive economic revitalization, but it did help influence the eventual impact.

In another example, a theater professor and her students formed a partnership with a nonprofit law firm representing the family of a victim of police abuse to create a performance about the abuse of police power and citizen oversight (output). Directly following the performance, the city council president (who had been in attendance along with the mayor) initiated conversations with activists who had been advocating for an office of police ombudsman; within six months, city officials established that office. It is impossible to know to what extent the theater performance can be credited for this outcome, but it does appear that the affective power of the arts was an effective tool for instigating a dialogue, which ultimately led to changes in oversight procedures that are having a long-term impact on the city.

Even when initial engagements provoked trepidation ("Can you believe that this is actually going to happen?"), as campus and community relationships became stronger, CBR interest matured. One biology faculty member smilingly described herself as being "stuck now! We've committed to the community." A second faculty member described himself as having "an amazing support community outside campus with the people who are doing this work, who are looking to me as one of the important components of their work, because I am bringing myself and I also bring students."

Personal transformation. Finally, a faculty member reported that "seeing the impact we are having on the community is really rewarding." Such changes brought "a satisfaction that . . . doesn't appear when you are working for academic issues. . . . I can look at Grand Avenue, I can look at West 7th. . . . It's a huge ego trip to work with the community."

Participating in opportunities to creatively live civic commitments and imagine broader social or institutional change also empowered faculty. As one stated, after examining the "whole question of university civic engagement, I just keep seeing new ways that universities can consider themselves as real partners in a real collaboration." This new perspective even developed when faculty were virtual "lone rangers" at their educational institutions.

Another reflected on her earlier experiences as a new professional and graduate student and remembered the words of her activist mentors:

> "You've arrived when you can make the institution that you're in take very seriously some needs of some people that are outside the [academic] community." So I've always wanted to see if there was a way for the institution I was related to, to seriously and openly dedicate resources to someone other than the kids who go there.

After six years of getting to know her adopted city, she was able to put her interests in CBR and social change into practice through a new course: Schools and Prisons.

Interest theory suggests that when individuals personally identify with the activity or subject of interest, they have achieved a mature phase of interest (Hidi & Renninger, 2006). This experience was true for many participants who described how engaging in CBR helped them forge new professional identities, such as in the following comment:

> I was trained as an economist, but my professional life almost never draws on economics in a very deep way. I'm now reading evaluation literature, health literature, community development and in CBR about partnerships. So professionally, CBR has taken me into a new professional world. I'm still an economist and bring those skills to the table in that content, but it's given me a whole new professional field that doesn't have very strong edges. It's very expansive, and that's what I like.

Another said,

> I've been able to create and carve out [a unique role] for myself both [on my campus] and beyond. People want me. The fire that keeps me going is wanting to continually hone my skills and if I do have something to offer, I do like to pass it along.

As one faculty member said, regardless of the length of their careers, "CBR offers a way to put different experiences that I've had that are important to me separately, into a more coherent package." Over time, repeated engagement with CBR also became a form of professional development: "This work in CBR continues to evolve and I continue to learn new things. So it's probably my own personal continual education, ongoing learning."

Data further showed CBR was a valuable venue for seamlessly combining research, service, and teaching. The geographer noted that he

> was no longer known as a great theorist or a postmodernist or a Marxist or whatever. I have made my reputation as someone who actually goes out and works with communities and helps them through some difficult times. And so whatever reputation I have in the profession is based on the creative ways I have linked that with teaching and inspired generations of geographers who have this sense of being grounded in reality.

One also described CBR as marrying "professional and personal commitments," or meshing personal aspirations with the question, "What's worth doing as an academic?" This integration starkly contrasted with earlier graduate school experiences of being taught to separate professional and personal parts of their lives. In comparison, CBR helped faculty derive meaning from both parts simultaneously; as one respondent stated, "Every time someone tries to take that [option] away from me, I resist." They appreciated this new context where work, politics, values, and commitments could "fit a little better" with teaching, especially research methods teaching. CBR made life more "energizing" and, as one faculty member put it, provided "a new focus in making me feel more relevant."

Lessons Learned

We learned several lessons from this research. First, faculty experiences in developing CBR interest do indeed parallel Hidi and Renninger's theory (2006) of how interest develops. In the beginning, external conditions and other related intrinsic passions could motivate initial expressions of interest in CBR. Over time, faculty members eventually conquered challenges that led to expanded knowledge, intensified value, and deeper personal satisfaction in practicing and teaching CBR. After interest matured, faculty attributed their continued CBR engagement to new levels of significance in who they had become and how the community viewed CBR teachers as a positive resource in helping them solve local problems. Such demonstrations of personal, public, and professional esteem built critical personal and social capital in faculty that was also valuable in larger cultural contexts.

Second, when pro-CBR centers or programs were present on campus, faculty members' interest development was undergirded, and CBR activities were more broadly validated. One former director of such a center, who now teaches CBR, envisioned sustained campus support becoming

> more central than it is. . . . I think anyone who'd claim they're interested in CBR is always pushing against this. It's that idea of moving from the margins to the center. And I know that not everyone has made great inroads in that and I think we have a ways to go. But conversations are happening; there are certainly places that are doing it.

Third, findings suggest that CBR also produces rewarding effects on campus. For example, students and faculty derived very noteworthy and valuable personal and professional benefits from engaging in CBR. They also cited its positive influence on disciplines, departments, programs, policies, and other initiatives associated with the organizational structures of higher education campuses. Additional data described how CBR improved learning goals in courses and added new vibrancy and potency to faculty performance evaluations.

Conclusion

Although the generalizability of our results is limited, findings consistently suggest that faculty members continue to engage in CBR because they witness its transformational effects in their classrooms, communities, and vocational paths. Despite encountering challenges, they freely choose to recommit to this form of research because of the benefits that accrue on multiple levels.

References

Ainley, M. (2006). Connecting with learning: Motivation, affect and cognition in interest processes. *Educational Psychology Review, 18*(4), 391–405.

Ainley, M., Hidi, S., & Berndorff, D. (2002). Interest, learning, and the psychological processes that mediate their relationship. *Journal of Educational Psychology, 94*(3), 545–561.

Bergin, D. A., Ford, M. E., & Hess, R. D. (1993). Patterns of motivation and social behavior associated with microcomputer use of young children. *Journal of Educational Psychology, 85*, 437–445.

Creswell, J. W. (2009). *Research design: Qualitative, quantitative, and mixed methods approaches* (3rd ed.). Los Angeles, CA: Sage.

Dewey, J. (1899). *Interest as related to will.* New York, NY: Herbart Society.

Dewey, J. (1913). *Interest and effort in education.* New York, NY: Houghton Mifflin.

Eren, A. (2012). Prospective teachers' interest in teaching, professional plans about teaching and career choice satisfaction: A relevant framework? *Australian Journal of Education, 56*(3), 303–318.

Gehlbach, H. (2006). How changes in students' goal orientations relate to outcomes in social studies. *Journal of Educational Research, 99*(6), 358–370.

Glesne, C. (2006). *Becoming qualitative researchers: An introduction* (3rd ed.). Boston, MA: Pearson Education.

Graham, S., & Weiner, B. (1996). Theories and principles of motivation. In D. C. Berliner & R. C. Calfee (Eds.), *Handbook of Educational Psychology* (pp. 63–84). New York, NY: Simon & Schuster Macmillan.

Hidi, S., & Renninger, K. A. (2006). The four-phase model of interest development. *Educational Psychologist, 41*(2), 111–127.

Inoue, N. (2007). Why face a challenge? The reason behind intrinsically motivated students' spontaneous choice of challenging tasks. *Learning and Individual Differences, 17*(1), 251–259.

Izard, C. E. (1977). *Human emotions.* New York, NY: Plenum Press.

Long, J. F., & Woolfolk Hoy, A. (2006). Interested instructors: A composite portrait of individual differences and effectiveness. *Journal of Teaching and Teacher Education, 22*(3), 303–314.

Murphy, P. K., & Alexander, P. (2000). A motivated exploration of motivation terminology. *Contemporary Educational Psychology, 25*, 3–53.

Prenzel, M., Kramer, K., & Drechsel, B. (1998). Changes in learning motivation and interest in vocational education: Halfway through the study. In L. Hoffmann, A. Krapp, K. A. Renninger, & J. Baumert (Eds.), *Interest and learning: Proceedings of the Seeon Conference on Interest and Gender* (pp. 430–440). Kiel, Germany: IPN.

Renninger, K. A. (1992). Individual interest and development: Implications for theory and practice. In K. A. Renninger, S. Hidi, & A. Krapp (Eds.), *The role of interest in learning and development* (pp. 361–395). Hillsdale, NJ: Erlbaum.

Renninger, K. A. (2000). Individual interest and its implications for understanding intrinsic motivation. In C. Sansone & J. M. Harackiewicz (Eds.), *Intrinsic and extrinsic motivation: The search for optimal motivation and performance* (pp. 373–404). San Diego, CA: Academic Press.

Renninger, K. A., & Wozniak, R. H. (1985). Effect of interest on attentional shift, recognition, and recall in young children. *Developmental Psychology*, *21*, 624–632.

Ryan, R. M., & Deci, E. L. (2000). Self-determination theory and the facilitation of intrinsic motivation, social development, and well-being. *American Psychologist*, *55* (1), 68–78.

Schiefele, U. (1998). Individual interest and learning: What we know and what we don't know. In L. Hoffmann, A. Krapp, K. A. Renninger, & J. Baumert (Eds.), *Interest and learning: Proceedings of the Seeon Conference on Interest and Gender* (pp. 91–104). Kiel, Germany: IPN.

Schiefele, U., & Csikszentmihalyi, M. (1994). Interest and the quality of experience in classrooms. *European Journal of Psychology of Education*, *9*(3), 251–270.

Schiefele, U., Krapp, A., & Winteler, A. (1992). Interest as a predictor of academic achievement: A meta-analysis of research. In K. Ann Renninger, S. Hidi, & A. Krapp (Eds.), *The role of interest in learning and development* (pp. 183–212). Hillsdale, NJ: Erlbaum.

Shen, B., Chen, A., & Guan, J. (2007). Using achievement goals and interest to predict learning in physical education. *Journal of Experimental Education*, *75*(2), 89–108.

Shirey, L. L., & Reynolds, R. E. (1988). Effect of interest on attention and learning. *Journal of Educational Psychology*, *80*(2), 159–166.

Sjoberg, L. (1984). Interests, effort, achievement and vocational preference. *British Journal of Educational Psychology*, *54*(2), 189–205.

Splitter, L. J. (2010). Dispositions in education: Nonentities worth talking about. *Educational Theory*, *60*(2), 203–230.

Strand, K., Marullo, S., Cutforth, N., Stoecker, R., & Donohue, P. (2003). *Community-based research and higher education*. San Francisco, CA: Jossey-Bass.

Tin, T. B. (2013). Exploring the development of "interest" in learning English as a foreign/second language. *RELC Journal*, *44*(2), 129–146.

Tobias, S. (1995). Interest and metacognitive word knowledge. *Journal of Educational Psychology*, *87*(3), 399–405.

Todt, E., & Schreiber, S. (1998). Development of interests. In L. Hoffmann, A. Krapp, K. A. Renninger, & J. Baumert (Eds.), *Interest and learning: Proceedings of the Seeon Conference on Interest and Gender* (pp. 25–40). Kiel, Germany: IPN.

Turner, J. C., Cox, K. E., DiCintio, M., Meyer, D. K., Logan, C., & Thomas, C. T. (1998). Creating contexts for involvement in mathematics. *Journal of Educational Psychology, 90*(4), 730–745.

Vispoel, W. P., & Austin, J. R. (1995). Success and failure in junior high school: A critical incident approach to understanding students' attributional beliefs. *American Educational Research Journal, 32*(2), 377–412.

Young, B., & Lanegram, D. (1995). *Grand Avenue: The renaissance of an urban street.* Clearwater, MN: North Star Press of St. Cloud.

PART TWO

GUIDING COMMUNITY-BASED RESEARCH TOWARD COMMUNITY OUTCOMES AND STUDENT LEARNING

Joyce F. Long

Each chapter in this volume emphasizes the potential of community-based research (CBR) for facilitating community change and impact for the common good. CBR's influence, however, is not just limited to the community. CBR can also have an empowering effect on instruction and student learning. The contributors in Part Two show how CBR can achieve dual roles: excellent instruction with significant student learning and community impact. Whether readers are novices or experts in the practice of CBR, these chapters provide guidance and share lessons learned for fulfilling both goals rather than sacrificing one option for the other. They also demonstrate how these tandem roles can be securely woven into the pedagogical structure of individual classes, research projects, academic disciplines, entire campuses, and transnational efforts.

In the remainder of this introduction to Part Two, we discuss the types of student learning outcomes a faculty member can expect from CBR. We then provide an overview of each chapter and explain how the overall content is intentionally arranged to highlight five important design elements that are part of any CBR project. We conclude with some general suggestions for prioritizing tasks and preparation.

CBR's Influence on Student Learning

On the first day of my educational psychology courses, I explain that psychology is the study of the soul, and the term *soul* refers to the mind, will, and emotions. We then devote the rest of the semester to exploring how these three internal resources can be engaged when learning.

Mental processes, such as acquiring, remembering, understanding, and using knowledge, are associated with the term *cognition* (Woolfolk, 2013). In comparison, the term *conation* describes activities of the will, which include motivation and volition. When the will is engaged, students invest effort into learning and have "the tendency to take and maintain purposive action or direction toward goals" (Snow, Corno, & Jackson, 1996, p. 264). Finally, emotional responses, values, and feelings—classified under the term *affect*—can enhance or inhibit learning processes and outcomes (Goleman, 1995). Since Bain (2004) describes the best college faculty as achieving "a sustained, substantial, and positive influence on how students think, act and feel" (p. 5), it is appropriate to assess CBR's effect on student learning within these three intrapersonal areas.

Only a few published reports by students describe their CBR experiences. One article was coauthored by undergraduates from four different campuses: Catholic University of America, Emory University, Georgetown University, and the University of Pennsylvania (Willis, Peresie, Waldref, & Stockmann, 2003). Each of the project descriptions varied by focus (i.e., program and process evaluation, curriculum development, welfare reform) and academic discipline, but the authors collectively compiled the following long list of cognitive processes and outcomes typical of their CBR experiences: learning how to use research tools and programs, gaining knowledge about people and communities, engaging in problem solving, critically and logically thinking, translating knowledge into action, reconceptualizing their abilities and roles, redefining their communities, achieving greater understanding of social problems, recognizing community needs, and successfully integrating academics and interest in service.

The undergraduates likewise mentioned conative outcomes when sharing how CBR enhanced their "dedication to working within our communities" (Willis et al., 2003, p. 42). They additionally cited a variety of emotions, including care, frustration, anger, sadness, and grief. Ultimately, they described their CBR experiences as transformative, because they incorporated cognition and affect.

CBR was emotional, connecting our minds and hearts. We have come to appreciate the power of understanding and passion. By combining academics and service through CBR, we developed the desire and ability to address community issues in a systematic and effective manner. (p. 42)

Another article was written by a medical student from the University of Toronto whose research led him to develop an online resource for those affected by pancreatic cancer; he similarly described his CBR experience using cognitive and affective terms (Perrin, 2012). He mentally constructed, revised, and polished online content; he also developed appreciation for the social determinants of health and enthusiasm for community work, which contrasted with the apathy he had previously felt.

The number of student-authored reports is quite limited, but their content echoes comments from Parroquin's undergraduate students in Chapter 6. They refer to cognitive engagement in "thinking constantly about the codes" and more critically reading the focus group transcripts they were analyzing. Indicators of emotional engagement also emerged: "I heard the parents in a focus group express apprehension that the NPLB [No Parent Left Behind] classes were ending; my heart went out to them." Students additionally said that the CBR unit reinforced their career goals (conation).

Student feedback related to these three internal sources of engagement in learning is additionally found in Chapter 14, which is teeming with Nicholson's experiences as a graduate student and the responses of undergraduate students she mentored in CBR. The following is just a sample of the rich cognitive concepts she uses: summarize, assess, consider, negotiate, adapt, reflect, process, apply, awareness. She also lists a range of affective outcomes (e.g., pleased with almost all aspects, confident, comfortable, satisfaction, pride) and shares several conative incidents of overcoming challenges through effort.

Articles from faculty (Chapdelaine & Chapman, 1999; Puma, Bennett, Cutforth, Tombari, & Stein, 2009) likewise cite examples of affect and conation in describing the excitement and appreciation their students experienced during CBR projects and the effort they exerted in maintaining constant contact with partners and attending extra meetings. The bulk of their evidence, however, points to cognitive results: enhanced critical thinking skills, new perspectives, improved understanding of methodological concepts, increased awareness of social issues, applied research skills, acquired knowledge about the strengths and limitations of each partner, and developed leadership and project management skills. Faculty members in Chapter 4 cite similar examples of multidimensional learning outcomes observed in their students and describe them as fueling their own motivation to engage in CBR.

Since only a few published reports exist, there is still much more work to be done in documenting student outcomes linked to CBR. A promising new assessment was developed (Lichtenstein, Thorme, Cutforth, & Tombari,

2011) to help faculty collect this type of data. The survey was constructed from interview and focus group data collected from 70 undergraduate students at six institutions with CBR experiences from across a wide range of disciplines. In analyzing the qualitative data, the authors found five categories of student outcomes they used to create the conceptual framework for the survey: academic skills, educational experience, civic engagement, professional skills, and personal growth. Since three of these themes are associated with cognitive and affective outcomes, the survey's results are likely to help us better understand how and why CBR influences students' minds, wills, and emotions.

Collectively, these initial reports suggest that our understanding of how CBR influences student learning will expand as more documentation occurs and further research is conducted on this subject. If extensive published results on student development through service-learning are any indication (e.g., Brandenberger, 2013; Fitch, Steinke, & Hudson, 2013), CBR faculty members have a very large open door for publishing in this area. More results on student learning outcomes related to CBR will also be beneficial for institutions of higher learning as they evaluate whether CBR helps fulfill their intended missions in the community (Lichtenstein et al., 2011).

Designing a CBR Course

What does a CBR unit or course look like? Instead of mechanically inserting CBR into a course or project opportunity, the following chapters offer suggestions and guidelines for thoughtfully adapting CBR into a variety of learning contexts or disciplines. The content of Part Two begins with a presentation of five core elements that should be part of every CBR project: partnership, objectives, working, evaluation, and reflection. In Chapter 5, Pigza sensibly explains each element in her conceptual framework and demonstrates its implementation through effective examples that can help readers readily understand how they function cohesively and why they are important. These guidelines are useful whether the CBR project is a single student's effort, a unit in a larger curricular context, or the focus of an entire course. The clarity of Pigza's presentation also helps faculty prioritize the community partner's needs without sacrificing student learning outcomes (Strand, Marullo, Cutforth, Stoecker, & Donohue, 2003).

Chapter 6, by Parroquin and her undergraduate student Geiger-Medina, describes CBR in a Romance language classroom. Their presentation has concrete connections with every element in Pigza's model and provides a snapshot of how to apply all five elements in one unit. Following this composite portrait, the remaining chapters in Part Two are arranged to highlight and elaborate on different parts of the POWER model, commencing with partnerships and ending with reflection.

Although Ruebeck's content in Chapter 7 also highlights every element in Pigza's model, he specifically emphasizes the building of partnership in his own marketing research course and describes the other partnerships that occurred during this CBR collaboration across three campuses. Chapters 8 and 9 portray the importance of defining objectives. In Chapter 8, Bartel and Nigro portray the numerous ways a CBR center initiates and sustains campuswide objectives in regard to faculty engagement in an array of undergraduate projects. Berkove, on the other hand, concisely illustrates in Chapter 9 how his CBR unit helped him fulfill the department's student learning objectives.

The authors of Chapters 10, 11, and 12 focus on the working element of Pigza's model. In Chapter 10, Holter and Frabutt describe their work of preparing graduate students to conduct CBR in multiple schools across the nation where they already work as teachers or administrators. These authors methodically build students' research skills through a four-sequence series of online courses. Tryon and Steinhaus, both of whom are associated with CBR-related centers, discuss CBR projects on several continents in Chapter 11. They give practical advice on how to prepare students for these important global ventures. By comparison, Owens-Manley in Chapter 12 evaluates her work as a director of a CBR center in supporting multiple projects across one campus.

To highlight the valuable role of evaluation, in Chapter 13, Persichetti, Sturman, and Gingerich offer guidance on building and assessing wide-scale support for CBR across a campus. In this broad evaluative context, they then describe how it provides space for an ongoing course and how this supports a long-term partnership that has achieved impact in reducing domestic violence. Part Two concludes with Nicholson's meaningful reflection in Chapter 14 on her experience as a psychology graduate student. She began researching lead levels for a local health task force and ended with a funded dissertation project that employed dozens of undergraduate students whom she trained as CBR researchers.

One final parting word of advice: Finding a suitable partner and crafting an appropriate research question can take time. Therefore, we recommend that faculty begin the process before the course starts, whenever possible. Once those two tasks are completed, faculty can more accurately define the remaining class structure and create realistic expectations for students relative to the CBR work.

In general, adequate preparation makes it easier for faculty to build a trust-filled working relationship with students and create a supportive environment that produces favorable results for students "and the subject matter under study" (Fenstermacher & Richardson, 2005, p. 192). Whether CBR is the primary focus of the entire course or simply a unit in the course, adequate preparation time yields great rewards in helping faculty productively facilitate students' conversations about the project. These conversations provide students with ample space to apply theory, develop explanations and understanding, defend their answers, reflectively enjoy the process, become confident in what the project is achieving, and grow as scholars in their respective disciplines (Bain, 2004).

References

Bain, K. (2004). *What the best college teachers do.* Cambridge, MA: Harvard University Press.

Brandenberger, J. W. (2013). Investigating personal development outcomes in service learning: Theory and research. In P. H. Clayton, R. G. Bringle, & J. A. Hatcher (Eds.), *Research on service learning: Vol. 2A. Students and faculty* (pp. 133–156). Sterling, VA: Stylus.

Chapdelaine, A., & Chapman, B. L. (1999). Using community-based research projects to teach research methods. *Teaching of Psychology, 26*(2), 101–105.

Fenstermacher, G. D., & Richardson, V. (2005). On making determinations of quality in teaching. *Teachers College Record, 107*(1), 186–213.

Fitch, P., Steinke, P., & Hudson, T. D. (2013). Research and theoretical perspectives on cognitive outcomes of service learning. In P. H. Clayton, R. G. Bringle, & J. A. Hatcher (Eds.), *Research on service learning: Vol. 2A. Students and faculty* (pp. 57–84). Sterling, VA: Stylus.

Goleman, D. (1995). *Emotional intelligence. Why it can matter more than IQ.* New York, NY: Bantam.

Lichtenstein, G., Thorme, T., Cutforth, N., & Tombari, M. L. (2011). Development of a national survey to assess student learning outcomes of community-based research. *Journal of Higher Education Outreach and Engagement, 15*(2), 7–33.

Perrin, A. J. (2012). A community-based transformation. *Journal of Cancer Education, 27*(1), 192–194.

Puma, J., Bennette, L., Cutforth, N., Tombari, C., & Stein, P. (2009). A case study of a community-based participatory evaluation research (CBPER) project: Reflections on promising practices and shortcomings. *Michigan Journal of Community Service Learning, 15*(2), 34–47.

Snow, R. E., Corno, L., & Jackson, D., III. (1996). Individual differences in affective and conative functions. In D. Berliner & R. Calfee (Eds.), *Handbook of educational psychology* (pp. 243–310). New York, NY: Macmillan.

Strand, K., Cutforth, N., Stoecker, R., Marullo, S., & Donahue P. (2003). *Community-based research and higher education: Principles and practices.* San Francisco, CA: Jossey-Bass.

Willis, J., Peresie, J., Waldref, V., & Stockmann, D. (2003). The undergraduate perspective on community-based research. *Michigan Journal of Community Service
Learning*, *9*(3), 36–43.

Woolfolk, A. (2013). *Educational psychology: Active learning edition* (12th ed.).
Boston, MA: Allyn & Bacon.

5

THE POWER MODEL

Five Core Elements for Teaching Community-Based Research

Jennifer M. Pigza

This chapter explores the very practical question, How do I teach community-based research (CBR)? Full-length books, websites, and scholarly articles all seek to answer this question from multiple angles of inquiry (e.g., Hollander, 2011; Stoecker, 2005; Strand, Cutforth, Stoecker, Marullo, & Donohue, 2003). In this chapter the basics of teaching CBR are presented through the mnemonic POWER: partnerships, objectives, working, evaluation, and reflection. Describing the teaching of CBR with a mnemonic enables faculty to readily employ a shorthand reference for the key elements of the CBR process that is useful for planning, implementing, and teaching students about the method. The mnemonic also creates a common language that can be easily used with community partners to build mutual accountability. In sum, the purpose of the mnemonic is not to dilute the complexity of the process of CBR, but rather to accentuate its key elements in a way that highlights CBR's complexity and provides suggestions on how to attend to each part of the process.

Although similar to the OPERA model (Welch, 2009), which is designed for the development of service-learning courses, using POWER to plan and implement CBR maximizes the fundamental orientation of CBR: long-term engagement to produce community impact. The POWER rubric includes some of the common elements of traditional CBR and service-learning but presents them in a manner consistent with the goals and processes described in this book. Before delving into the definitions and actions associated with each element of POWER, it is important to consider why POWER is an appropriate shorthand representation of impact-oriented CBR.

Why POWER?

First, POWERful CBR reflects a solidly community-oriented approach. Rather than beginning with the objectives of faculty or higher education institutions, POWERful CBR begins with participatory partnerships and long-term objectives for community impact that are mutually determined within POWER's CBR process. As Figure 5.1 indicates, partnerships are the starting and returning point that encircles each succeeding step.

Second, POWER is an apt mnemonic that relates to the question, Who has power in the CBR process? As Stoecker and Beckman (2009) assert, impact-orientated CBR emphasizes "a form of community development that builds the leadership and power of those who have been most excluded and are the most vulnerable" (p. 2). Naming the CBR process POWER reminds faculty and community partners to remain vigilant about how the process is shared among students, faculty, community partners, and community members engaged in the project.

Third, impact-oriented CBR has the power to transform institutions, faculty, and disciplines. Thus, a POWERful orientation expands the expectations of the institution's relationship with its neighbors, the purpose of the disciplines, and the types and duration of investment higher education makes in advancing the public good. As Dempsey (2010) found, engaging in CBR can transform faculty personally and professionally even when contributing to change requires faculty efforts beyond the traditional

Figure 5.1 Elements of POWERful CBR

boundaries of an academic term or research team (see Chapter 4). Keeping this change goal in mind and achieving community impact may encourage faculty to maintain the sometimes demanding commitments required by CBR.

Next, we examine each of the elements of POWER and describe how faculty can use the POWER acronym as a road map to engage in impact-oriented CBR. The following five sections begin with orienting questions that serve as a useful guide to faculty and community partners as they engage in the CBR process.

Partnerships

Guiding Questions for Partnerships

- What assumptions and expectations might faculty, community partners, community members, and students bring to a CBR relationship?
- In what ways can a faculty member's growing relationship with a community partner reflect equal participation and ownership of the process?
- How does my partner's community development goal match my research abilities and interest as a faculty member?

For many faculty, grounding research and pedagogy in a relationship with external partners may result in feeling unmoored and perhaps even threatened. In POWER's conceptual framework, impact-oriented CBR requires opening up the academic enterprise and welcoming other voices and objectives into the process. Forming POWERful partnerships begins with simply establishing connections, an element that is critical to the long-term success of faculty's efforts and the attainment of community goals and potential impact.

Establishing Connections and Developing a Partnership

How do you find a community partner? Potential campus sources for such introductions might be an office of community service or service-learning, academic departments that have field-based components, a campus community liaison office, and fellow faculty who are regularly involved in CBR. A basic Internet search can also reveal nonprofit and governmental agencies that are engaged in mutually beneficial efforts. Consider meeting with these individuals, groups, and multiagency coalitions to identify an issue or question that is important and actionable.

Navigating through the early stages of the CBR partnership requires faculty to set aside their expert agendas and focus on building relationships. Ultimately, this is human work that requires time, transparency, authenticity, trust, accountability, and clear communication. The best questions that engender trust and confidence "are questions asking people about what they are doing, what is working for them, what is not working for them, where they think they are heading, and what capacity gaps they are experiencing" (Stoecker & Beckman, 2009, p. 5).

In its most ideal form, CBR in the community impact framework gives preference to the needs and goals of the community over those of higher education or of particular faculty or courses, which is a radical departure from the norm in higher education. As your partnership develops, try to nurture the following practices: effective problem solving, building in best practices, colearning and mentoring, sharing resources, and putting an emphasis on producing results (Marullo, Moayedi, & Cooke, 2009). The successful implementation of these practices happens across the life of a POWERful CBR partnership, and the initial stages of a relationship provide the foundation for these practices to occur and to establish equality of participation and influence.

Potential Challenges and Solutions

There are multiple challenges to establishing and nurturing the participatory partnerships required for POWERful CBR; a few of these are preconceptions, time horizons, methods of communication, and language.

Faculty should consider their institution's past and present impacts and engagements with the community and community partners (Dempsey, 2010). This history and present engagement may have created positive, negative, or neutral impacts and impressions. Who on campus is involved in the existing partnership? Are these projects successful? What is working? What has been challenging? Is there a desire to expand efforts? Answers to these questions from institutional and community perspectives will enable a more informed early relationship.

Time horizons are also a factor. Higher education is organized on quarters, semesters, or trimesters, and summers may be active or fallow. Potential community partners' calendars might align well with this, or they may drastically differ. Additionally, long-term community-impact strategies do not coincide with the typical length of a course; they take years to achieve. Finally, the campus-based processes of the institutional review board (IRB), course approval, and resource allocation take time that may or may not match the planning patterns of community partners. Acknowledging these expectations and limitations early in the process provides an opportunity to devise a plan that meets both parties' needs in regard to time.

Methods of communication may also differ, so it is necessary to determine the best way to communicate as soon as possible, by e-mail, phone, text, a wiki, or in-person conversations. What combination of these will most effectively facilitate your relationship and collective work? How might each of the parties involved adjust their conflicting styles of communication to collaborate effectively? Taking time to establish expectations among participants will save time and effort in the long term.

Finally, the language of the academy and of community expertise might create a barrier for finding common ground. Particularly in the early stages of relationship development, be sure to ask for clarification as you listen and work to establish a common language for the work you aim to do. For example, one faculty member proposed a project to community partners about "alternative economies and energy." Community members countered with "poverty and sustainable development, [which] better represented the language they used in their own work" (Dempsey, 2010, p. 370).

Objectives

Guiding Questions for Objectives

- Whose objectives matter? How do you integrate faculty's writing and research, students' learning, and the community's impact goals?
- How do faculty and partners determine if CBR can assist in reaching a desired impact?
- How do these goals need to be prioritized or sequenced?
- What are reasonable short- and long-term goals?

With a foundational partnership in process, creating objectives and actions naturally flows. One way to think about objectives and POWERful CBR is to imagine nested objectives based on three perspective points that range from wide to narrow and include the partnership, the CBR project, and the course.

Objectives of the Partnership

Beginning with the widest perspective, faculty and community partners should work together to determine the overall objectives of the partnership. As relationships begin to form, the collective determines how the long-term efforts of this partnership will contribute to communities becoming "stronger, safer, more powerful, happier collectives of people" (Stoecker & Beckman, 2009, p. 8). For example, chemistry professor Steve Bachofer has a long-term relationship with the Contra Costa Watershed Forum in the county where Saint Mary's College of California is located. The long-term desired impact for this partnership is to maintain and develop water resources as "healthy, functional, attractive and safe community assets" (Contra Costa Watershed Forum, n.d.). The long-term desired impact of the partnerships can become its de facto mission statement.

Objectives for a Project

By creating project objectives collaboratively, faculty and community partners begin to stage progress toward the long-term impact goal, taking into account other factors, such as funding cycles, major events, the development of organizational strategic plans, or deadlines for academic publications. Moving from a long-term goal to short-term strategic objectives can be complicated. In this process, faculty and partners may recognize the need for multidisciplinary projects, or even a multicampus approach to meet the long-term community development objective (see Chapter 7). The community design process (Stoecker, 2005) suggests that CBR can be useful in diagnosing a community issue, prescribing a course of actions or interventions, identifying necessary resources, implementing an intervention, and evaluating progress and process.

Project objectives are also the starting point for creating action plans that delineate individual action items, deadlines, responsible parties, human and financial assets, and potential collaborators. The action plan is a mutually agreed-upon document that moves the idea of a project to reality; it becomes a tool for evaluating progress and accountability.

Course Objectives

Concurrent with the development of partnership objectives and project objectives, faculty must also attend to course objectives. For some courses, course learning objectives are strongly related to teaching CBR theory and practice. For others, the learning objectives are related to the discipline, and CBR is used as a tool in the study. In most courses, however, teaching research techniques and exploring a subject area will be combined. For faculty who are engaged in impact-oriented CBR, course objectives should include readings and discussions about the purpose of this particular type of research, education about the community, and perhaps guest lectures from community partners or community members.

In light of the long-term goals and periodic research objectives, faculty and partners can ask, What is the research question for this term? and What part of this research project can students accomplish given our time horizon? In Bachofer's case, the project objectives coincided with his course objectives. With his partners, he developed a multiyear research and action plan that included mapping nearby Las Trampas Creek, gathering and evaluating soil samples, and creating experiments and lesson plans for elementary classrooms. These courses occurred over a four-year period and contributed to the overall desired impact of the partnership.

A Note About Practicalities

Before moving from partnerships and objectives to the working portion of POWERful CBR, it is critical to pause to discuss practicalities. Each college and university has policies and processes that affect the CBR process and partnership. Administrative details include memoranda of understanding and course agreements with community partners, potential human subjects review, liability for student participation, and funding for research activities and transportation. Here faculty recognize they most likely will collaborate with other campus entities such as general counsel, the service-learning or CBR office, and centers for teaching and learning to proceed successfully. Some institutions have formalized policies and processes for these issues, others do not. Faculty must allow ample time to work out these parts of the CBR process, or their research efforts can become stalled.

Working

Guiding Questions for Working

- Have students, faculty, community partners, and community members fully agreed to an action plan, and do they all understand their responsibilities?
- What academic and popular venues can we explore for promoting and sharing our CBR and change efforts?
- How can faculty involve community partners in facilitating and witnessing the growth and development of students?

In the working portion of POWERful CBR, the research plan is enacted, students enter the field, stories are told, and things happen. In this model, working implies a range of actions, including the CBR itself, facilitating student learning and development, and disseminating lessons learned.

The Work of Research

During this phase, the action plan that was created during the objectives process becomes the road map for action, although the need for more details will likely arise. For example, if students are conducting surveys in public spaces, the action items need to include details such as design and approval of the instrument, training of student and neighborhood canvassers, logistical planning of conducting surveys, and supervision and emergency planning. Faculty and partners should identify not only parameters and time lines of the project but also contingency plans if plans go awry.

Facilitating Learning and Development

POWERful CBR involves not only working toward the change objectives of the partnership but also facilitating student learning and development (Lichtenstein, Thorme, Cutforth & Tombari, 2011). Current research identifies five dimensions of student learning outcomes related to CBR participation: academic skills, educational experience, civic engagement, professional skills, and personal growth (Lichtenstein et al., 2011). Faculty should consider some questions in advance, such as, What academic skills will students gain through this experience? What personal and professional skills might they enhance? How will CBR participation prompt questions of civic engagement and discipline in action? and How might someone be personally challenged by taking this course? Advanced consideration of these questions can help faculty become more intentional in their teaching and more skilled in responding to emerging student challenges throughout the term.

Politics professor Patrizia Longo has direct experience in working with her students in academic and nonacademic learning prompted by CBR. Longo worked on a multiyear project with Berkeley Women for Peace to document the oral histories of women who initiated the antinuclear movement in Northern California. In addition to supporting students in learning how to gather oral histories, she also guided students through transportation and time-management challenges, cross-cultural issues in the class and community, and larger discussions about nuclear proliferation and students' potential roles in the peace movement today.

The Work of Dissemination

For community partners, sharing results of the research is critical for progressing toward the community impact goals. For this type of dissemination, faculty, students, and partners will probably produce executive summaries, research reports, newspaper articles, and text for grant proposals; they should also be prepared to offer presentations at community and board meetings and professional conferences. It is incumbent on faculty to ensure that agreed-upon product deliverables are completed.

Faculty can identify outlets for publishing, presenting, and document-ing their CBR efforts, with a community partner or students as coau-thors. In addition to considering traditional disciplinary journals and associations, faculty can look more broadly for dissemination opportuni-ties. For example, they can use multiple teaching and learning journals, issue-oriented publications, and professional associations and publications concerned with civic engagement in higher education. The tenure and promotion process is a key moment for documenting CBR partnerships and projects. Therefore, faculty should be encouraged to include CBR as research and innovative pedagogy. Sharing their stories internally across campus further strengthens the institution's culture of CBR, active pedago-gies, and community engagement.

Evaluation

Guiding Questions for Evaluation

- To what degree has the CBR process contributed to the desired impact?
- Where and how should evaluation happen in a CBR project?
- How will faculty and partners evaluate the partnership itself?

Evaluation appraises the strengths and weaknesses of the CBR project and partnership with the goal of improving effectiveness. Evaluation is thus necessary to gauge whether a project is moving toward its goals and creates opportunities for adjustment along the way. Faculty can build evaluation into the CBR process in several practical ways, such as reviewing the research implementation time line and identifying natural places for an evaluative pause, which is often pedagogically useful as well. If a CBR project involves students conducting multiple focus groups with several community members and community partner staff, pausing after the first round of focus groups to debrief successes and challenges can inform the next round of focus groups. This not only enables students to self-evaluate but also provides commu-nity partners with an opportunity to determine whether the focus group was executed in a way that will provide the information they seek. At this phase of the CBR project, modeling shared power and influence in the research process is critical for teaching students about impact-oriented CBR.

Evaluating the Project: Outputs, Outcomes, and Impact

In the early stages of a CBR partnership, evidence of impact may be difficult to achieve. This is one reason why POWERful CBR is based on the assumption of a long-term relationship among faculty members and community partners. Evaluate your CBR efforts on three levels: outputs, outcomes, and impact (see Chapter 2). Outputs are short term in their vision and provide the initial results of the research (Beckman, Penney, & Cockburn, 2011). To evaluate outputs, faculty must ask, To what extent did the proposed CBR project follow its implementation plan? and Were the results summarized for the community partner in a usable fashion?

In comparison, outcomes are medium term and refer to application of the results. To evaluate outcomes, faculty must ask, How was the community partner able to use the results? and What effect did the outputs have, now and in the future, on individuals and organizations? For example, sociologist John Ely has a long-standing partnership with the Northern California Service League, a nonprofit organization dedicated to reducing crime by helping offenders and ex-offenders become responsible and productive citizens. Ely's students are conducting an ongoing research project evaluating the effectiveness of one of the leagues' educational programs. After each implementation cycle, he asks the league whether the project report was effective (outputs). He also inquires about how the results of the research informed the refinement of educational programs for ex-offenders (outcomes).

Another question of evaluation is concerned with impact, the long-term view of the CBR partnership and how the research contributes to the community's stated long-term goals of systems change, economic development, or social justice. In the preceding example, Ely and the league members ask themselves to what degree this CBR project assists the league in reducing crime (desired impact).

Evaluating the Partnership

POWERful CBR also engages faculty and partners in an evaluation of the partnership itself, occurring at natural breaks and shifts in the action plan to allow necessary corrections, and it should occur as a summative experience on a biannual or annual basis. These conversations with community partners are a time to reinforce (or change) the shared goals and desires of the group, assess how well power is being shared, make adjustments to future plans, and consider whether the activities of the CBR partnership are leading toward the desired impact.

Faculty and community partners may choose to evaluate the partnership using the transformational evaluation relationship scale (TRES)

(Clayton, Bringle, Senor, Huq, & Morrison, 2010), which explores how partnerships can be exploitative, transactional, and transformative. Although this scale was developed to evaluate campus-community partnerships for service-learning, its elements translate well to POWERful CBR. An exploitative relationship reflects a disproportionate allocation of power and benefits to one partner. Transactional relationships are short term, limited, project based, and work within systems. Transformational relationships are long term, dynamic, issue based, and create new systems and group identities. As CBR partnerships develop, they are likely to experience transactional and transformational elements.

While it may be impractical for faculty and community partners to conduct a formal evaluation using TRES, a conversation inclusive of all stakeholders based on TRES's eight dimensions of partnership can be incorporated into an annual retreat. The eight areas of TRES, adapted to POWERful CBR are as follows:

1. Common and interconnected goals
2. Collaborative decision making
3. Relative contribution of resources
4. Responding to and managing conflict
5. Work and identity formation
6. Distribution of power
7. How the partnership matters
8. Satisfaction with personal and organizational change

For a session such as this, some time should be allotted for individual reflection followed by a group conversation on the eight dimensions. It is also possible to collectively choose which dimensions seem most relevant for evaluation at a particular time. Ask participants to evaluate the present status (Where are we currently on this dimension?) and their desires (Where should we go in the future?).

Engaging Students in Evaluation

In terms of evaluating CBR at the course level, faculty can make use of a few assessment tools that will help them ascertain how students are learning and implementing the model and maintaining focus on long-term impact. During class, faculty can ask students to discuss what is and is not working in their CBR efforts. This conversation creates an opportunity to praise the group for what is going well, clarify expectations, and solve problems as needed. Another discussion or writing prompt midway through a course can request students to state what they believe the purpose of CBR is. The ensuing discussion becomes an evaluation of current efforts, a reminder of the bigger goals of impact-oriented CBR, and an invitation to students to make meaning of their CBR experience in light of larger goals and course learning objectives.

Reflection

Guiding Questions for Reflection

- How have faculty, students, and the community intentionally engaged in reflection throughout the CBR process?
- Does the reflection provide openings for personal, academic, and communal learning?
- How does this reflection influence the continual formation of the partnership and CBR?

Freire defined *praxis* as "action and reflection upon the world in order to transform it" (1970/1994, p. 33). His notion of praxis is helpful in the pursuit of impact-oriented CBR and is reflected in the earlier discussion of the elements of POWER. If we truly seek the transformation of the people and places that constitute community, inside and outside the academy, we must be equally engaged in action and reflection. Reflection without action can produce academic navel gazing in which our best knowledge and skills are never realized in community partnerships that can transform lives. On the other hand, action without reflection ignores opportunities for learning.

The value of reflection in student learning and development is well documented, and the inclusion of reflection in the POWER mnemonic emphasizes its role not only in student learning and development but also in the learning and development of faculty, community partners, and community members. The process of reflection deepens learning, provides knowledge for future action, attends to the collaborative evolution of the partnership, and provides a space for unexpected insights and new questions. The fields of service-learning and student learning and development provide ample resources for facilitating reflection (e.g., Angelo & Cross, 1993; Pigza, 2010; Reed & Koliba, 1995). These resources can be translated into CBR use with faculty, community partners, and community members as well.

Reflection as an Ongoing Practice

Although reflection occurs at the end of POWER, faculty should establish a reflective orientation throughout the CBR process by imagining a project time line or semester with peaks and valleys where reflection can take place. For example, before visiting a community for the first time, faculty might facilitate a conversation that allows students to explore their preconceptions and misconceptions (Angelo & Cross, 1993). This enables faculty to affirm accurate perceptions and knowledge, correct information, and model an asset-based perspective on the people and place for their CBR. It may be equally useful to hold a similar conversation in reverse with community partners to describe their preconceptions of students and faculty.

In the middle of a CBR project, consider a reflection activity that might help all participants gauge their learning and development. For example, a one-word journal (Angelo & Cross, 1993) activity with a group of students, community partners, and faculty might be effective. Begin by asking participants (and yourself) to provide a one-word answer to an open-ended question, such as, What am I learning through this CBR experience? Then ask them to write one or two paragraphs explaining why they chose that word. Discussing their writing in pairs or small groups provides an opening for multiple forms of learning (academic, personal, civic, etc.) and reinforces that the exercise is a learning process for all.

Concluding reflections provide students, faculty, community partners, and community members with an opportunity to make meaning of the entire CBR project in the context of the community impact goal. For example, at a celebratory meeting at the end of a semester or phase of the project, dedicate time for thee-minute speeches (Reed & Koliba, 1995) that answer a common question such as, Why does this partnership make a difference? For students, this could be a brief written assignment; for other partners, it could be an impromptu topic for discussion. During the gathering create time for students to give their three-minute speeches and for you and community partners and members to offer their reflections as well.

Lessons Learned

Engaging in impact-oriented CBR in the classroom and in the community is about "thinking about a community-driven, system-oriented approach versus a campus-driven individual oriented one; thinking of larger, longer term action, done in a highly participatory manner that involves ongoing evaluation and redirection" (Stoecker & Beckman, 2009, p. 8). My description of POWERful CBR reflects this sentiment and challenges *why* and *how* faculty collaborate with community partners. My own experience of such partnerships bears out the importance of POWERful CBR as process and product alike.

My department at Saint Mary's College of California has renewed its partnership with the Prescott-Joseph Center for Community Enhancement, in Oakland, California. Our initial collaboration in 2011 involved the placement of two summer research interns at the center, and we now share an AmeriCorps VISTA member whose salary is paid 50/50 by the college and the center. The collaboration's long-term desired impact is halting generational poverty and increasing the educational attainment of residents in West Oakland. A one- to two-year outcome is the establishment of a multifaceted family resource center supported by academic and cocurricular initiatives of the college. More immediate outputs have been the result of research interns' asset mapping and data gathered from the AmeriCorps VISTA member's focus groups and community surveys. We are currently laying the groundwork for faculty to be engaged in CBR, service-learning, and cocurricular initiatives.

I have been establishing and nurturing this partnership while simultaneously writing about the elements of POWERful CBR, which has triggered several personal thoughts and emotions. I am cautioned by my desire to move quickly, reminded of the time and sensitivity required to build relationships, and eager to involve faculty from multiple disciplines in the project. However, I am overwhelmingly humbled by the power of the invitation to me and my colleagues to join this important work.

And herein, I believe, lies a critical lesson: POWERful CBR does not happen because faculty and students impose themselves on a community, *it happens because we are invited*. It happens because we share power. It happens because we approach these relationships with thought and care. It happens because we recognize the expertise within communities. It happens because we develop the ability to balance confidence in our knowledge and skills with humility about how they can best contribute to creating change. It happens because we genuinely want to be part of generating the long-term change a community seeks. The remaining chapters of Part Two are examples of faculty, students, and institutions attempting to do just that.

References

Angelo, T. A., & Cross, K. P. (1993). *Classroom assessment techniques: A handbook for college faculty*. San Francisco, CA: Jossey-Bass.

Beckman, M., Penney, N., & Cockburn, B. (2011). Maximizing the impact of community-based research. *Journal of Higher Education Outreach and Engagement, 15*(2), 83–104.

Clayton, P., Bringle, R. G., Senor, B., Huq, J., & Morrisson, M. (2010). Differentiating and assessing relationships in service-learning and civic engagement: Exploitative, transactional, or transformational. *Michigan Journal of Community Service Learning, 16*(2), 5–22.

Contra Costa Watershed Forum. (n.d.). *Welcome to the Contra Costa Watershed forum*. Retrieved from www.cocowaterweb.org

Dempsey, S. E. (2010). Critiquing community engagement. *Management Communication Quarterly, 24*, 359–390.

Freire, P. (1994). *Pedagogy of the oppressed*. New York, NY: Continuum. (Original work published 1970)

Hollander, J. B. (2011). Keeping control: The paradox of scholarly community-based research in community development. *Community Development, 46*(2), 265–272.

Lichtenstein, G., Thorme, T., Cutforth, N., & Tombari, M. L. (2011). Development of a national survey to assess student learning outcomes of community-based research. *Journal of Higher Education Outreach and Engagement, 15*(2), 7–33.

Marullo, S., Moayedi, R., & Cooke, D. (2009). C. Wright Mills's friendly critique of service learning and an innovative response: Cross-institutional collaborations for community-based research. *Teaching Sociology, 37*(1), 61–75.

Pigza, J. M. (2010). Developing your ability to foster student learning and development through reflection. In B. Jacoby & P. Mutascio (Eds.), *Looking in, reaching out: A reflective guide for community service-learning professionals* (pp. 73–94). Boston, MA: Campus Compact.

Reed, J., & Koliba, C. (1995). *Facilitating reflection: A manual for leaders and educators*. Retrieved from www.uvm.edu/~dewey/reflection_manual

Stoecker, R. (2005). *Research methods for community change: A project-based approach*. Thousand Oaks, CA: Sage.

Stoecker, R., & Beckman, M. (2009). *Making higher education civic engagement matter in the community*. Retrieved from www.compact.org/wp-content/uploads/2010/02/engagementproof-1.pdf

Strand, K. J., Cutforth, N., Stoecker, R., Marullo, S., Donohue, P. (2003). *Community-based research and higher education: Principles and practices*. San Francisco, CA: Jossey-Bass.

Welch, M. (2009). O.P.E.R.A.: A first letter mnemonic and rubric for conceptualising and implementing service learning. *Issues in Educational Research, 20*(1), 76–82. Retrieved from www.iier.org.au/iier20/welch.html

6

APPLYING THE POWER MODEL IN A SECOND-LANGUAGE CLASS

Rachel Parroquin with Emily Geiger-Medina

Community-Based Spanish: Language, Culture, and Community is a three-credit course offered each semester by the Department of Romance Languages and Literatures (ROLL) at the University of Notre Dame. The class is designed to help advanced intermediate Spanish students gain more expertise in language knowledge and skills as they study issues and engage in service-learning opportunities in the local community. In this case study, I briefly introduce the course and then employ Pigza's POWER model (see Chapter 5) to discuss my experience in integrating a research partnership with a parent involvement organization into the course.

I asked my student, Emily Geiger-Medina, to provide her perspective on the course's month-long community-based research (CBR) unit because after the semester ended, she approached me about continuing to work on the project. At the time, she was enrolled in a course on inequality in the American education system and desired to continue her engagement in education-focused research in the Hispanic community while simultaneously expanding her knowledge via her course work. It seemed a natural fit to have her help write our experiences for this case study as Emily was a sociology and psychology double major with a keen interest in education, especially as it relates to the Hispanic community.

The Course

Community-Based Spanish is one of several options students have for a fifth semester bridge class between a four-semester sequence of language and culture courses and studying literature. Students tend to enroll in the course to learn more about the Latino community and culture, in addition to enhancing their Spanish language skills. Those who take the course have a range of language ability that varies from completion of minimum prerequisites to study or service abroad immersions, and many are Spanish majors. The course already has a community-based learning (CBL) component because research irrefutably shows it is beneficial in providing "linguistic relevance and cultural context" (Long, 2013, p. 202) to the second language (L2) field. In contrast to the documentation of CBL in L2 pedagogy, the field has few examples of CBR partnerships.

The CBR Unit: Analyzing Interviews and Focus Groups of Latino Parents

The CBR model in Chapter 5 is based on the POWER acronym whose letters represent five concepts that Pigza argues should be part of any CBR project: partnership, objectives, working, evaluation, and reflection. Although each essential component is highlighted in this case study, Pigza emphasizes that partnership is the starting and ending point of the process, and therefore envelops the remaining components.

My community partner, No Parent Left Behind (NPLB), primarily serves low-income parents of children who struggle in school. Its curriculum trains parents in learning processes, language arts, and math, so they are better equipped to give their children academic support. Although the director of NPLB does not speak Spanish, she had interview and pre- and post-focus group audio files from NPLB workshops offered to Spanish-speaking parents at three schools and community sites. She needed that data analyzed to determine if the program was effective for Latino families.

Partnership

Six months before the CBR unit began, NPLB's director and I were part of a CBR team that was awarded a minigrant from the Center for Social Concerns (CSC) at Notre Dame to fund this CBR project. Before agreeing to work with NPLB, I considered several issues. First, as most L2 faculty, I did not have training in CBR. Thus it was imperative that my community partner either have a good understanding of this approach to research or that we could get assistance from CSC staff. Second, as a teacher in the humanities, I was concerned that I lacked the research tools needed to complete the project. If NPLB's director did not possess those skills, we would need an additional faculty partner from the social sciences. Third, and perhaps most important, faculty in the Spanish program need partners who provide students with opportunities to use Spanish as much as possible, so we had to find a partner that could give my students opportunities to use their skills in Spanish so they could meet their learning goals.

Because I had already served with NPLB's director for 16 months on the Latino Task Force for Education (LTFE), I knew she had the requisite understanding of CBR and qualitative research skills. Therefore, our backgrounds complemented each other's in terms of research and linguistic and cultural skill sets. It also became clear that my students would have ample opportunity to use Spanish. Moreover, our past experiences in helping to develop, plan, and present workshops to parents and students confirmed our mutual interests in closing the education gap, so I knew we would be able to work together well. Therefore, I felt comfortable having my class work with this community partner.

Objectives

As we planned the CBR unit, we gave equal consideration to NPLB's objectives and to student learning outcomes linked to course objectives. NPLB's main objective was to have the data analyzed and coded by bilinguals who had an understanding of the local Latino population and culture, and sufficient intercultural competence to note group differences in bilingual Spanish-English parents, monolingual Spanish parents, and codes developed for English monolingual parents.

I realized that completing the CBR unit could help students acquire research skills and meet the following learning goals formulated by ROLL for the course in knowledge, skills, and dispositions: (a) "understand most points of extended speech and . . . begin to recognize nuances of meaning, and (b) "develop a better understanding of the target language and culture(s) through authentic materials and . . . gain more profound insight into the relationship between the two" (Department of Romance Languages and Literatures, 2008). Beyond these departmental learning outcomes, the CBR unit could additionally enable students to fulfill three of my course goals: (a) engage deeply with the community, (b) become educated about the richness of the Latino community and what it offers to the larger society, and (c) more thoroughly understand the challenges the community faces that also affect the larger society. Ultimately, my hope was that students might begin to see how they could work to affect community change through CBR, an aim the CSC and ROLL could support in our faith-based university with its mission to further social justice.

Working

NPLB's director met with me several times to plan the unit, choose its timing in the semester, and determine what content to cover with the students prior to the CBR unit. She also instructed me on the data analysis procedures students would use. We discussed how students should be prepared and how to ensure that students were capable of completing the assigned tasks. I carefully selected and sequenced readings prior to the CBR unit to include research briefs focusing on local Latino issues that had been written by upper-level Spanish students as well as work by local scholars relevant to Latino education and parent involvement (see Sidebar 1).

Sidebar 1: Lessons Learned From the Readings

Emily Geiger-Medina

The readings helped me recognize that Latinos bring their own unique array of different talents, priorities, experiences, and perspectives into the U.S. education system. I also learned Latinos are more likely to suffer rather than prosper in the current system because they face a cumulative disadvantage stemming from a plethora of factors. One of the most influential factors is their limited English proficiency. Across the United States, Hispanics have the highest dropout rate of any racial or ethnic group (Motel & Patten, 2013, p. 27), and locally 39% of Hispanic third graders fail Indiana's state math and language arts standardized test (compared to 20% in math and 15% in language arts for Whites). This gap continues to grow for fifth- and eighth-grade students in language arts (Indiana Department of Education, 2013).

After reading that everything parents "do or don't do affects [their] children" (Dabbah, 2006, p. 5), I realized that parents without proficiency in English are less likely to talk to teachers or ask questions. Instead, they prefer to remain quiet because, as one parent put it, "I don't know how to pronounce it. I don't know how to express it correctly, so I better remain silent" (Chamberlain & Sleevi, 2011, p. 4). I discovered the communication barrier with parents was the biggest regional challenge teachers faced working with Latino children (Guzmán, Reyes, Palacios, & Carolan-Silva, 2011), but all factors related to limited English proficiency create a huge obstacle for children to succeed in school because they prevent many monolingual, Spanish-speaking parents from believing they can help their children with homework (Dabbah, 2006). Another handicap is related to the fact that 21.9% of Hispanic parents have completed less than the equivalent of a ninth-grade education (Motel & Patten, 2013), and 25.9% of U.S. Hispanics live in poverty. This lower socioeconomic status affects the frequency of reading at home and the number of words in a child's vocabulary (Hart & Risley, 1995; Rothstein, 2004).

By the time the CBR unit began, students had literally faced many of the local Latino issues through their CBL experiences at several community sites. Students had also directly interacted with parents and middle and high school youths at a Preparing for College Workshop organized by LTFE and financially supported by a grant from Notre Dame's Provost Initiative on Engaging the Community. All these experiences, class discussions, and course readings introduced students to the human face and reality of the issues they were studying in class and would work with in the CBR unit.

The unit consisted of eight classes (12 contact hours) plus a follow-up session for students to present their findings in the target language (Spanish) to interested community members and NPLB. On day one, NPLB's director introduced the group to the program, gave instructions on how to code qualitative data, and explained the concept of inter-rater reliability. She then described the a priori codes students would use and guided them through a practice exercise of coding a sample English-language transcript until they understood the process. Each transcript was given to a pair of students; their homework consisted of listening to an audio file, reading the corresponding transcript, and coding it.

On day two, she returned to evaluate their accuracy in coding, model the process again, and answer questions. Students compared their coding homework with that of their peer partner and discussed differences until they established high levels of inter-rater reliability in coding. We also discussed trends across groups. Students generally took detailed notes, which they incorporated into their written summaries with cited quotes from the transcripts as evidence of their coding and trends. This same procedure was followed for the remainder of the unit until each data set (individual interviews, pre- and postfocus groups) was analyzed. Following the CBR unit, students read other articles (predominantly in Spanish) from theology, economics, political science, and health care with national and international foci related to migration and its impact on migrant communities, which continued to challenge their critical thinking on issues from their CBR/CBL experiences.

Evaluation

Pigza (Chapter 5) describes an evaluation framework with three types of CBR relationships. The partnership with NPLB was transactional, meaning it was limited, short term, and focused on a specific project. While there is the potential for creating a transformational relationship given our common goals and ongoing work with LTFE, it is not yet fully developed.

I was not aware of all eight areas outlined in the POWER model until after the project was completed, so NPLB and I did not formally evaluate the project using all those elements; I incorporated that process into future projects. We did keep partnership outcomes in mind from the beginning of our planning to ensure that work done by students would benefit NPLB directly. NPLB's director and I were working toward a common goal of reducing the education gap among Latino families. We also had an interconnected goal of helping my students gain linguistic and cultural knowledge and practice through working with the Spanish language data.

All decision making related to the organization and scheduling of the CBR unit was collaborative; each partner provided expertise, resources, and time according to her capacity. Since we had collaborated together previously, we had a good working relationship. We had no conflict, but if we had I am confident that we would have been able to address it quickly and appropriately, given our shared history. Because of that shared history and our complementary skill sets, the power dynamic was an equal one. The development of our partnership over the course of working with LTFE and the CBR unit has continued as we move ahead to address the education gap in our local Latino community, demonstrating the importance of the partnership to both of us. While I cannot speak about my partner's satisfaction with personal and organizational change, I have gained professionally and personally by having participated in the CBR unit with NPLB.

Pigza also suggests in Chapter 5 that students engage in evaluation as well. This was accomplished during the CBR unit and at the end of the semester by various means. Class discussions offered students the opportunity to question the process, clarify points of misunderstanding, and solidify their comprehension of CBR. Students also recorded oral dialogues with a partner reflecting on the process and connecting the CBR experience to the course as a whole and personal student learning outcomes. These discussions and dialogues were used to make adjustments midunit. Finally, students were prompted to include the CBR unit in their metareflection papers at the end of the semester in which they were asked to evaluate their learning process through CBL and CBR and to consider how those pedagogies might have enhanced their learning outcomes (see Sidebar 2).

Sidebar 2: Student Evaluations

Emily Geiger-Medina

Perhaps the only thing I would have changed about this course would be our preparation for the research component. I had no previous research experience, and the expectations at first glance were quite overwhelming. I was responsible for reading transcriptions and listening to recordings of interviews and focus groups, coding the transcripts, summarizing the findings, and discussing the analyses with my peers. It would have been helpful to have better understood the process itself before being completely immersed in it. Through the course readings and lectures, I initially learned about general issues facing the entire Latino community; in the CBR unit, I was then able to fully understand how those trends applied in a more individualized and personal perspective. I strongly believe that simultaneously working from both perspectives helped me gain even more from this course. I learned how community work benefits those being helped and those doing the helping, and I learned to appreciate the Latino culture.

Reflection

Pedagogical lessons. I learned three valuable pedagogical lessons about the logistics of teaching a CBR unit. First, I would schedule the time differently, and I would have the partner spend more time explaining the project and process to ensure that students clearly understood CBR and the project. Students also needed more time to process the data, as this challenged them. Additionally, I would do a better job of sequencing due dates for other subsequent assignments, like the final research paper.

Second, given the need to work in both languages, I would take time to better craft the written assignments students used to process, analyze, and report results. There is value in students doing all the work in the target language and then translating the coding sheets, summaries, and their reflections into English for NPLB. However, it was time consuming for students, and they regarded it as redundant. A more efficient use of their time would achieve the partner's output and student learning needs by dividing the process between languages. For example, after listening to audio files and coding the Spanish language transcriptions, students could create bulleted lists in English with examples of parent comments organized by code categories. These lists could then function as a prewriting tool for composing more elaborated summaries in the target language of Spanish while providing useful information to the partner.

Third, throughout the CBR unit, students raised difficult questions that went beyond the scope of what an L2 class can address. They wondered how to affect local partners' programming, what they could do with their new knowledge, and how they might have an impact on policies related to the partner's issues. Although discussions about these issues can take place, the L2 faculty member needs to be open to directing students to other courses that can help them progress from assessing data to becoming agents who influence long-term impact.

Student learning outcomes. In addition to what I learned about how to teach with CBR, I also found that student reflections, course evaluations, and final exam questions highlighted six significant learning outcomes that either differed from or were deeper than previous student reports associated with this CBL course. First, with CBR's emphasis on collaboration and blurring the levels of hierarchy (Strand, Marullo, Cutforth, Stoecker, & Donohue, 2003), I found students were more likely to value and share their expertise gained in other courses (e.g., anthropology, psychology, sociology, and theology) and through their cultural and linguistic CBL immersion experiences abroad and domestic rather than deferring to me as the expert. This thinking and shared reflection greatly enriched class discussions and students' collective learning. Second, because students were analyzing the data in Spanish, they gained confidence in their linguistic skills, which improved more than by simply reading materials. Third, students repeatedly noted they engaged more deeply with the material, which resulted in an enhanced understanding of issues. According to one student:

> Since I had to think constantly about the codes, I was reading the transcripts in a critical way that I would not have done if I had not had to code them. After coding the transcripts, writing the summaries of the transcripts helped me to think about everything I had read and to highlight certain themes that stood out. . . . This helped me a lot to make connections to our readings.

Fourth, while reading critically, many students reported their cultural understanding was enhanced through experiencing the literal and figurative voices of the parents. A student explained it this way, "Listening to the voices and reading the transcripts, we have put a face to these problems, and we can understand them better." This process helped all students broaden their awareness of what Latinos faced in school. One summarized the unit as helping

> accumulate a well-developed understanding of the reality of the educational experience of Latinos in our country and the general challenges this demographic group faces in obtaining access to high quality educational programs and being successful in the world of education.

Fifth, this enhanced understanding of deep issues faced by Latinos led a few students to question what they could do as citizens or in their future careers to make policy and structural changes needed to have a true impact. One student commented,

I think my real interest began to take hold of me when we worked with [NPLB]. When I heard the parents in a focus group express apprehension that the NPLB classes were ending, my heart went out to them. In that moment, and many afterwards, I wanted to do what was necessary to continue this program for them.

Sixth, students learned a great deal about doing research including the importance of not imposing their own suppositions on data and letting the data speak for itself, carefully reading transcripts at least twice when coding rather than only once, and the importance of inter-rater reliability and understanding other coders' thinking in establishing accurate data analysis. While working with CBR's messy nature and the continual refinement of research at times frustrated the students, it also helped them learn to address the kinds of challenges that often arise in research. For example, it quickly became apparent that they needed additional codes to represent Spanish-speaking parents' responses when they sometimes contrasted with responses of English-speaking parents. Differences in trends between monolingual and bilingual parents also surfaced, requiring further discussion and fine-tuning of the codes. Dealing with these challenges helped students gain a better understanding of the qualitative research process (see Sidebar 3).

Sidebar 3: Student Reflection

Emily Geiger-Medina

My paternal grandparents were born in Mexico. Neither of my parents completed college. I grew up in an environment that statisticians could easily argue would not give me a bright future or high school diploma, let alone a college degree from a prestigious university. I believe part of the reason I want to go into education is because I want to show students like myself, who grow up with every statistic pointing against them, that there is a way out of the cycle and a way to prove the statistics wrong. Working with residents of South Bend increased my interest in learning more about the Latino community, further strengthened my ability to draw connections between multiple components of my life, and reinforced my passion to work in education.

Being involved in this CBR project was an incredible experience. Hearing individuals tell their stories was extremely eye opening. I was shown that statistics represent real people facing real difficulties. Moreover, I learned how widely experiences vary. Too often Latinos are thought of as one large community and are grouped together on a large scale. Although there were significant similarities between stories and experiences in the data, there were also noteworthy differences. Participating in the research project reinforced a lesson I had learned in my introductory statistics course: Aggregated data can be useful in understanding trends, but individual stories must not be ignored. I was also able to develop an understanding of where the findings I read about were coming from. It was one thing to read about how Latino parents were less likely to understand the educational system (Crosnoe, 2006), but it was entirely different to hear a mother personally explain her current understanding on the audio file.

Studying sociology and psychology, I realized that research would likely be a part of my future, especially if I decide to attend graduate school. Working with NPLB helped me understand the research process more clearly. I learned how many people are necessary to perform qualitative research and how important communication is in the research process. Accurate and valid research is nearly impossible without communication among researchers and subjects, as well as among researchers and assistants.

In regard to our community partner, students presented several outputs to NPLB, including coded transcripts that were cross-checked by partners to ensure inter-rater reliability, analysis of the parent interviews and focus groups, and summaries of trends noted within and across groups as determined by class discussion. NPLB's director used this information to create several outcomes, including a presentation of the results in a poster session at a university awards dinner the following spring. NPLB has likewise incorporated the results and analysis into subsequent grant proposals for NPLB and LTFE. In terms of our CBR project helping NPLB achieve community change and impact, it is early in the process, but the results are continuing to inform NPLB's efforts and LTFE to work toward increasing achievement and graduation rates among local Latino youth.

References

Chamberlain, S., & Sleevi, J. (2011). Educación primaria de niños latinos en South Bend y los Estados Unidos: el pasado y el presente [Primary education of Latino children in South Bend and the United States: The past and the present]. *Student Research Series, 7*(3), 4.

Crosnoe, R. (2006). *Mexican roots, American schools: Helping Mexican immigrant children succeed.* Stanford, CA: Stanford University Press.

Dabbah, M. (2006). *Ayude a sus hijos a tener éxito en la escuela: Creando el hábito de buena asistencia a temprana edad* [*Help your child succeed in school: Creating good attendance habits at an early age*]. Naperville, IL: Sphinx.

Department of Romance Languages and Literatures, University of Notre Dame. (2008). *Learning goals for the major in Spanish.* Retrieved from romancelanguages .nd.edu/assessment/learning-goals-for-spanish-major/

Guzmán, J. C., Reyes, J. R., Palacios, J., & Carolan-Silva, A. R. (2011). *Latinos in north central Indiana: Educational challenges and opportunities.* Goshen, IN: Goshen College.

Hart, B., & Risley, T. R. (1995). *Meaningful differences in the everyday experience of young American children.* Baltimore, MD: Paul H Brookes.

Indiana Department of Education. (2013). *DOE compass.* Retrieved from http:// compass.doe.in.gov/dashboard/istep.aspx?type=corp&id=7205

Long, S. S. (2013, June). Editor's message: Focusing on the scholarship of community engagement. *Hispania, 96*(2), 202.

Motel, S., & Patten, E. (2013). *Statistical portrait of Hispanics in the United States.* Retrieved from www.pewhispanic.org/2013/02/15/statistical-portrait-of-hispan ics-in-the-united-states-2011/

Rothstein, R. (2004). *Class and schools: Using social, economic, and educational reform to close the achievement gap.* Washington, DC: Economic Policy Institute.

Strand, K., Marullo, S., Cutforth, N., Stoeker, R., & Donohue, P. (2003). *Community-based research and higher education.* San Francisco, CA: Jossey-Bass.

7

MULTICAMPUS PARTNERSHIPS STUDYING THE FEASIBILITY OF BUYING LOCAL

Christopher S. Ruebeck

D uring a single semester, faculty members and college students from three schools engaged in a multi-institutional community-based research (CBR) study of the demand for and supply of local food in eastern Pennsylvania's Lehigh Valley. The study was motivated by the expressed needs of the Greater Lehigh Valley chapter of Buy Fresh Buy Local (BFBL), a group with local and national connections to the movement toward greater use of locally grown food. Students from Muhlenberg College worked as part of an independent biology study project, a group from Lehigh University participated in a community consulting practicum, and students at Lafayette College completed group projects as part of my marketing research class.

In this chapter I relate my experience in this interinstitutional effort as an assistant professor in the Department of Economics at Lafayette College. The first section places this experience in the pedagogical and conceptual framework of the marketing research and economics literatures. The chapter then continues with an elaborated description of our project using the elements of Pigza's POWER theoretical model (featured in Chapter 5) to provide an authentic example of how her model can be applied in practice.

The Literature

Economics and marketing research use the term *service-learning* (SL) more frequently than *community-based learning* or *community-based research*

(CBR). This reflects the significant variance in the degree to which students' projects may be community driven or focused on measuring outputs in relationship to their value in the community. Unfortunately, only a fraction of those existing programs are documented in either discipline's mainstream literatures, perhaps because CBR/SL projects focus on outcomes, the inherently interdisciplinary nature of community-based activities, or a lack of academic recognition that there is worthy scholarship in CBR.

The economics pedagogy is more recent and less widespread; it is connected to current excitement over developments in active learning (Salemi, 2002). Some examples of community-driven service-learning in economics appear exclusively on Web pages. For example, Whitehead (2009) describes a cost-benefit project that is part of a larger program at Appalachian State University (Mortensen, 2010). Other programs may be connected to or have grown out of community development efforts such as those at Simon Fraser University (*Center for Sustainable Community Development*, 2010), or are part of a larger policy program such as those described by Minkler and Blackwell (2010).

Elliot (2009) advocates improved methods for student reflection based on service-learning projects in a development economics class and uses the Kolb (1981) learning cycle (described later) to organize a discussion of outcomes. Elliot's motivation is to demonstrate that service-learning "remains underrepresented in disciplines that value objectivity," (p. 265) and he uses data collected from Campus Compact. The student experience in this example remains one of volunteerism, but Elliot carefully works through the question of service-learning's utility and applicability. His collaboration with local agencies resulted in a partnership effort in which agency representatives talked to the class and requested the assessment tool. As a result of this request, his traditional student journal assignments were replaced by an assessment of the agency's operations with recommendations for improvements that were reported directly to the agencies.

Brooks and Schramm (2007) describe another comprehensive program at the University of Vermont and conclude that a research-teaching-service model offers benefits to all participants. Although initially uncomfortable with the nontraditional type of course, the students responded very positively to the hands-on, applied, and obviously relevant nature of the work. Their project spanned multiple semesters, drawing on a wider range of economic theory, under the umbrella of urban economics. Although the project I describe also connects research, teaching, and service, it is less integrative in nature, with more of the semester devoted to traditional lecture.

The marketing literature in this area, by comparison, is more developed because student projects have long been an important part of marketing and marketing research courses. More than 20 years ago, Ramocki (1987) stated, "The client-sponsored research project is no longer a novel approach to the marketing research course or to the marketing curriculum in general" (p. 24). After reviewing favorable descriptions in the literature from the early 1980s, he then describes his own empirical study of a student research project that was successful in significantly increasing the students' self-reported research proficiency. He validated this finding by comparing student and client opinions about the results' utility and achievement of the project's purpose. Today, student self-assessment is still used widely in marketing and other courses. (Bernhardt, Jones, Ruebeck, & Isaacs, 2010), but fewer empirical studies assess the courses' impact in the community (Ziegert & McGoldrick, 2008).

The economics and marketing research literatures discuss Kolb's model of experiential learning as instrumental for understanding the benefits of service-learning (McGoldrick, 1998; Petkus, 2000). Indeed, in a service-learning context, one can start at any point in Kolb's (1981) cycle of four stages: (a) abstract conceptualization, (b) active experimentation, (c) concrete experience, and (d) reflective observation, with the cycle returning to (a) abstract conceptualization. In an economics classroom, the cycle is usually initiated through lecture at the abstract conceptualization stage. New applications are then often illustrated as part of lecture, homework, and exams. We can also see concrete experience and reflective observation provided through current events coverage and assignments, but that standard practice seldom loops back through the stages. By incorporating CBR, we enable cycling through the levels more than once, provide more concrete experiences, and increase the frequency and relevance of reflective observation.

Although the program McGoldrick (1998) describes is more concerned with community service than CBR, an edited volume by McGoldrick and Ziegert (2002) contains many more examples of the range of economics service-learning projects. Some chapters also make a connection between these classroom efforts and faculty research. Ziegert and McGoldrick (2008) accurately characterize the current state of pedagogy in economics with the following statement: *"Thinking like an economist* has become the buzz phrase for describing lifelong learning in undergraduate economics education" (p. 39). A literature is developing in economics around "the use it or lose it" pedagogy advocated by Hansen, Salemi, and Siegfried (2002). These programs usually advocate simpler approaches than CBR through classroom activities (also known as experiments), small-scale projects, and activities such as journal writing. In advanced courses like marketing research—with its statistics, econometrics, and intermediate microeconomics prerequisites—the large-scale nature of the project described in this chapter is a natural extension of those experiences students may have gained in earlier classes.

Alignment With the POWERful Model of CBR

In addition to this project fulfilling the academic goals of the economics and marketing research disciplines, it also practically demonstrates Pigza's (see Chapter 5) theoretical model for teaching CBR. I next use her five core concepts (partnerships, objectives, working, evaluation, and reflection) as the structure to describe what can be seen as an example of a POWERful course project in CBR.

Partnerships

In Pigza's framework, a partnership should open up the academic enterprise and welcome other voices and perspectives into the process. This marketing research project inherently had broad community participation and partnership because we studied an industrial supply chain bringing local food to diners' plates at home or in a restaurant. These supply chains are diverse, connected communities, and our study considered the various impacts that farmers, distributors, grocers, restaurateurs, and consumers have on each other. *Community* is too often used as a reference only to consumers, excluding the people behind the production of the intermediate and final goods and services purchased by consumers. In our study, however, we included producers as part of the community and differentiated among the producers at each level of the supply chain in terms of their local, national, and global reach. Thus students could understand the local community better by perceiving it through the eyes of people in business as well as consumers. They began to see more clearly the people who are the links in this chain as connections in an economic partnership, and they discovered their own value connections to like-minded entrepreneurs, including the small farmers who mattered most to the BFBL organizer with whom we collaborated.

The academic research community was also a partner because in addition to an expanded research relationship with my students, I was in closer contact with CBR scholars at other local institutions and my own college as well as being involved in this book project. All these additional connections expanded my sense of the community that is involved in CBR.

Moreover, this multi-institutional partnership brought together a wide range of faculty and students who were collectively pursuing shared goals. Our work was coordinated with a biology group at Muhlenberg College and an economics and marketing group at Lehigh University throughout the entire project. The cooperation of faculty at all three schools was flexible, recognizing the constraints and differing goals in each group's academic environment. Fortunately, all three of these higher education institutions are loosely affiliated through the Lehigh Valley Association of Independent

Colleges (LVAIC), a 40-year old organization that provides connections for students, faculty, and administrators in the member schools. One of the more recent components of LVAIC is the Lehigh Valley Research Consortium (LVRC), which initiated and organized this project. The organizational and funding encouragement from these other groups was important, given that there was little support at the college level for CBR projects at that time.

Objectives

In Chapter 5 Pigza elaborates on the fact that there can be project and course objectives. Project objectives include a project description and detailed time line of when particular elements of CBR will happen; course objectives should include long-term plans and short-term actions.

Project objectives. The LVRC sought partners to help advance the goals of our local BFBL chapter as well as learning goals for students and research interests of students and faculty. The following five goals were part of a larger contract that specified faculty should also produce a written report after the student presentations to document our methods, data, results, and recommendations. The document was produced through discussions with BFBL.

1. Identify regional food production capacity using such measures as the number of farms, farm acreage, types of food production, and monetary value of food sold locally.
2. Characterize consumption of locally grown food, including households, food distributors, and restaurants.
3. Understand the decision-making process of stakeholders in the demand for and supply of locally grown food, including how they make their decisions, time scales they use, and market or policy variables that might affect their decisions.
4. Identify challenges to a greater use of the local food supply and increased consumption of local food.
5. Identify best practices, market conditions, and policies for increasing the wealth of stakeholders in this region and addressing obstacles for bringing together food suppliers and consumers.

Course objectives. Marketing research (as a course, discipline, or practice) concerns survey design, data collection, qualitative analysis, and statistics. Student learning objectives focus on applying the classroom knowledge in practice, and helping students understand the tight integration of the academic learning objectives into the community members' objectives is a natural part of this process. For this project, students needed to build an understanding of the features of the local food supply chain and the project's goals. These course goals from the syllabus expect students to demonstrate the following:

1. Apply their previous econometrics knowledge and additional advanced statistical techniques.
2. Understand the pitfalls, trade-offs, and importance of survey design.
3. Appreciate and apply statistical concepts important to sampling design.
4. Understand various survey methods' strengths and weaknesses, and their appropriate application.
5. Use their knowledge to build a report with information relevant to our local community.

Working

Pigza uses the term *working* in Chapter 5 to describe how the research plan is enacted. At Lehigh, three students devoted the entire semester to this component of the project as their capstone course; in comparison, the three Muhlenberg students worked in conjunction with faculty-directed research. My component of the project had the largest number of students involved (15) and operated within a more conventional course framework.

Collectively, the three different faculty members allocated work to each group across two dimensions. The first dimension was geographic because Lafayette and Muhlenberg are at opposite ends of the Lehigh Valley, and Lehigh is in the middle. The second dimension was the nature of the tasks given to each group. At Muhlenberg the students focused on biology, which naturally applied to farm production at the beginning of the supply chain, while the students' major at Lehigh, marketing economics, led to their investigation of restaurants' local food use at the other end of the supply chain. My own research program sponsored by the National Science Foundation, to study other aspects of the supply chain, fit nicely with my challenge to provide Lafayette students with sufficient project dimensions and meaningful work. These allocations across the three schools helped us avoid duplicated efforts and kept student groups from overwhelming any farmers or restaurateurs, for example.

In my marketing research course, three students were assigned to each of the following group tasks:

1. Group A: Research consumers' *current* food purchase behaviors and decision processes.
2. Group B: Investigate reasons for consumers to *change* what they do and their associated decision-making processes.

3. Group C: Survey six farmers (from a list of 10 provided by BFBL) to identify what is currently sold locally, how decisions can change, and how they define *local food.*
4. Group D: Survey four to 10 of our town's restaurateurs on their current locally bought food and how it might change.
5. Group E: Survey personnel in local distribution networks (who bring food from farms to grocery stores) and personnel at groceries to determine what is currently purchased, how decisions can change, and how they define *local food.*

Students had a chronology of the semester delineating the development, testing, administration, and analysis of their surveys. They also understood that their work would be peer critiqued in an electronic discussion board and that they would receive informal feedback on progress in classroom sessions. To better understand BFBL's goals, we invited the community organizer in for a presentation before we got started and asked her to return for the final student presentations. Naturally, she and I also had discussions before and after her presentation to help me guide the students' development.

Her presentation not only began a dialogue between the students and her but it also allowed the students to observe my interaction with her. They asked questions and received clarifications from both of us. Our classroom discussions after the presentation (as well as our modifications to the plan as the semester progressed) continued to refer to the knowledge gained from this initial meeting. I also know (through comments on the course evaluation forms and from observing their work) that students were very invested in helping the community organizer achieve her goals. Her presentation thus helped students make a personal connection and become more invested in the project, as they knew from the start that she would return to observe their final presentations. Because this was the first time she had made such a presentation, the opportunity also enabled her to develop a message that could help her act as an agent of change elsewhere.

Interviewing supply chain members also contributed to students' interest in and empathy toward the producers. The students in groups C, D, and F were meeting people in food supply professions that the students hadn't thought about before or had only viewed from a consumer's perspective. Preparing for these one-on-one data collection meetings also helped students carefully craft specific open-ended questions.

Evaluation

In Chapter 5 Pigza defines *evaluation* as an ongoing appraisal of the project's strengths and weaknesses to help achieve change. As such, my evaluation of the project focuses on four areas: agreement among constituents, regional and campus support for CBR, student engagement, and the strategic design process.

Agreement among constituencies. The original request from BFBL was to create an estimate of the differential impact that locally bought food can have on the Lehigh Valley economy compared to food from outside the region. Although that information can be valuable, such a study did not fit the academic goals of the course, which focused on gathering attitudes, behaviors, and opinions using various survey methods. We could help develop the groundwork for understanding the economic effect of buying local food, but the project needed to serve all three goals of the projects' constituencies: student learning, the community's needs, and my existing research goals. Through the LVRC's administrative process (including a written contract), we were able to iron out those differences before we started the project. That process helped us learn about each other's constraints and goals, in addition to increasing the community organizer's appreciation of the contributions that students could make to her goals.

The project was ultimately successful because we did provide BFBL with new information that supported its efforts to increase use of the local food supply chain, which was information that complemented its original intent. We also laid the groundwork for future efforts to follow those same goals. By creating a better understanding of the workings of the supply chain, future investigations can research the flow of the consumer's dollar back into the community via a local food purchase compared to money paid for food that originates outside the Lehigh Valley.

Regional and campus support for CBR. For this project, the LVRC acted as the aggregator that brought the schools and the community together. Its mission includes identifying and facilitating these projects by connecting scholars from institutions in Pennsylvania's Lehigh Valley with local governments, nonprofits, and businesses. This suggests that the LVRC is at the beginning of the partnership process that Stoecker and Beckman (2010) describe. Through the LVRC's aggregation efforts, CBR enabled our separate institutions to recognize shared goals and the benefits from engaging the community as a group, which made our individual work more relevant and facilitated a longer lasting impact.

In economics, a need for better public relations in two areas is providing impetus for more CBR projects. According to Ziegert and McGoldrick (2008), the economics discipline should (a) enlarge our existing focus on "self-interest" to include the benefits and understanding provided by various models of self-interested behavior, and (b) provide students with more community context to understand economic theory. They conclude, "Through service-learning, students have opportunities to make a difference in their communities while at the same time developing the habits and skills of an engaged citizen" (p. 43). In their course evaluations, my students expressed this same value as an important dimension of their experience in the project.

Other active programs at a faculty member's institution can similarly increase the critical mass necessary for administrative support of CBR. At our institution, courses such as statistics and the mathematics of social justice can include CBR experiences (Bremser, Kimber, Root, & Weaver, 2010; Root & Thorme, 2001; Root, Thorme, & Gray, 2005). Additionally, a long-standing program at Lafayette College, the Tech Clinic, is a two-semester course that integrates community, industrial, and college needs with interdisciplinary teams of students and instructors. It inhabits a middle ground between the academic projects run by faculty as part of a course and the pure community service efforts organized by the dean of students and Lafayette's Landis Center. Other options include opportunities with groups like Engineers Without Borders, which allows students (who get no academic credit) to use skills associated with their academic (and anticipated professional) discipline to assist communities around the globe.

We also have a new collegewide committee on community-based learning and research. One of the committee's first acts was to hold an expo showcasing faculty activities in community-based learning and CBR, all of which existed before the committee was created. Much more recently, staff and resources have transformed the committee into a Center for Community Engagement (CCE). These events and initiatives reflect the respect faculty members have for CBR after observing students' learning and their own research efforts. This growing component of Lafayette's mission further reflects a nationwide trend in pedagogy.

All these efforts combine to create a culture of community involvement on campus, which can lead to connections that will help CBR-oriented faculty. Although individual faculty and administrators' efforts are crucial to the success of the projects they spearhead, the faculty member involved in CBR may also rely on larger aggregator groups such as our region's LVRC to help make the connections with community members. Likewise, the faculty member who has a pedagogic agenda in a particular course or a scholarly agenda in a research program can be a significant resource of specialized knowledge to larger programs such as our college's CCE focused more purely on community needs.

Student learning and engagement. The students who interviewed farmers, distributors' staff at groceries, and restaurateurs had the most active community engagement. Those who surveyed consumers, on the other hand, were more focused on our own college campus. All the groups learned from each other's experiences as they discussed their progress in class and online. Critiquing each other's plans, progress, and anticipated results not only helped to improve students' final products, but also engaged each of them in critical thinking about what they and others were doing.

Student learning was enhanced by the following factors: training in data analysis and survey design in prerequisite courses, lecture, and homework; awareness of the sponsor's needs through an initial presentation; direct interaction outside the classroom with producers and consumers of local food; discussions among the student groups to review and critique each other's progress; and final presentations with the community organizer in attendance. These components reinforced the project's value, emphasized student groups' accountability, and generated more high-quality ideas for each group's contribution.

In the context of Kolb's learning cycle, Ziegert and McGoldrick (2008) make clear the distinction between deductive and inductive reasoning. They assert that economics instruction is usually deductive, from the general to the specific, but service-learning and CBR allow students to think inductively, taking examples from their particular experiences and using them to inform useful generalizations. We can take this idea further, recognizing that the Kolb (1981) cycle is about moving back and forth between inductive and deductive reasoning, without giving primacy to either mode. We therefore improve learning when asking students to move through this alternating cycle, whether that cycle occurs exclusively in class or in tandem with experiences outside the classroom. The CBR paradigm not only facilitates that movement for students but also creates greater utility for the community, especially nonprofit entities and small businesses that may be too constrained by their limited resources to pursue such research themselves.

Ziegert and McGoldrick (2008) also make the case for using formative and summative assessments. In my course, formative assessments came from critiques on the electronic discussion board and classroom discussions. Summative assessment occurred naturally as the project developed and at the semester's end, facilitated by clear rubrics for each stage of project completion.

Although each of the three collaborating faculty had planned to have their student groups attend the other two presentations, it was not possible because of their busy schedules and students' lack of desire to leave their campuses for too long. We found it was somewhat easier to involve students in the community than in activities on other campuses. No presentation was given at Muhlenberg, but the community organizer and I attended the Lehigh and Lafayette presentations. The Lehigh student group also compiled a separate report with their reflections on the project in addition to the report (Ruebeck & Niesenbaum, 2009) based on the students' work.

CBR might appear suspect to some observers if its inclusion simply decreases time students could spend acquiring additional disciplinary knowledge. We do know, however, that students will learn more if they can process new insights through applications of their classroom knowledge. Thus we need to consider how we tie together the community and the classroom portions of a course, bringing the classroom to life. As Bain (2004) has noted, students do not really understand or retain what we teach them unless it changes the way they view the world. We know they will remember that they had fun with activities outside class, but what we really want is for that excitement to translate into a changed view of the world, increased understanding, and wider perception.

The strategic design process. Stoecker and Beckman (2010) describe the three crucial research areas as diagnosis, prescription, and evaluation in a four-phase cycle of the strategic community design process, which also includes implementation. Our work with BFBL addressed two phases, diagnosing a community issue and prescribing action. The community organization, BFBL, recognized the community's need to analyze the current situation and was able to bring the question to academics through a local forum. Because those academics (the chairman of Lehigh's Department of Economics and the director of the LVRC) were on the lookout for projects in which their constituencies could help the community, they were able to connect the local food growers' need with my pedagogical goals and research program.

It was important for students to be involved in the process of describing prescriptions and choosing strategy criteria, as marketing research should be designed, collected, and analyzed with an eye toward the effect it will have on decision making. That part of the process can be forgotten in the hullabaloo of survey design, data collection, and statistical tests. If the decision makers are not paying attention to the questions, either because they do not trust the data collection methods or because the questions are not relevant, any time spent on market research is wasted effort. In our classroom sessions and online discussions, we therefore focused our hypotheses, survey design, and data collection methods by asking each other, How can the answers we find change decision makers' actions? We could thus hope that the written report (Ruebeck & Niesenbaum, 2009) would enhance the project's potential for achieving outcomes and impact.

Reflection: Lessons Learned

In addition to earlier descriptions of the student reflective activities that were an ongoing part of the project, Pigza suggests in Chapter 5 that faculty and community partners should also reflect on overarching personal, academic, and communal forms of learning. From my perspective, the community service component of the course was always important, which is why I had previously urged students to consult campus experts (in athletics, the library, or the dean of students) for projects they could pursue in this course. During prior semesters, I had invited those experts to the students' final presentations, and projects naturally evoked individual students' interest. Therefore, I was not actually looking for what I thought to be a complication of the successful structure I had already developed in this class. In considering a project that originated with a community group's interest and synergized with my own research and course goals, I was personally unsure whether it would be successful.

I was further concerned that students would chafe at a project driven by the community's wishes rather than their own. Instead, I discovered that the connection to a community's needs inspired students' commitment and imagination, so concern was unfounded. Students understood the project's relevance to their classroom knowledge and vice versa; they were likewise motivated by the community sponsor's participation in defining the goals. I had also worried there would not be enough work for me to assign to five different groups of students. As it turned out, because students collaborated on each dimension of the project, the groups provided each other with useful input during the process, resulting in a richer understanding of the community's larger social goal.

Reflecting on the factors that contributed to the successful community interaction we had in this course, two characteristics stand out. First, it was an upper-level course with a strong econometrics prerequisite and meant for students who were economics majors. Therefore, they were more likely to be innately comfortable with business interactions or at least motivated to overcome any initial trepidation. This seemed to confirm Ramocki's (1987) observation that "clients must be properly screened to ensure that they are enthusiastic and possess realistic expectations" (p. 29). Second, my experience agreed with Petkus's (2000) finding that it is important to have clients who are likely to cooperate, because our community partner's enthusiasm definitely affected the students' commitment to the project. In contrast, students did find it challenging to locate food distributors and grocers who had the time or inclination to help us.

Originally, the course objectives did not include aspects related to service in the community beyond campus, but drawing up a contract with a partner and stating clear project objectives provided important guidance in this area. The students and I also worked together to understand how we could apply the knowledge they had from the course to the contract's objectives. These efforts made it possible to achieve a balance, important in all pedagogy, between the specificity of the instructor's directions and the creative latitude given to students. I discovered that my students probably grew more, and likely enjoyed the project more, precisely because the objectives were somewhat open ended. The community sponsor likewise received more useful information from this collaboration across campuses, even with little integration of student experiences across campuses.

Finally, I learned how important support structure is. Although a significant initiative was required by me as the instructor, community partnerships are more likely to be productive if organized across an institution's departments or institutions in the local area. Nascent forms of such support have continued to expand at Lafayette College and across Lehigh Valley schools since this project's time, and Lafayette has recognized that it is necessary to develop a critical mass to support its continued existence. As such, we have started to marshal resources to sustain these efforts as long-term components of the student experience.

A complement to that internal support from each academic institution is the need to develop and maintain relationships with local grant-giving entities and government agencies. A last link in the chain is to have private companies support the CBR work that goes on between institutions. It may be difficult for several schools to organize across a region like the Lehigh Valley, yet every institution would gain from better coordination of efforts across institutions, and each individual institution can most clearly see the cost and benefits of ceding some of its territory to the umbrella group.

Conclusion

Because a variety of learning styles can be addressed by service-learning, Peterson and McGoldrick (2009) place their economics course examples in the field of public scholarship so that experiential learning can be seen in the larger context of pluralism in economics education. They and other scholars pull together several strands of the education and economics education literatures to describe how "economics educators have struggled to find evidence that the learning we assume is occurring in our courses has any lasting effect" (p. 78). They believe that "economists are already, perhaps unknowingly, developing experiences consistent with facets of this approach" (p. 87). My experience was a slow realization that what I was trying to do with my class was part of this larger effort. As opportunities have continued to become available to expand this research and pedagogy program (Fortwangler, Rue-beck, Grover, & Taylor, 2012), I have continued to connect my efforts to this larger experience, and I have been heartened by my students' appreciation of this stronger community orientation, even though it has resulted in a somewhat more prescriptive design of their projects' goals.

It is thus clear that CBR can enhance student learning in a marketing research course, and it goes further than simply satisfying course objectives for learning quantitative and qualitative methods. The students gain a greater appreciation of the scope of a large project, and they enjoy contributing to a larger research program. More substantial goals can be accomplished by partnering efforts across academic institutions. By connecting community members, the value exceeds the sum of the pedagogical, scholarly, and industrial parts.

Author's Note

Thanks to Michele Deegan, director of the LVRC, for including me in her efforts to bridge academia and community; Lynn Pryor, of the Lehigh Valley chapter of BFBL, for her support of my students and our work; Jim Dearden at Lehigh University for his collaboration; and Chawne Kimber for supporting further efforts in CBR. Thanks also go to the students in Econ 361 for embracing this project, and especially Sarah Christy for additional research assistance. Joyce F. Long's editing work significantly improved this chapter. The LVRC website is www.lehighvalleyresearch.org. Work was also supported in part by grants from Pennsylvania State Representative Robert L. Freeman and from National Science Foundation grants HSD BCS-079458 and CPATH-T0722211/0722203. The opinions, findings, and conclusions or recommendations expressed in this material are those of the author and do not necessarily reflect the views of the National Science Foundation or the other groups.

References

Bain, K. (2004). *What the best teachers do*. Boston, MA: Harvard University Press.

Bernhardt, K. S., Jones, S., Ruebeck, C., & Isaacs, J. (2010, June). *Assessing the effectiveness of using a computer game to bridge a research agenda with a teaching agenda*. Paper presented at the annual conference of the American Society for Engineering Education, Louisville, KY. Retrieved from http://users.rowan.edu/~jahan/asee/env_asee09/New%20Folder/papers/2010_bestpaper.pdf

Bremser P., Kimber, C., Root, R., & Weaver, S. (2010). Mathematics of, for, and as social justice. In K. Skubikowski, C. Wright, & R. Graf (Eds.), *Social justice education: Inviting faculty to transform their institutions*. Sterling, VA: Stylus.

Brooks, N., & Schramm, R. (2007). Integrating economics research, education, and service. *Journal of Economic Education, 38*(1), 36–43.

Center for Sustainable Community Development. (2010). Retrieved from http://www.sfu.ca/cscd

Elliot, D. (2009). What is the comparative advantage of the service learning pedagogy? Insights from development economics. *Forum for Social Economics,* 38(2/3), 263–278.

Fortwangler, C., Ruebeck, C., Grover, H., & Taylor, A. (2012). *Gardening in Easton's West Ward neighborhood: Local perceptions of the value and operation of community gardens.* Retrieved from http://www.lehighvalleyresearch.org/files/articles/wwnp_final_report.pdf

Hansen, W. L., Salemi, M. K., & Siegfried, J. J. (2002). Use it or lose it: Teaching literacy in the economics principles course. *American Economic Review, 92*(2), 463–472.

Kolb, D. A. (1981). Learning styles and disciplinary differences. In A. W. Chickering & Associations (Eds.), *The Modern American College* (pp. 132–255). San Francisco, CA: Jossey-Bass.

McGoldrick, K. (1998). Service-learning in economics: A detailed application. *Journal of Economic Education, 29*(4), 365–376.

McGoldrick, K., & Ziegert, A. (2002). *Putting the invisible hand to work.* Ann Arbor: University of Michigan Press.

Minkler, M., & Blackwell, A. (2010). *Promoting healthy public policy through community-based participatory research: Ten case studies.* Retrieved from depts.washington.edu/ccph/pdf_files/CBPR_final.pdf

Mortensen, T. (2010). *ACT: Appalachian and the Community Together.* Retrieved from community.appstate.edu/program/act-appalachian-and-the-community-together

Petkus, E. (2000). A theoretical and practical framework for service-learning in marketing: Kolb's experiential learning cycle. *Journal of Marketing Education, 22*(1), 64–70.

Peterson, J., & McGoldrick, K. (2009). Pluralism and economic education: A learning theory approach. *International Review of Economics Education, 8*(2), 72–90.

Ramocki, S. (1987). Measured effectiveness of client-sponsored consulting projects in the marketing research course. *Journal of Marketing Education, 9*(1), 24–30.

Root, R. & Thorme, T. (2001). Community-based projects in applied statistics: Using service-learning to enhance student understanding. *American Statistician, 55*(4), 330–335.

Root, R., Thorme, T., & Gray, C. (2005). Making meaning, applying statistics. In C. Hadlock (Ed.), Mathematics in service to the community: Concepts and models for service-learning in the mathematical sciences (pp. 89–100). Washington, DC: Mathematical Association of America.

Ruebeck, C., & Niesenbaum, R. (2009). *Local food and local taste: A study of supply and demand.* Retrieved from http://s3.amazonaws.com/zanran_storage/nercrd.psu.edu/ContentPages/2450443657.pdf

Salemi, K. (2002). An illustrated case for active learning. *Southern Economic Journal,* *68*(3), 721–731.

Stoecker, R. (2005). *Research methods for community change: A project-based approach.* Thousand Oaks, CA: Sage.

Stoecker, R., & Beckman, M. (2010). *Making higher education civic engagement matter in the community.* Retrieved from www.compact.org/news/making-higher-education-civic-engagement-matter-in-the-community/9748

Whitehead, J. (2009). *ECO 4660 course syllabus: Benefit-cost analysis.* Retrieved from www.appstate.edu/~whiteheadjc/ECO4660

Ziegert, A. L., & McGoldrick, K. (2008). When service is good for economics: Linking the classroom and community through service-learning. *International Review of Economics Education, 7*(2), 39–56.

8

MEETING THE OBJECTIVES OF FACULTY ENGAGEMENT IN UNDERGRADUATE COMMUNITY-BASED RESEARCH PROJECTS

Anna Sims Bartel and Georgia Nigro

The goals of community-based research (CBR) are ambitious: "social action and social change for the purpose of achieving social justice" (Strand, Marullo, Cutforth, Stoecker, & Donohue, 2003, p. 8). As these authors acknowledge later in their text, CBR at an institution of higher education must also have goals of pedagogical integrity and student intellectual growth. At many campuses with professional degree programs, CBR can merge seamlessly with the institutional mission to generate powerful student and faculty work, often on a large scale. For example, information technology students might join forces to develop new media applications for area nonprofits, or public health students might design strategic interventions for regional nutrition programs with detailed assessment protocols. Similarly, institutions with graduate programs in professional fields can connect community agencies with students who possess high levels of expertise, such as master's of engineering candidates undertaking substantive research projects to fulfill their thesis requirement. These students are likely to provide community partner organizations with the equivalent of professional consulting services.

In comparison, neither model works at a four-year liberal arts college where community collaborators must rely on the relative inexperience and varying levels of expertise of undergraduates. Meeting community research needs can also be limited by the smaller scale of students' individual or group projects produced in a single course. Offsetting these challenges is the fact that many students enter a liberal arts college with a commitment to making a difference in the world. They may also seek community engagement early and build relationships that can span all four years.

To build substantive CBR at this kind of college, students need faculty members who can help them cultivate experience in research and community engagement. Students can achieve these dual purposes if faculty members help students develop their expertise in disciplinary research methods, foster long-term partnerships, and nurture a hunger for and training in intellectual work that advances the public good. At Bates College students are able to attain these goals because the campus culture has a fluid yet complex network of support for students and faculty members. Moreover, this systemic support enhances the possibility that research projects will produce outputs and outcomes that can be parlayed into impact under the right conditions.

Network of Support for CBR

CBR has deep roots at Bates College. Founded by abolitionists, the college has a long-standing commitment to issues of social justice and equality, and its location in one of Maine's largest, poorest, and most diverse cities offers multiple opportunities for engagement. Although partnerships between local schools and the college date to 30 years ago, the college formalized a commitment to service-learning and community volunteerism in 1997 by creating the Center for Service-Learning, which in 2004 transformed into the Harward Center for Community Partnerships.

Additionally, the college released a new mission statement in 2010 that highlighted two features of a Bates education aligned with CBR. First, the statement stressed that the college educates the whole person through "creative and rigorous scholarship in a collaborative residential community" (Bates College, n.d.). In practice, one of the ways Bates has achieved this element of its mission is through a senior thesis requirement, which nearly every department and program at the college has. Almost every student writes a senior thesis that involves original scholarship. Second, the mission statement mentions that the college cultivates not only intellectual discovery but also informed civic action. Thus, it made sense to support CBR at the institutional level, because this form of research has the potential to amalgamate and fulfill the key features of the college's mission.

In fact, Bates committed to these practices decades before they were specified in the new mission statement. One of the first courses supported by the new Center for Service-Learning in the 1990s was an action research course taught by Georgia Nigro and another colleague in the college's five-week short term. That course soon entered the regular curriculum as a cross-listed course in the psychology and education departments. This kind of consistent engagement from faculty members and departments has produced disciplinary support for CBR ranging from individual courses with a community-engaged component to multiple courses in a few departments designed to intentionally build CBR expertise.

Environmental studies, for example, offers a capstone course for juniors and seniors in which students can work collaboratively on CBR projects that instructors develop beforehand with community partners based on a single theme. During the first two years the course was offered, students collaborated with multiple agencies that were involved in completing a community food assessment. For the next two years, the projects focused on the Androscoggin River with multiple community partners who sought research collaborations ranging from creating interpretive signage for river walks to a business plan for a kayak rental service, which opened soon after and is still functioning today. Similarly, students in the biochemistry program have worked with area health providers to develop culturally sensitive practices for interactions with the Somali immigrant and refugee community that included testing pictograms to increase the immigrants' understanding of and compliance with prescription medication regimes.

Students in other departments or programs with curriculums that tie increasingly complex community engagement to a progressive series of courses can culminate their studies with one rigorous and relevant CBR project as a senior thesis. In the Department of Sociology, for example, students can take a first-year seminar on social inequality and work in direct service with a community organization that addresses inequalities. As sophomores, those same students might take a required research methods course in which they work on a research project loosely informed by a community partner's needs that have been previously identified. At this level, some elements of the project may answer a question posed by the community partner, and other elements can guarantee that students receive practice in a range of methods common to the discipline. In their junior year, students might take a seminar in which they work fairly independently with a community partner to craft a research question and identify appropriate methods to produce a final product that more fully meets the partner's needs (output). As seniors, these same students are now prepared to become partners with seasoned community collaborators who already know their research capabilities. Thus, sociology students who first learned of a community food assessment in their sophomore methods course could conduct more advanced research in a junior seminar by surveying all emergency food providers in the area. As seniors completing a thesis, these students could examine the issue even more deeply (e.g., a comprehensive community assessment of food deserts).

Support by the Harward Center for Community Partnerships

This level of CBR activity by students and cooperating faculty members receives ample support from our Harward Center for Community Partnerships, which answers to the vice president for academic affairs and the dean of faculty. Although the center's work extends beyond support for CBR, community-engaged learning in general and CBR in particular have been core center activities since its founding. The center also provides grant opportunities for departments and individual faculty members who want to infuse civic engagement into their curricula.

The environmental studies program used such a grant to develop the capstone course described earlier. Likewise, individual faculty members can apply for grants to support their own public work, individual course development, or both. A philosophy professor received one of these grants to support his sabbatical travel to an international center on biomedical ethics. He plans to include Islamic medical ethics in his courses when he returns and work with local health-care organizations serving immigrant and refugee populations.

Other center activities may indirectly support student CBR. For example, faculty members and students can present their ongoing CBR work at a lunchtime series called Public Works in Progress, sponsored by the Harward Center, which is open to campus and community members. Our Bonner Leaders program further encourages students to deepen their involvement in civic engagement by taking at least two courses with a community-engagement component.

Although individual student CBR projects benefit enormously from the network of support we have created at Bates, it is important for faculty to know that not every student project needs that much support. In fact, we have discovered that our CBR culture can spawn opportunities and practices that flourish without extensive support. One spring, for example, the Harward Center used funding left over from another initiative to launch the Short-Term Action/Research Team during the college's five-week spring term. One team of eight students functioned as a rapid-response research team, offering community partners quick turnarounds on community-based research projects or research-based action projects. Two faculty members and two staff members from the Harward Center launched the team, but once the group acquired the eight community requests, it functioned fairly independently, completing many projects ranging from grant prospecting for four different agencies to a detailed analysis of visits to a local hospital during one year and an analysis of inexpensive tablet computer applications for a local school (outputs).

The team may sound like a technical assistance team with limited expertise and little reflection, but it functioned as more than that. Students talked with hospital personnel about the hospital's faith-based commitment to social justice that undergirded the hospital's worries about how the emergency room was used. They discussed school funding formulas that drove teachers to request computer applications that cost 99 cents or less. They also considered an economic climate in which adolescent girls thought having a baby was the pathway to a paycheck. With the team's broad range of disciplinary backgrounds (economics, psychology, sociology, environmental studies, English), students did not need faculty or staff members to prompt their discussions, although we willingly joined in on occasion.

Community-Engaged Research Fellowships

The center activity that most directly supports students doing CBR is the Community-Engaged Research Fellowships program (formerly the Community-Based Research Fellows Program). In 2007 Harward Center associate director Anna Sims Bartel wrote a successful proposal to the National CBR Networking Initiative to create the program. Fellows are typically upper-level students with experience in research methods and community partnership work who develop their own proposals in concert with community partners, faculty members, and Harward Center staff. All fellows have disciplinary advisers and meet regularly in a noncredit seminar devoted to CBR theory and practice, which is taught by a dedicated faculty member (Bartel until fall 2009, Nigro until 2012, and now Ray).

The noncredit seminar for fellows meets seven times each term. Readings vary, but parts of Strand and colleagues' (2003) *Community-Based Research and Higher Education* are consistently featured. In recent years, readings have covered the history of the institutional review board and its role in protecting individuals, but not whole communities, from harm in research (Hyatt et al., 2009; Minkler, 2005), the sustainability of community work (Schensul, 2009), and cultural considerations (Brodsky & Faryal, 2006). The readings have also targeted specific topics, such as community gardening, or specific research methods, such as Photovoice, a form of participatory photography. Faculty members and community partners are invited to the seminar, but their schedules rarely permit these visits.

Fellows' projects generally serve, extend, and deepen existing collaborations within established relationships but may also build new partnerships.

Fellows often write senior theses based on their CBR projects that involve intense disciplinary grounding and guidance as well as support from the fellows seminar, its participants, and the instructor. Fellows also receive a stipend, which frees higher-need students to pursue CBR rather than search for employment. Any student may apply for CBR fellowships for one semester or one summer, and time frames can be adjusted to meet project needs.

Although a fellow sketches a goal for his or her CBR project in the program application (which must include a letter of reference from a faculty member and community partner), each project is explained in greater detail through a planner, which is a template titled Designing the Community-Based Research Project. The template follows the steps in a community-based research project as outlined in Chapter 5 of Strand and colleagues (2003) and guides fellows, in concert with faculty members and community partners, through a process of inquiry aimed at crafting a meaningful and realistic CBR project. For some fellows, filling out this template is the first time they realize the intensity, complexity, and multifaceted nature of CBR.

CBR fellows benefit from and operate within the following overlapping and mutually dependent matrices of meaningful support: (a) a vibrant and healthy network of campus-community partnerships, established over the past decades and nurtured through sustained commitment to shared interests; (b) close mentorship by a faculty member; and (c) affiliation with other students engaged in community work. The Harward Center is helping craft these pathways and opportunities for deepening engagement through the curriculum and cocurriculum. Most important, the fellows program enhances the substantive research collaborations between Bates and community partners, while it cultivates a greater understanding of academic work for the public good among students and faculty.

Pursuing Impact

By illustrating in detail the network of support for individual student CBR projects, we hope readers see the many entry points into CBR that faculty members can use. In our experiences as staff and faculty members, we have found that faculty colleagues undertake this work for many reasons. Many are mission-driven and want to develop the next cadre of leaders to do the hard work of democracy. Some want to address a persistent injustice, such as a minimum wage that is too low on which to live. Others want to support the economic development of their region or desire to enrich their communities by promoting local gardens or after-school programs. In addition, some faculty members embrace CBR as a mechanism for living a spiritual commitment or a commitment to a healthier planet. Although the college's mission may suggest that social justice is the only issue faculty pursue with CBR, individual faculty member positions complicate such a singular notion. Regardless of their motivation, any faculty member can find support for CBR at the Harward Center.

Even with the extensive support for CBR that Bates provides for faculty and students, real, measurable community impact has been elusive. Some scholars of service-learning and civic engagement have argued that higher education's efforts in these areas have produced limited community impact (Butin, 2010). Certain philanthropists agree, contending that despite spending vast sums of money, their efforts to produce community change have resulted in few "improved outcomes at the individual, family, or community level" (Kubisch, Auspos, Brown, & Dewar, 2010, p. 9). Nevertheless, we believe that Bates' fluid, complex network of support for student CBR projects enhances the possibility for undergraduate CBR projects to move from creating outputs (e.g., tutoring sessions for struggling K–12 students) to outcomes (e.g., better grades) and then to impacts (e.g., higher high school graduation rates). We now provide several examples of different student projects that support this claim.

Products or outputs of student CBR projects can vary greatly and include a report for the community partner or a public presentation. In most cases, the nature of this product is negotiated beforehand; in some instances, however, community partners can adjust their requests after they better understand a student's capacities. A 2010 Harward Center survey of 31 community partners reinforced how important the delivery of these outputs is, which is why the center staff works closely with students and faculty members to ensure that community partners receive the promised work. In the fall of 2012, for example, students in a community psychology class worked with three different partners on projects related to restorative justice. Each partner clearly specified a desired product or output, and although the three products differed significantly, each was delivered.

As faculty members establish and maintain close involvement with student CBR projects, they increase the probability that not only outputs but also outcomes will be achieved through a project. In some fields, planning for and even predicting outcomes has become an important stage in the research process. When one CBR fellow was asked by a local nutrition center to determine if its summer gardening program with adolescents had an effect on family members, the undergraduate was able to work with a faculty member to create a two-generational model that predicted effects of teen gardening. The student also designed a questionnaire to test the predictions with results showing that family food shopping and meal preparation habits did change as a result of teens' involvement in the program.

At Bates, we have discovered that meaningful outputs and outcomes result from the web of complex relationships with community partners that the Harward Center has forged collaboratively with faculty members. Some of these relationships began in classrooms years earlier, because in the past decade, more than a handful of students have graduated and moved into partnership positions in the community. It also helps that students sometimes work with a community partner multiple times. Often, they learn the partner's needs as first-year volunteers and return later as researchers with a commitment to CBR.

This web of relationships increases the chance that the work of students and faculty members will have real community impact. Staff members from the center, along with some faculty members and students, participate in regular discussions with important stakeholders from different sectors who are committed to crafting a common agenda for solving particular community problems. Although these discussions have not yet produced the broad cross-sector coordination known as collective impact (Kania & Kramer, 2011), they have helped foster the kind of communication patterns and the sort of mutually reinforcing activities that are conditions for successful collective impact.

Peer support, especially that provided by the CBR fellows program, likewise enhances the possibility that student projects will produce meaningful outcomes with the potential to result in community impact. CBR fellows, for example, take very seriously Strand and colleagues' (2003) concerns about "doing CBR in the middle" (p. 73); that is, working with agencies that support communities rather than directly with community members. In one case, this issue prompted a student to return to the community partner with a new research design that included the voices of community members who were left out of an earlier design. In another case, a lively discussion about the possibility of some partners pacifying or disempowering community members resulted in a student adding a new dimension to the research design to intentionally disrupt the existing power dynamics.

Students can also help each other develop projects that are more responsive to community needs. After one fellow was stymied in her attempt to develop learning modules for children, the science major received valuable advice from another fellow who was minoring in education. These examples reflect how the CBR fellows program often helps students who desire and strive for more than outputs to be part of sustainable community initiatives that support lasting social change.

Although the outputs and outcomes planned for student CBR projects are important to describe, the serendipitous benefits that sometimes accrue are equally significant. As the following example demonstrates, these unexpected benefits can be as vital to the economic, civic, and spiritual life of a community as any planned outcome. One summer, a fellow had concerns about climate change and its effects on coastal communities. She had the following goals: (a) create a series of public lectures for a coastal community she was tied to personally and (b) explore, via conversations with community elders, the history of the community's relationship to the coast and salt marsh, and their perceptions of changes over time to these ecosystems. She met her goals handily; the lectures drew 50 to 80 attendees each time, and elders willingly shared their knowledge with her. Surprisingly, by summer's end, she learned that the community began to use the information she shared in its building decisions. Furthermore, the community also expressed a commitment to continue investigating the issues and offered funding to support a Bates student in a future partnership role. This example shows how community benefits can serendipitously emerge from initial outputs and outcomes related to a student-initiated project.

In comparison, not every CBR project has the potential to achieve a community impact because some projects do not produce outputs that community partners are ready or able to use. After a CBR project demonstrated that a preschool intervention to increase children's executive functioning produced significant gains, especially in children with special needs, school personnel's initial excitement was quickly dashed by the realization that a commercial curriculum designed to improve executive functioning was too expensive for the district to purchase. In some cases, however, community partners can use the outputs they initially requested—an evaluation, a survey, a tool—to help create impact.

All these possibilities are acceptable to us because we understand that it is unrealistic to expect that our work or even our partners' work will always result in immediate, meaningful outcomes, let alone impact. Impact will result from combined efforts, aligned circumstances, appropriate strategy, and wise use of resources, all of which depend on a range of factors, many outside our control. At Bates our goal is to support students, faculty members, and community partners in their efforts as best we can while pursuing community impact with a realistic disposition. As a small undergraduate institution, we may always struggle to achieve the degree or scale necessary for significant community impact, especially if comprehensive community initiatives operating over a 10-year period, such as the Neighborhood Improvement Initiative funded by the Hewlett Foundation, have failed to bring about major improvements in well-being for people in distressed communities (Kubisch et al., 2010). Therefore, we have to be realistic about the impact we can expect from undergraduate projects, even well-resourced ones. Nevertheless, we are anxious to build our capacity for impact and draw inspiration from different corners.

One inspiring source is the work by practitioners of community-based participatory research designed to reduce health disparities. In describing a logic model of pathways and processes that can lead to outcomes and impacts, Wallerstein and colleagues (2010) present testable hypotheses that can be examined in our work. Similarly, the Assessing the Practices of Public Scholarship work group of Imagining America, a national consortium of higher education institutions and allied organizations, has developed an approach to assessment that integrates community impact with project and partnership designs in the arts, humanities, and design (Bartha & Nigro, 2013). These initiatives have in common a commitment to sustained, reciprocal, equitable partnerships in which community partners have a voice in defining what impact should look like. They also lead us to confidently conclude that our partnership practices at Bates are laying a solid foundation for attaining community impact, even though we are still mindful that the wicked problems tackled in our work will not yield to easily measurable solutions.

Whereas the impact of CBR projects in communities has been hard to assess, there is extensive research measuring impact relative to students. In psychology, for example, a meta-analysis of learning outcomes associated with service-learning for students from kindergarten through college (Conway, Amel, & Gerwien, 2009) included 103 independent samples from 78 published studies. The authors found the largest effect sizes for academic outcomes, followed by social outcomes, and then personal and citizenship outcomes. Publication of a volume devoted to research scales that assess student experiences in service-learning (Bringle, Phillips, & Hudson, 2004) is further evidence of the robust attention given to student impact. A comparable volume that assesses community impact is needed.

Lessons for Faculty

Over time we have learned that faculty development in CBR can naturally co-occur with student development if the institution has a fluid and complex network of support like ours. At a meeting of advisers for one term's CBR fellows, faculty members were envious of the space created for students to explore the goals and challenges of CBR; they also wanted to use the interdisciplinary set of readings assigned to students. In another term, a faculty member with training in experimental methods asked the faculty convener of the CBR fellows to guide him in learning about qualitative approaches to research so he could better advise his student's work with area lesbian, gay, bisexual, transgender, and questioning youths. These examples illustrate what can happen when faculty members are open to learning about the philosophy, tools, and strategies of CBR.

Another lesson we have learned is that faculty members may support student CBR even when they themselves do not embrace it. There are probably as many reasons for not embracing CBR as there are motivations for trying it. Some faculty members believe it is a pedagogically sound approach but not rigorous enough to meet their disciplinary standards for research. These faculty members can feel comfortable advising student projects but will not seek out opportunities for further involvement because they are concerned that the faculty reward structure does not recognize public work. This may be one reason community partners do not achieve the level of interaction with faculty members they would like, even though the Harward Center's survey of community partners found that they almost universally wished for more interactions with faculty members.

Other faculty members contend that the constraints of their teaching loads, disciplinary goals, and divergent perspectives make these interactions undesirable or impossible for them. Changing demographics among faculty and fewer faculty members on the tenure track can further exacerbate this trend (Butin, 2006). But as colleges and universities here and abroad begin to recognize and reward multiple forms of scholarship, more faculty members may shed their discomfort with CBR (Rice, 2005). Of course, if they feel too much pressure to collaborate with students on research projects that can lead to publication, they may eschew CBR altogether because the scale of projects at small colleges in small towns may increase a partner organization's capacity without yielding publishable data within some disciplines.

A final lesson learned is that the desideratum (some would say requirement) for a community-driven process, rather than an academics-driven process, is a stumbling block for some faculty members who share a desire to carry out research for the common good. For these faculty members, CBR should include the possibility of interacting with the community over research questions that originate in their disciplines but have important implications for the community. For example, one faculty member thought the local schools needed to do more to address the prejudice and stereotyping of new immigrant and refugee populations, mainly from Somalia. She wanted to involve students in research that would test a theory-driven, evidence-based intervention that had been developed by an international team of researchers in her discipline. Although the work has moved forward, it raised questions for some people who thought it fit poorly with the ethos of community partnership work the college was cultivating. We believe, however, there should be room for academic-driven research like this. As in any CBR project, norms of reciprocity and mutual benefit can support the project, even if the research question originates in the academy.

Final Reflections

In this chapter we describe a network of support for individual undergraduate CBR projects that includes many practices well known to faculty members from other campuses and a few that are homegrown, such as our CBR fellows program. Taken together, these practices mark our campus as an engaged institution (Butin & Seider, 2012) that has opened academic space for CBR in individual departments with the help of a well-resourced center rather than offering a major, minor, or certificate in community engagement (or a related field). We point this out because we share Butin and Seider's (2012) belief that CBR is part of an important intellectual movement that deserves the same type of scrutiny as other academic practices. While such scrutiny will undoubtedly come from structures that systematize and solidify the practices of community engagement in majors, minors, and certificate programs, it also needs to come from existing departments as their administrators try to accommodate the needs of their students and faculty members for whom the linkage of academic practice and public relevance is central. Questions about the assumptions, aspirations, and practices of community engagement will accompany that level of scrutiny, yet a noisy multitude of answers is just what we need right now to further build and support our communities.

References

Bartha, M., & Nigro, G. (2013). Assessing the practices of public scholarship. *Diversity & Democracy, 16*(3), 20–21.

Bates College. (n.d.). *Mission statement.* Retrieved from www.bates.edu/about/mission

Bringle, R. G., Phillips, M. A., & Hudson, M. (2004). *The measure of service learning: Research scales to assess student experiences.* Washington, DC: American Psychological Association.

Brodsky, A. E., & Faryal, T. (2006). No matter how hard you try, your feet still get wet: Insider and outsider perspectives on bridging diversity. *American Journal of Community Psychology, 37*(3/4), 311–320. doi:10.1007/s10464-006-9015-x

Butin, D. W. (2006). The limits of service-learning in higher education. *Review of Higher Education, 29*(4), 473–498.

Butin, D. W. (2010). *Service-learning in theory and practice.* New York, NY: Palgrave Macmillan.

Butin, D. W., & Seider, S. (Eds.). (2012). *The engaged campus.* New York, NY: Palgrave Macmillan.

Conway, J. M., Amel, E. L., & Gerwien, D. P. (2009). Teaching and learning in the social context: A meta-analysis of service learning's effects on academic, personal, social, and citizenship outcomes. *Teaching of Psychology, 36*(4), 233–245. doi:10.1080/00986280903172969

Hyatt, R. R., Gute, D. M., Pirie, A., Page, H., Vasquez, I., & Dalembert, F. (2009). Transferring knowledge about human subjects protections and the role of institutional review boards in a community-based participatory research project. *American Journal of Public Health, 99*(Suppl. 3), S526–S531.

Kania, J., & Kramer, M. (2011). Collective impact. *Stanford Social Innovation Review, 9*(1), 36–41.

Kubisch, A. C., Auspos, P., Brown, P., & Dewar, T. (2010). Community change initiatives from 1990–2010: Accomplishments and implications for future work. *Community Investments, 22*(1), 8–12.

Minkler, M. (2005). Community-based research partnerships: Challenges and opportunities. *Journal of Urban Health: Bulletin of the New York Academy of Medicine, 82*(Suppl. 2), ii3–ii12. doi:10.1093/jurban/jti034

Rice, R. E. (2005). The future of the scholarly work of the faculty. In K. O'Meara & R. E. Rice (Eds.), *Faculty priorities reconsidered: Rewarding multiple forms of scholarship* (pp. 303–312). San Francisco, CA: Jossey-Bass.

Schensul, J. J. (2009). Community, culture, and sustainability in multilevel dynamic systems intervention science. *American Journal of Community Psychology, 43*(3/4), 241–256.

Strand, K., Marullo, S., Cutforth, N., Stoecker, R., & Donohue, P. (2003). *Community-based research and higher education.* San Francisco, CA: Jossey-Bass.

Wallerstein, N., Oetzel, J., Duran, B., Tafoya, G., Belone, L., & Rae, R. (2010). What predicts outcomes in CBPR? In M. Minkler & N. Wallerstein (Eds.), *Community-based participatory research for health: From process to outcomes* (2nd ed., pp. 373–392). San Francisco, CA: Jossey-Bass.

9

MATHEMATICAL MODELING + A COMMUNITY PARTNER = THE FULFILLMENT OF STUDENT LEARNING OBJECTIVES

Ethan Berkove

Case Studies in Mathematical Modeling is a semester course offered annually by the Department of Mathematics at Lafayette College. As students focus on analyzing real-world problems, this course is an excellent candidate for serving the community through community-based research (CBR). In the following case study, students were partners with a community loan fund. After a brief explanation of the case studies course, this project is described.

The Course

Students take Case Studies in Mathematical Modeling to gain experience in working through the types of problems they may encounter in their careers after college. It might come as a surprise that almost no mathematical techniques are taught in the course. Instead, an overarching course objective is for students to apply appropriate techniques from their undergraduate background to come up with solutions to projects with a real-world connection. Past projects have included an analysis of insurance pricing and the development of a treatment plan for controlling invasive plant species.

Case Studies in Mathematical Modeling is open to any student who has taken the calculus sequence and linear algebra as prerequisites. In terms of nuts and bolts, the course meets twice a week for 14 weeks, and the class size varies from 12 to 20 students. Students work on their projects in groups of three to four and present their solutions orally to the rest of the class at the end of each project. In addition, each student submits his or her own written solution for grading. Because this class brings together ideas from many other courses in mathematics and other fields, it is usually taken during the junior or senior year. Students in the joint mathematics-economics major are particularly well represented in the class because it is one option for the capstone course requirement and plays something of a unifying role in the major.

The course sometimes offers students an experience in CBR. A community partner who provides a problem for the course benefits from the in-depth analysis and conclusions that result from student explorations. At the same time, students learn how actual problems can differ from those in a textbook. Students have to consider unfamiliar aspects of problem solving, such as how their assumptions can simplify (or oversimplify) a problem. They also learn the need to evaluate whether their answers are reasonable and can be implemented. Working with a community partner gives students the added benefit of contributing to the community, which we hope students will continue to do after they graduate.

The Project: Economic Self-Sufficiency for Rising Tide

As one successful CBR project undertaken through the case studies course, students collaborated with the Rising Tide Community Loan Fund (Rising Tide), a subsidiary of the Community Action Committee of the Lehigh Valley (CACLV). Rising Tide's mission is to provide microloans ($5,000 to $35,000 at the time of the project) at affordable rates to small businesses in the Lehigh Valley that are unable to secure loans on their own from more usual sources. Its purpose is to promote economic development in our community. When the project was assigned, Rising Tide had one full-time and one part-time employee who oversaw the loan process and provided additional business consulting. Rising Tide is financially supported through a number of sources including low-interest bank loans, federal funding, donations, and interest from its loan portfolio.

As their final course project, students were asked to develop a five-year business plan to make Rising Tide more economically self-sufficient. When this project objective was assigned, roughly half of Rising Tide's budget came from loan interest, the main source of self-generated revenue. This meant that students had to determine a way to increase Rising Tide's portfolio holdings.

As they worked on the project, students also had to consider a number of issues including how the portfolio was to be funded (because Rising Tide had to raise capital from banks and other sources before it could loan that money to businesses), the size and distribution of the loan portfolio, and whether Rising Tide would need to hire another employee to help manage the additional workload. Each group had roughly five weeks to complete these tasks.

At the start of the project, student groups received basic information about the size and distribution of Rising Tide's loan portfolio, a yearly budget report, and a general description of the organization. Students quickly realized that the material they were given was less complete than in their previous experience and requested clarification. To keep Rising Tide employees from having to answer a constant string of student requests, the class assembled a list of questions and had Rising Tide staff address them via e-mail about a week after the project was first assigned. Those clarifications were enough; even the groups that were having particular trouble getting started were able to make significant progress in their analyses. At the end of the semester, every group presented its solutions to the entire class and the employees of Rising Tide who had an opportunity to ask questions after each presentation. After the semester ended, Rising Tide received copies of all student reports.

The project was successful on many levels. Rising Tide had previously completed an analysis of how it might expand over time, and the student reports, although varied, reached similar conclusions. In the short term, the students' independent assessments therefore supported and strengthened Rising Tide's internal analysis. Four years after the project, Rising Tide had doubled its maximum loan size and added an additional part-time employee, both suggestions by student groups that became outcomes. Although various market forces clearly shaped these Rising Tide decisions, student work helped plant these seeds of change, which took a number of years to reach fruition.

The project was a similarly significant experience for the students. At the conclusion of the course, students were asked in an exit survey to reflect on whether knowing that Rising Tide was interested in their analysis changed their approach to the final project. Of the 19 students in the class, 12 responded, and 11 commented that their approach to the problem changed because of the community partner's involvement. Among the differences cited were an increased effort to provide a reasonable and flexible solution for the partner, a more careful consideration of the project's underlying assumptions, and greater attention toward crafting a clear and concise final presentation. One student mentioned that the main difference for him was that he was "motivated by more than academic reasons. [He] wanted to find an answer for the people of Rising Tide." Another student remarked that working on the project "provided [her] with a sense of responsibility, since Rising Tide's main goal is to help members of the community improve their standards of living."

Finishing the case studies course with a CBR project was a satisfying experience. Student reaction to this project was very positive, and based on the exit survey and course evaluations students felt that the project added a deeper dimension to the course. Overall, the sentiment was strong that such a project should remain part of future versions of the course. From the teaching standpoint, working with a community partner motivated students to think about problems more broadly, deeply, and carefully.

Lessons Learned

One of the more challenging aspects of incorporating a CBR project into a math class is finding a community partner with an appropriate project at the right level. Many potential partners have interesting questions to investigate, and even though five weeks may seem like a lot of time for an assignment, students need to be able to make progress toward a solution within a week of starting if they are to have a reasonable report at the end.

My most successful projects are the ones I've had the most time to prepare. Ideally, I try to arrange to have a community partner and develop some reasonable questions before the start of the semester. An early start provides a number of advantages. In some cases I've been able to incorporate background for the CBR material earlier in the semester, which can be helpful for this final project. I can also promote the project during the first part of the semester, motivating students to hone their oral and written skills. Finally, the more time I have to craft a project, the easier it is to tailor it to a particular class.

Students also work harder when they find a problem particularly engaging. Setting up a visit with the community partner, either in class, or better yet, on site, really helps draw in the students. I try to arrange the visit within a day or two of assigning the project and encourage the class to come up with questions. At the other end, I make a point of inviting the partner to the students' final presentations, and I encourage the partner to come to the meeting with questions. The human connection is a great motivator—students can do truly exceptional work when they believe someone will use their conclusions.

It is difficult to fully evaluate how a CBR experience in the classroom changes a student's outlook. However, I have received more feedback from alumni about the case studies course than from any other course I teach.

Former students comment about seeing similar problems in their professional experiences, or how they discussed their projects in job interviews. Anecdotally, I believe the CBR project provides students in the case studies course with an outstanding experience for their educational backgrounds, one that sticks with them long after they graduate.

10

STRATEGIC TRAINING GOALS

Preparing Graduate Students to Conduct School-Based Action Research

Anthony C. Holter and James M. Frabutt

Public and private organizations face growing accountability pressures to document program effectiveness, outcomes, and community impact. Aside from external pressures, however, a hallmark of high-achieving organizations is that they simply want to know whether what they are doing works and how it can work better. Said another way, highly effective organizations are steadfastly committed to their mission, and they use data frequently to assess how well the mission is achieved.

Effective and high-functioning leaders are no different. They are skilled in posing poignant questions, systematically gathering and evaluating pertinent evidence, and following through to make mission critical decisions that are informed by data. This chapter suggests that leaders of this ilk are an invaluable commodity for leading today's Catholic schools and recounts a graduate-level training and formation model designed to prepare mission-driven and data-informed leaders for Catholic schools via community-based action research.

Contemporary Catholic school leaders face a constellation of challenges heretofore unseen in the nearly 200-year history of Catholic education in the United States (Grace & O'Keefe, 2007; Nuzzi, Frabutt, & Holter, 2012). As instructional and spiritual leaders of their schools, Catholic school principals must ensure a vibrant Catholic identity and a sound educational experience for their students amid drastic shifts in school demographics and financial viability. Most pointedly in Catholic schools, these shifts have centered on an increasingly non-Catholic student population, decreased numbers of men and women in religious orders who serve as teachers and leaders, and increased tuition costs (McDonald & Schultz, 2010; Notre Dame Task Force on Catholic Education, 2006). While the genesis of these myriad challenges is complex, one major symptom of these root causes is often made manifest through concrete financial realities, such as the growing gap between tuition charged and the actual cost to educate each child.

Despite these many challenges, Catholic schools continue to provide powerfully effective education, especially for the multiply disadvantaged, minority students from low-income families with parents who are not college educated (Greeley, 1982; Neal, 1997). What remains troubling, however, is that the schools most likely to serve multiply disadvantaged urban students have been vanishing at an alarming rate (O'Keefe & Scheopner, 2007). Between the years 2000 and 2006, 564 Catholic schools closed in urban centers across the United States, displacing over 250,000 students (National Center for Education Statistics, 2008).

These sobering statistics clearly indicate that nationally, the Catholic school community is facing staggering and mounting challenges. Moreover, these national trends are affecting the vitality and vibrancy of individual neighborhoods and communities across the United States (Brinig & Garnett, 2012; White House Domestic Policy Council, 2008). A publication from the National Catholic Educational Association, *Endangered Species: Urban and Rural Catholic Schools*, highlighted the precarious position many historically healthy and vibrant Catholic schools currently find themselves in: on the brink of extinction (Haney & O'Keefe, 2007).

Yet the demise of U.S. Catholic schools is not a foregone conclusion (Frabutt & Holter, 2009; Holter & Frabutt, 2012). It may be the case that the very institutions threatened by growing fiscal and demographic challenges hold the answers to their own renewal. In fact, O'Keefe (2007) concluded his analysis of the challenges and possibilities awaiting Catholic schools with the reminder that "the great strength of Catholic schools is their autonomy, the ability to craft creative responses to meet current needs" (p. 55). He went on to state that schools that beat the odds and respond well to these challenges have leaders and personnel who "innovate, they reach out to the local community, they form partnerships" (p. 55).

So how do these leaders meet the increasing demands of Catholic school leadership? What tools do they have to ensure they are making the best decisions with their precious resources and engaging the local community and forming fruitful partnerships? Research indicates that precious few leadership preparation programs are designed to prepare candidates with the theological and administrative skills, knowledge, and dispositions required of the contemporary Catholic school leader (O'Keefe, 1999; Schuttloffel, 2007).

In contrast, Catholic school principals who engage in community-based action research are "poised to address myriad challenging issues at work in their schools" by employing sound educational research methodology to identify and meet the urgent needs in their school community (Frabutt, Holter, & Nuzzi, 2008, p. 1). When these individuals address pressing needs in their local community, they also advance the broader goal of school renewal as they "systematically use data to answer questions and take an inquiry-based approach toward educational improvement" (Frabutt et al., 2008, p. 1; see also Goldring & Berends, 2009). This approach to community-based action research for Catholic school leaders is rooted in Catholic theology and is responsive to the administrative demands of contemporary leadership (Frabutt et al., 2008).

A Few Caveats About Our Approach

While there are indeed many models for engaging undergraduates in community-based research, our commentary here is based on the model proposed by Stoecker and Beckman (2010) and Beckman and Penney (2010), which is referred to in several chapters of this book. Before we examine the specific case of Catholic school leaders' use of the community impact framework, it is important to briefly discuss several key differences between our approach and the typical undergraduate model for implementing community-based research more broadly in the academy.

The first and perhaps most obvious difference between our approach and the traditional undergraduate model is that we teach graduate courses in educational research methods in a master of arts in educational administration degree program. What makes this an important distinction is that our students enter and graduate from the program as a cohort and complete a set course of study that requires them to engage in community-based research (Mary Ann Remick Leadership Program, 2012). In fact, one of the essay prompts for their application to the program asks them to identify the needs, challenges, or opportunities at their school that are appropriate for a community-based action research project.

Second, these nascent ideas for a community-based action research project are fully addressed and developed through four courses (10 credit hours) of educational research methods and applied community-based action research. This sequence of course work dedicated to community-based research allows students to extend their research experience and projects beyond the one-semester experience typical of undergraduate programs. In fact, our students are able to dedicate nearly an entire calendar year to their community-based action research project (see Table 10.1).

TABLE 10.1
The Step-by-Step Process of Action Research in the
Mary Ann Remick Leadership Program

Program Phase	Course Number or Requirement	Stages of Action Research
Preprogram (Application)	Applicants are asked to respond to an essay prompt regarding an issue in their school community that is appropriate for action research project	**Stage 1: Planning stage** Identifying and limiting the topic Gathering information Reviewing related literature Developing a research plan
Summer 1	No official course work; individual consultation with faculty members	
Academic year 1	No official course work; individual consultation with faculty members, completion of action research topic selection rubric	
Summer 2	EDU 73777: Educational Research and Methodology. Candidates develop an action research plan that is implemented in their school community	
Academic year 2	EDU 73886: Action Research in Catholic Schools I. Candidates implement the action research plan developed over the summer, collect data, and begin data analysis plan	**Stage 2: Acting stage** Collecting and analyzing data
	EDU 73887: Action Research in Catholic Schools II. Candidates finalize data collection and analysis, evaluate the impact of their intervention or inquiry, and formulate recommendations and next steps	**Stage 3: Developing stage** Developing an action plan
Summer 3	EDU 73888: Leadership in Catholic Schools. Candidates reflect on the action research process and prepare a research brief and conference poster to disseminate their findings at the school level and to the broader Catholic leadership and action research communities	**Stage 4: Reflecting stage** Sharing and communicating results Reflecting on the process

Note. From "Mission Driven and Data Informed Leadership," 2012, by A. C. Holter & J. M. Frabutt, *Catholic Education: A Journal of Inquiry and Practice, 15*(2), 253–269. Adapted with permission.

Third, and most important, our candidates are all teachers or leaders in Catholic schools. They are key stakeholders in and representatives of their school communities. We are not deploying students to foreign or unknown communities. Rather, we are enrolling members from a particular community, empowering them with the tools necessary for systematic research, challenging them to apply those tools to their own community needs, and supporting them in the evaluation of the projects and interventions they are assessing. They generate the questions, and we supply the framework and technical assistance to ensure they have the proper tools and resources to accurately identify and assess their pressing questions.

These practical and programmatic differences mean that we are able to design our community-based action research courses—the entire four-course sequence—around the needs of community members seeking real answers to the educational issues in their schools. Put another way, our entire approach to community-based action research *starts with community*.

Finally, we are using the term *community-based action research* to designate our specific approach to community-based research. The term *action* is an intentional addition meant to connect with the vast literature on action research that informs our practice (Cochran-Smith & Donnell, 2006; McNiff & Whitehead, 2006). The term *action research* defines an array of inquiry from teacher self-reflection on classroom instruction to a broad examination of social issues with the intent to change policy and structure. For the purposes of our courses, and for clarity in this chapter, we operationally define *action research* as systematic; oriented toward positive change in the school community; and participatory, practitioner-driven inquiry (Frabutt et al., 2008; Holter & Frabutt, 2011, 2012).

The Community Impact Framework

The community impact framework described in Chapter 2 supports a model of higher education civic engagement that fundamentally "shift(s) how community is viewed" (Stoecker & Beckman, 2010, p. 1). Moreover, this approach to community-based research "enhances the chances that substantial positive change would occur in our communities out of the research" (Beckman & Penney, 2010, p. 35). The impact pyramid, described in Stoecker and Beckman (2010), provides a good visual structure and helpful language to guide action toward impact. The pyramid is used to outline this chapter's discussion of strategic community development as it is implemented in the community-based action research sequence in the Mary Ann Remick Leadership Program at the University of Notre Dame.

Community development is at the foundation of the impact pyramid. This means that the work of attaining impact should address entire communities and not just individuals in those communities. For example, if the community is a neighborhood and the issue is crime, the desired impact could be a safer neighborhood for all. Measures that ensure safety for some, such as alarm systems for a few residents or fences for others, would not suffice as impact. Once the community is identified, developing relationships becomes the next important activity. The work toward impact begins with getting to know those who will be involved in action. Who has expertise to contribute? Who has need? What perspectives and interests will assist the effort? Once relationships develop so it is clear who will be involved at least initially, a next level of the pyramid is strategic design. Effective methods must be developed to reach the desired goal. Finally, impact is situated at the peak of the pyramid, ultimately a collective manifestation of greater well-being.

Community Development

The foundational cornerstone of the community impact pyramid and our research sequence for school leaders lies with the notion of *community development*, which is defined as "a set of principles and practices for changing communities [that] . . . builds the leadership and power" of those in the community (Stoecker & Beckman, 2009, p. 2). Community is viewed as a system of interconnected parts; it is the entire community, not a few individuals. For our students, the unit of community is their school, so all considerations for research questions, interventions, and action planning begin in that locally situated ecological niche.

Community as a social system. Our teachers and educational leaders are acutely aware that their work unfolds within a complex, multilayered social system. Individual classrooms are systems, as are departmental units, grade-level groups, and indeed the entire school community itself. This broad system consists of various stakeholders such as students, teachers, parents, administrators, community residents, priests, and parishioners. The system is value laden as well, so a particular value system cannot be absent from the discourse on community-based research. Our community of Catholic school teachers and leaders share common Catholic values that are the genesis and foundation of their inquiry, but their inquiry is not "some special form of Catholic research" (Holter & Frabutt, 2011, p. 2). These values guide the animating questions, method of inquiry, and dissemination of findings that all lead to positive change, even school renewal at their research site. Thus, there is great symmetry and synergy between the condition of community participation in the research and the "strong community life that is at the heart of the Catholic school" (Moore, 2004, p. 172).

As instructors, we recognize and stress that the most effective action research projects are those conceived of and developed within that multilayered system. In fact, we state emphatically that the research question must be generated by and be important to the local community. The following are two concrete examples of how this is accomplished:

1. When our students are choosing and developing research topics, we provide a series of reflection questions to key them in on the most interesting and pressing issues in their school community (e.g., What aspects of your school and parish life are most interesting? What are some of the perceived areas of need at your school?) and encourage them to seek the counsel of colleagues (e.g., school principal, teachers, guidance counselors) to derive the most appropriate set of research questions.

2. When our students are vetting the many and often competing needs of the community, we challenge them to evaluate the feasibility of their proposed research topics based on time constraints, the required resources for various aspects of the project, and their access to the data their topic requires. This process also ensures that the research project will be completed in the allotted time.

Navigating these early project checkpoints ensures that our students stay attuned to local need and community context and envision their work transpiring in an active, dynamic social system.

Building leadership and power from within. Another key tenet of community development is that communities must develop their own leadership potential, thereby building their own power, to effect positive change. Our action research process aims to "support community members in harnessing their collective capacity to solve their own problems with minimal outsider assistance" (Stoecker & Beckman, 2010, p. 2).

What does it mean to *harness collective capacity*? Most simply, this phrase turns on the notion of empowerment as accessing and using individual and collective power. When teachers and school leaders claim this locus of control (Mertler, 2012) they gain a voice to pose the questions that need to be asked and the assertiveness to find the answers. In short, the school leader is recast, neither as a top-down recipient of instructions and directives, nor as a consumer of outside services and consultation. Instead of a school hiring an external consultant to develop a marketing strategy for increasing Latino enrollment, an empowered principal can involve a faculty- and parent-led team in tackling that issue, thus increasing individual/collective skill, competence, and confidence in the process.

The other term that is so crucial to community development work among teachers and school leaders is *problem solving*. Relevance, utility, and immediate application are hallmarks of well-crafted community-based action research. In fact, to qualify as community-based action research at all, our students' research topics and questions must be change oriented. This means that community-based action research must aim to make a positive change in the school from the outset. The data must be shared with key stakeholders so that these important changes can be carefully considered. We find that the process of community-based action research empowers these practitioner researchers to seek a "leadership role in resolving the problem" that prompted their inquiry in the first place (Stoecker & Beckman, 2010, p. 3).

Participatory Relationships

Above the foundation of the pyramid, community development, is the next value of importance in reaching impact in communities is participatory relationships. For community development to be attained, such relationships are essential (Stoecker & Beckman, 2010). Community-based research at its core is "fundamentally about relationship[s]" (Stoecker & Beckman, 2010, p. 4). These relationships shape the scope and trajectory of the research activities explored in and with the community. The quality of relationships among key stakeholders is a direct correlate of the strong Catholic school community in which they are forged. Because our students are already leaders in the Catholic schools where they will conduct their research, the process of establishing relationships is considerably less daunting but no less important. The following three factors illustrate the important and nuanced participatory relationships that characterize this research in Catholic school contexts: engage multiple stakeholders, model reflective practice, and continually monitor relationships.

First, by design, our students strive to involve colleagues and stakeholders at every phase of the research process. As we have already discussed, the research questions themselves are derived from conversations with faculty and staff, students, parents, and other stakeholders in the school community, often building solidarity around a common issue or concern. Next, through the use of sound sampling techniques, our students seek the most appropriate methods for selecting participants in the study. These sampling procedures often require additional steps to ensure that the quietest, least involved, or most marginalized members of the school community are equally represented in the study. And finally, students develop a dissemination plan to share the results of their inquiry with the very community that helped define the issue and provided data for the inquiry. The resulting recommendations or plan of action is thus embedded in ongoing work with the community stakeholders. At each step of the process, stakeholders are affirmed as valued and contributing members of the school community.

Second, we believe that a powerfully instructive example of participatory relationships is provided by the sheer example of our school leaders. When it comes to encouraging others' reflective practice and their own growth as change agents, "modeling is still the best teacher" (York-Barr, Sommers, Ghere, & Montie, 2006, p. 245). A school leader who asks pointed and challenging questions and listens attentively to the answers is better positioned to engender the support and participation of a broader cross-section of school stakeholders.

Third, it is important to note that the participatory relationships established and affirmed through community-based action research must also be closely monitored. In Catholic school communities, as in many other communities, participants and researchers are often friends, colleagues, or mentors. Respecting confidentiality and anonymity where appropriate will bolster these important relationships, foster honest participation and feedback, and protect the integrity of the research process. Thus we intentionally reflect on researcher positionality or the researchers' place in and relationship with the community they are studying (Herr & Anderson, 2005).

Strategic Design

Assuming a strong orientation toward community development and valuing participatory relationships, attaining impact involves the strategic design of activities toward the desired change. Just as the stakeholder relationships in a community are essential to effective community-based research, so too are the relationships and boundaries between local communities, institutions of higher education, and even specific faculty in the academy who engage in community-based research (Stoecker, 1999, 2005). In the community impact framework, these boundary definitions are part of the "strategic design" or plan of action, evaluation, and reflection wherein community members articulate "what parts of institutions are needed to accomplish community goals" (Stoecker & Beckman, 2010, p. 7).

The community-based action research projects our candidates design and implement are in many ways an expanded strategic design. Following the format and structure of social sciences research, students develop compelling research questions, review relevant research, design a rigorous and systematic method to collect and analyze data, and use these data to evaluate their interventions and answer their questions of interest. As instructors of the course and faculty members of the academy, we take on a variety of roles along this research trajectory. The following three examples highlight specific instances of community-university partnerships and the expectations and boundaries inherent in each.

Although some school and community leaders are familiar with the structure and requirements of community-based research, many likely approach it with some trepidation, asking, What is community-based action research, anyway? How will I have time to tackle this research while fulfilling my normal job responsibilities? How do I know this is actually going to make a difference? To assuage these concerns and ensure the locus of control remains with the community leader, we have developed a framework for leaders to conduct valid and reliable research for positive change in their school community (Holter & Frabutt, 2011). In this action phase of the strategic design, our role as faculty and instructors is to provide a road map or plan that will meet course requirements and ultimately lead to positive change in the school community. Although the process is a creation of the academy, school leaders can respond to and modify the tools and general prompts we have developed to design their own unique high-quality and community-specific research project.

Another important relationship in this community-university partnership exists in the ongoing evaluation of the community-based action research project. As social scientists and experts in educational research, our skill in the design, method, and analysis of educational inquiry helps students avoid potential pitfalls in assessment and evaluation, and challenges them to make the best decisions for their community-based inquiry. Our position as faculty advisers is an important departure from the typical consultant or service provider positions traditionally occupied by university faculty in participatory or community-based research (Stoecker, 2005; Stoecker & Beckman, 2010). We do not do the research for the community. Rather, we empower our students to become proficient in the skills necessary to conduct their own research while providing the structure and support they require as novice researchers. In other words, the strategic design of evaluation components fuses our expertise in design with their expert knowledge of school leadership and the local community to arrive at a compelling and methodologically sound community-based action research project.

In addition to statistical analysis of the data and formal evaluation of the project, strategic design also calls for broader reflection on the research process. Reflection as a formalized component of the course is manifest in assignments such as research journals and regular communication with students' action research group (a small subset of classmates who discuss, critique, and reflect on their projects). Additionally, the final course in the research sequence serves as a capstone to the experience, offering our students a platform to reflect on the ongoing impact of their research project and challenging them to share their site-based inquiry with the greater community of Catholic school researchers (see ace.nd.edu/leadership/actionresearch). These course components provide our students with the opportunity to develop "a framework for knowing where they have come from in order to understand where they are going" (Hendricks, 2006, p. 26).

Although we provide the general framework for this year-long empirical investigation, it is far from a rigid or static template for school leaders to simply drop or plug in their site-specific project and data. Instead, the template serves as a road map for the accomplishments of the calendar year, and we believe it is important to have transparency in the process before a single question is posed or a data point is collected. At every step of the way, our students are making important decisions about what to study, how to study it, and who will be their partners and collaborators. In this way, our strategic design is a collaboration between community members and university faculty, between local community and higher education at every step of the way.

Community Impact

Community impact is at the top of the impact framework, resting on the foundation of community development and supported through participatory relationships, as described by Stoecker and Beckman (2010). We next describe course-level outputs and general outcomes that unfold in the school community using two case examples and explain how the outcomes result in broad-level community impact pertaining to Catholic education.

Course Outputs

Beckman and Penney (2010) define *output* as the "shortest term, immediate product of the community-based research" (p. 36). In our sequence of graduate research and methodology courses, the research report is the most immediate product. Similar in scope and content to a master's thesis, the report each student produces details the animating research questions, relevant research literature, primary findings, and future directions of the project.

As a requirement of graduation, each student also presents his or her research at the annual Remick Leadership Conference on Notre Dame's campus. Students condense their report into a conference poster and involve other graduate and undergraduate students, faculty and staff, and community members in a discussion of their research. They create simple, engaging briefs that are meant to provide a concise and nontechnical overview of their work for multiple stakeholder audiences. Additionally, many of our students present their research at other regional or national conferences and publish their work in academic journals and popular news media outlets (e.g., Beltramo, 2012; Klich, 2011; Mullarkey, 2011).

These outputs are an important component of our courses and reflect our commitment to community-based action research. They also fulfill the course objectives relative to challenging students to become critical and competent consumers and producers of educational research. Moreover, as they share the major findings and new questions inspired by the research, students engage in the process of conducting educational inquiry more broadly (Mertler, 2012).

General Outcomes

The general outcomes of community-based action research can be thought of as second-order outputs or "something that can be accomplished because of the output" (Beckmann & Penney, 2010, p. 36). For students in our program, these outcomes are typically achieved in two primary categories: policy and procedural changes in the school community and changes in personal disposition, stance, or orientation to educational inquiry.

Changes to policy and procedure in the school community. As discussed earlier in this chapter, a hallmark of community-based action research is that the "information derived from such a process will be used to guide action or a series of actions" to change policies or procedures and improve conditions in the community in general (Frabutt et al., 2008, p. 6). To put it succinctly, "without action, there is no action research" (Holly, Arhar, & Kasten, 2009, p. 217).

Planning for positive social change is so important to our conceptualization and practice of community-based action research that a specific subsection requires students to reflect on the implication and application of their results in their research reports (Holter & Frabutt, 2011). One way to measure these outcomes is to read the final reports or attend the research conference where our students present and discuss their research projects. Past participants have examined the effectiveness of reading programs for English language learners (Asmar, 2008) or students with learning disabilities (Moreau, 2009) in their school. They have studied coaches' efficacy in the spiritual formation of student athletes (Zelenka, 2009) and the impact of gender-based math classes on the learning environment (Keller, 2009). In each case, school leaders used sound research methodology to learn more about the needs in their school community and make real, positive changes for students and staff alike. The following case studies highlight the kinds of outcomes our students implement and achieve in their school communities as a direct result of completing the research report.

In 2009, Sister Mary Agnes Greiffendorf, principal at Saint Pius V Catholic School in Providence, Rhode Island, set out to examine the "unique characteristics that attract families to Saint Pius V Catholic School, and thereby use that information to strengthen the school enrollment" (Greiffendorf, 2009, p. 5). Sister Mary Agnes designed an original survey instrument based on relevant marketing literature and administered it to more than 100 new and current families in the school community. Her collaborative inquiry confirmed that parent, parishioner, and nonparishioner participant responses "coincided well with the four pillars of a Dominican school: prayer, study, community, and preaching" (2009, p. 41).

These results led to a new marketing strategy and message that highlighted the school's Dominican charism (i.e., the religious order's special orientation and unique mission) and targeted families from outside the parish boundaries. Thus the research was directly responsive to the school's expanding need to increase enrollment amid growing competition from other public and private schools and inclusive of key school stakeholders. This new and more effective marketing approach highlighted essential elements of the school community that "encapsulate[d] what is important to the school and what it stands for" (Cook, 2004, p. 18). As a result of Sister Mary Agnes's research and more accurate marketing, enrollment has been steadily climbing at her school.

In another example, Scott Kmack (2008), dean of students at Trinity Catholic High School in Newton, Massachusetts, used community-based action research to better support at-risk students during the transition into ninth grade. Although "Catholic social teaching compels Catholic schools to include and serve traditionally marginalized students, including students in poverty, those with special needs, and English language learners," fully engaging these students requires significant attention to services, staffing, and support systems (Scanlan, 2009, p. 1). To address this need, Kmack's project centered on designing, implementing, and assessing the effectiveness of a new advisory program for ninth graders who had been accepted to the school on conditional status, based largely on low test scores.

As part of the action research, these students were placed into a newly structured advisory system directed by a trained and experienced educator. This adviser mentored students individually, and in a group setting the adviser provided "basic academic and organizational skills, led community building activities, and served as a guide for transition to high school" (Kmack, 2008, p. 145). The study tracked students' grades, assessed organization skills weekly, and sought process-oriented feedback from students, teachers, and the adviser. These data sources indicated a pattern of success for a majority of students in the program and revealed that focused, well-articulated efforts can indeed create positive learning environments for even the most marginalized students. Using an inquiry stance to address a far-reaching educational goal, Kmack found solutions "to address the unique needs of every student who is present in Catholic schools" (p. 171).

Changes to personal disposition toward educational inquiry. It is admittedly more difficult, however, to measure the following outcome of community-based action research: the changes in personal disposition, stance, or orientation to educational inquiry (Holter, Frabutt, & Nuzzi, 2012). Rather than a simple tally of positive changes in the school community, this kind of outcome is measured in incremental movement toward an appreciation and practice of data-driven leadership. Cochran-Smith and Lytle (1999) refer to this shift in leadership as a change in "stance" that "describe[s] the positions teachers and others who work together in inquiry communities take toward knowledge and its relationship to practice" (p. 288).

Graduates often call, e-mail, or write their instructors to relay updates on the ongoing development of their projects, new positions, or responsibilities that have come about because of their inquiry, and they share the many ways community-based action research continues to enrich their work. This general change in stance or disposition as an outcome of community-based action research is reflected in the words of one of our recent graduates:

> No longer must I feel imprisoned by anecdotal evidence, which is far too often used to make important decisions regarding fundamental aspects of the life of the school. Now if there is a problem, I have a systematic approach to examining existing research on a topic, collecting data, and analyzing results that will allow me to instead be data informed. (T. Jarotkiewicz, personal communication, June 18, 2009)

These dual and complementary outcomes of community-based action research—positive change in the school community and student growth and development—move beyond the traditional focus on faculty research interests and student learning experiences for the sake of "effects on communities," which is a potential barrier to advancing community-based research in the academy (Beckman & Penney, 2010, p. 40).

System-level impact on Catholic schools. Finally, *community impact* is broadly defined as "the accumulated consequences of [multiple] outcomes" (Stoecker & Beckman, 2010, p. 8) and "the effect of the research on the large issue or goal within the given discussion" (Beckman & Penney, 2010, p. 37). To rightly understand the community impact achieved by our Catholic school leaders' research, we must return to the scenario presented at the beginning of the chapter. In light of the financial, demographic, and other challenges Catholic schools face, our singular community impact focus is to sustain and strengthen Catholic schools, which means we seek to use all outcomes of community-based action research to effect Catholic school renewal.

Advancing the renewal and revitalization of American Catholic schools one principal at a time will be neither quick nor easy. Yet, in the six years that this research sequence has been a component of the Remick Leadership Program, we have formed and educated nearly 150 Catholic school teachers and leaders who are making positive, mission-driven, and data-informed differences in their school communities. As these Catholic school leaders are empowered to ask questions about the status quo, they use sound research methods to systematically assess the issues that are most pressing in their schools. At the same time, their studies advance and improve the spiritual and intellectual formation of the children entrusted to their care. These teachers and principals can provide a powerful and instructive example to their immediate circle of influence by modeling the types of leadership behaviors and practices that Catholic school renewal demands.

Lessons Learned and Conclusion

We began developing this community-based action research framework in 2007 when Notre Dame formally approved the master's degree in educational leadership program. After six years of delivering and refining our instructional methods and approach, we provide a brief and nonexhaustive set of lessons learned. We have selected a few examples in three categories: lessons learned about the content and format of the action research sequence, practicalities for the instructional delivery of the course sequence, and challenges the learners faced.

The first lesson learned was to incorporate a summative component into the action research sequence so participants could fully examine their community-based research experience. This became a fourth course: an integrative one-credit hour seminar, which was added after a few cohorts graduated. Participating students now carefully and systematically look back on their cycle of community-based research, highlighting successes, challenges, road blocks, and solutions. Sharing those highs and lows in a structured group exchange allows students to see the commonality of their experience. In this same seminar, students who are just about to graduate are also prompted to project how the skills and competencies they have gained will serve them in their own leadership. They not only describe in concrete terms how their behaviors and values will differ as a result of this graduate course work but also speculate on what specific change-oriented projects or issues they hope to take on in the future.

Second, as instructors we have grown to more deeply appreciate the art and skill of flexibility and adaptation. Students' projects and their diverse contexts are subject to the real-world fluctuations of day-to-day life in a Catholic school, so the pristine research plan introduced in the summer session invariably comes face-to-face with the reality of the school year. They may discover the scope of the project is too great or too difficult because of new leadership or political forces; there may be issues of access to data or an outright crisis at the school (i.e., school consolidations or potential school closure). We have indeed dealt with each of these examples, and it has required guiding students in recalibrating or adapting their project or its main goals and methods. In so doing, we have found frequent communication (e.g., e-mail, phone, and even in-person site visits) to be indispensable for reshaping a project that is still relevant, doable, and in accordance with the graduate program's expectations.

Third, student voice and input during the final integrative seminar helped us comprehend that becoming a mission-driven and data-informed leader is a developmental process. To obtain, practice, and refine one's competency in CBR takes time and benefits from the wisdom of experience. We now realize that what we seek to effect—a paradigm shift in one's approach to leadership—does not occur immediately. In fact, Schoen (2007) has explained that an action research orientation is a developmental process, encompassing an acquisition phase, a fluency phase, and a generalization phase. The graduate course work experience we have designed purposefully facilitates acquisition and develops fluency. Only continued experience, trial and error, and reinforcement can lead to the generalization phase when leaders embrace an inquiry stance on their own in new contexts. Ultimately, our hope is that the stance our students take toward issues in their school communities affirms inquiry as "a continual process of making current arrangements problematic; questioning the ways knowledge and practice are constructed, evaluated, and used; and assuming that part of the work of practitioners individually and collectively is to participate in educational and social change" (Cochran-Smith & Lytle, 2009, p. 121).

In conclusion, the model of community-based action research that we have outlined runs contradictory to traditional models of inquiry where academics conduct research "on people" rather than "with people" (Stoecker, 2005, p. 29). In fact, our entire orientation to community-based action research is one of empowerment: using our skills as teachers and educational researchers to instruct and guide our students from roles as novice researchers to school leaders who prize and use the collective talents of the school community to identify, assess, and change pressing educational issues. Far from being a static directional indicator, this change in stance is a change in "worldview, a critical habit of mind, a dynamic and fluid way of knowing and being" (Cochran-Smith & Lytle, 2009, p. 120) that is the foundation and driver of school renewal (Goldring & Berends, 2009; Ontario Principals' Council, 2009). More precisely, this orientation toward inquiry is most effective when it moves beyond the individual and is characteristic of entire communities of people, such as the Catholic school communities described in this chapter.

It is true and well documented that Catholic schools today face a growing constellation of challenges. While these challenges are daunting, they are not insurmountable. As our work with Catholic school leaders is beginning to indicate, the individual and cumulative efforts to address community-based issues with action research contribute to the renewal of individual schools and the apostolate of Catholic education. Such "prudent innovation" is indeed what is required for the "courageous renewal on the part of the Catholic school" (Congregation for Catholic Education, 1998, para. 3). Although we have focused exclusively on the context of the Catholic school, this model is likewise applicable to a wide array of community and educational contexts.

References

Asmar, K. M. (2008). The effect of an English language acquisition program on the academic literacy, English fluency, and reaching achievement of second grade ELL students. In J. M. Frabutt, A. C. Holter, & R. J. Nuzzi (Eds.), *Research, action, and change: Leaders reshaping Catholic schools* (pp. 119–134). Notre Dame, IN: Alliance for Catholic Education Press.

Beckman, M., & Penney, N. (2010). Improving the results of CBR: Moving toward community impact. In J. M. Pizga & M. Beckman (Eds.), *New directions in community based research* (pp. 34–41). Princeton, NJ: National Community-Based Research Networking Initiative.

Beltramo, J. A. (2012). Response to student literacy needs at Mother of Sorrows Catholic School. *Catholic Education: A Journal of Inquiry & Practice, 15*(2), 295–324.

Brinig, M. F., & Garnett, N. S. (2012). Catholic schools and broken windows. *Journal of Empirical Legal Studies, 9*(2), 347–367.

Cochran-Smith, M., & Donnell, K. (2006). Practitioner inquiry: Blurring the boundaries of research and practice. In J. L. Green, G. Camilli, & P. B. Elmore (Eds.), *Handbook of complementary methods in education research* (pp. 503–518). Mahwah, NJ: Erlbaum.

Cochran-Smith, M., & Lytle. S. L. (2009). *Inquiry as stance: Practitioner research for the next generation.* New York, NY: Teachers College Press.

Cochran-Smith, M., & Lytle. S. L. (1999). Relationships of knowledge and practice: Teacher learning in communities. *Review of Research in Education, 24,* 249–306.

Congregation for Catholic Education. (1998). *The Catholic school on the threshold of the third millennium*. Boston, MA: Pauline Books and Media.

Cook, T. (2004). Charism: A Catholic school's mark of distinction. *Momentum, 35*(1), 18–21.

Frabutt, J. M., & Holter, A. C. (2009). Ensuring vital schools through action research. *Community Psychologist, 42*(4), 51–53.

Frabutt, J. M., Holter, A. C., & Nuzzi, R. J. (2008). *Research, action, and change: Leaders reshaping Catholic schools*. Notre Dame, IN: Alliance for Catholic Education Press.

Goldring, E., & Berends, M. (2009). *Leading with data: Pathways to improve your school*. Thousand Oaks, CA: Corwin Press.

Grace, G., & O'Keefe, J. (2007). Catholic schools facing the challenges of the 21st century: An overview. In G. Grace & J. O'Keefe (Eds.), *International handbook of Catholic education: Challenges for school systems in the 21st century* (pp. 1–11). Dordrecht, The Netherlands: Springer.

Greeley, A. M. (1982). *Catholic high schools and minority students*. New Brunswick, NJ: Transaction Books.

Greiffendorf, M. A. (2009, June). *Marketing research to strengthen enrollment at St. Pius V school*. Paper presented at the annual Remick Leadership Conference, Notre Dame, IN.

Haney, R. M., & O'Keefe, J. M. (2007). *Endangered species: Urban and rural Catholic schools*. Washington, DC: National Catholic Educational Association.

Hendricks, C. (2006). *Improving schools through action research: A comprehensive guide for educators*. Boston, MA: Pearson.

Herr, K., & Anderson, G. L. (2005). *The action research dissertation*. Thousand Oaks, CA: Sage.

Holly, M. L., Arhar, J. M., & Kasten, W. C. (2009). *Action research for teachers: Traveling the yellow brick road* (3rd ed.). Boston, MA: Pearson Education.

Holter, A. C., & Frabutt, J. M. (2011). *Action research in Catholic schools: A step-by-step guide for practitioners*. Notre Dame, IN: Alliance for Catholic Education Press.

Holter, A. C., & Frabutt, J. M. (2012). Mission driven and data informed leadership. *Catholic Education: A Journal of Inquiry and Practice, 15*(2), 253–269.

Holter, A. C., Frabutt, J. M., & Nuzzi, R. J. (2012, November). *Leading the way: Action research for school leaders*. Paper presented at the annual meeting of the University Council for Educational Administration, Denver, CO.

Keller, D. (2009, July). *Gender-based 8th grade math classes: Do they improve the learning environment?* Paper presented at the annual Remick Leadership Conference, Notre Dame, IN.

Klich, S. (2011). A secondary intervention in reading: Word skills for junior high. *i.e.: inquiry in education, 2*(2), 1–21. Retrieved from digitalcommons.nl.edu/ie/vol2/iss2/3

Kmack, S. (2008). The effects of an advisory program for at-risk first-year high school students. In J. M. Frabutt, A. C. Holter, & R. J. Nuzzi (Eds.), *Research, action, and change: Leaders reshaping Catholic schools* (pp. 135–178). Notre Dame, IN: Alliance for Catholic Education Press.

Mary Ann Remick Leadership Program. (2012). *Program handbook*. Notre Dame, IN: Alliance for Catholic Education.

McDonald, D., & Schultz, M. M. (2010). *United States Catholic elementary and secondary schools, 2009–2010: The annual statistical report on schools, enrollment, and staffing.* Arlington, VA: National Catholic Educational Association.

McNiff, J., & Whitehead, J. (2006). *All you need to know about action research.* Thousand Oaks, CA: Sage.

Mertler, C. A. (2012). *Action research: Teachers as researchers in the classroom.* Los Angeles, CA: Sage.

Moore, L. P. (2004). Community. In T. C. Hunt, E. A. Joseph, & R. J. Nuzzi (Eds.), *Catholic schools in the United States: An encyclopedia* (Vol. 1, pp. 172–174). Westport, CT: Greenwood.

Moreau, L. (2009, June). *Efficacy of the Fast ForWord program for increasing reading achievement of students identified with learning disabilities.* Paper presented at the annual Remick Leadership Conference, Notre Dame, IN.

Mullarkey, J. (2011, April). *Service that serves students: Looking practically at service learning.* Paper presented at the meeting of the National Catholic Educational Association Annual Convention, New Orleans, LA.

National Center for Education Statistics. (2008). *Private school universe survey.* Washington, DC: Author.

Neal, D. (1997). The effects of Catholic secondary schooling on educational achievement. *Journal of Labor Economics, 15*(1), 98–123.

Notre Dame Task Force on Catholic Education. (2006). *Making God known, loved, and served: The future of Catholic primary and secondary schools in the United States.* Notre Dame, IN: Alliance for Catholic Education.

Nuzzi, R. J., Frabutt, J. M., & Holter, A. C. (2012). Catholic schools in the United States since Vatican II to present. In T. C. Hunt & J. C. Carper (Eds.), *The Praeger handbook of faith-based schools in the United States, K–12* (Vol. 2, pp. 317–349). Santa Barbara, CA: Praeger.

O'Keefe, J. M. (1999). Leadership in urban Catholic elementary schools. In T. C. Hunt, T. O. Oldenski, & T. J. Wallace (Eds.), *Catholic school leadership: An invitation to lead* (pp. 225–243). New York, NY: Falmer Press.

O'Keefe, J. M. (2007). Catholic schools at a decisive moment: Challenges and possibilities. In R. M. Haney & J. M. O'Keefe (Eds.), *Endangered species: Urban and rural Catholic schools* (pp. 43–57). Washington, DC: National Catholic Educational Association.

O'Keefe, J. M., & Scheopner, A. (2007). No margin, no mission: Challenges for Catholic urban schools in the USA. In G. Grace & J. O'Keefe (Eds.), *International handbook of Catholic education: Challenges for school systems in the 21st century* (Vol. 1, pp. 15–35). Dordrecht, The Netherlands: Springer.

Ontario Principals' Council. (2009). *The principal as data-driven leader.* Thousand Oaks, CA: Sage.

Scanlan, M. K. (2009). *All are welcome: Inclusive service delivery in Catholic schools.* Notre Dame, IN: Alliance for Catholic Education Press.

Schoen, S. (2007). Action research: A developmental model of professional socialization. *Clearing House: A Journal of Educational Strategies, Issues, and Ideas, 80*(5), 211–216.

Schuttloffel, M. (2007). Contemporary challenges to the recruitment, formation, and retention of Catholic school leadership in the USA. In G. Grace & J. O'Keefe (Eds.), *International handbook of Catholic education: Challenges for school systems in the 21st century* (Vol. 1, pp. 85–102). Dordrecht: The Netherlands: Springer.

Stoecker, R. (1999). Are academics irrelevant?: Roles for scholars in participatory research. *American Behavioral Scientist, 42*(5), 840–854.

Stoecker, R. (2005). *Research methods for community change: A project-based approach.* Thousand Oaks, CA: Sage.

Stoecker, R., & Beckman, M. (2009). *Making higher education civic engagement matter in the community.* Retrieved from www.compact.org/news/making-higher-education-civic-engagement-matter-in-the-community/9748

White House Domestic Policy Council. (2008). *Preserving a critical national asset: America's disadvantaged students and the crisis in faith-based urban schools.* Washington, DC: Author.

York-Barr, J., Sommers, W. A., Ghere, G. S., & Montie, J. (2006). *Reflective practice to improve schools: An action guide for educators.* Thousand Oaks, CA: Corwin Press.

Zelenka, M. (2009). Coaching coaches to see spirituality as a character trait. *Momentum, 40*(4), 20–23.

11

WORKING THROUGH THE CHALLENGES OF GLOBALLY ENGAGED RESEARCH

Elizabeth Tryon and Norbert Steinhaus

Many community-based researchers in the United States are interested in taking their practice to a new level by actively seeking partners in other countries and incorporating students into these projects. In addition, U.S. researchers experienced in working with more traditional one-way or translational research abroad are beginning to question the effectiveness of their methods and seek ways to improve the quality of community impact. One initiative is the growing global movement of universities dedicated to community engagement, system change, and social justice (e.g., Langman, 2005; Smith, 2002; Smith, Chatfield, & Pagnucco, 1997). Because we are from the United States and Germany, we have experience in global community-based research (CBR) and are uniquely poised to address some of those issues in this chapter. We describe projects in several countries, highlighting practices and models in which undergraduate and graduate students can be central participants (Strand, Marullo, Cutforth, Stoecker, & Donohue, 2003).

University community engagement in Europe began at the end of the 1960s (Hagen, 2008; Sclove, Scammell, Holland, & Alimohamed, 1998) and resulted in many different forms of engagement through multiple mechanisms. The nature of this historical period gave rise to much grassroots activism and drove innovations in university engagement activity, including worker education and policy advice. One significant example of this type of innovation is the emergence of the science shop concept in the Netherlands (Mulder, Der Hyde, Goffer, & Teodosiu, 2001), described in detail later. The science shop movement spread quickly throughout the rest of Europe

and is now established in Asia, Africa, South America, and Canada (see www
.livingknowledge.org).

This movement has followed a similar track in the United States (Sclove
et al., 1998; Wachelder, 2003). Starting in the mid-1980s with student
volunteerism and continuing with the rise of service-learning in the early
1990s (Sclove, 1995), nationally recognized notions of the engaged campus
have challenged universities to reconsider their civic responsibilities (e.g.,
Battistoni, 2002; Checkoway, 2001; Cruz & Giles, 2000; Jacoby, 2009).
Although some universities have novel structures and programs (e.g., Duke-
Engage, http://dukeengage.duke.edu; Wisconsin Without Borders, www
.livingknowledge.org/science-shops/about-science-shops/) that cross disciplines and national boundaries on their campuses, the majority are only now
discovering the global networks that exist to support CBR. As Americans
individually join groups such as Living Knowledge (the international science
shop network) and the Global Alliance for Community Engaged Research
(GACER), they learn about the work being done on a global scale and report
back to their peers (Lemish, 2013).

In many parts of the world, national and regional networks to promote
university engagement with the communities from which they draw and
serve are growing in size and strength. Impressive examples include the Latin
American Center for Service-Learning; Ma'an Arab University Alliance for
Civic Engagement, based in Cairo, Egypt; South African Higher Education Community Engagement Forum; AsiaEngage; Engagement Australia;
and Campus Engage in Ireland (see talloiresnetwork.tufts.edu/what-we-do/
regional-partnerships/). Such regional and national networks are important
for the exchange of experience and capacity building between faculty and students, community-based researchers, and community organizations, which
are called civil society organizations (CSO) in the European Union. They
also provide a collective voice in policy advocacy. Through collaboration
with global networks such as the Global University Network for Innovation,
GACER, the Talloires Network based at Tufts University (talloiresnetwork
.tufts.edu/who-we-ar) and Living Knowledge, support is provided to create student experiences that range from local to global. Further evidence of
this growing momentum is GACER, a platform for creating a worldwide
knowledge democracy, whose founders cochair the Committee for Social
Responsibility in Higher Education for the United Nations' Educational,
Scientific and Cultural Organization. According to GACER (2015), practitioners should be linked to a global network to "share effective practices in
strengthening engagement of communities." The Research Universities Civic
Engagement Network of Campus Compact has also endorsed the GACER
platform (Tryon, Hood, & Taalbi, 2013).

Those in U.S. higher education can benefit immensely from examining the community-based work and research other nations' universities are doing across borders. Engaged universities, whose faculty and students are involved in mutually beneficial relationships that cross national boundaries, become a more integral part of the communities where they are working and learning (Porter & Monard, 2001; Stachowski & Mahan, 1998; Volet, 2004). As colleges and universities participate in these networks, they produce knowledge with their community partners based on local and indigenous wisdom, addressing local social challenges. The global cross-linkage of engaged universities and grassroots CSO's, and the accompanying possibilities for service-learning or CBR, provides enormous potential for intercultural, civil-society-oriented learning for students. Within this developing global context, U.S. higher education institutions face an urgency to develop cross-national partnerships and educate in a way that is no longer only about transference of learning but also emphasizes engagement in the community through various learning methods, such as community-based participatory research and service-learning programs.

Terminology: Global and International

Clarity of terminology is important when communicating with partners domestically and beyond in the development of CBR. The same terms may take on different meanings because of differences in cultural frames of reference. For example, in the United States, we've noted that colleagues often tend to use the term *international* interchangeably with *global*. In the authors' experiences, however, the European Union seems to use these terms in a more nuanced manner. In the European Union, *international* commonly means an exchange between just two countries. In this chapter we use *global*; we have found it is used commonly in the European Union to refer to a large number of countries on at least two continents, if not across the whole planet, that are affected by an issue or project, or are partners on a project.[1]

Models

Throughout the world, different types of interfaces exist between academic researchers and civil society. Several good CBR models exist in the United States (Stoecker, 2012; Strand et al., 2003), and documented good practices of high-quality CBR in the United States or the European Union can naturally be applied in a global context. It is especially important to study these models and follow good practice in these contexts to create successful global impact, given the extra variables entailed in cross-cultural exchange (Lewin, 2009).

The community development model from Stoecker, Beckman, and Min (2010) is useful whether working domestically or globally. In this model, CBR and service-learning are often integrated into the following cyclical process: diagnose, prescribe, implement, and evaluate (Stoecker, 2012). The activities stem from discovering, in a community-based participatory fashion, the community's issues and priorities, and its preferred methods of addressing them. Because of the cultural differences often evident in global practice, it is critical to spend time determining what research will be valued and used by the population involved with it before forming hypotheses or taking students into a project area to begin data collection.

In the science shop model prevalent in the European Union, organizations referred to as science shops are created as mediators between community groups (trade unions, nonprofit organizations, social and advocacy groups, environmentalists, consumers, residents associations, etc.) and research institutions (universities, independent research facilities). Science shops are important actors in brokering CBR. Because they function within different sociopolitical, cultural, and organizational contexts, there is no one standard science shop (Mulder, Der Hyde, Goffer, & Teodosiu, 2001). One commonly held view, however, is that they provide "independent, participatory research support in response to concerns experienced by civil society" (Mulder et al., 2001). Moreover, there are indeed important parallels among the many different types of science shops because of their common demand-driven and bottom-up approach. They also share an interactive dialogue with community and advocate strongly for community involvement in research (Mulder & De Bok, 2006). Science shops are also often (but not always) linked to or based in universities where students do research as part of their curriculum. Through this type of extension and support activity, science shops attempt to create access to science, knowledge, and technology for social groupings that would not or could not ordinarily interact with these related disciplines.

Case Studies

In globally engaged CBR, there are as many trajectories as there are unique partnerships between academics and community members, depending on local contexts, issues, and politics. All successful work involves intentional relationship building over time, which is crucial in cross-cultural partnerships. The following four distinct, interdisciplinary CBR projects from the University of Wisconsin–Madison (UW-Madison) and a cooperation of

Science Shop in Europe are useful for faculty because they illustrate practices of globally engaged research. After these case descriptions, we present some lessons learned to round out our exploration of how faculty or instructional staff might incorporate global CBR into their curriculum.

Women's Reproductive Health and Malaria Prevention in Rural Kenya

> When I first arrived in Lunga Lunga, in the summer of 2009, I learned that the inhabitants of a nearby village set fire to all mosquito nets because a two-year old child died with a white net [entangled] around his neck. In the minds of the villagers, the white net served as a demonic symbol and the mother was held accountable for the strangulation of her child since women are responsible for . . . [mosquito] net caring, although they do not necessarily sleep under one. In fact, this mother slept on the floor with no net while her husband and their two children slept protected under the net. (A. Alonso, personal communication, December 15, 2012)

Although the Kenyan Ministry of Health reports that malaria is the leading cause of illness and death in Kenya, challenges are great in collecting reliable epidemiological data because 90% percent of attributed cases are dealt with through witch doctors and traditional healers. A program for distributing mosquito nets had been in effect since 2001 but was not appreciably decreasing rates in rural populations. Araceli Alonso, a professor of gender and women's studies at the UW-Madison and a former nurse, found through participant observation, personal accounts of villagers, and interviews with malaria experts that women and therefore their children do not receive equal protection against or treatment for malaria because of the government's allocation policies as well as gender and cultural issues. Real headway against malaria can only be made by understanding cultural influences and incorporating gender-sensitive analysis in policies and implementation of prevention and treatment programs.

Alonso first visited Kenya alone, without any preconceived ideas about completing research. She just wanted to visit her pen pal of several years. After a brief stay as a guest, her observation was that many houses might have a net, but not all women slept under one. Could it be because of cultural expectations about gender relations in the household? She discovered that her hypothesis did not account for all the reasons. Prior research and government accounting had focused only on net ownership. Curious and passionate about taking action, she received a small grant to return to Kenya with several graduate students in her program. They completed some informal research with the local nurse. They interviewed the townsfolk, and discovered several causes of women not using the nets. Only women of childbearing age received government nets, so postmenopausal women did not receive them. Some of the younger women could not walk 12 miles to the nearest clinic to deliver their babies, which was a requirement for receiving a net. And some women had to ask permission from their husbands to use or sleep under the nets but were unable to secure their consent. A superstition had also developed and was perpetuated by oral transmission about demons being in the white nets because a baby had strangled itself in one. As a result, some women only used the nets for fishing or to drag fruits and vegetables home from the market. In these cases, all the netting's insecticide pretreatment was thus lost and no longer effective even if later used for its intended purpose.

These preliminary findings caused the research team to adjust its recommendations, leading to education sessions about malaria in women's health meetings and then to an undergraduate initiative organized as an independent study. Students in UW-Madison's undergraduate theater program were recruited to create street theater and role-play with local actors to get the message out in a way people could decode, helping villagers understand that the mosquito could actually be viewed as the demon. Nets were also dyed blue to make them demon free. After these successes, local women requested more information about reproductive health and became empowered to take control of family planning. Ongoing evaluation is now under way with a new graduate and undergraduate student cohort to determine the impact of these new modes of intervention, which appear to have resulted in rural villagers taking strides forward. For this work, Alonso was awarded the United Nations Public Service Award for Gender, Health, and Development. The model will soon be replicated in 11 countries in Africa and in some of the most isolated indigenous communities of Guatemala.

Green City, Freiburg, Germany: Sharing Green Technology With UW-Madison

Researchers in the United States are accustomed to approaching developing countries and offering help from what is often presumed to be a more highly evolved standpoint. This project in Germany constitutes a different model, a sort of reverse CBR with an advocacy component. It began in Freiburg where experts had answers to questions about sustainable economic development in the United States. In reciprocation for providing this assistance, the Freiburgers asked for help in determining how to market their green products and technology in the United States (Frey, 2011). They asked the following questions: What prices could the U.S. market bear? How much would it cost to import products to the United States or manufacture certain components of various products and systems there? What motivates the U.S. buyer to act sustainably?

Madison was in an enviable position for this collaboration, because Freiburg, the Solar Capital of the European Union, is its German sister city. Freiburg's city officials and representatives of the GreenCity Cluster (a business district in the city designed to promote the renewable energy economy) were interested in being of service. Their desire was to not only reach new U.S. Midwest markets but also inform Americans of the European Union's stance on energy (see www.greencity-cluster.de/?L=1). As one Freiburg energy consultant said, "It's not sustainable for you Americans to continue using up 25% of the world's resources!" (T. Dresel, personal communication, June 21, 2008).

Because of the long-standing exchange program (more than 50 years) between UW-Madison and the University of Freiburg, the many contacts developed over time prepared a fertile ground for this new study. UW-Madison undergraduates traveled to Freiburg in the summer of 2011 in a credit-bearing summer field course co-led by an academic staff instructor and a community partner from the Madison-Freiburg Sister City group with expertise in sustainable development. A faculty partner at the University of Freiburg gave an overview of the renewable energy landscape and the environmental economics of its Green City program in a month-long seminar. Interdisciplinary UW-Madison research teams interviewed staff at environmental firms, architects, landscape designers, transportation engineers, city planners, people with civil society organizations, and administrators of the Fraunhofer Institute (which studies energy policy and solar research), and they researched material components for their cost-effectiveness and availability. When the students returned to Madison in the fall, they presented their findings at city meetings, on campus, and to civic groups. One student used the trip as a springboard to successfully compete for a research scholarship, which enabled her to return to Freiburg two more times to collect data on green policies in local and regional government. She is now completing a thesis comparing the policy differences between the cities of Freiburg and Madison.

This initial knowledge transfer was followed by what could be called a tag-team approach to keeping the information exchange going for additional years. In the summer of 2012, a GreenFreiburg in Madison course was taught at UW-Madison with a guest lecturer from Freiburg who put German ideas into a U.S. context. Students wrote reports for independent study credit, and one student presented the research he had done on types of highly efficient building materials in Freiburg at a professional association. He then completed a related modeling study as part of an internship at a local engineering firm that fall and was subsequently hired after graduation.

The following year, faculty and students returned to Freiburg in a summer field course and created an even more robust exchange of technological skills ("know-how transfer" in the German vernacular). A new green energy/efficiency center is being planned in Madison with input from the previous research team's findings. Faculty and students will continue to provide an important ongoing research link between the two cities in the future, and a subsequent team will investigate well-defined questions from Madison architects, planners, and businesses, in hopes of finding answers to inform the Madison center's development and research use.

Ecuador: Community Water Research

Water quality is an issue of great magnitude around the globe. The environmental and public health impacts of water quality are often magnified in rural socioeconomically challenged areas such as the Jama county of coastal Ecuador where the population lacks access to information to effectively manage its resources. Six rivers originating in the coastal mountains descend toward the Pacific Ocean, flowing through tropical forest remnants, pastures, plantations, and villages. The inhabitants who rely on these water sources are affected by upstream activities and their own uninformed management practices. The high incidence of diarrheal disease is one public health impact of poor water quality (Woodward, n.d.).

Catherine Woodward's approach was a systematic, multilayered one. She spent considerable time in Ecuador, along with her partner, Joe Madden, a marine biologist and environmental consultant. They assessed the needs of deforested areas and ultimately founded the Ceiba Foundation for Tropical Conservation (www.ceiba.org) in 1997. After several years of doing research independently, and after speaking to the president of the village of Tabuga on water quality concerns, Woodward conceived of a Land Use, Water Quality and Human Health project in 2011. Realizing that "because of differences in local ecosystems, you have to get local knowledge" (C. Woodward, personal communication, December 13, 2012), she contacted the local government *presidentes* of each community who had credibility with the villagers. The first piece of indigenous wisdom she learned was that forest conservation protects the water because forests prevent runoff.

The initial participants in Woodward's project were UW-Madison undergraduates who came to Ecuador as water quality interns on a Wisconsin Idea Fellowship grant from the university's Morgridge Center for Public Service. They established monitoring sites on four rivers based on procedures learned through the Water Action Volunteers (WAV) program in Wisconsin (watermonitoring.uwex.edu/wav). They worked closely with Tabuga high school students and teachers to introduce a water-quality-monitoring curriculum and create instructional materials related to the project for community education programs. In the following years, independent study students participated in a multidisciplinary, long-term CBR project with local teachers, high school students, and landowners to collect and analyze data on land-use practices, water quality, and incidences of waterborne disease, and they piloted the use of simple sand-filtration systems for water sanitation. An additional new service-learning course now recruits students each summer from a wide variety of disciplines for hands-on work in a developing country where they expand their awareness of global challenges in natural resource management and human health.

Woodward asked local intellectual leaders whose findings would be trusted by the townspeople to join the student research teams, knowing that a lasting solution requires inhabitants to be actively involved. Community research team members attended an intensive three-day training, based on Spanish-version WAV manuals, that was regionally relevant for physical, biological, social, and ecological factors. Each team received $50 per data set, which was a strong motivator for participation. The teams have now established and mapped 19 monitoring points on four rivers and have sufficient equipment for four water-quality-testing kits. Plans are under way to develop a standard monitoring protocol for the rivers of coastal Ecuador. The success of these activities inspired Ceiba administrators to expand the project to include a water quality undergraduate service-learning course.

Once this process was running smoothly, Woodward brought in several new graduate student researchers. Because preparation is critical, students received a substantive orientation in the United States and a three-day, intensive, on-the-ground cultural training session in Ecuador using the asset-based community development model (Kretzmann & McKnight, 1996). During the summer of 2013, they completed their theses based on this project.

As the work expanded, Woodward created additional opportunities for students. Summer conservation internships have been developed and integrated into field research teams. She also applied for a new grant to support participants in building a database and publishing reports on water quality for local, regional, and national dissemination.

Science Shops in the United Kingdom, Norway, and Belgium: Framing a European-wide Research Question

The following case is a little different from the previous examples because no students were involved. However, it does describe issues that arise in formulating a cross-cultural study. It is included here because coordinators of any similar project involving students would have to be aware of these issues. Research in the past 20 years has made it clear that violence is a significant factor in maternal and prenatal morbidity (Andries et al., 2011). Pregnant women in the European Union are victims of domestic violence at the rate of 2% to 8% (Gazmararian et al., 1996; Taillieu & Brownridge, 2010). In the United Kingdom, Norway, and Belgium, three CSOs, each in its own way, battle violence in general, and violence against pregnant women more specifically. To better help these women, the CSOs need more knowledge about the phenomenon and possible ways to deal with it. Scientific knowledge available from international literature is mostly Anglo-Saxon and needs to be adapted to the larger European context. As of 2012, Europe hosts 35 million migrants (exclusive of asylum seekers and illegal immigrants) from outside the European Union. It is therefore essential to take these different ethnic backgrounds into account, as they likely have an impact on prevention of domestic violence during pregnancy.

Public Engagement with Research and Research Engagement with Society (PERARES) was a four-year project funded by the European Commission's 7th Framework Programme that enabled science shops in three countries to create CBR initiatives that helped these CSOs. The first step in this process was to map the different needs of the CSOs' key partners: Stavanger Shelter (Norway), Cambridge Women's Aid (UK), and Beweging tegen Geweld (Belgium). The second step was to frame one research question that led to a comparative study performed in all three partner countries.

In the preparation stage, members of the science shops and partner CSOs assembled information, exchanged experiences, and discussed needs related to domestic violence during pregnancy. This resulted in drafting a framework of existing needs. During this gathering process, it became apparent some clear distinguishing features could be tracked to the work of the CSOs. As two of the CSOs are women's housing shelters, needs were directly derived from victims and social workers' experiences; the third CSO is not a shelter and is focused on intermediaries. To frame a mutual research question, a transnational workshop with CSOs, experts, and science shops was organized in February 2011 in Brussels. During this workshop, the topic was reframed to domestic violence and pregnancy instead of domestic violence during pregnancy because violence can occur before a pregnancy is detected or confirmed or even after the mother has given birth.

Working in different countries unavoidably involves different circumstances, and thus the group encountered barriers to framing a research question. In the United Kingdom and Norway, student researchers are allowed to work directly with victims, but in Belgium this posed ethical issues. In the United Kingdom and Norway, it is common for pregnant women to go to a midwife for their prenatal care, and women are mostly cared for by gynecologists in Belgium. These international differences challenge the framing of one mutually accepted research question; any faculty, staff, or student research team from the United States attempting to engage in a transnational project would likely have to be attentive to such issues.

By sharing experiences, including the most urgent needs, and agreeing on barriers and definitions, the group managed to formulate a common goal: Explore how to overcome the barriers health-care providers face in identifying and responding to the needs of pregnant women experiencing domestic violence. An additional focus was on immigrant women in that group. The formulation of the goal was a very intense process, which led to a mutual understanding of the topic and the cultural and legislative differences of the partner countries and organizations.

Lessons Learned: Good Practices for Conducting CBR in a Foreign Country

Although these four cases present different types of projects on different continents, they hold clues for addressing the challenges global CBR can involve. Next we present some of the strategies researchers have found useful in working across cultures and time zones regarding six different issues: logistics, establishing trusting partnerships, cultural understanding, data collection, institutional review boards (IRBs), and ownership of the data.

Logistical Issues

Community-based researchers in another country, particularly if leading students, face issues similar to those of concern in any study abroad program. First and foremost, their students must be well prepared. They should also consider ahead of time such issues as risk, liability, and health; language; transportation; and financial challenges. Because much information is available on dealing with these issues elsewhere (e.g., de Schweinitz et al., 2009; Puffer, Pian, Sikkema, Ogwang-Odhiambo, & Broverman, 2013), we just touch on them here.[2]

Risk, liability, and health issues. These potential hazards are enough to make a university legal adviser's hair stand on end. For example, a global field course instructor shared in a debriefing that a student was bitten by an elephant in India (T. Petith, personal communication, March 12, 2013). Was the instructor negligent for not warning the student beforehand, "Don't put your hand in the elephant's mouth"? This may sound far fetched, but it is surprising how often such situations arise. Furthermore, health issues, including mental health, may emerge in students who have not traveled abroad and experience insecurity in unfamiliar settings where they are far from regular support systems. Insurance, good support networks in a country, and tested protocols are critical. The most efficient way to deal with these areas of concern is to delegate them to or consult with someone in the university's study abroad office, or whatever unit is responsible for general foreign study requirements.

Language differences. Even if one speaks the lingua franca, grammar or jargon can get in the way, especially when technical language is involved. Using even simple verbs in the wrong position in a sentence can create serious misunderstandings. Here is where the strength of the community partner relationship is worth its weight in gold. Hiring an interpreter, working with the partner on site, or holding regular meetings to smooth communication problems will keep projects on track.

Getting around. Whether or not one is familiar with the country, the added responsibility of leading students puts the burden on the university to make sure that scheduling does not leave students stranded somewhere because of missed trolleys or other transportation problems. It is important to have contingency plans; imagine the most likely scenarios, and maybe a few unlikely ones, and give the students, their home campuses, and everyone on the leadership team a complete list of cell phone numbers that can be used in the assigned country.

Financial challenges. Community partners often invest considerable time as coeducators when they participate in student/faculty projects. It is often appropriate to compensate partners or their organizations for this investment. However, the partners often cannot accept a check from a U.S. bank, and U.S. dollars are generally of no value. The researcher may also be in places where carrying large sums of local currency is not prudent, and credit cards are not accepted. PayPal, perhaps surprisingly, can be used as a fairly workable solution if a cybercafé is available. The barter system is one alternative to e-payment in rural areas where cash has little value. There can also be challenges with this approach, as illustrated by Alonso's street theater project whose actresses are

> paid with rice, beans, sugar, chickens, goats, and also with currency when it's appropriate. The problem is that very often when women get paid in currency, their husbands have the right to take that money from them since they are the "heads" of the household. They can use it as they please (many times they drink it all). So it is the women themselves who ask to get paid in goods instead of money because that way they make sure there is food on the table. (A. Alonso, personal communication, January 4, 2013)

Unexpected expenses can result from missed flights or trains that have to be rebooked, loss of personal items such as wallets or phones, and even corruption at customs. This occurred with a UW-Madison project in Ho Chi

Minh City where students traveling with a nonprofit reported that they had to bribe officials by giving them some of their equipment before the group could enter the country. Extra funds must be available so such occurrences do not derail the project.

Establishing Partnerships

The main challenge in designing and carrying out robust CBR in a global setting is relationship building, which takes time and energy. The first serious challenge to global work, then, is simply time, which can thwart the best intentions of U.S. academics who must also be attentive to publishing pressures, grant deadlines, and other pressures

Nonetheless, unless a long-standing relationship has already been established, one should never attempt to arrange a CBR project involving students without making a reconnaissance trip first, if for no other reason than to check out the potential pitfalls. Alonso felt she already knew her Kenyan literacy pen pal, but nonetheless she decided to spend 36 hours on planes, trains, buses, Jeeps, and finally a moped to reach the remote village of Lunga Lunga to deepen her understanding of the setting. When a research opportunity presented itself later, she had already done her due diligence in studying her environment and building trust among her hosts.

She had shared the bed of the children, whose mosquito net had holes in it. She was aware of the depth of their poverty and the gender and power structure of the village. Thus her advice to faculty wanting to create that same bond is "Go to the houses, dance, sing, live with the community. Become trusted, engage with community. Eat the same food, sleep in the same houses with the women" (A. Alonso, personal communication, December 15, 2012).

Using Cultural Understanding to Gain Authentic Data

Many resources are available about creating study abroad experiences or business partnerships across cultures. The importance of deriving authentic data is particular to CBR in a global setting. To accomplish this, understanding the host culture is essential. Even inside the United States, the case of the 1993 outbreak of hantavirus, a rare and lethal viral infection, on a Navajo reservation near Four Corners in the American southwest is illustrative. Since Navajos were the only ones dying, the press labeled it a contagious Navajo flu and banned Native Americans from stores and restaurants in the nearby town (Bales, 1994). Once the media had fanned the flames of the story, medical researchers descended in droves but made no headway trying to interview grieving tribal members who told the scientists whatever they thought they wanted to hear to get rid of the unwanted interlopers during their time of mourning. Unbeknownst to the Western medical community, the Navajo shamans or elders had predicted the epidemic based on the rainy season, when the rodent population rises. The mice were carriers of the hantavirus, not people. If researchers had only interviewed the shamans first (Stoecker & Tryon, 2009), lives could have been saved.

When cultural understanding is sufficient, the dialogue for defining a project can be productive and pleasant. Processes familiar to the host country should be used instead of imposing typical U.S. approaches, such as an efficiency model mind-set. If cultural norms require taking longer than a standard U.S. time frame, then that is what it will take. It is important to conduct the study in a manner that respects the values of the involved cultures. The cooperative project of domestic violence and pregnancy in three EU countries illustrates that the process is likely as important as the findings. In other words, taking great care with the process is what leads to authentic findings, which results in better research and better student learning.

Hazards beyond the readily apparent ones ought to be anticipated when collecting data globally, such as when asking for community input, negotiating an agreement for participatory research, and hiring community researchers for pay. Woodward learned a few hard lessons when hiring townspeople to do data collection in Ecuador. People who were not hired and were envious of the sudden rise in status of their fellow villagers caused friction. She held a few town meetings to assuage feelings of jealousy by supporting the new hires, explaining the reasons for her picks, and promising that as the program gained funding more positions could become available.

An often overlooked way to seek help in data gathering is to ask local universities to work in partnership with you; they may already have on-the-ground knowledge and data and could be offended if not at least given a courtesy call. Even if offense is not an issue, reaching out can avoid reinventing the wheel and will likely move the research closer to results and action faster by taking advantage of community wisdom and finding out what knowledge already exists.

IRBs in Other Countries

As complex as submitting IRB protocols for research in the United States is, it can get even more complicated in global research. In some cases, researchers are asked to apply for an IRB protocol in the United States and in the country where data will be collected. Each country may have its own protocols as well as forms of submittal. The European Union has ethics committees governed by law that are very similar to IRBs but with slightly different language and focus. The overall objective is to ethically evaluate research projects that are carried out on living beings and to legally and socially protect individuals from the consequences of (clinical) research. For EU collaboration projects, an Ethical Issues form must also be submitted. Also, private (not organized by public law) ethics committees, established by organizations to support their own ethical standards and gaining in popularity, offer services to research institutions, individual researchers, CSOs, or patient groups being studied. An ethics committee on energy supply security was consulted during the nuclear disaster in Fukushima, Japan, concerning the risks and social implications of nuclear power and other energy forms.

Who Owns the Data?

Faculty members and academic staff who work with coinvestigators in the United States have guidance in negotiating issues of ownership and credit. However, when collaborating across borders, the laws might be different. For example, The European Union's governing body called Intellectual Property Rights guides such decisions. According to this body, findings from research funded with public money are public. This is important for the European-funded Science Shop projects because Science Shops can retain their policy of open access to their research results. It is prudent to check national rules first, find a mutual understanding, and then come to clear agreements and contracts.

Rewards

While undertaking CBR and global travel at the same time can seem quite daunting, the rewards can be well worth the risks and the extra planning required. Groundbreaking research is being conducted all over the world by many, such as Alonso and Woodward, and these partnerships can provide an extremely robust and rich experience for campuses and their global community partners. Often, partners are able to work on phases of development previously undreamed of, such as the water-quality research in Ecuador that had no resources until Woodward's team approached the village leaders. In addition, faculty and staff often forge lifelong bonds with community partners in other countries (A. Alonso, personal communication, December 15, 2012).

American society stands to benefit as well, as illustrated in the example of the Freiburg exchange with Madison on sustainability and the more traditional model of working with developing nations. A mindful community-based approach to research in other countries can create newfound respect for what might previously have been negative associations about charitable attitudes of U.S. researchers. It can also create more authentic and deeper student learning (Baldwin, Buchanan, & Rudisill, 2007; Cashman & Seifer, 2008).

Good frameworks for practice, including strong backup support systems and well-built, long-term relationships, help move CBR away from an activity that would have an isolated impact to a more holistic, ongoing alignment of results across national boundaries. As this is accomplished, globally engaged research can support faculty scholarship and student learning as well as capacity building across the world.

Notes

1. The rise of what is being called *world English* is a controversial topic that is outside the scope of this chapter but bears further study in the context of communicating with colleagues in countries where English is not the native language (Pennycook, 2014). Suffice it to say that agreeing explicitly on terminology can help avoid potential misinterpretations about project content.

2. See also researchadministration.yale.edu/ora-services/conducting-research-internationally and www.lang.nagoya-u.ac.jp/proj/genbunronshu/31-1/toraiwa.pdf

References

Andries, C., Buckley, N., De Bal, I., Roelens, K., Studsrød, I., Temmerman, M., . . . Willumsen, E. (2011). Domestic violence and pregnancy: The challenge of framing a European-wide research question. *Living Knowledge, 9*(1), 11–12.

Baldwin, S. C., Buchanan, A. M., & Rudisill, M. E. (2007). What teacher candidates learned about diversity, social justice, and themselves from service-learning experiences. *Journal of Teacher Education, 58*(4), 315–327.

Bales, F. (1994). Hantavirus and the media: Double jeopardy for Native Americans. *American Indian Culture and Research Journal, 18*(3), 251–263.

Battistoni, R. M. (2002). *Civic engagement across the curriculum: A resource book for service-learning faculty in all disciplines.* Boston, MA: Campus Compact.

Cashman, S. B., & Seifer, S. D. (2008). Service-learning: An integral part of undergraduate public health. *American Journal of Preventive Medicine, 35*(3), 273–278.

Checkoway, B. (2001). Renewing the civic mission of the American research university. *Journal of Higher Education, 72*(2), 125–147.

Cruz, N. I., & Giles, D. E. (2000). Where's the community in service-learning research. *Michigan Journal of Community Service Learning, 7*(1), 28–34.

de Schweinitz, P., Ansong, D., Manortey, S., Amuasi, J., Boakye, I., Crookston, B. T., & Alder, S. (2009). Evaluating international collaboration: Differential perceptions of partnership in a CBPR project in Ghana. *Journal of Empirical Research on Human Research Ethics: An International Journal, 4*(4), 53–67.

Frey, W. (2011). *Green city Freiburg, Herder Verlag GmbH.* Retrieved from www.freyarchitekten.com/en/sustainability/sustainability.html#ecologic

Gazmararian, J. A., Lazorick, S., Spitz, A. M., Ballard, T. J., Saltzman, L. E., & Marks, J. S. (1996). Prevalence of violence against pregnant women. *Journal of the American Medical Association, 275*(24), 1915–1920.

Global Alliance on Community Engaged Research. (2015). *Global Alliance on Community Engaged Research*. Retrieved from communityresearchcanada.ca/?action =alliance

Hagen, S. (2008). From tech transfer to knowledge exchange: European universities in the marketplace. In L. E. Engwall & D. Weaire (Eds.), *The university in the market* (pp. 103–117). London, UK: Portland Press.

Jacoby, B. (2009). *Civic engagement in higher education: Concepts and practices*. San Francisco, CA: Jossey-Bass.

Kretzmann, J., & McKnight, J. P. (1996). Assets-based community development. *National Civic Review, 85*(4), 23–29.

Langman, L. (2005). From virtual public spheres to global justice: A critical theory of internetworked social movements. *Sociological Theory, 23*(1), 42–74.

Lemish, P. (2013, April). *Knowledge mobilization via two Canadian examples: York's knowledge mobilisation unit and Guelph's The Research Shop—Institute of Engaged Community Scholarship*. Presentation at the semiannual meeting of the Midwest Knowledge Mobilization Network, Indianapolis, IN.

Lewin, R. (Ed.). (2009). *The handbook of practice and research in study abroad: Higher education and the quest for global citizenship*. London, UK: Routledge.

Mulder, H. A. J., & de Bok, C. F. M. (2006). Science Shops as university-community interfaces: An interactive approach in science communication. In D. Cheng, J. Metcalfe, & B. Schiele (Eds.), *At the human scale: International practices in science communication* (pp. 285–304). Beijing, China: Science Press.

Mulder, H. A., Der Heyde, T. A., Goffer, R., & Teodosiu, C. (2001). Success and failure in starting Science Shops (SCIPAS Report 2). Retrieved from www.living knowledge.org/livingknowledge/wp-content/uploads/2012/02/wp2-so.pdf

Pennycook, A. (2014). *The cultural politics of English as an international language*. New York, NY: Routledge.

Porter, M., & Monard, K. (2001). "Ayni" in the global village: Building relationships of reciprocity through international service-learning. *Michigan Journal of Community Service Learning, 8*(1), 5–17.

Puffer, E. S., Pian, J., Sikkema, K. J., Ogwang-Odhiambo, R. A., & Broverman, S. A. (2013). Developing a family-based HIV prevention intervention in rural Kenya: Challenges in conducting community-based participatory research. *Journal of Empirical Research on Human Research Ethics: An International Journal, 8*(2), 119–128.

Sclove, D. (1995). *Democracy and technology*. New York, NY: The Guilford Press.

Sclove, R., Scammell, M., Holland, B., & Alimohamed, F. (1998). *Community-based research in the United States: An introductory reconnaissance, including twelve organizational case studies and comparison with the Dutch science shops and the mainstream American research system*. Los Angeles, LA: Loka Institute.

Smith, J. (2002). Bridging global divides? Strategic framing and solidarity in transnational social movement organizations. *International Sociology, 17*(4), 505–528.

Smith, J. G., Chatfield, C., & Pagnucco, R. (Eds.). (1997). *Transnational social movements and global politics: Solidarity beyond the state.* Syracuse, NY: Syracuse University Press.

Stachowski, L. L., & Mahan, J. M. (1998). Cross-cultural field placements: Student teachers learning from schools and communities. *Theory Into Practice, 37*(2), 155–162.

Stoecker, R. (2012). *Research methods for community change: A project-based approach.* Thousand Oaks, CA: Sage.

Stoecker, R., Beckman, M., & Min, B. H. (2010). Evaluating the community impact of higher education civic engagement. In H. E. Fitzgerald, D. L. Zimmerman, C. Burack, & S. Seifer (Eds.), *Handbook of engaged scholarship: The contemporary landscape* (2nd ed., pp. 177–196). East Lansing: Michigan State University Press.

Stoecker, R., & Tryon, E. (2009). *The unheard voices: Community organizations and service learning.* Philadelphia, PA: Temple University Press.

Strand, K., Marullo, S., Cutforth, N., Stoecker, R., & Donohue, P. (2003). Principles of best practice for community-based research. *Michigan Journal of Community Service Learning, 9*(3), 5–15.

Taillieu, T. L., & Brownridge, D. A. (2010). Violence against pregnant women: Prevalence, patterns, risk factors, theories, and directions for future research. *Aggression and Violent Behavior, 15*(1), 14–35.

Tryon, E., Hood, C., & Taalbi, M. (2013). *Examining institutional frameworks for global service learning and community-based research.* Retrieved from www.nafsa .org/uploadedFiles/Chez_NAFSA/Find_Resources/Supporting_Education_ Abroad/Examining-Institutional-Framework.pdf

Volet, S. (2003) *Challenges of internationalisation: Enhancing intercultural competence and skills for critical reflection on the situated and non-neutral nature of knowledge.* In 2003 Biennial Language and Academic Skills in Higher Education Conference, 24–25 November 2003, Student Learning Centre, Flinders University, Adelaide pp. 1–10.

Wachelder, J. (2003). Democratizing science: Various routes and visions of Dutch Science Shops. *Science, Technology, & Human Values, 28*(2), 244–273.

Woodward, C. (n.d.). *Land use, water quality and human health in rural coastal Ecuador.* Unpublished manuscript.

12

DEEPENING LEVELS OF ENGAGEMENT

What Works, What Doesn't, and the Important Role of a Community-Based Research Center

Judith Owens-Manley

How should colleges and universities respond to the problems affecting the towns and cities around them? These institutions are key community assets equipped to contribute to their local neighborhoods in a myriad of ways (Maurrasse, 2001; Weinberg, 2003), and there is currently much exploration of this question in higher education literature.

Community-based research (CBR), which focuses on answering questions posed by communities, is an approach schools can use to help their communities in important ways. Strand, Marullo, Cutforth, Stoecker, and Donohue (2003) have outlined three generally accepted principles to guide CBR. In essence, they suggest that CBR should be collaborative across campus and community, value multiple sources of expertise and methods, and have the ultimate goal of fostering social justice. This chapter aims to show that the more fully these elements define a CBR endeavor, the deeper the engagement, and the deeper the engagement, the more likely the project will be associated with helpful community change.

To assist a faculty member or academic staff to design and carry out effective CBR, this chapter describes four CBR projects and explores the ways each fulfills the three definitional elements. The discussion also highlights some of the roles that faculty or academic staff in community engagement centers can play in ensuring the success of CBR.

The Context

The CBR projects discussed here are affiliated with Hamilton College, a small liberal arts college in upstate New York where I was the sole person responsible for directing and managing CBR projects. Hamilton College has an enrollment of about 1,800 students on an idyllic, traditional, hilltop-situated campus. Its most immediate neighbor down the hill is the relatively well-heeled village of Clinton, population 1,942. The nearby city of Utica, population 62,235 (U.S. Census Bureau, 2010b), is much less prosperous. Utica is an old, postindustrial city with the decline in population and economic base that is typical in the northeast. It has become known as the town that "loves refugees" (Wilkinson, 2005, p. 9) because the Mohawk Valley Resource Center for Refugees is responsible for resettling more than 15,000 refugees in the area since 1979 (see www.mvrcr.org/about).

Although the college's senior administrators perceive their town-gown relationship with the village of Clinton as important, faculty who are interested in community-based teaching and learning typically want their students engaged with community members and community organizations in the city of Utica, where the needs are far greater and the population much more ethnically diverse. In Utica 76% of children in the Utica City School District K–12 are eligible for free or reduced price lunches (New York State District Report Card, 2012b), compared to 13% of youths in Clinton (New York State District Report Card, 2012a). Nearly 95% of the population of Clinton described itself as "White only" in the 2010 census (94.1%), compared to 69% in Utica (U.S. Census Bureau, 2010a, 2010b). In Utica city schools, 14% of the students are limited in English proficiency compared to 1% in Clinton (U.S. Census Bureau, 2010a, 2010b). The population of the city of Utica, which includes African Americans and Latinos, also has a significant number of refugees from the former Yugoslavia, Ukraine, Southeast Asia, and several African countries. Burmese refugees from refugee camps in Thailand and the Bhutanese from refugee camps in Nepal are among the latest arrivals.

In 1999 the chief administrator of Oneida County urged Hamilton College to form a partnership with a group of community funders to hire me as an associate director in the Arthur Levitt Public Policy Center. The group envisioned my role as enhancing the partnership between college and community and coordinating projects that produced CBR helpful to municipal, educational, and nonprofit organizations in the county. Initially I worked with a coalition of organizational executives called the Funders Council to produce CBR.

Three years into the position, I was entirely funded by the college, and the community leaders functioned more as an advisory group. By that time, the Funders Council could not agree on a consistent and aligned vision, the county leadership had changed in an election year, and local priorities had changed. They could not agree on a direction for joint funding of projects. In comparison to that changing environment, Hamilton was continuing its service-learning and CBR work funded by a series of small grants. We were sending students into the community to work with refugees and immigrants, to help with after-school programs, and to assist in completing tax returns with low-income families.

When the college took full control of the position, I continued to teach a seminar in program evaluation in Hamilton's government department and to guide a community-based learning program I had developed in collaboration with other faculty and students. The following four projects, drawn from the departments of public policy, computer science, women's studies, and government, were supported through my position.

Four CBR Projects

As mentioned earlier, Strand and colleagues (2003) offer a definition of *CBR* composed of the following central elements that practitioners can use to more effectively fulfill its potential:

- CBR is a collaborative enterprise between academic researchers (professors and students) and community members.
- CBR projects validate multiple sources of knowledge and promote multiple methods of discovery and dissemination of the knowledge produced.
- CBR embraces social action and social change for the purpose of achieving social justice, goals that may differ considerably from those of traditional research.

These three principles may also be thought of as levels of engagement. For instance, most of the community-based research projects undertaken by campuses and communities can be characterized as collaborative enterprises, suggesting that they fulfill the first element of the definition, although the nature of the partnership may differ across projects in quality and degree. Fewer project administrators, however, may take the necessary steps to validate and exchange knowledge with community members, expand methods of discovery beyond those traditionally used, and take care to disseminate the results of the project in a user-friendly and mutually agreed-upon manner. Even fewer reach what many consider to be the highest level of engagement: action to achieve social justice. When all three of Strand and colleagues' (2003) features are evident, the likelihood of reaching the deepest level of engagement is greater.

For each of these projects, I attempt to show which levels were attained and how this was accomplished. Individual faculty members developed the first two projects. One had no involvement with the policy center, and the other had the center's support. As the associate director of the public policy center and director of the CBR program in the center, I created and managed the remaining two projects, emphasizing the valuable role faculty or academic staff can play through a similar center.

Initial Level of Engagement

Short-term, unrelated projects in one course. In this first example, a public policy professor regularly solicited projects with real-life policy questions each year from government and nonprofit agencies at the state and local levels. His upper-level students, working individually or in pairs, selected a project and then worked as partners with the corresponding community organization. They usually completed the research over one, or in the case of a thesis, two semesters. Although the extent of community engagement varied considerably, each student generated a report as a final paper. Students were further encouraged but not required to make a final presentation to the partner.

Is this a collaborative enterprise between academic researchers (professors and students) and community members? Although it is generally accepted that the research question should arise from the community, in practice, an institution's CBR director, faculty, or students may also initiate a project or at least a relationship with a community organization that later results in a research request from the partner (Maguire, 1987; Reason, 1994; Stoecker, 2003). This model's chief strength, however, is that the question of interest truly did originate entirely from the community partner.

Beyond that, though, student and community partner involvement was inconsistent. Students were sometimes disappointed with the limited attention the agency devoted to the project. Community partners may also have had elevated expectations of what the undergraduate students could provide. This lack of ongoing interaction led to some dissatisfaction on the part of students and community partners. The faculty member also had limited interaction with the community because this person's main activity was to solicit the projects and oversee and provide direction for the students' work.

Do the CBR projects validate multiple sources of knowledge, promote multiple methods of discovery, and encourage dissemination of the knowledge produced? The main weakness in this model is the lack of depth in the relationships. This model is predicated on the proposition that the student functions as the expert and discovers knowledge that is then given to the community partner. The faculty member provides a great deal of excellent feedback to individual students to assist with the structure of the projects; however, he or she does not explicitly teach them the methodology of community-based research. The students may use various methods of research they have learned, but they are not taught to respect and incorporate the knowledge of community partners nor how to collaborate. Similarly, community engagement tends to be limited in writing about the product or disseminating it.

A student report to United Way provides an example of a difficulty that can arise when there is so little interaction between the campus and community. A student presentation for the United Way was one of the first products from this class. Agency directors complained that the student had used names and features of clients in his research report in a way that made them identifiable to the general community. This of course violated traditional research guidelines as well, but the demands of collaboration in community-based research accentuated the violation, and the members of the community complained that the professor overseeing the course did not protect them and their clients from the violation. The student worked independently and only contacted community agencies for access to data. He presented his findings only after a report had been written, accepted by his professor, and bound and printed for dissemination to community organizations.

Is there a goal of social action and social change for the purpose of achieving social justice? These unrelated, short-term projects were not intended to create ongoing results in the community, and they were not focused on social action or social justice issues. When the semester was over, the projects came to an end, and the cycle of soliciting projects by the faculty member began again with no continuity from the efforts of the previous semester.

Ongoing projects in one course. This second example also originated with a Hamilton faculty member, a computer science professor, who was the recipient of a multiyear grant that required forming a partnership with the public school system. The professor designed a computer science course for undergraduate nonmajors, which entailed multiple ongoing semester projects. I was the liaison and relationship builder with neighboring public schools where the course was enthusiastically embraced by administrators and teachers.

One project from this course focused on public school student safety in the use of computers. Hamilton students in the computer science course were taught the basics of computer security and personal safety in the first few weeks of the class. They were then assigned in groups to specific ninth grade classrooms in two districts that they visited to introduce themselves and the project. They left a pretest to be administered to the high school students to measure the students' beliefs and behaviors relevant to computer safety. The completed pretests were collected and responses entered into a database. Several weeks later, Hamilton students returned to the ninth grade classrooms after creating and practicing a lesson on computer safety and security that they presented to the class. Perhaps a week following the lesson, the high school students completed a posttest, and the results were also entered into a database.

Is this a collaborative enterprise between academic researchers (professors and students) and community members? School personnel were dealing with a number of issues related to safety and security. They worried about students' use of social media and the Internet in general because students did not appreciate implications to their personal safety or possible legal consequences (M. Vetros, personal communication, September 15, 2008). Although the project was intended to address this issue of concern for the school, it was designed at the college and presented as a finished product to the schools. After the initial meeting with the school personnel and students, which the faculty member did not attend because of time constraints, most of the contact with the schools was via e-mail or telephone with me as the liaison. Also, collaborative decision making and planning was limited.

Did the project validate multiple sources of knowledge and promote multiple methods of discovery and dissemination of the knowledge produced? An intention of this project was to produce a report for the schools using the data from the testing. From the start, it did not aim to draw on the expertise of community partners. Furthermore, the data had not been analyzed 18 months into the project. If and when a report was generated, school administrators were legitimately concerned that it would only fulfill the needs of the faculty member's grant and not be useful to the schools. The participatory relationships were few, and the participation was minimal.

Was there a goal of social action and social change for the purpose of achieving social justice? Although the impetus for this project was the requirement for a faculty member's grant, there was an articulated need on the part of the schools, and the school administration was in support of it. Furthermore, the high school students, college students, faculty member, and school administrators expressed informally a high level of satisfaction with the project. The public school students seemed to have enjoyed the lesson on computer safety presented by the college students. Although the project appeared to be popular, based in part on the expectation that the data would be analyzed and useful information provided to the schools, it was not clear when it would be finished. The evidence was not convincing that the project accomplished much without the data analysis and a long-term outcome. Without a larger commitment to community engagement and participatory principles, the project's potential for long-term outcomes and impact is limited. The faculty member also admitted that greater communication and collaboration would have improved the project, but he felt he did not have the additional time for these two elements.

Lessons Learned

These two projects are not without merit, yet they did not fulfill CBR's potential to help achieve impact as described throughout this book. Although the questions for investigation either arose from or were clearly of value to the community partner, there was no depth to the partnership or relationship, and trust did not build over time. There were no extended opportunities for the community partner to draw on the expertise of the campus partner. The research did provide immediate information that was used in obvious ways by the partners, but in both cases, the relationship was conceptualized using a short-term perspective. These efforts only attained the first level of engagement in Strand and colleagues' (2003) model.

Deeper Levels of Engagement

Ongoing project linked to a variety of courses. The Status of Women Project originated with a community group, the Women's Fund of Herkimer and Oneida Counties, which requested a status of women study for the region. Women's fund organizations across the country had completed similar projects, and members of the local organization were interested in developing measures on the status of women in this region. Through a series of meetings that included a luncheon for women faculty and Women's Fund members at the college, members of both groups and I planned a multiyear project for which our small campus was responsible. Each year the research questions were mutually developed and explored either through academic courses or hiring student workers to complete pieces of the project in the public policy center.

Two faculty members, one from the government department and one from women's studies, agreed to include CBR assignments in the Politics of Gender course and a seminar on women and aging. Neither of the courses was designed as a CBR course in its entirety; the research for the project was just one assignment students were asked to complete. In the first year of using CBR in the course, students interviewed representatives from agencies that provide services to women, which were at least purported to support women's self-sufficiency. These interviews complemented course readings relative to domestic violence, single parents, displaced homemakers, refugee women, and women with physical or mental health limitations.

The plan for a second stage of the project, interviewing women who were recipients of those agency services, floundered because the faculty member took a sabbatical leave. Members of the Women's Fund and I worked together to find a sociology professor at another local university who was enthusiastic about having her students participate through a research methods course, which furthered our work in those next years. In the last stage of the project, a seminar on women and aging required students to interview older women caregivers to generate information about their needs, services they accessed, and gaps that the Women's Fund could advocate for or fund.

Each year I looked for courses that could link to the work requested by the Women's Fund but was not always successful in matching the request with an academic course, especially because some courses were not offered every semester or even every year. In semesters without students in an active course working with the project, we hired students to do background research; gather data on local and statewide conditions; and, in one case, create a literature review on caregiving.

Overall, I acted as the project director and generated a report that combined and edited the individual student papers. We produced a general status of women report in 2003, and a second report in 2005–2006 on women of working age with limited economic opportunities. The third report in 2008–2009 focused on older women caregivers who provided support for someone in their home, usually a spouse or a parent (for the three reports, see www.womensfundhoc.org/resources.php).

Was it a collaborative enterprise between academic researchers (professors and students) and community members? I met regularly throughout the year with Women's Fund representatives, members of other community organizations that served women in the project, and faculty from another university. The chair of the Status of Women Committee, a committee of The Women's Fund, worked with the director to edit reports, and the direction for each year was mutually determined by the committee members' questions and our capacity to respond with students and faculty. Faculty who worked on the project attended the Women's Fund Annual Luncheon each year and helped disseminate the project results (output) to more than 200 community members. This project largely met the criteria for collaboration, although women served by the project were not directly involved. Flexibility and open communication on both sides enabled creative development of the projects each semester and the identification of available resources. Women's Fund members and I agreed that this model worked very well.

Did the CBR projects validate multiple sources of knowledge, promote multiple methods of discovery, and encourage dissemination of the knowledge produced? The chair of the committee worked side by side with faculty members and me, bringing her own experience and that of other Women's Fund members to the project and to any decisions about and preparation for disseminating the findings each year. This was a sound example of working together and promoting multiple methods of discovery.

Was there is a goal of social action and social change for the purpose of achieving social justice? The courses taught as a part of this project included a focus on social action or social justice. The Women's Fund board of directors used each report in deliberations to determine advocacy positions and actions (outcome). Findings also informed decisions on which projects to fund (outcome), as they typically made four or five awards of $2,500 to $5,000 each year. The community partner used the status of women reports to aid their strategic use of resources in the community (S. Eghigian, personal communication, April 16, 2009).

Long-term project in a regularly offered CBR course. HOPE VI is a federally funded housing initiative to replace older and dilapidated public housing with newer housing. It also provides services that improve the lives and increase the self-sufficiency of public housing residents. This project with the Utica Municipal Housing Authority aimed to tear down the Washington Courts housing project, which was built in 1949; move the residents; and build scattered-site housing for single and multifamily homes in a completely different neighborhood in the city.

The HOPE VI Project represented Hamilton's most extensive involvement with any CBR endeavor. A community agency, three neighborhoods, and a group of clients were all involved. Because of the relationship I had with community organizations, the college also received a paid contract to complete the project's program evaluation over a five-year time span.

I planned the overall design for the evaluation, taught a yearly program evaluation course in which students undertook the evaluation, hired and mentored student workers to supplement the research when students in my class were not able to carry it out, and generated a report each year from the student research. Each year the policy center worked with the Utica Municipal Housing Authority to set the research agenda and resolve difficulties with aligning an academic schedule, the community partner schedule, and federal Housing and Urban Development regulations. In Year 1, the students and

I interviewed displaced residents and reported their level of satisfaction and gaps in services. During Year 2, we interviewed residents in their new housing. Students used geographic information system mapping to visually graph the characteristics of the old and new neighborhoods in Year 3, conducted key informant focus groups in Year 4, and updated the quantitative data and reinterviewed original residents in Year 5.

Students interned over five summers to complete pieces of the project, including one student who had a double major in public policy and art; she created a photo essay of the displaced individuals and families.

Was it a collaborative enterprise between academic researchers (professors and students) and community members? Key members of the community informed the research and its direction, and Hamilton was a regular and collaborative partner with the staff of the Utica Municipal Housing Authority. The housing residents, however, were subjects of the research rather than participants in our planning. In an ideal project, the research community partners actually consist of "people whose lives are directly affected by the issues at hand" as well as community organizations that interact with them, and "outsider organizations" such as our institutions (Stoecker & Beckman, 2010, p. 3). In this case, we interacted with the community agency and its staff, but the clients were a separate stakeholder group with different needs, opinions, and purposes that needed to be considered. Nonetheless, this project went a long way toward fulfilling the ideal of collaboration.

Did the CBR projects validate multiple sources of knowledge, promote multiple methods of discovery, and encourage dissemination of the knowledge produced? The project made a good attempt to value the knowledge of the housing authority staff and its residents. In addition, the people affected by the HOPE VI intervention were empowered by our research in two important ways. First, their stories and the history of their neighborhood were recorded (see www.hamilton.edu/cache for video clips and history). One student's work resulted in a permanent exhibit of 16 portraits (output) that were professionally framed and paired with an excerpt of each person's life composed by a community member and project consultant. We displayed the photo essay exhibit at a reception honoring residents and their guests at the public library (outcome), and in the final year of the project, each person who was interviewed was given a framed copy of his or her portrait. A luncheon, planned as a celebration and remembrance, was held for all of the original residents at the end of the project. We provided transportation and produced a video from resident interviews. Each resident received a DVD of the video, which included key figures in the community as they recalled their experiences at Washington Courts.

Was there a goal of social action and social change for the purpose of achieving social justice? The project probably does not meet the gold standard for the displaced residents, who lost a way of life and the neighborhood they valued. Most of them remained poor because the population left in the housing complex by the time HOPE VI forced the move was largely elderly or disabled. Most were able to move to other public housing, but the social networks they counted on were disrupted. Some who expressed satisfaction in the first year were dissatisfied with three factors in Year 5: their neighbors, the quality of the different public housing, and unfulfilled promises made to them for better housing and better lives. Although this CBR project ensured that residents' voices were heard and their words were respected through recording and remembering their history, the community organization's positive outcome did not achieve the broader goals of a social change project. Stoecker (2003) recommends that academics doing work with the community should not think about the right way to do the research project but instead think of CBR as "a social change project of which the research is only one piece" (p. 102). Additionally, it is yet to be determined whether the project has had an impact on future housing policy decisions.

Lessons Learned

In both of these projects, more elements of Strand and colleagues' (2003) explanation of CBR were met. Both projects substantially involved the community partners in planning, decision making, and carrying out the activities required by the project; community partners were likewise instrumental in the dissemination of results. The results of the research also contributed to next steps for the organizations involved, and thus led to outcomes, if not toward a long-term impact. The substantial role I played as a director of the CBR program in ensuring the definitional elements were in place was significant in these cases.

Conclusions

This chapter focuses on three defining principles of CBR. However, it is also important to note a few additional requirements the faculty member should fulfill if CBR is to develop its potential for influencing impact.

Students must be well prepared for CBR assignments. Strand and colleagues (2003) suggest students need substantive knowledge about the research problem, familiarity with and sensitivity to the community, an understanding of CBR, and good basic research skills. Although covering this instructional content presents its own challenges in the course of a semester's time frame, faculty can provide students with a foundation for their work (Weinberg, 2003). This also requires the faculty member to understand the principles of CBR.

Just as in well-done service-learning, it is important for students to have opportunities for reflection on what they are experiencing in the community. Students engaged in the Women's Fund and HOPE VI projects found themselves altered by the experiences, which is often the case, as those who have been engaged with CBR will attest. Some students were confronted with the loneliness and social isolation of the elderly caregivers when they were asked to "please come back and visit." Other students visiting displaced residents in their new apartments were sometimes overwhelmed by the levels of poverty they had never seen before and the serious health issues of the people they interviewed. How do we mesh what students need to confront, reflect on, and learn about in their academic disciplines with their experiences as members of a larger community with social issues that affect real people? In addition to assisting students to make meaning of their experiences through reflection, ethical considerations and tensions need to be negotiated through courses and projects that are different from our traditional academic work.

Nonetheless, including community-based research in an academic course can be a powerful way to produce future leaders and actively engage young adults as citizens, an espoused goal of many institutions of higher education today. Willis, Peresie, Waldref, and Stockmann (2003) suggest that community-engaged experiences provide students with

- practical, real-life experience;
- enrichment of traditional academic course work;
- sense of empowerment;
- greater understanding of social problems; and
- integration of academics and service.

In addition to these benefits, students also acquire valuable skills while learning to work in teams and community groups. For example, they are

> managing myriad tasks, identifying resources, asking for and providing assistance, giving and receiving constructive criticism, listening to conflicting points of view, recognizing differing strengths and weaknesses, resolving disagreements, keeping track of information, speaking up when it matters, and otherwise merging abilities and efforts toward the accomplishment of a common goal. (Strand et al., 2003, p. 135)

Finally, it is important to highlight the critical role of a center whose mission is to assist with community-based educational efforts. Stoecker and Beckman (2010) point out that our commitment to achieving impacts beyond token participation with communities requires real work that "is an ongoing, coordinated, year-round, long-term team effort" (p. 8). Projects with significant community collaboration are time and relationship intensive but critical for trust and collaboration. The role of a CBR center in coordinating that ongoing, long-term effort is pivotal. The academic staff and faculty of such centers are employed to put in the time it takes to develop and nurture ongoing relationships in the community. Academic courses can be organized around long-term projects these centers have helped develop, and continuity can be provided for a project. This enables the incorporation of rotating new groups of students and faculty over several semesters so that deeper levels of engagement can occur than those fostered through the single and sporadic courses individual faculty may attempt. Work initiated under this fuller commitment of a college center differs substantially from one-shot efforts that ask the community to conform to faculty needs and student objectives rather than the other way around.

When colleges have a center that is focused on community engagement, the long-term relationships with community partners the center fosters can serve students in ways that go beyond individual course work, including offering them year-round work as research assistants. Students can also work as research assistants for specific project needs through cocurricular service or independent research projects. They can likewise hold issue forums with a social action or social justice focus and empower community networks that support the work being done while engaging constituencies who are not yet at the table.

There are inherent difficulties in forming and maintaining community CBR partnerships that are committed to outcomes for student learning and for the reciprocity of community benefit. When colleges or universities take this higher road for working with community partners, life can get complicated, but it ultimately leads to more meaningful experiences for students, faculty, and community members. Indeed, "through community partnerships, institutions of higher education may gain more than they actually give" (Maurrasse, 2001. p. 182).

The following are general recommendations for faculty members to reach deep levels of community-based research.

1. Learn how to think about, design, and implement community-based research as distinct from traditional research.
2. Provide students with fundamental understanding of the principles and practices of CBR.
3. Make good use of the community-based education center and its academic faculty and staff.

These recommendations can help ensure that community-based research is a powerful tool and resource for the long-term investment most likely to affect students, the academy, and ultimately the community.

References

Maguire, P. (1987). *Doing participatory research: A feminist approach.* Amherst: University of Massachusetts, Center for International Education.

Maurrasse, D. J. (2001). *Beyond the campus: How colleges and universities form partnerships with their communities.* New York, NY: Routledge.

New York State District Report Card. (2012a). *Accountability and overview report 2010–11. Clinton Central School District.* Retrieved from reportcards.nysed.gov/files/2010-11/AOR-2011-411101060000.pdf

New York State District Report Card. (2012b). *Accountability and overview report 2010–11. Utica City School District.* Retrieved from reportcards.nysed.gov/files/2010-11/AOR-2011-412300010000.pdf

Reason, P. (1994). Three approaches to participative inquiry. In N. K. Denzin & Y. S. Lincoln (Eds.), *Handbook of qualitative research* (pp. 324–339). Thousand Oaks, CA: Sage.

Stoecker, R. (2003). Are academics irrelevant? In Minkler, M., Wallerstein, N. (Eds.) *Community-based participatory research for health* (pp. 98–112). San Francisco, CA: Jossey-Bass.

Stoecker, R., & Beckman, M. (2010). *Making higher education civic engagement matter in the community.* Retrieved from www.compact.org/news/making-higher-education-civic-engagement-matter-in-the-community/9748

Strand, K., Marullo, S., Cutforth, N., Stoecker, R., & Donohue, P. (2003). *Community-based research and higher education: Principles and practices.* San Francisco, CA: Jossey-Bass.

U.S. Census Bureau. (2010a). *Census summary file 1; Table QT-P3, Race and Hispanic or Latino, Clinton, NY.* Retrieved from http://factfinder.census.gov/faces/tableservices/jsf/pages/productview.xhtml?src=CF

U.S. Census Bureau. (2010b). *Census summary file 1; Table QT-P3, Race and Hispanic or Latino, Utica, NY.* Retrieved from http://factfinder.census.gov/faces/tableservices/jsf/pages/productview.xhtml?src=CF.

Weinberg, A. S. (2003). Negotiating community-based research: A case study of the "Life's work" project. *Michigan Journal of Service Learning, 9*(3), 26–35.

Wilkinson, R. (2005, April). A marriage made in heaven. *Refugees Magazine,* 4–25.

Willis, J., Peresie, J., Waldref, V., & Stockmann, D. (2003). The undergraduate perspective on community-based research. *Michigan Journal of Service Learning, 9*(3), 36–43.

13

ENGAGEMENT WITH THE COMMON GOOD

Curriculum and Evaluation of a Long-Term Commitment

Amy Lee Persichetti, Beth Sturman, and Jeff Gingerich

In 1989 Cabrini College became one of the first institutions nationally to integrate community service-learning into the core curriculum (DeBlasis, 2006). As an early adopter, Cabrini College has had significant time to develop strong community partnerships and centralize community engagement support through a community engagement center. With the support of administrators and presidents, the college encourages faculty participation in community service-learning through a promotion and tenure process that recognizes civic engagement as important elements of service and scholarship. These are trademarks of a program fully engaged in best practices (Furco, 2002).

Although the college could have been satisfied with its existent service-based core curriculum, Cabrini leadership recognized in 2007 that it was time to reevaluate the curriculum to incorporate newly emerging practices such as community-based research (CBR) and advocacy into the curriculum. After three years of intensive faculty discussion, committee work, course pilots, and consultation with outside experts, Cabrini College rolled out a newly approved core curriculum in 2009.

As do many other Catholic institutions of higher education, Cabrini College attempts to provide students with a liberal learning experience that simultaneously preserves its Catholic identity. This results in a signature educational experience—a unique Cabrinian educational experience—for the college's students. This common experience is the core of every student's general education at the college and a shared experience for all students. In this curriculum, known as Engagements With the Common Good (ECG), all students take thematic and community engagement course work, culminating in a capstone in the major field. *The common good* refers to the long-standing educational tradition at the college of building student knowledge, habits, values, and skills that can be used to benefit others. The goal is not to forsake the self but to create conditions for all people to find fulfillment. The desired outcome of ECG is that students will be civically engaged, working for peace and justice and against poverty and oppression, and grow in their compassionate concern and ability to advocate for all human beings. More specifically, this core and common curriculum focuses on achieving responsibility for social justice, a specific student learning outcome at Cabrini.

ECG is extended by a sequence titled Explorations, a modified distribution requirement structured to provide students with broad exposure to various disciplinary experiences, help students achieve other established learning outcomes, and complement the work of the Engagements curriculum. In particular, the Explorations sequence teaches students to understand themselves as products of and participants in institutions, creative traditions, the historical process, and value-driven decision making.

The four-year ECG curriculum, which is required, asks students to investigate their personal beliefs and backgrounds in the first year, complete service with a community partner in the second year, and work toward sustainable, structural change in the third year through CBR and advocacy projects. In the fourth year, departmental capstone courses integrate this learning with students' personal and professional interests. Throughout the courses, students simultaneously study the philosophical and academic issues underlying societal problems and seek change through partnership with community leaders. At the time of this writing, the first three years of the series have been piloted successfully, and ECG 100, 200, and 300 are in full implementation. The 400 level is still in development.

Important Content in the Curriculum

A great deal of social justice education is provided in the 100- and 200-level courses, which prepare students and faculty to focus on CBR at the 300 level. In their first year, all Cabrini students take an ECG 100 course, which concentrates on awareness of self and the world around them. This writing-intensive course approaches the common good from a variety of perspectives by exposing and interrogating the tension between the individual and society. It also examines the individual's position in various communities: family, nation, race, class, gender, and other categories of identity. Often the relationship between individuals and others is thought of as competitive.

This course complicates that understanding by exploring relationships that work toward greater dignity, solidarity, and equality. This course prepares students to see solidarity, reciprocity, and mutual engagement as expressions of social justice. Through reading, writing, classroom discussion, and cocurricular activities, students come to a greater understanding of the formal and informal social structures that help build their identities. Important questions help to situate such discussions, including the following: Who are we as community members, national citizens, and global citizens? How can our circle of empathy be extended? and What constitutes happiness, security, and dignity, and who has opportunities to attain them?

At the 200 level of the ECG series, students are introduced to a specific local or global organization working on complex issues of social justice. In addition to continued rigorous writing instruction as well as academic readings on the social issue determined for the course, students at the 200 level are required to work directly with service providers or community members on a community engagement project related to the course topic. The combination of academic and hands-on experiences allows students to continue studying the philosophical and academic aspects of a social issue while grappling with the real-world limitations of service, solidarity, dignity, and justice. It is our hope that this will continue to develop empathy in our students and also highlight the tensions and challenges of direct service work, providing students with a more complicated and realistic view of what it means to work for social justice. After completing ECG 200, students are better prepared to recognize the need for systemic change. The ECG 300 course is designed to model ways that students, our future leaders, can learn the skills necessary for facilitating policy-level systemic change.

Engagement With the Common Good 300

The student learning outcomes for this junior-level core course, ECG 300, are intentionally written broadly enough for instructors to select the topic and community partnership that most naturally fit their interests, relationships with community partners, and personal or professional expertise. Thus, participation from faculty members from a wide array of disciplines is encouraged. Likewise, this approach enables students to select courses based on their own social justice interests, fostering the opportunity for personal investment in an otherwise mandatory course. The ECG 300 description and outcomes are listed in the undergraduate catalog as follows:

> ECG 300 is an interdisciplinary, writing intensive course that helps students utilize their assets and the assets of community partners (local or

global) in the pursuit of social justice. Students will work with community partners, contributing to research that will be used to expand the capacity and quality of the partner organizations while providing students with life-long tools for civic engagement. This research may also be used to advocate for systemic changes that will affect greater solidarity with local and global communities. Students will develop skills and strategies to advocate for policies with U.S. and international public and private decision-makers. The learning outcomes for this course are:

1. Students will *reflect* on the tensions among their individual beliefs and personal interests, political realities, and the common good in local and global communities.
2. Students will *demonstrate* a sustained commitment to the practice of social justice through community-driven projects designed to create social change.
3. Students will *demonstrate* in practice (by developing their research and advocacy skills) and in reflection the difference between seeking justice through charity and through social change.
4. Students will *critique* their personal philosophy of social justice grounded in dignity, equality, and solidarity through

   - their community involvement,
   - their growing solidarity with diverse communities, and
   - their intellectual understanding of philosophical, historical, and contemporary movements that sought to create social justice (through the lens of oral and written reflection; Cabrini College, 2010, p. 70).

The ECG 300 course discussed in the remainder of this chapter focuses on domestic violence education and is one of the sections Cabrini students can choose to meet their junior-level core requirement. The course was first introduced in 2006 as part of a former social justice seminar series created in 1989. Since that time, more than 15 sections of the class have been offered, and the course has been successfully replicated by two other professors at the college. These course sections are always filled very quickly, signifying a large demand for the course and a vested interest on the part of the student body.

CBR in ECG 300: Dating and Domestic Violence

Dating and Domestic Violence, one of the sections of ECG 300, reflects a partnership between Cabrini College and Laurel House, a local domestic violence shelter. Over the course of the semester, students become provisionally certified in domestic violence crisis counseling according to Pennsylvania Coalition Against Domestic Violence (PCADV) standards. The PCADV provides oversight of all training programs in Pennsylvania domestic violence shelters. To attain full certification that would allow students to work or volunteer at any Pennsylvania domestic violence shelter, they must complete an additional eight hours of on-site training at Laurel House. This step is optional and is one benchmark we are using to gauge students' commitment to domestic violence education beyond the semester.

In addition to completing the domestic violence training modules, students are required to design and conduct research on dating and domestic violence among college and high school students. The purpose of this CBR is twofold: to inform the educational efforts of Laurel House and to reinforce course-based knowledge with real-time statistics. One of Laurel House's sustainable long-term goals in its work with colleges is to create *lifelong ambassadors*, defined, people who are aware of the warning signs of domestic abuse; understand the available resources; and possess the skills and tools to help a friend, family member, neighbor, or colleague. Regardless of the field these young adults go into after graduation, knowledge about dating and domestic violence is something that will serve them and their communities well throughout the course of their lives. From the perspective of Laurel House's administrators, having the opportunity to work closely with students from Cabrini in a variety of capacities helps ensure that many students leave college well prepared to help further part of Laurel House's mission, which is "to raise public awareness about domestic violence and to advocate for social change against domestic violence" (Laurel House, n.d.).

Pedagogically, this course follows best practices of CBR (Strand, Marullo, Cutforth, Stoecker, & Donohue, 2003), in part, because the teaching load is jointly shared by Amy Lee Persichetti, a Cabrini College professor, and Tommie Wilkins, director of community education at Laurel House. Over the course of the semester, Wilkins teaches several of the modules required by the PCADV. The curriculum of the training (and therefore, the course) is written by the PCADV staff, and the modules are standardized, creating a natural division of labor between the faculty member and the community partner. It was decided very early that the modules that required the most applied knowledge would go to Wilkins, who has worked on the frontlines of domestic violence for 10 years. More broadly themed modules such as cultural competency and historical perspectives on domestic violence were delegated to Persichetti. Similarly, Persichetti assumes responsibility for all course-based assessment, while Wilkins ensures that students are being taught in accordance with PCADV standards.

The commitment to Laurel House is also sustainable because ECG 300 is affiliated with Laurel House each semester, although each semester brings a new set of students whose knowledge and skills must first be developed and then put to work with Laurel House. Just as academic research often leads to more research questions, the work from one semester builds on the findings of the previous semester. For example, in the first semester that the course Dating and Domestic Violence was offered, the investigation was directed toward college students' experiences with dating violence. During the next semester, the empirical work asked similar questions of high school students. The third time replicated earlier studies and expanded the research to identify critical junctures in student development when dating violence rates increase. The fourth group polled high school and college students to learn if they saw dating violence as a problem and to identify the most effective ways to design intervention programs. This fifth year's study is focusing on how much preservice and in-service teachers know about domestic violence and how equipped they are to handle domestic violence issues that may arise in their classrooms. As the partnership progresses, Laurel House and Cabrini College are committed to improving and strengthening the research to address the overarching, systemic issues that enable domestic violence to proliferate.

Using Research for Informed Action and Community Impact

At the end of the semester-long course, students present their research results to the executive director of Laurel House in a student-led, professional-level PowerPoint presentation containing all the research findings to be used as needed and to be available to subsequent students in the course. While the research informs day-to-day domestic violence educational programming, the results also inform and shape educational programming at the state level. PCADV is undertaking the development of a new three-year strategic plan. Pennsylvania is on the cusp of joining several other states that have already enacted legislation requiring dating violence prevention to be part of the high school curriculum. PCADV has worked hard to ensure that this new legislation will require certified domestic violence agencies to be included in the development and delivery of the curriculum.

Working with college students helps PCADV in several ways. For example, the agency is learning more about the most effective ways to provide information to high school students and ensure that colleges also educate their students about dating violence. These outcomes are a natural extension of the work PCADV is already doing in community education. Additionally, Beth Sturman is Laurel House's executive director and a member of PCADV's Strategic Planning Committee, which has been actively meeting for the past six months. In this capacity, she has been and will be able to use these outcomes (i.e., lessons learned and the model codeveloped with Cabrini) to help inform PCADV's new strategic plan in regard to the education of young adults to achieve more community impact. Thus these nascent phases are affecting a more long-range social change as described in Chapter 2 and in the broader CBR literature (DeBlasis, 2006; Strand et al., 2003).

It may seem improbable that such a partnership could be replicated at other institutions. However, several important components illustrate why and how this CBR partnership could be effective elsewhere. First and most important, Laurel House and Cabrini College share a commitment to social justice that is explicitly articulated in organizational mission statements. Second, in addition to this alignment in the big picture, Cabrini and Laurel House share an educational mission (Strand et al., 2003). As director of community education at Laurel House, Wilkins is exclusively devoted to bringing information about dating and domestic violence to schools in the region. Her relationship with Cabrini not only helps Cabrini students learn but also helps Wilkins meet the expectations of her own role in her agency. This confluence of missions facilitates the team-teaching model, allowing Wilkins to make a time commitment to team-teaching the course without overextending her own position or adding extra responsibilities to her job. Third, there is a strong relationship with the executive director of Laurel House, one of the greatest champions of this partnership. Having access to the top administrative structure of Laurel House not only helps disseminate data but allows frequent and collegial conversation about how Cabrini and Laurel House can maximize their relationship to reach as broad an audience as possible. At the time of this writing, this relationship has led to a grant from the U.S. Department of Justice as well as the creation of a Domestic Violence Task Force composed of leaders from schools, police forces, health-care providers, and child service agencies in the region working together to address and eliminate domestic violence in local communities.

In addition to the operational aspects of this partnership, there is a high level of communication and genuine appreciation between the community partner and the professor. A large part of this is simply a natural affinity, but it is strengthened by a common commitment to ending domestic violence and a clear understanding that each party brings her or his own set of strengths to the table. The domestic violence movement, itself, is rooted in feminist pedagogy, which strongly values academic and experiential knowledge and seeks to "subvert the tendency to focus on only the thoughts, attitudes, and experiences of those who are materially privileged" (hooks, 1994, p. 185). This philosophy is embraced by the professor and the community partner, who are able to view each other's contributions as complementary and equally valuable, an essential piece of successful CBR collaboration (Strand et al., 2003).

Assessment of the Curriculum

Because Cabrini has a strong tradition in community engagement, much of the initial curricular reform that began in 2007 used existing administrative structures and practices. However, as the program was implemented, it became clear that a programmatic assessment of the ECG core curriculum was necessary to inform important decisions about resource allocations and to support this central and important part of the Cabrinian experience (Hollowell, Middaugh, & Sibolski, 2006). Because the ECG curriculum is a multidisciplinary effort taught by full-time faculty across the campus, the responsibility of assessment could not fall under the auspices of any single department.

To accommodate the need for assessment, the role of dean of academic affairs was redefined to incorporate oversight of the ECG curriculum, and currently an overarching assessment plan is being developed. Each level of ECG (100, 200, 300 and 400) is administered by a faculty leader whose duties include staffing and overseeing the implementation of the course in exchange for a course release. An ECG coordinator is responsible for the oversight of the entire ECG series, a faculty member provides writing instruction, and a faculty member oversees inclusion of diversity in the courses.

Course Assessment and Potential Impact

Drawing from pertinent literature in assessment and community engagement best practices, we have developed seven questions to guide community-based research practitioners and their partners in the assessment process. The first part of each question provides a general understanding of its importance followed by how this step was accomplished in the Cabrini/Laurel House partnership. As is the case with all assessment, this is simply a guide. It is essential for assessment to be specifically tailored to meet the needs and culture of a given institution and community-based research partnership.

Who are the stakeholders in the course? Before beginning an assessment process, it is important to establish the list of stakeholders (Hollowell et al., 2006; Walvoord, 2004). The data each stakeholder seeks may differ significantly and can be a source of tension when creating assessments. In the case of our course, a list of stakeholders includes Cabrini College students in the course, the course instructor, Laurel House, PCADV, the dean for academic affairs, the Academic Planning Committee, and other governance bodies charged with overseeing the core curriculum. In creating assessment tools, it is essential to design an assessment procedure that addresses the needs of all stakeholders.

What are the questions we need our assessment to answer? To begin the assessment process, it is essential to know what questions this assessment seeks to answer (Stassen, Doherty, & Poe, 2001), a process that is particularly difficult when dealing with the abstractions of social justice (Langworthy, n.d.). In our case, the assessment must also contribute to the overall progress of the core curriculum and fulfill the needs of stakeholders in Cabrini's governance and administrative structures. Finally, assessments should also answer questions essential to the operations and funding of the community partner that may be concerned with issues unrelated to the academic endeavor. It is clear that this could rapidly become a Sisyphean task without a clear focus. Therefore, focusing the assessment to address the concerns of all stakeholders is essential.

In evaluating ECG 300, we decided on three main questions, driven largely by the stakeholders.

1. Are students meeting the learning outcomes of the ECG 300 class?
2. How does community-based research advance or contribute to the mission of Laurel House?
3. Does the class help meet the learning outcomes of the core ECG curriculum?

What are you already doing in your course that can answer these questions? Given the time constraints of all of the stakeholders, it is important to make assessment convenient (Stassen et al., 2001; Walvoord, 2004). During the creation of the outcomes, faculty generated a list of possible indicators for student learning, for example, "Students will *demonstrate* in practice (by developing their research and advocacy skills) and in reflection the difference between seeking justice through charity and through social change" (Cabrini College, 2010, p. 71).

While this is an interesting learning outcome, it is admittedly challenging to assess and even more difficult to monitor across disparate sections of the course. To prevent drift across sections, faculty designing the core provided a list of how students might achieve this outcome. For example, they could

• participate in a community-based research or advocacy project throughout the semester that has direct applications or benefits for a community partner;
• formally present research findings in an oral presentation and written document to the community partner;

- discuss progress and implications of the project weekly or biweekly; and
- collaborate (preferably with the community partner) to complete a critical assessment of the research, the impact on the community partner, the partner's impact on the students, and the potential for social change.

This list serves to create continuity across sections while allowing instructors to work in accordance with their own pedagogical strengths and the needs of community partners. To ensure quality across sections, each new section of the class is evaluated by the ECG task force, which is charged with approving the creation of new sections.

Is the assessment plan realistic and sustainable? Even the best assessment plan will fail if it is not sustainable. In higher education, balancing the increasing demands of faculty workload becomes trickier by the year (Sorcinelli, 2007). Budgetary concerns are also of great concern in our current economy. Social service providers are similarly stressed. Therefore, it is important that the assessment process does not place an unreasonable or unsustainable burden on workloads or budgets.

Currently, the responsibility for gathering and presenting assessment data is shared by ECG faculty leaders who gather data from signature assignments in each discrete ECG course. These documents are then read and assessed by paid faculty who are trained in norming sessions to use a common rubric. The report is given to the college's Assessment Committee, but results are also shared with ECG faculty leaders who bring the results back to faculty teaching in the ECG series for discussion and action.

What benchmarks can be used to define success? Just as colleges and universities must answer to stakeholders, community partners must also satisfy the expectations of funders, grant providers, and other governing bodies. For this reason, it is essential to come to a complete understanding of how all parties define success. In the beginning of the process, Cabrini faculty asked Laurel House staff members to articulate their needs, define the research they would like conducted, and assess the applicability of the research to day-to-day operational work. However, it is also important to ask community partners how they assess their own programming so that, when possible, the college and the partner can benefit from the assessment process. To this end, Cabrini asked Laurel House what information they tracked for reporting to funders. Based on Laurel House's response to this question, the following course benchmarks were designed:

- number of presentations to middle and high school and college students

- number of middle, high school, and college students who attended the presentations
- number of students from Cabrini who completed the state-approved domestic violence training
- number of other contacts initiated by Cabrini students outside the classroom for other projects (news articles, awareness events, etc.)

By agreeing on a common set of benchmarks, Cabrini and Laurel House share a vision for the course and focus on those elements important to the college and the community partner.

Have we effectively integrated results so a complete picture of the course emerges? The possible assignments described in the faculty-generated list do meet a great number of criteria set forth in best practices for assessment. Used in tandem with the benchmarks set by Laurel House, these assignments and measures are descriptive and diagnostic (Holland, 2001). They also rely on direct measurements that demonstrate skills (e.g., writing and critical thinking) as well as more indirect measurements that are more reflective (Stassen et al., 2001; Walvoord, 2004). Given the nature of the social justice curriculum, the assessment is understandably heavy in subjective self-assessment, but an attempt has been made to be objective where possible.

No singular assignment or benchmark is completely perfect. Each has its strengths and weaknesses. The idea is not to find the perfect measure; instead, it is to find measures and assignments that are strong, and when used with other measures and assignments, can provide a fair and accurate picture of what is happening both in the course and with the community partner.

Also, if the budget permits, an outside evaluator is an excellent investment, in part because internal evaluations are more positive than external evaluations more than 75% of the time (Furco, 2009). Course-based and programmatic assessments can be strengthened by meeting with an external evaluator who can review your assessment plan; conducting focus groups with students, faculty, and community partners; and providing feedback to improve assessment practice as well as instruction.

How can we revise or improve the course and partnership based on this information? Throughout this process, it is important to keep in mind that "flexibility, experimentation, and openness to innovation are essential during the exploratory phases of change" (Holland, 2001). While these primary assessment processes are important, they are by no means permanent. As the curriculum and CBR components progress, and data are collected, a clearer view will emerge on what questions need to be asked and what instruments need to be revised. However, this does not discount the importance of following best practices in assessment.

New Directions From Lessons Learned

Administrators of Cabrini College, as those in an increasing number of colleges and universities, recognize the importance of community engagement in enhancing the educational experience of students. However, designing programs that mutually benefit the college and the community partner is a continuous challenge (Strand et al., 2003). ECG 300 is only one of many possible models for community-based research, but it illustrates how a shared vision can genuinely benefit all parties. It is likewise important to note that this course is the product of several revisions. In the same vein, there are far-reaching systemic goals that we are still struggling to address (Furco, 2002).

Over the course of the past four years, this course has undergone considerable refinement. In the research component, we now use QuestionPro software that captures and collates data through an online survey link. Previously, students administered surveys manually and created databases for results. This was extraordinarily time consuming and limited the academic course learning as well as the pool of possible respondents. The time we saved by refining the data collection process is now used to complete a literature review assignment. Students are now asked to compare their findings with those of peer-reviewed articles, a step that has enhanced the educational experience of students and legitimized student research findings.

Additionally, using a language that is valuable to the college and the community partner is important. Currently, we are in the process of revising the syllabus to include a strict accounting of how and when PCADV hourly training standards are being met by the course. This is important to Laurel House, whose training program is regularly audited by the PCADV. Earlier versions of the course met PCADV standards, but the syllabus was not written in a way that would be clear to PCADV auditors. This revision will produce a document that is relevant for academic purposes with the added benefit of streamlining Laurel House's compliance process.

The Cabrini/Laurel House partnership has continued to strengthen through a three-year U.S. Department of Justice grant awarded to Cabrini for domestic violence education. The purpose of the grant is to improve domestic violence training for preservice and in-service teachers. For the duration of the grant, Laurel House will be paid as a consultant throughout the course of Cabrini's work with the Norristown School District. In this way, the knowledge and expertise of Laurel House staff will remain an essential part of the project, and Laurel House will be compensated for that knowledge and expertise as well as for the accompanying staff time. This helps us to further strengthen our program in regard to best practices, and it is our first foray into joint efforts to seek funding (Strand et al., 2003). The partnership between Cabrini and Laurel House has engaged other community agencies in the fight against domestic violence. They meet each semester to discuss ways these essential organizations can work together to address domestic violence and educate and pool resources to assist victims and their families, thus potentially increasing the impact of our CBR alliance.

Since the inception of this joint CBR initiative, thousands of surveys have been completed. As this body of research completed by Cabrini students grows, administrators of Laurel House and Cabrini agree that a large-scale synthesis of all the research completed to date would be an asset to Laurel House's educational approach. Looking through research from the past four years could create a comprehensive list of recommendations that could be presented to the board of Laurel House as a data-driven action plan to inform Laurel House's educational programming for teens. Similarly, Laurel House and Cabrini staff are interested in following up with students who have already participated in the course to find out how, if at all, they believe the course is informing their work or personal lives. To this end, Laurel House interns could follow up with previous Cabrini students each year to find out what impact this course has had on former students after they move on to postgraduate life.

Presently, two additional professors, Darryl Mace, chair of the history department, and Laura Groves, chair of social work, have been trained to teach this course. Both professors have found the course to be easily replicated, straightforward, and highly effective. This suggests that the model not only works well within our current structure, but also is highly replicable at other institutions.

While much lies ahead in this partnership, Cabrini and Laurel House are reaping benefits from the CBR work being done by students. Now that the program is established, Cabrini and Laurel House administrators and staff look forward to using the completed research to inform larger, policy-level changes. Additionally, we will more diligently measure and track the effects of this partnership consistently. The past four years have provided our partnership with the collaborative problem-solving skills that will serve as a strong foundation as those at Cabrini and Laurel House continue to work together to prevent domestic violence.

References

Cabrini College. (2010). *Undergraduate catalog*. Radnor, PA: Author.

DeBlasis, A. (2006). From revolution to evolution: Making the transition from community service-learning to community based research. *International Journal for Teaching and Learning in Higher Education, 18*(1), 36–42.

Furco, A. (2002). *Self assessment rubric for the institutionalization of service-learning in higher education.* Retrieved from www.servicelearning.org/instant_info/links_collection/index.php?popup_id=485

Furco, A. (2009, February). *Effective methods for assessing the impact of service-learning on students, institutions, and communities.* Paper presented at the meeting of the Western New York Service-Learning Coalition, Buffalo, NY.

Holland, B. (2001, March). *Exploring the challenge of documenting and measuring civic engagement endeavors of colleges and universities: Purposes, issues, ideas.* Paper presented at the meeting of the Campus Compact Advanced Institute on Classifications for Civic Engagement. Retrieved from www.compact.org/advancedtoolkit/pdf/holland_paper.pdf

Hollowell, D., Middaugh, M. L., & Sibolski, E. J. (2006). *Integrating higher education planning and assessment: A practical guide.* Ann Arbor, MI: Society for College and University Planning.

hooks, b. (1994). *Teaching to transgress: Education as the practice of freedom.* London, UK: Routledge.

Langworthy, A. (n.d.). *The challenge of benchmarking community engagement: The AUCEA pilot project.* Retrieved from http://research.usc.edu.au/vital/access/manager/Repository/usc:4234

Laurel House. (n.d.). *Mission statement.* Retrieved from http://laurel-house.org/about-laurel-house/our-mission/

Sorcinelli, M. D. (2007). Faculty development: The challenge going forward. *Peer Review, 9*(4), 4–8.

Stassen, M., Doherty, K., & Poe, M. (2001). *Program-based review and assessment: Tools and techniques for program improvement.* Retrieved from www.umass.edu/oapa/oapa/publications/online_handbooks/program_based.pdf

Strand, K., Marullo, S., Cutforth, N., Stoecker, R., & Donohue, P. (2003). *Community-based research and higher education.* San Francisco, CA: Jossey-Bass.

Walvoord, B. A. (2004). *Assessment clear and simple: A practical guide for institutions, departments and general education.* San Francisco, CA: Jossey-Bass.

14

REFLECTIONS ON A GRADUATE STUDENT'S DISSERTATION EXPERIENCE USING COMMUNITY DATA FOR RESEARCH AND MENTORING

Jody Nicholson

My experience with community-based research (CBR) began when I enrolled in a community psychology course as a graduate student at the University of Notre Dame. A member of the Lead Alliance in South Bend, Indiana, contacted my graduate adviser about a potential project for an interested graduate student that would target a specific aim of the alliance: the high prevalence of children suffering from lower levels of exposure to lead in the local community. These lower levels were concerning, as they were too low to require from the local health department but still put them at risk for short- and long-term developmental consequences. After hearing about the request, I committed to writing my white paper (a final course requirement) on lead exposure in children. At the time, I had only a mild interest in pursuing that topic further beyond the course; however, the white paper turned into an application for an internal CBR grant at Notre Dame, which began the funding for what became a three-year, $80,000 intervention that turned into my dissertation.

Over the past 50 years, the United States has drastically lowered the action level for when children should receive services to reduce their exposure to lead. The action level was as high as 60 micrograms/deciliter (µg/dl) in the 1960s, and after more than 20 years of remaining at 10 µg/dl, it was successfully lowered to 5 µg/dl in 2013. The lead-exposure community is trying to remove the terms *threshold* and *poisoning* from the literature because they result in unintended consequences. People perceive that lower levels are acceptable because levels are below the threshold, or because levels are below the threshold, people believe they are not poisoned. The national average of children's blood lead levels (BLLs) responded to the stricter exposure regulations and decreased from 15 µg/dl in the 1970s to a current average of around 1.3 µg/dl (Bellinger & Bellinger, 2006; Centers for Disease Control and Prevention, 2013; Hubbs-Tait, Nation, Krebs, & Bellinger, 2005). Although there has been success in lowering the national average for children's BLLs, consensus exists among lead exposure experts that any amount of exposure is detrimental to young children and has similar negative behavioral, academic, and physical outcomes at levels of exposure above detection (Bellinger & Bellinger, 2006; Needleman & Gatsonis, 1990; Tellez-Rojo et al., 2006). Research and intervention programs, however, have tended to neglect children with BLLs below the action level (Sandel, Phelan, Wright, Hynes, & Lanphear, 2004) and instead mainly target families with children above this level for educational and environmental initiatives (Yeoh, Woolfenden, Wheeler, Alperstein, & Lanphear, 2009).

At the time of my dissertation, experts in the field of lead exposure were in the midst of advising the Centers for Disease Control and Prevention to revise earlier policy guidelines to get more help for children with BLLs below 10 µg/dl (Betts, 2012). This same concern was being mirrored in our community by the South Bend Lead Alliance, a group of university and community members that had spun off a larger Lead Task Force housed in the county health department for the purpose of examining the local lead exposure problem. To meet the Lead Alliance's research need, the intervention I developed for my dissertation built upon existing educational and environmental approaches and targeted children with lower BLLs (<10 µg/dl) in a community sample of low-income families.

Specifically, I hoped to identify the most effective low-cost initiatives for teaching parents how to protect their children from lead dust exposure in the home through education, cleaning strategies, or environmental home risk assessments. To test the effectiveness of these educational and environmental intervention tactics on a sample of children with levels of exposure below 10 µg/dl, families were randomly assigned to receive education on lead exposure (i.e., active control group), a cleaning kit including a high-efficiency particulate air (HEPA) vacuum, a home risk assessment, or a cleaning kit and a home risk assessment. This research design tested an existing hypothesis that a combination of environmental interventions through home risk assessment and cleaning would be more effective (Lanphear, Dietrick, Auinger, & Cox, 2000).

Participation in the study resulted in a significant decrease in children's BLLs regardless of group assignment. Furthermore, children whose families participated in my intervention saw a significant reduction in their BLLs compared to a matched comparison group of children from the same community with similar levels of exposure who did not participate in my study. No children increased to a level considered lead poisoning, and 95% of the sample saw a decrease in their BLLs. I have been able to disseminate these findings nationwide through conferences and personal networking and, at the writing of this chapter, am working on the manuscript to submit for publication.

The road from the white paper to my dissertation was filled with learning experiences for me and a small army of undergraduate students at Notre Dame whom I recruited from two sources: (a) a formal course, Chemistry in Service to the Community, offered through the chemistry department in conjunction with Dennis Jacob's analytical chemistry lab and (b) psychology majors who were interested in pursuing medical professions (i.e., I posted flyers around the psychology building). Throughout the three years of my study, I incorporated six undergraduate students with their own projects of interest related to my study and helped them gain summer funding so they could remain working on the study between semesters. We presented the results of their experiences at regional and national conferences. These students received course credit for their work as well. Two students collected health information with a chart review of participants' Women, Infants, and Children (WIC) files to see how iron levels affected children's BLLs. Another student interested in risk factors for lead exposure (e.g., poverty, race, children under six years) created a Google map of where the participants lived in town and overlaid it with census track data to demonstrate how those most at need in the community were from areas demonstrating the most risk. A premed student, who was just returning from a study abroad in Spain, joined my project to help interview families whose primary language was Spanish and tested a protocol for measuring lead dust contents in vacuum cleaner bags that we collected from our participants. One research assistant, who aspired to be a psychiatrist, helped me research and choose the best child assessment tool to use for investigating children's cognitive and behavioral development and was trained to administer and score these tests.

In addition, about two dozen other students assisted me on smaller scales with tasks that helped them learn more about research methods through data entry, data management, or accompanying me in home interviews or meetings in the community. With practice, seasoned research assistants were able to conduct interviews on their own. I needed this many students because my study required a great deal of project management (i.e., interviewing 84 participants three times in a community setting, phoning each participant once a month over five months), and my sample was not reliable in completing interviews as scheduled, which required rescheduling many visits. Each interview needed to be entered twice into a data set, and participant recruitment continued for two and a half years.

I enlisted students in all aspects of my project to deliberately provide them with an applied experience in research. In hindsight, I viewed myself as a teacher, facilitating an interdisciplinary research experience based on social learning, but I was also a student of the CBR environment, gaining from the same experiences I provided to my undergraduate research assistants.

Student Benefits

One advantage for the undergraduate students was their better understanding of the course content; psychology students gained experience in applying research methods, and the students in the Chemistry in Service to the Community class were able to better contextualize the issue as they tested the samples in their analytic chemistry lab. Difficult subjects to grasp, such as random assignment, internal and external validity, and attrition, were discussed regularly and seen through a different lens than what was explained in the classroom. For example, even though students understood the necessity of random assignment for being able to interpret causality from their research methods course, they benefitted from having to explain the importance to a social worker at Head Start who felt a specific family really could use a vacuum and needed to be assigned to the cleaning kit group.

As a result of their engagement with my CBR project, students reported that they did better in other research-related courses. However, the lessons learned went beyond applying course material to serving as a form of career development. The majority of students who were research assistants on my study are currently finishing medical school. They reported that they gravitated toward discussing their work on my project during their medical school interview process. These students spent their interviews describing concrete experiences that helped them gain a much more holistic perspective of patients that takes into account contextual components that may affect childhood health, such as the home environment and factors related to poverty.

In addition to these very practical and tangible benefits for students, I also observed great character development as students gained a more mature perspective about their role in society. At the University of Notre Dame, this lesson of social justice is entrenched in the Catholic affiliation of the university, but at my current position at a non-faith-based institution, the lesson is no different. CBR encourages the satisfaction and pride one feels when helping someone in need, whether at the individual or organizational level.

Making students aware of their potential for creating change can be empowering but also daunting. I feel this experience is incredibly timely and developmentally appropriate as students make the transition from adolescence to emerging adulthood and become working members of society. I enjoy seeing students begin to feel a greater responsibility for creating change as they also learn to consider taking another person's perspective on the change that is needed.

Lessons Learned

As previously mentioned, I was a teacher as well as a student in this CBR experience. The lessons learned by my students (e.g., better understanding of course content, career advancement, and character development) were also benefits for me. Above and beyond the strengths I gained from my program, CBR gave me the opportunity to become a better student, a more effective teacher and researcher, and a more conscientious citizen.

First, my graduate program provided me with a strong foundation in methodology and research design, but my CBR experience taught me how to carefully consider if the intervention designed on paper could be realistically disseminated. In my study, I designed an aspect of my intervention as providing a client cleaning instructions accompanied by a cleaning kit containing a vacuum with a HEPA filter. In these instructions, I explained a three-bucket mopping system that would help families clean more effectively to reduce lead dust, which was recommended in the research I had reviewed. Parents were told to have one bucket with rinse water, one with soapy water, and an empty bucket for wringing out the mop. I quickly got feedback that the three-bucket mopping system was unrealistic for mothers—they only had two arms! I had to adjust and adopt a two-bucket system. I started to consider how recommendations in the literature fit the practical application. The most empirically grounded intervention will fall flat if recipients are unable to implement them. This experience benefitted me in multiple ways compared to the more typical experience of my fellow graduate students who were working on data collection on campus for their advisers' projects. After beginning my faculty career, I see my contemporaries feeling uneasy starting their own projects and dealing with the uncertainty of data collection, while I can confidently and comfortably strike a balance between research rigor and practical application.

Second, as I developed my philosophy of teaching, I learned quickly how easy it was to provide rich learning experiences for students. For example, taking an undergraduate with me to appointments in the community, such as meetings for the county's Lead Task Force and the South Bend Lead Alliance, took no extra work on my part and gave the student a fresh perspective on problem solving and interacting with other entities to try to create change. Driving to the meeting, we would talk about who may be there and what would be discussed; driving back from the meeting, I would help the student process and reflect on the experience. In a similar manner, I would bring students along on interviews at families' homes with the drive time spent in discussion. Having these en route discussions before and after community engagement with undergraduates often forced me to summarize, reflect, and apply the experience to information the student would be learning in class. For example, I was already comfortable discussing research method topics or psychology courses, but after asking students about the courses in which they were currently enrolled, I could typically come up with a meaningful discussion for any course content. As we discussed and processed our experiences on these interviews, I became aware of concepts I knew well and those I needed to learn better. I was also able to practice helping the undergraduate students reach a higher level of understanding by honing my skills in asking the right question instead of just telling them the answer. These informal instructional opportunities helped me grow and build my confidence in teaching. In the end, giving undergraduate students a CBR learning opportunity probably helped spur my personal growth as much as theirs.

Third, my dissertation has provided me with strong research to build a fundable line of study in my new faculty position while giving me a strong learning experience in CBR. One of my first lessons was the importance of becoming a part of the community rather than being an outsider who is merely visiting the community. This task is especially difficult for graduate students who typically are temporary residents of communities. To become entrenched in the South Bend community, I attended meetings with the Lead Alliance and the county health department's Lead Task Force and built relationships with people outside my discipline. These relationships necessitated flexibility and the ability to communicate effectively with people who had not been trained as I had. In this manner, CBR and interdisciplinary work traveled hand in hand. Because of the interdisciplinary nature of the Lead Alliance members and the topic of lead exposure, I collaborated with researchers in chemistry, anthropology, and geology. I became more aware of terminology that was specific to my field and how to reword sentences accordingly so I could communicate effectively and subsequently build quality relationships with community members and academics outside my field of training.

To help develop this relationship with my community partners, I thought of our goals in terms of a Venn diagram. I visualized how our goals might overlap and how we also might have unshared, independent goals. In my dissertation study, we had a shared goal of getting children tested in the community. My rationale behind this goal was different from that of my partners. I needed to get the children tested so I could find children within the proper range of exposure to recruit for my study; my community partners needed the children tested to monitor them for lead exposure and provide evidence of this monitoring to their funders. I learned to be transparent about goals that were more specific to my study and not necessarily shared by my community partners (e.g., getting the children retested in a timely manner after completing my study). I had to make it clear that my aim was to support their personal goals in exchange for their support of my personal goals. For example, I coordinated a lead testing day at the local Head Start school, which satisfied a need that had been expressed during two years of attending Lead Task Force meetings but also helped me expand my recruitment and increase my study's sample size.

In a similar manner, I learned to think of resources in a Venn diagram. I assessed the resources we all had, the assets I had that they could use (i.e., grant-writing skills, university equipment and resources, funding opportunities), and the resources they possessed that I needed (i.e., participants, trust in the community, funding opportunities). Sometimes I even found that I only needed to connect the dots between one community partner's needs and another's resources. In the Head Start screening days, the health department needed to meet a screening quota in the community, so having the health department conduct the lead screening for Head Start helped connect two community partners' needs. Building those relationships enhanced my project but required careful communication and consideration of the issues of goals and resources.

Finally, just as my students reported how CBR helped their career advancement, I am a testament to how CBR helped me obtain my current tenure-track faculty position; the job advertisement included a community-based focus. At my current institution, the University of North Florida, community-based learning (CBL) is integrated into its 10-year accreditation plan. Through the university's Center for Community-Based Learning, I became a Community Scholar in my first year and an Engaged Scholar in my third year. Through both of these programs hosted by our center, I met with like-minded professors to discuss CBL and CBR in research and teaching. I have completed two similar CBR projects with a local Head Start school and am working on a community-wide study to be completed prior to my going up for tenure. In addition, I am conducting a study on campus to examine the effectiveness of CBL experiences in student development. These studies have continued to help me provide experiences for graduate and undergraduate students to gain field experience in collecting data in the community.

Final Thoughts: Challenges for Sustainability for Graduate Projects in CBR

My dissertation provided a rich CBR experience for me as a developing teacher and researcher. I am pleased with almost all aspects of my experience, but there was one point of frustration. I was striving to make a sustainable impact on the community, which is the gold standard in CBR. However, I am not sure this was accomplished. After my dissertation was completed, and I headed off to my postdoctoral fellowship, one of my community partners asked, "Who will be the next Jody?" I did not have an answer for her. Most graduate students I knew were tied to their adviser's data. My opportunity was extremely rare, and I couldn't think of any upcoming doctoral student who would be able to step in to the position after I was gone.

I know my project had an impact on individuals in the community because children's lead exposure was significantly reduced. I was also able to make changes at the organizational level by giving my time and energy to connect resources between the university and community (i.e., the Head Start school and the health department). Did this create a form of systemic change in which the local health department and Head Start schools always do lead screening together, or did I only create a short-term solution? At this point, I am unsure if my efforts were maintained.

References

Bellinger, D. C., & Bellinger, A. M. (2006). Childhood lead poisoning: The torturous path from science to policy. *Journal of Clinical Investigation, 116,* 853–857.

Betts, K. S. (2012). CDC updates guidelines for children's lead exposure. *Environmental Health Perspectives, 120*(7), A268.

Centers for Disease Control and Prevention. (2013). Blood lead levels in children aged 1–5 years—United States, 1999–2010. *Morbidity and Mortality Weekly Report, 62*(13), 245.

Hubbs-Tait, L., Nation, J. R., Krebs, N. F., & Bellinger, D. C. (2005). Neurotoxicants, micronutrients, and social environments: Individual and combined effects on children's development. *Psychological Science in the Public Interest, 6*(3), 57–121. doi:10.1111/j.1529-1006.2005.00024.x

Lanphear, B. P., Dietrich, K., Auinger, P., & Cox, C. (2000). Subclinical lead toxicity in US children and adolescents. *Pediatric Research, 47*(4), 152A.

Needleman, H. L., & Gatsonis, C. A. (1990). Low-level lead exposure and the IQ of children: A meta-analysis of modern studies. *Journal of the American Medical Association, 263,* 673–678.

Sandel, M., Phelan, K., Wright, R., Hynes, H. P., & Lanphear, B. P. (2004). The effects of housing interventions on child health. *Pediatric Annals, 33,* 474–481.

Tellez-Rojo, M. M., Bellinger, D. C., Arroyo-Quiroz, C., Lamadrid-Figueroa, C., Mercado-Garcia, A., Schnaas-Arrieta, L., & Hu, H. (2006). Longitudinal associations between blood lead concentrations lower than 10 μg/dL and neurobehavioral development in environmentally exposed children in Mexico City. *Pediatrics*, *118*, E323–E330.

Yeoh, B., Woolfenden, S., Wheeler, D., Alperstein, G., & Lanphear, B. (2009). Household interventions for prevention of domestic lead exposure in children. *Cochrane Library*, 1–46.

PART THREE

COMMUNITY-BASED RESEARCH IN COMMUNITY-WIDE LONG-TERM EFFORTS

Mary Beckman

In contrast to the chapters in Part Two that focus on instruction, the following chapters describe community-wide efforts in which community-based research (CBR) is only one possible tool or means of contributing to positive local social change over time. In some chapters, the local change sought involves one issue that affects an entire geographic area, such as coffee production in Haiti in Chapter 17 or parent involvement in public schools in Chapter 18. In other cases, the work of the group aims to affect community development in general. This type of effort is described in Chapter 15, which focuses on eradicating poverty in a region of Virginia, and in Chapter 16, which discusses the Los Angeles Urban League's broad multi-issue agenda. Whether the orientation is on one issue or community development more generally, each chapter presents either a community-initiated effort into which higher education was invited or a collaboration jointly initiated by community and campus representatives. All the contributors explain how CBR assisted the work of their groups.

The primary purpose of Part Three is to help readers consider how they might align CBR with larger ongoing work. However, a secondary purpose is to offer guidance regarding ways to proceed with the larger group effort itself. To this end, each chapter also points out challenges in beginning and furthering a community-wide initiative, gives pointers for addressing such challenges, shares outcomes for communities, and displays the possible benefits for everyone involved when such work is sustained.

To set the stage for this last section of the book, it is helpful to revisit Chapter 2, "The Role of Community-Based Research in Achieving Community Impact." The authors lay out a community impact framework that consists of four central elements. They argue that keeping these components in mind will enhance the possibility that community development will be achieved over time. The elements are a group that has an institutional design suited to the work and commits to a long-term effort toward a goal, a long-term goal and plans to reach it, involvement of diverse participants most helpful to reach the goal, and commitment to regular monitoring of outcomes and revision of strategies in light of the information attained through monitoring. This framework is one of several features of Chapter 2 that is used or expanded on, implicitly or explicitly, throughout Part Three. Other features include definitions of *outputs*, *outcomes*, and *impacts*.

Part Three begins with Chapter 15 in which a city official asked a professor at Washington and Lee University to enlist his students in an investigation that would help the city government learn more about poverty in the region. Two of the professor's poverty studies undergraduates took up the task. The presentation of the results was so well received that an area-wide poverty commission was formed to make use of the findings. CBR, rooted in several academic disciplines, assisted a number of the activities that followed the formation of the commission.

Chapter 16 focuses on research involving graduate students in the University of Southern California's Rossier School of Education. In this case, the local Urban League office had previously created a number of goals to address a variety of social challenges in Los Angeles. When it invited the University of Southern California into this long-term, ongoing enterprise, the Rossier School agreed to actively work with the initiative. This chapter shows how graduate students were able to use the CBR process in a unique way for their own learning as well as to contribute to a subgroup of the larger Urban League coalition that focused on a specific public high school.

Chapter 17 follows with a description of the Global Solidarity Partnership, a collaboration between a small Catholic college in Florida and coffee growers and artisan organizations in Haiti. Scholars from multiple disciplines contributed to this effort, including electrical engineers and solar physicists. These faculty members worked on developing sustainable energy projects in Haiti, showing that CBR is not the only type of contribution students and faculty can make to such endeavors. This chapter features other student and faculty engagement options as well, such as nonresearch internships.

Chapter 18 focuses on the issue of parental involvement in schools. It follows work that emerged from a collaboration of public school administrators and university faculty and staff. In addition to highlighting some of the challenges in sustaining a long-term effort aimed at addressing a community issue and illustrating the role CBR can play in informing issues across time, it provides information that is of value to those with specific interests in parent involvement.

15

THE POVERTY INITIATIVE IN ROCKBRIDGE COUNTY, VIRGINIA

Don E. Dailey and David Dax

Beckman and Long focus their introduction to this book on the role of community-based research (CBR) in supporting positive social change at the local level. As faculty and staff participating in CBR on a college campus, we can easily lose sight of this objective by placing our attention entirely on student development. Student projects tend to be seeded on the college campus; the community is more of a venue for action than the primary focus. In this view, a successful project is one that helps students develop more nuanced insight into social problems and sharper analytical skills as they integrate their applied learning with the more theoretical knowledge they acquire through course work. If the project dies in the community or has little to no effect, while not ideal, no one on campus will lose any sleep.

These two objectives—student development and community improvement—can and should, however, work in tandem. This dual development of students and community is best accomplished when student work is initially focused on what the community needs as defined by the community. As faculty and students respond to these needs, students can grow in ways that are difficult to achieve in the classroom.

The Poverty Initiative at Washington and Lee University (W&L) is an example of a community-wide effort in which a community research project undertaken by two students served as a catalyst for community-wide organizing and additional student and faculty research, which in turn influenced a range of changes in local policies and their long-term impact. Over the course of a year, the initial research project bloomed into a full initiative that involved community research, learning, and action. It began with an idea from a single member of the community and remained focused on the community throughout. At the same time, the students involved in the initial CBR project and later community organizing activities have described these experiences as among the most significant in their college experience. Thus, this project did further the dual aims of student development and community change.

Campus-community relationships are usually focused on the needs of one agency at a time, and this reality too often reflects the fragmented nature of agencies that are operating in most communities. Although problems such as poverty are multifaceted and cut across the work of several agencies, these agencies tend to only experience limited communication rather than shared systems or authentic collaboration. Thus, whether a CBR group on campus seeks to learn from the community about which problems are most critical, or someone from the community requests projects at the CBR office, this communication usually occurs with one agency at a time.

In contrast, the following describes efforts in which leaders in the field are supporting a community-wide lens for identifying and addressing problems, and a focus on systemic change. This involves more of a focus on supporting structures and processes that encourage community-wide communication and collaboration, structures that empower a diversity of community voices to engage in democratic deliberation and a deeper integration of campus CBR with the community and its structures and processes to foster broader community collaboration. This approach has important implications for how CBR identifies issues and projects, the nature of those projects, and the catalytic role they can play in supporting change.

Our Poverty Initiative began with a student assessment of poverty in Rockbridge County, Virginia, requested by the city manager of Lexington. Rockbridge County is located in rural southwest Virginia and consists of two small towns, Lexington and Buena Vista. Throughout the county there are large pockets of poverty and wealth. Some families live in cabins with dirt floors, no indoor plumbing, and have never traveled more than 20 miles outside the county.

The students conducting the local poverty needs assessment developed a well-written report that received positive reviews from CBR colleagues in the field beyond campus. The report was also presented by staff at a national CBR conference sponsored by the Bonner Foundation, an organization that supports college-community partnerships designed to mitigate poverty (www .bonner.org). The president of Bonner and colleagues from other institutions described the study and report as an exemplary model of what student-faculty collaboration can accomplish. Following publication of the report, community leaders, CBR staff, faculty, and a large group of students collaborated in hosting a Community Forum on Poverty that provided an opportunity for the community to learn about findings from the assessment and begin to articulate and organize their own voices on these issues. This eventually led to intentional community organizing, the creation of a community-wide Commission on Poverty, and the organic growth of grassroots community groups that took charge of change. In turn, these local groups became a source of relationships, ideas, and information that generated additional CBR projects involving more students in local poverty issues. Students played key roles in supporting the Commission on Poverty and worked with smaller community groups focused on particular issues, facilitating meetings, conducting new research, and identifying promising policy options found in other communities. The Bonner Foundation supported this evolving work.

This chapter describes this initiative in greater detail and draws on this experience to develop larger observations for the field and specific recommendations for faculty.

Poverty Initiative

Needs Assessment

In the spring of 2007 Jon Elestad, city manager of Lexington, contacted Harlan Beckley, professor and director of the Shepherd Program for Poverty Studies at W&L to request an assessment of poverty in the area that would identify the prevalence of poverty, the most critical poverty-related needs among the local population, and gaps in service. Elestad, Beckley, and Shepherd staff formed a kickoff meeting to introduce the study to faculty and community leaders. Following this meeting, two students, Melissa Caron and Chris Martin, were selected to conduct the needs assessment under the guidance of Beckley and Don E. Dailey, a visiting associate professor at W&L. Both students had already completed a concentration in poverty studies through the Shepherd Program, giving them a solid foundation in the issues they were addressing. They were graduating at the top of their class at W&L and were known as students who could deliver high-quality work. These handpicked students were also supported by a group of community leaders who provided guidance on research questions, met with the students for interviews, and later provided guidance on how to bring the results of the study to the community. The assessment found critical needs concerning access to public transportation, lack of affordable housing for low-income residents, lack shelter for the homeless, and a range of other concerns related to loss of jobs in the area (Caron & Martin, 2008).

Beyond these particular concerns, the study identified a need for greater communication and collaboration among agencies organized to address varying aspects of poverty. Agencies were not coming together to address problems in a holistic manner to plan or communicate, share data, or make needed referrals.

Community Forum

The study report gained attention from the local press, W&L's website, and informal exchanges between agency and political leaders. As W&L staff and students came together with local community leaders to discuss the study, they found local agency leaders and care providers were frustrated and anxious about the conditions of poverty existing in the community. Just after the needs assessment was launched, the nation underwent a critical economic downturn that was felt overnight in the local region. Agency leaders were uninterested in more research; they wanted concrete help to address the human concerns they were dealing with, such as loss of jobs, hunger, need for shelter, problems with credit, rising utility bills, and stress. Demand for food assistance was doubling. Reports of domestic violence and abuse were rising. They talked about individuals and families facing long-term poverty and the new face of poverty. As one agency director said:

> I'm working face-to-face with folks living in desperate circumstances. Their only access to food beyond the local food pantries is what they kill in the woods. This type of poverty has been here a long time. But I'm seeing a new face on poverty, people coming in who have never struggled before. Food assistance allows them pay their utility bills and get by for another month. But people are desperate and I'm feeling the pressure. We all are. How is research going to solve this? (community service director, personal communication, January, 2009).

As community members and W&L students, faculty, and staff talked through these issues, they began to find common ground in their sense of urgency to take action. All agreed that the next step was to host a special Community Forum on Poverty that would give community members an opportunity to learn about findings and recommendations generated by the needs assessment and to talk about concerns beyond what was addressed in the assessment. All hoped the forum would provide an impetus for building capacity to communicate and collectively collaborate on issues of local concern.

Given that the economy and poverty were recognized as national as well as local concerns, and the word-of-mouth buzz the study generated, the forum drew nearly 100 participants, including political and business leaders, agency heads, local religious leaders, and concerned citizens. Following a plenary session in which community members, students, and faculty and staff from W&L passionately shared and discussed area needs, forum participants broke into small groups to discuss the following topical issues raised in the report: transportation, education, health care, food security, the criminal justice system, and housing. Ultimately the forum led to creation of a Commission on Poverty, grassroots community groups aligned with particular issues, and a steering group that managed these processes.

Creation of Commission on Poverty

Poverty is multifaceted, and addressing it involves the work of various agencies. Despite this complexity, services of this nature in Rockbridge County are normally delivered in isolation and not supported by an adequate referral system or a means for hands-on collaboration. These issues were highlighted in the needs assessment (Caron & Martin, 2008) and in the community forum. There was particular interest in developing a unifying structure to support a more coherent approach to addressing poverty.

To this end, staff and faculty from the Shepherd program at W&L and local community leaders joined forces to form the Commission on Poverty. Each of the governing councils from the communities that make up Rockbridge County voted to support the establishment of the commission in principle, and asked authors Dailey (representing W&L) and United Way director David Dax to work with community leaders in launching the commission, which was envisioned as an overarching organization aimed at raising awareness about poverty in the community; facilitating exposure to effective policies, programs, and tools in the field; providing opportunities for greater collaboration and democratic deliberation across agencies and community groups; and empowering the human and financial capital in the community to reframe problems and pursue collective action. More than 40 leaders from local agencies, education systems, businesses, and the local governing councils, along with concerned citizens, attended the first meeting of the commission in September 2009.

Grassroots Community Groups

During the first year following Caron and Martin's (2008) needs assessment and the community forum, the commission sought to form small community groups to more closely study issues identified at the forum, review policies and interventions developed by similar communities to address these issues, and serve as advocates for needed action. The concept was proposed and organized by staff and faculty at W&L, drawing on a model for supporting community decision making developed by the Bonner Foundation. It was hoped that students, through courses, independent studies, internships, work-studies, or extracurricular services, could provide critical support to the groups as coordinators, researchers, and consultants.

As a result of formal planning and discovery of issues that naturally emerged in the community after publication of the poverty report and after the forum met, groups were eventually formed on transportation, housing, credit and financial literacy, and women's and children's health. This work has had a direct impact on local policy. A number of the resulting activities and impact of these groups are discussed next.

Restructuring and expanding public transportation. Transportation is an enormous concern in rural communities, affecting low-wealth individuals in many important ways. It can influence a person's ability to find and keep a job, obtain health care, shop for groceries, or respond to other basic needs that require travel.

In most rural communities in Rockbridge County, public transportation is nonexistent. In Rockbridge County, where 96% of the population is rural, the student study found that 14.2% of individuals in its two cities, Buena Vista and Lexington, do not own a vehicle (nearly double the state average), and the rate is even higher for the elderly (around 24%; Caron & Martin, 2008). Many essential services such as the Free Clinic and child support services fall outside of walking range and can only be accessed by vehicle. The study undertaken by W&L students reported that the lack of adequate public transportation is the most pressing and severe issue in the county.

The only public transportation service available for use by the general population in Rockbridge County was the Rockbridge Area Transportation System (RATS), which provides demand-responsive transit to those who meet strict income eligibility requirements or receive benefits from federal and state governments. RATS helps clients make medical appointments and take emergency or quasi-emergency trips to the grocery store, but there is no stable public or private transit system for individuals seeking daily, non-emergency rides to work, day care, or to conduct daily business, especially outside the 9:00 a.m. to 5:00 p.m. time frame, when many low-income workers hold jobs.

Caron and Martin (2008) recommended establishing a coordinated system of bus services to reduce inefficiencies, eliminate duplicative services, and simplify the area's transportation strategy. They also recommended coverage to outlying communities, supported by a computer-based routing system, and urged the community to provide demand-responsive, point-to-point, and circuit-routed services. Finally, they recommended some form of subsidization, whether from the local government or state grants, to offset costs until operations were at an adequate level to sustain operations.

The community group that formed to focus on transportation was led by the director of RATS and members of the community who served on the RATS board. The group studied options and models for how to expand services. Based on these deliberations, a plan was proposed and put forward to the county board of supervisors for restructuring and expanding services. Representatives from the Commission on Poverty, W&L, United Way, and a group representing African American residents in the community spoke about this proposal at a public hearing. Predominantly African American neighborhoods have been continually excluded from access to adequate services. Leaders from the commission joined these residents in demanding that any new system address this issue.

The board of supervisors approved the new plan and funding to support the plan. Using local appropriations, a new local transportation operation was launched in 2010–2011, with expanded bus and shuttle services to outlying areas, increasing access for largely African American neighborhoods and providing a standard system of fixed routes.

Housing. Caron and Martin's (2008) needs assessment noted lack of quality, affordable housing as the second most severe issue in the community, according to social service agency leaders. This issue received considerable attention at the community forum. The most significant component of this issue was the prevalence of low-quality units, resulting from a housing stock that is, on average, older than the median age of housing units in Virginia and the United States.

According to the 2000 census data, owner-occupied units on the average were built in 1974, with 18.9% percent built before 1940, and renter-occupied units dated on average from 1966, with 22.9% built before 1940 (Caron & Martin, 2008). As a result, occupants reported inadequate kitchen facilities, plumbing, and heating units, and reported that requests for repairs were ignored by landlords. Furthermore, the overall price for housing in the community is above average for the region, and subsidized housing is only available for the elderly and the disabled. Habitat for Humanity builds a limited number of homes each year, and these homes are not available to individuals with bad credit. Finally, new housing and property-maintenance inspection programs are nonexistent outside the Lexington and Buena Vista city limits because the county has chosen not to enforce this optional state code. This results in dilapidated homes owned by landlords who are not willing to making necessary repairs.

Following the forum, United Way director Dax played a key role in forming a group on housing consisting of leaders of the Rockbridge Area

Housing Corporation, Habitat for Humanity, Rockbridge County Rental Housing Office, Lexington City Planning and Building Office, and Total Action Against Poverty. The group grew to include concerned local citizens, a diverse group of religious leaders, and a member of the Lexington city council. This group was supported by a W&L student, Caroline Head, who provided research on best practices and promising policies found in other communities. She also played a key role in keeping the groups organized, focused, and meeting on a regular schedule. In this role, Caroline served as research assistant with Dailey; her position was sponsored by work-study funding from W&L and support from the Bonner Foundation.

The housing group found one policy option that pertained to affordable housing in a review of promising strategies in the field by additional W&L student researchers. Armed with this new information, the group concluded that the state maintenance and inspection code needed to be enforced across the county to prevent landlord negligence and ensure a better quality of housing stock. They also recommended the institution of additional regulation to strengthen rules governing housing standards and landlords, as well as placing a numerical limit on the number of nonrelated tenants allowed to occupy an apartment. Regulations and limits are designed to fortify protection for the poor and prevent university students from driving up housing prices as they move in together and pay higher rent. Since enforcing an inspection code is expensive and labor intensive, the housing group proposed that in the meantime agencies take on the responsibility of doing home repairs, particularly for the elderly. They further proposed that this work could be enhanced with social venture programs that train at-risk youth to perform productive, community-oriented construction.

Credit and personal finances. Caron and Martin (2008) did not focus specifically on credit and personal finance issues, although participants at the forum stressed the importance of this issue among low-income individuals, families, and others experiencing problems with debt as a result of the economic downturn. Subsequently, Beckley organized an independent study under the guidance of a W&L finance professor. Two W&L students who were enrolled in the Shepherd Poverty Program, Katherine Donnelley and Katie Harris, signed on and used this project as the foundation for their capstone paper that was required for their fulfillment of a concentration in poverty studies. Before launching the project, Donnelley and Harris presented their initial thoughts about the study to the Commission on Poverty. The presentation generated a great deal of excitement among the more than 40 members in attendance, and a small group was formed to help the students define the study, provide access to other resources in the community, and serve as a sounding board.

These processes helped the students focus on identifying the specific issues residents face in struggling with credit. After gathering interview and survey data from community agency leaders, bank leaders, and Rockbridge County residents in a variety of income brackets, Donnelley and Harris found numerous financial issues that contribute to an individual's access to credit. These included lack of availability of credit, unstable employment, difficulties overcoming bad credit once it is incurred, use of predatory lenders as a short-term solution for quick cash, difficulty saving money over extended periods of time, debt accrued from nonrecurring unexpected expenses, and general mismanagement of money.

After studying policies in other communities and discussions with members of their community advisory group, the students made the following recommendations: (a) establish a new student-run organization to tackle local personal finance issues through financial education seminars, weekly credit counseling, creation of a savings matching program, and providing support for local agencies; (b) establish local support groups for individuals experiencing financial crises; (c) establish a local credit union; and (d) strengthen and enforce payday lending regulations. These findings and recommendations were presented at a community meeting consisting of their small community group, elected officials, business leaders, and W&L students, faculty, and staff.

Birthing center and access to health care. In the summer of 2010 the only birthing center in the county was closed by the hospital because of inadequate physician coverage. The decision was made independent of community input and drew a strong local reaction. After the closing, a variety of groups from the community and university began to separately meet to discuss the closing. Professors and students from the Women's and Gender Studies Program at W&L, the Commission on Poverty, and a small group of health-care providers were concerned about the implications for women and children living in poverty who would not have the means to travel 30 miles for prenatal care and birthing services. Still others at the university and in the business community were concerned about the challenge this could pose in recruiting faculty and other professionals to the area. Leaders from the commission collaborated with the mayor of Lexington to form a common group consisting of local residents, concerned health-care providers, academicians, and local elected leaders representing Lexington and the county government. This group met with the executive director of the hospital to discuss these issues and the more long-term issue of access to quality health care for all residents. After the first meeting, the hospital and other health providers responded with a new plan for organizing local midwives and other health providers to meet the needs of expecting mothers. The community group also began working with local health-care providers and the Department of Public Health to study alternative policies, including a long-term proposal to create a central community health center focused on women's and children's health with satellite health clinics in remote areas. Leaders of other clinics around the state were brought in to meet with the group, and plans were developed for visiting selected clinics.

W&L students and faculty participated in this discussion, led primarily by Domnica Radulescu, professor of romance languages and director of the Medieval and Renaissance Studies Program and an affiliated faculty member in the Women's and Gender Studies Program at W&L. Radulescu initially became involved as a concerned citizen, and students supporting this project worked directly with her as volunteers providing extracurricular service. While the creation of a health center is a long-term issue, this group has kept the immediate concerns of the community in the forefront, leading the hospital to become more responsive in its communication with the community and more responsive to these issues. During the winter of 2011, the hospital hired a new obstetrician to meet the needs of women and families in the area.

Key Attributes of the Change Process and Recommendations for Faculty

In reflecting on this history, certain factors appear to be worth considering as themes or lessons that help explain the success of this initiative. First, student knowledge, motivation, and reflection made up the cornerstone for the needs assessment that was a touchstone for all other events in this initiative. Second, the variety of groups formed during this initiative made progress by responding to critical issues as learning communities supported by student research. Third, the initiative evolved in an organic fashion that provided opportunities for generating life into new projects. Fourth, a small group of campus and community catalysts and facilitators played a key role in deliberately moving the initiative along from one point to the next. Two leaders in this group took responsibility to watch for opportunities that could be strategically seized on in promoting the initiative. Fifth, maintaining momentum over time is challenging and complex.

Student Knowledge, Motivation, and Reflection

The Caron and Martin needs assessment was the cornerstone for the initiative, and it was fortunate that two exceptional seniors undertook it. These seniors were adept at drawing on their own expertise in poverty studies and that of faculty as new issues emerged. The report developed by the students was excellent; it needed only limited editing. Beckley, who provided invaluable guidance on poverty issues throughout the assessment and helped the students deepen their reflection on what they were learning, handpicked the two students. The students also had the benefit of guidance from Dailey, who served as their professor for a credit-bearing independent study based on their work on the project.

Recommendations for Faculty

The first point here is not simply to select high-performing students but to be aware that student characteristics do make a difference. If possible, for a signature event of this nature it is important to find motivated students who have developed knowledge that can be applied. Doing this as part of a course with open enrollment brings more uncertainty in regard to student motivation and knowledge, while independent studies and funded internships are ideally suited to finding the right student match. As a project of this nature unfolds, later stages of organizing and additional research can incorporate a wide variety of perhaps less specifically prepared students to get involved through courses and extracurricular service.

The second point is that faculty play an important role not only in helping students make use of their knowledge but also in guiding them through reflection. The importance of reflection in student community-based learning outcomes is well documented (Eyler, 2002). However, teachers cannot take it for granted that students will engage in the type of reflection that helps them make sense of what they are learning. Deliberate efforts to facilitate reflection is recommended.

Reflection should be continuous rather than a single event, occurring before, during, and after the project is launched. Challenging students to think in new ways is also an important element; at the same time, they need support as they are sometimes unsettled by the shifts in beliefs or life choices their experiences might seem to be urging. Strategies for reflection may differ based on prior student knowledge and preparation as well as learning style. Campus Compact has assembled resources that can be helpful to faculty in designing and facilitating reflection during service-learning projects (www .compact.org/disciplines/reflection).

Learning Communities

Each phase of the initiative was enhanced by learning communities. For our purpose, a learning community is when a group of diverse participants come together to share perspectives, knowledge, and experience and to learn from each other about a particular topic. A learning community supporting a CBR project is characterized by collaborative inquiry, sharing, critical feedback, and colearning (Senge & Scharmer, 2006). The following learning communities were developed as part of the Poverty Initiative: informal poverty study advisory group; community forum; small steering group; community grassroots issue groups; and Commission on Poverty. In one form or another, each group consisted of community members and W&L students, faculty, and staff. The learning community supporting Caron and Martin (2008)—the informal poverty study advisory group—was involved in the research design, reviewed survey questions, engaged in collaborative inquiry with collected data, and was intensely involved in planning follow-up activities.

As participants in the learning communities made observations, offered interpretations, constructively argued, and shared ideas, the group and individual members were exposed to multiple perspectives representing cultures different from their own. Conditions existed for considering points of view reflecting racial, gender, ethnic, and age differences as well as differences in professional experience, training, and rural-versus-urban and community-versus-academic orientations. Community involvement engendered a sense of ownership in the initiative, and community motivation to act on the research was enhanced. This process of community partnership also planted seeds for grassroots organizing.

As this initiative evolved into other community groups (transportation, housing, financial literacy, women and children's health), similar processes involved a variety of other students who were challenged to learn, question their own basic assumptions and beliefs, and integrate knowledge gained from their classroom on campus with the knowledge developed through experiences in the community as a classroom. The learning communities that emerged further strengthened the richness of data available to the student researchers and the relevance of insight brought to data analysis. Data collected from university researchers in isolation of community partners may provide only a cursory snapshot of events and questions being studied, but when community members engage in ongoing discussions about their experiences with an issue, student and faculty researchers gain a more nuanced perspective.

Recommendations for Faculty

Our project shows the important and varied roles faculty members can play in this systemic change process. They can bring conceptual leadership to the design and facilitation of learning communities and assist in identifying expertise from other faculty not involved. Two of the grassroots community groups' core activities were assessing problems and exploring interventions to address those problems. Faculty researchers can contribute to such a process as well.

In a participatory research project, however, a learning community challenges faculty to be open to knowledge from nonacademic sources. This requires openness to rethinking how learning occurs in a group context with each member bringing valued perspectives (Strand, Marullo, Cutforth, Stoecker, & Donohue, 2003). Research processes can be significantly enriched and appropriately contextualized as community members review and expand on data. As students and faculty come forward with potential interventions found in their research, openness to community members to bring their own insight into learning and strategy formation is crucial. This valuing of and incorporating expertise beyond the academy is possibly the most essential bridge to creating impact found in the Poverty Initiative.

Organic Change Versus Deliberate Action

Evolution of the initiative from a single CBR project occurred through organic and deliberate process interaction. In one respect, these are contrasting concepts. Organic change occurs as a natural, adaptive, flexible process whereas to deliberate processes involve predetermined structures and an emphasis on planning, order, and control. The strength of organic change is that it flourishes and lives with what naturally and authentically emerges as important in the community. Its inherent weakness is that it can potentially move in aimless directions or fail to move at all, even if change is needed (Mintzberg & Huy, 2003).

In contrast, planned, deliberate change can provide strategic focus on goals for change, allocate resources to support change, and address challenges or resistance to change. Its inherent weakness is that it may impose efforts to mobilize structured change in ways that are irrelevant to community needs, fail to garner authentic support, produce artificial changes, and cut off opportunities for growth where change is needed (Mintzberg & Huy, 2003).

The Poverty Initiative appears to be an example of how planned change and organic growth came together. Using the community for change in this initiative occurred through events and structures designed to support follow-through after the research and report were completed. Through the commission and smaller groups, the community developed immediate structures where student research could continue to live and lead to change. This developed through a combination of deliberate design and responsiveness to events naturally emerging in the local context. A few specific examples can illustrate these points.

Participation in the commission was perceived as a highly visible activity for community involvement that initially provided status and a feeling of being in the loop of an important event. A number of community leaders and service directors specifically requested to be included. This was not the case for the grassroots community groups where more hands-on action and time-consuming hard work would likely occur. W&L staff developed a formal mission and goals statement for the small community groups, outlined responsibilities for the group facilitators, and contacted individuals to serve as facilitators. All community leaders, with one exception, declined to serve in this capacity. Calls and e-mails to other community members simply requesting their participation in a small group were rejected. There was no sense of urgency to form the small groups, and the group work sounded like an additional time-consuming job.

In response, commission leaders intentionally adopted a hands-off approach and focused attention on addressing issues and using groups that emerged outside the commission's formal plan. For example, no one on the commission anticipated the closing of the birthing center, but once this happened it emerged as an issue that pushed people to take action. A variety of groups began to naturally form, at which point the commission asserted itself as a focal point for bringing together these groups as a single grassroots community entity focused on local heath. As another example, the credit issue was identified as a major issue at the forum, although initially a community group was not formed to address this issue. The group developed as students, under faculty guidance, began to tackle the issue and bring it back into the community through the commission. The credit group was formed as commission members from different agencies and local banks began to support the students undertaking that study.

In contrast, transportation followed the path of more deliberate planning and made use of an existing structure rather than responding to unanticipated opportunities. The group on transportation was formed primarily through RATS and leadership from its executive director who also served on the commission. By extension, RATS recruited its existing board to serve as the core of that community group.

Recommendations for Faculty

This vision embraces the notion of forming groups to address short-term crises and then using that momentum to start building the infrastructure for more long-term community groups focused on grassroots transformation. Although each event led to the next, the initial student poverty study served as a continuing touchstone and credible force for change.

The lessons learned in the W&L initiative encourage a combination of predetermined design with responses to demand that more naturally occur in the community. At the very least, openness to such demand enables a space in the community where people can start thinking about organizing for change. Community needs and demand do not necessarily follow the same pattern for all projects, but opportunities for organizing will likely emerge in each case. Opportunities often arise in existing community groups that are open to responding to community needs. In other cases, where groups are either nonexistent or uninterested, a new group can be formed to bring fresh ideas to the table.

Faculty can participate in this type of work in a variety of ways. At the most fundamental level, this means simply embracing a mind-set that is flexible and open to discovery, regardless of the specific activities in which the faculty member is involved. It might also mean participating in deliberate planning for supporting the impact of the research through presentations or literally assisting in organizing structures. Faculty conceptual leadership can also be important to support the evolving nature of initiatives that move from initial research to a larger system of action.

Faculty, Staff, and Students Facilitating Progress

At different intervals the larger initiative could have died. Any project of this nature faces several points in time where future progress is vetoed, it fades from lack of attention and competing agendas, it is significantly altered, or it continues and grows. Table 15.1 identifies key transition points where some form of veto could occur for the Poverty Initiative.

TABLE 15.1
Key Points of Transition

Milestone	Examples of Failure to Move Forward
Report completed	• Audiences fail to review report • Audiences review report but fail to take action
Community forum	• Low attendance and low engagement • High attendance but low engagement
Community action	• Report and recommendations for a commission are put on the shelf • Recommendations considered by governing bodies but not approved • Recommendations approved but not implemented
Commission launched	• Community apathy, participation is low • Community participation is high but fails to meet expectations, no impact
Initiative sustained	• Ceases to exist after initial start • Ceases to exist as a permanent structure, although impact on policy continues separate from the structure

At each transition point, positive action was deliberately encouraged by a small group of seven community catalysts who came together during the initial poverty study and as a smaller self-appointed steering group advocating for change after the report was published. The group was formed and led by both authors of this chapter but also consisted of the city manager of Lexington, executive director of Rockbridge County Government Services, executive director of the Free Health Clinic, director of social services for the county, and a leader from Total Action Against Poverty in Roanoke. This group later expanded to include one of the local school district superintendents and a member of the Lexington City Council.

Recommendations for Faculty

Community members bring credibility to the process and relationships that are essential. They are also immersed in the daily routines, deadlines, and emergencies that need to be addressed, and this can distract their attention from a larger community initiative. University faculty, on the other hand, live outside the fray of these issues. From this position, they can support change by assuming the natural role they have as a partner: listening, observing, and collaborating with staff in mobilizing resources as needed. Faculty, staff, and students are able to step back, anticipate challenges, plan ahead, take advantage of local political connections, and build interest through informal meetings in the community with concerned citizens, churches, and various movers and shakers. This being said, it is essential for someone or a small group with credibility in the community and university (whether faculty, staff, or community members) to deliberately facilitate progress.

Stable Leadership and Time

Sustaining community initiatives usually requires some form of stable leadership that can be maintained over a sufficient time period for implementation, with commitment to ongoing learning and flexibility. From the beginning, the initiative was supported with strong leadership. The city manager's request for the study and Beckley's attention to the needs assessment as a signature project gave the initiative special status in the community and on campus. Caron and Martin brought outstanding leadership to the poverty assessment, and their subsequent presentations impressed local audiences. The student report generated by the assessment was extensively covered in the local media, and a wave of momentum began to emerge as the Community Forum and establishment of the commission created a sense of excitement. The campus and community steering group that eventually emerged encouraged this momentum over a two-year period, during which the initiative continued to make progress in shaping local deliberations on policy, facilitating stronger relationships and sharing among community agencies, and encouraging higher democratic participation among local citizens.

This momentum ended during the third year as the three most active members of the original steering group left the community for other positions, including both of us. The ideas and action generated during the initiative led to change in local policies and services, although the infrastructure supporting community-campus networking, democratic participation, learning, and continuous generation of new groups and projects is uncertain and less readily visible. The need for strategic collaboration still exists, but at this stage the momentum sparked by the Caron and Martin needs assessment, Community Forum, and Commission on Poverty has diminished. This illustrates the need for stable leadership in launching a new initiative, carefully planning and executing the transfer of leadership, investment of financial resources, and time to institutionalize structures that formed through the initiative.

Recommendations for Faculty

Tenured faculty and long-term university staff can bring stable leadership to initiatives as partners and consultants for the community, even if as individuals they do not see it as part of their professional responsibility to stay with the emerging entity for the long run. Sustained faculty-staff leadership can provide the time to build additional leadership and an infrastructure that can withstand changes in leadership over time. Key components of the infrastructure can include communication structures, a model for facilitating leadership transition, and access to needed financial resources. This is not to say that all initiatives must be sustained. They are created to mobilize needed change, not necessarily as permanent structures. Faculty may be able to play an ideal consulting role to work with the community and students to assess the value of an initiative and need for sustained commitment.

Conclusion

This case study provides an example of designing CBR that results in generative impact, which is something like a multiplier effect in which an initial event, idea, or project generates additional ideas, projects, and effects beyond the scope of the initial effort. Branches are then formed, generating more ideas and projects. This notion of generative impact draws on ideas of generative leadership designed to foster innovation and creativity through a balance of autonomy, transparency, and connectedness (Surie & Hazy, 2006). Some new organizations operate on this principle: An initial investment of seed into a small project leads to multiple branches of impact, each with its own story. Through the Poverty Initiative, an initial student needs assessment, requested by a local community partner, created greater awareness of poverty in the community, and specific issues cited in the students' report led to specific changes in local policies and services. Generative impact developed as community structures such as the Commission on Poverty and grassroots community groups were formed. In turn, these structures generated more research, deliberation on poverty issues, knowledge of effective interventions, and shared communication among diverse community partners touching on issues such as public education, criminal justice, transportation, housing and homelessness, financial literacy, and access to quality health care.

Faculty and staff collaborated with students and community members in making this possible. In summary, faculty seeking to design or participate in a similar initiative might consider the following.

1. Ground the initiative in a solid needs assessment that makes use of student knowledge, motivation, and reflection as well as the rich experience and knowledge community members bring to the table. Student reflection can be integrated in a way that supports student learning while also enriching the effects in community.

2. Facilitate small learning communities consisting of faculty, staff, students, and community members. A learning community can engage the student-community research team in meaningful exchanges that enrich understanding of issues and generates collective problem solving.

3. Support design at each iteration of the initiative with a combined sense of predetermined structures and plans for organizing, while being open to listening, discovering, and responding to unanticipated opportunities in the community

4. Consider serving as a stable voice or catalyst in building the community infrastructure necessary for sustained impact.

Among all partners, faculty are the most likely to bring content, conceptual and methodological expertise, and an informed critical lens to support strong initiatives. They are also generally the ones to bring students into the experience. To be effective, their expertise must be entwined with the strengths other partners bring to the effort.

References

Caron, M., & Martin, C. (2008). *Rockbridge poverty assessment 2008: A community-based research project supported by the Shepherd Program at Washington and Lee University.* Retrieved from www2.wlu.edu/documents/shepherd/Rockbridge_Poverty_Report.pdf

Eyler, J. (2002). Reflection: Linking service and learning—linking students and communities. *Journal of Social Issues, 58*(3), 517–534.

Mintzberg, H., & Huy, Q. N. (2003). The rhythm of change. *MIT Sloan Management Review, 44*(4), 79–84.

Senge, P., & Scharmer, C. O. (2006). Community action research: Learning as a community of practitioners, consultants, and researchers. In P. Reason & H. Bradbury-Huang (Eds.), *Handbook of action research: Concise paperback edition* (pp. 195–206). Thousand Oaks, CA: SAGE.

Strand, K., Marullo, S., Cutforth, N., Stoecker, R., & Donohue, P. (2003). *Community-based research and higher education: Principles and practices.* San Francisco, CA: Jossey-Bass.

Surie, G., & Hazy, J. K. (2006). Generative leadership: Nurturing innovation in complex systems. *Emergence: Complexity and Organization, 8*(4), 13–26.

16

LEARNING TO CO-CONSTRUCT SOLUTIONS TO URBAN SCHOOL CHALLENGES IN LOS ANGELES

Adrianna Kezar and Sylvia Rousseau

In 2006 the Los Angeles Urban League (LAUL) introduced the Neighborhoods@Work Initiative (or Neighborhoods at Work), one of the most ambitious community redevelopment projects. This project is an effort organized by a consortium of the LAUL, the Department of Public Works, the City Attorney's Office, the Los Angeles Police Department, and multiple other Los Angeles partners. The goal of the project is to improve the standard of living in five domains simultaneously—housing, education, employment, safety, and health—in the concentrated area of the 70-block neighborhood anchored by Crenshaw High School in south Los Angeles. This initiative creates a new vision for community redevelopment and university work with communities.

This project is obviously multidimensional, and it is also interdisciplinary, because the research brings in scholars from not only the five domains, but also policy, urban development, social work, and economics. Neighborhoods@Work does not just aim generally for improvement but has very specific goals and targets for each area (e.g., health, safety) the project is planned to reach within a certain timeline to demonstrate impact. This project epitomizes the key components of the community impact framework discussed in this book, which is the long-term strategic plan proposed by diverse collaborators, evaluated and revised along the way, toward the attainment of community development. Research, particularly community-based research

(CBR), plays an important role. To date, the project has raised $15 million to fund this comprehensive approach to community redevelopment.

In this chapter, we present three co-constructive solutions to urban school challenges. First, we discuss the Neighborhoods@Work Initiative in general, showing how it has evolved toward the development of long-term goals and strategies for the attainment of important improvements in the local area. Second, we describe the Greater Crenshaw Educational Partnership (GCEP) that evolved from the overall Neighborhoods@Work project and is a partnership among the Rossier School of Education at the University of Southern California, Crenshaw High School, and a number of other partners in the community and the university. We were involved with the Greater Crenshaw Partnership, and Sylvia Rousseau was a member of the the Crenshaw community as well. Third, we present a unique type of CBR involving graduate students conducting their doctoral dissertation work in collaboration with community organizations. The findings of this thematic dissertation research group highlight challenges and opportunities that emerge in trying to create a complex and multifaceted partnership among the community, school, and university.

We conclude with some overall observations about the benefits and potential of this type of CBR for faculty and students. After reading this chapter we hope that readers will leave with excitement about the potential of such a revolutionary vision for CBR projects that can be a part of academic courses and also some moderated realism about the difficulty of creating such important partnerships in our existing and sometimes limited structures and cultures in communities and universities.

Neighborhoods@Work Initiative

Long-Term Goals, Strategies, and Revision Toward Impact

In 2006 the LAUL released its strategic plan called Neighborhoods@Work, based on a study it had conducted the same year. A year earlier, the LAUL and the United Way released the report *The State of Blacks in Los Angeles* (Nicols, 2005) that documented how many of the gains made in the 1970s and 1980s on measures such as access to housing and employment essentially had been lost. The authors described the expansion of low-income populations and the shrinkage of the middle class among African Americans in Los Angeles and noted the continued decline of neighborhoods in African American communities. The implications of this report were significant, and the report concluded that if those trends remained, they would not have an impact on the African American community alone but could also affect the broader Los Angeles community. The report also suggested that existing community redevelopment efforts were not working, and a new approach was needed.

Responding to the report, Neighborhoods@Work signaled a new approach to thinking about community redevelopment, rooted in a systems perspective that had been emerging in the 1990s. Its key proponents had declared, "Pre-requisites to health (for example) are no longer simply disease prevention, or 'proper' lifestyles, but include peace, shelter, education, food, income, a stable ecosystem, social justice and equity" (Eisten, 1994, p. 237). This statement reflected the essence of the systems approach, which contrasted with the earlier paradigm of community redevelopment's focus on each group with expertise working to solve single problems such as housing, safety, or education. Within that previous framework, the links and interconnections among these issues were largely ignored. Neighborhoods@Work, however, adopted a systems philosophy in which multiple aspects of the community were addressed simultaneously with connections among these phenomena. Moreover, the Urban League organized Neighborhoods@Work around key interrelated areas significant for the designated community: health, safety, education, employment, and housing.

In addition to a systems approach, early participants in this process were convinced that community redevelopment efforts needed to be grounded in demonstrating impact. Critical to the formation of the project was creating benchmarks on the community's current performance on the chosen measures and metrics and then creating specific future targets for 3, 5, and 10 years beyond 2006. The LAUL also contracted with the Bridgespan Group, the same group that worked with the Harlem Children's Zone, a successful model of disrupting the cycle of generational poverty in central Harlem, to develop metrics for the project. At present, the project has identified multiple indicators of success for each of the five domains. For example, in the area of safety the LAUL is following the reduction in several different types of crime and better relationships between the police force and the community.

Because it is difficult to measure benchmarks unless an area of impact is designated, the comprehensive initiative targets a 70-square-block neighborhood around Crenshaw High School in south-central Los Angeles. Neighborhoods@Work chose a bounded geographic area building on the work of the Harlem Children's Zone (2002), which advised selecting a neighborhood that is "large enough to include all the essential components of community life—schools, churches, recreational facilities, commercial areas, common space—and small enough to allow programs and services to reach every willing member" (p. 2). These benchmark areas are important for demonstrating success but are also important for creating research on the project. This was especially important because Urban League staff realized that almost no community redevelopment projects they could identify had conducted research on the process or outcomes so successes could be easily replicated. Therefore, one of the major goals for the project was to be able to create a replicable model of urban redevelopment that could be brought to other locations.

The project thus began by commissioning several research reports to obtain baseline data on the five indicators. Healthy Cities, a research consultancy, was commissioned to collect initial indicator data. Because research was such a central aspect of the community redevelopment effort, the Urban League also approached the University of Southern California as well as several other Southern California colleges and universities to become partners with them. Faculty and administrators (including both of us) from various schools and units of the University of Southern California began meeting with staff at the Urban League to design an evaluation project that would follow the process of rolling out Neighborhoods@Work and also help in measuring the various impact metrics over the life of the project.

A Highly Participatory Process

The five areas of concern for Neighborhoods@Work—housing, education, employment, safety, and health—emerged from conversations with residents and key stakeholders in the community. After those areas were identified, the project moved rapidly, building excitement in the community through meetings with various constituencies related to the five components. For example, the staff at the Urban League held town hall meetings, established safety priorities and accountability metrics and goals, and integrated safety initiatives with the antigang and clean streets initiatives from the City Attorney's Office, the Los Angeles Police Department and the Department of Public Works. The staff also conducted extensive asset mapping of the community to move toward achieving the goals and soon realized that outside expertise and resources were often not needed.

Placing the community first is related to another unique quality of Neighborhoods@Work—co-construction—a notion adopted from Freire's (1970) work with communities. In co-construction the project design and implementation are carried out in collaboration with the community and the external stakeholders. The issues identified in the Neighborhoods@Work plan required solutions that none of the individual organizations or agencies had the capacity to create alone; the various stakeholders had to work together to co-construct unique solutions from the individual participating organizations' statements of belief. Each of the organizations had its own belief statements, as well as missions and vision statements.

The project is based on an assumption that the revitalization of a community requires the collective efforts of multiple parties, all of which are essential to address the complex issues typically found in urban communities. The design of Neighborhoods@Work likewise reflects an understanding of the interconnectedness and interdependency of the multiple segments of a community, and it places education at the point of intersection. For such a partnership to be co-constructed, Freirian-type dialogue, marked by trust, mutual respect for all stakeholders' knowledge, and love for one another must be present (Freire, 1970). Each partner must be recognized for the unique contribution it brings to the partnership, and all partners must be focused on the common goal of creating something new that benefits everyone collectively.

Although CBR was part of the overall project, and faculty and students were part of the work in various ways, we next focus on a CBR project we were directly involved with that became a major initiative of the Neighborhoods@Work Initiative called GCEP. This particular CBR project was part of a process evaluation and specifically looked at the process of co-construction as a unique feature of the project. We briefly describe GCEP before we review the CBR effort.

Greater Crenshaw Educational Partnership

The Neighborhoods@Work model placed education at the center. Its premise was that schools in the community are the causes and the victims of dire circumstances. Therefore, the LAUL created GCEP to focus on transforming community schools, starting with the community high school. GCEP has four members: the Los Angeles Urban League, the University of Southern California, the Tom and Ethel Bradley Foundation, and Crenshaw High School, which is a partner rather than the object of the partnership's work. Each year the LAUL publishes an annual report about Neighborhoods@Work with an update on this project.

The transformation that Crenshaw High School is undergoing is unlike the typical reform efforts taking place in many urban schools across America because it involves this extensive network of partners and the multidimensional model of the Neighborhoods@Work Initiative. The work on behalf of the school proved to be challenging; sustaining substantive change required a nontraditional comprehensive approach such as co-construction that engaged the school and community as true partners (Bringle & Hatcher, 2002; Mayfield & Lucas, 2000; Suarez-Balcazar, Harper, & Lewis, 2005). Furthermore, in traditional partnerships universities often "posture [themselves] as 'know-it-alls,' having all the expertise that communities need with little or no regard for the history and culture of communities" (Wilson, 2004, p. 20).

When GCEP began, Crenshaw High School was close to being reconstituted. Reconstitution of schools is a process by which the Los Angeles Unified School District restaffs the entire school, requiring all teachers, including the principal, to reapply for their jobs. Only a select number of teachers is allowed to return. This process is considered one model of school reform by the Los Angeles Unified School District because of its underperformance on No Child Left Behind metrics for multiple years. In the six years prior to the formation of GCEP, the school had four different principals appointed by the district with no consultation from the community or faculty. The school temporarily lost its accreditation in early 2000, only to be restored on a conditional basis after much intervention and many promises from the district. The school has maintained a relatively stable faculty, but no standards-based systemic process for evaluation of teachers had been in place to ensure the quality of teaching. Students were failing classes at a rate close to 60%. For several years the school posted low standardized test scores, and in 2007 the school failed to test a sufficient number of students to qualify for an Academic Performance Index score, which is issued by the state to indicate schools' annual academic progress. Although the district pumped hundreds of thousands of dollars into the school, it appeared to be unwilling or unable to create the systemic change the school needed.

Although some parents had withdrawn their children from the school, other parents decided to stay and work for the change that was needed. They joined with equally discontented teachers, community members, and a handful of students in informal meetings to do something. This group, known as the Crenshaw Cougar Coalition (CCC), met for more than two years, supported by the Tom and Ethel Bradley Foundation, to identify the underlying causes for the school's demise and develop a plan of action. During those years, Neighborhoods@Work also established a presence in the CCC, and LAUL formed a relationship with the University of Southern California to conduct research and evaluate its work in the community. All these elements were in place when the Los Angeles Unified School District created a new unit called iDesign for the purpose of facilitating external partnerships to guide change in schools that had demonstrated low academic performance for multiple years. Efforts by the parents, students, and teachers who were members of the school-based CCC led to a vote by parents and teachers to join this district unit and come into partnership with the GCEP. CCC's highly active role in promoting GCEP was the main factor in obtaining a positive vote from teachers and parents to accept GCEP.

This historic action marked a major change in the relationship between a neighborhood school and the school district because people in a community had decided to choose their own partners and take back their school. In this new relationship, the university brought its traditional resources of professional development, grants to fund small projects with clusters of teachers, and an available supply of graduates from the teacher education program as potential teachers. However, the university was also now positioned to learn about working as partners with the community in ways that required extensive dialogue, patience, and trust in the ability of the community to act as a partner in co-constructing the terms of the relationship. This was the difficult work essential to creating democratic schools (Dewey & Dewey, 1915; Epstein, 2001; Freire, 1970) that required a model of co-construction to ensure that traditional hierarchical relationships among communities, schools, and universities would not prevail. The community was thus determined to develop a partnership in a different way (Carroll, LaPoint, & Tyler, 2001).

With this action to form GCEP, the school dynamics immediately changed. The district used to have primary accountability, but now faculty, parents, and the newly selected partners held an unprecedented level of responsibility and accountability for the school. In assuming this new role for its own transformation, the school formed a School Transition Team made up of teachers, parents, students, community members, and school administrators, elected by each group's constituents. The University of Southern California's Rossier School of Education, at the request of two other partners and Crenshaw High School, invited Sylvia Rousseau, a clinical professor who was a former superintendent in a nearby area and lived in the general vicinity of the community, to function as the interim executive director. She spent 15 months on site working with teachers, parents, and administrators to help them implement the changes they envisioned for the school. Other professional schools in the University of Southern California, including the School of Social Work, the Annenberg School of Communication, the Viterbi School of Engineering, and the Marshall School of Business, collaborated with the high school to provide additional services and support.

In the next year, a flurry of activity began to transform the school. Large numbers of teachers spent their after-school and weekend time to convert the school into four theme-based small learning communities, create a ninth grade house, and maintain two preexisting magnet schools. The ninth grade house serves as a setting to orient all students entering the school in ninth grade to the high school community and to prepare them for enrolling in a small learning community in the 10th grade. Their work drew commendations from the review committee that approved their restructuring plan. By converting to block scheduling, the school was able to create an additional period in the school day that enabled students to recover credits from failed classes or take classes at the local community college. The larger Neigbor-hoods@Work program used its partnerships with the Los Angeles Police Department and the Los Angeles Sheriff's Department to create safe passage for students to and from school. The LAUL also drew grant money from a variety of foundations and corporations to implement change and award minigrants for teachers to implement innovative instructional practices. Staff from community-based service agencies met weekly with the school psychologist, psychiatric social worker, administrators, and grade counselors from each small learning community to establish a case management process for addressing the psychosocial issues for struggling students. As noted earlier, research is a key aspect of Neighborhoods@Work and GCEP; therefore, administrators of the Rossier School of Education realized it would be important to document the important work occurring as part of Rossier's involvement with GCEP, particularly this unique model of school reform and transformation in which the community was an active partner that required the university to assume a new role as learner and equal participant.

CBR With Doctoral Students

As a result of the commitment to conduct research using the Neighbor-hoods@Work model, Rossier faculty and administration dedicated a thematic dissertation group to study the GCEP and its process of forming a community-school-university partnership. In addition to assisting with meeting the larger project's research goals, administrators at the school of education recognized the potential of this study to add knowledge for carrying out its mission "to strengthen urban education, locally, nationally and globally" and "guide and develop practitioner leaders in urban educational settings." Also, Rousseau proposed a theme focused on community-school-university partnerships and saw its potential for expanding the understanding of professors who are continually engaged in rethinking curricula to prepare graduates to teach and lead in urban schools. Studying a complex model such as GCEP that shares the principles of the larger Neighborhoods@Work project (i.e., an interdisciplinary, impact-focused and co-constructed process) for transforming an urban school had the potential to enhance the university's pedagogy and school curriculum. Thus, the study held potential benefits for both partners, GCEP and the Rossier School of Education and highlights a valuable and perhaps unique way of bringing graduate students into CBR.[1]

The thematic dissertation group exhibited several characteristics of CBR. As described in more detail later, the lead researcher of the project (Rousseau) was also a member of the Crenshaw community. Students likewise spent considerable time out in the community and with community groups before they started focusing and narrowing their approach to the research. Thus the community was actively involved in conceptualizing the research project's focus and design and remained involved in the entire research process. In sum, all the researchers were present in the community and were part of the unfolding partnership between the university and community.

Furthermore, the thematic dissertation group also adopted principles used in the Neighborhoods@Work model into their classroom experience, making this CBR process unique. In particular, the notion of co-construction became a foundational aspect of the group's work, expanding notions of collaboration with the community to include collaboration among students and working in groups to design research together. Co-construction, of course, is an important principle of CBR and became a major philosophical underpinning for the education process as well. Co-construction in the groups involved ongoing face-to-face and electronic communications to deepen everyone's knowledge about the problems or issues related to the common dissertation theme and discussion about the literature to expand their collective body of knowledge. This process not only represented a new cultural model for conducting dissertation research, but also prepared the higher education students for creating cultural models for dialogue and co-construction in solving the problems in urban schools.

Ten students joined the group to study community-school-university partnerships. Four public school teachers, a principal, an assistant principal, a director of an on-campus program, an on-campus residence coordinator, and a curriculum developer were also involved in providing advice and feedback. Thus, multiple perspectives were represented in group discourses and action.

Although there were many different interesting aspects of this model of community-school-university partnerships to study, the group, working collectively, developed several research questions to guide their study of GCEP, grouped into two broad categories: (a) What is a process that enables communities, schools, and universities to co-construct partnerships for the purpose of transforming K–12 urban schools? What are the persistent barriers to establishing such partnerships? and What are some effective strategies that have the potential for overcoming barriers? (b) What attributes of partnerships capable of creating a new cultural model in urban schools can result from the process of co-constructing community, school, and university partnership with the intent to transform a K–12 school?

The group decided to study the process of co-construction because it was a unique aspect of the partnership or model. They created a working definition of *co-construction* as a process by which two or more parties engage in an interactive and equitable relationship to create shared understandings and agreed-upon outcomes leading to a new creation. *Co-constructed partnerships* among communities, schools, and universities in urban settings, as defined by their study, were a convergence of knowledge, resources, and assets through dialogic relationships with the potential to create models for eradicating historic, social, economic, and political barriers on behalf of urban school transformation.

Process

Engaging in co-construction was very much a part of the thematic group process from the formation of the research questions to the literature review to peer editing to working with the community mutually. The thematic dissertation group met every week in the start-up phase and then less frequently to discuss the core body of literature the chair had assigned and alert one another to additional research literature that shed light on the problem of co-constructing community-school-university partnerships.

Typical of CBR, prior to initiating their formal study, the dissertation students went into the community in teams and drove around to observe the day-to-day activities of the community. They also shopped in stores, attended community meetings, and had informal conversations with community residents. This process, carried out while students were conducting their literature review, helped the dissertation group balance real-life impressions of the community with the data (via statistics) that mostly portrayed the community as broken and dysfunctional. During the exploratory period of shaping the study, the group also invited lead persons in the partnership, teachers at the targeted school, professors from the university, and community residents, including parents, to discuss their perspectives on the history leading up to the GCEP. They shared their perspectives on the community and expressed their hopes for what GCEP would accomplish for the school. These conversations, along with the students' literature review, played an essential role in helping the doctoral students gain a perspective for designing the study. These experiences further helped the research team understand not only the problems but also the assets found in the community.

Research Design and Data Collection

The thematic dissertation group chose a case study research design to examine the partnership, informed by community members' perspective garnered through community visits and meetings. Following the unique model of co-construction, the research team collaboratively developed protocols for conducting interviews, observations, and analysis of artifacts to collect and triangulate the data. The interview protocols were based on research questions and theoretical frameworks co-constructed from their collective research literature. Using their observation protocols, the group examined documents including the vision and mission statements of each of the partner organizations, each partner organization's constitution and by-laws, and minutes from the organizations' meetings independent of GCEP. They also reviewed the GCEP bylaws and examined minutes from GCEP board meetings, transition team meetings, and the CCC. The group likewise examined the portion of GCEP's business plan that included the transition goals created for the school to exit program improvement status and regain full multiyear accreditation from the Western Association of Schools and Colleges.

The thematic dissertation group used another co-constructed protocol to conduct formal observations of school hallways and classrooms, board meetings, transition team meetings, community meetings, and Crenshaw Cougar Coalition meetings. They conducted more than 35 interviews in two-person teams using the jointly constructed interview questions. With the permission of the interviewees, the research team audiotaped the interviews in addition to taking notes. Their interviewees included parents, teachers, classified staff, administrators, lead persons in each of the partner organizations, and community residents. The number of members of the research team made collecting this rich and extensive body of data possible. The team constructed schedules and assignments to distribute the work in a coordinated manner and even co-constructed a codebook based on the findings of all members for analyzing the data. The codebook was available electronically for all members to contribute to using criteria set through a norming process conducted by the group.

In CBR the final results of research are usually brought to the community for member accuracy checks. The researchers did not do this. Rousseau, who was also a community member, was struggling with norms from the university about how involved the community could or should be in research processes and worried about whether colleagues would find it legitimate if community members had an impact on and shaped the findings of the research. She was also concerned whether students' work would be considered legitimate by the other faculty members, which led to less community involvement in the project than what is the ideal for CBR. Thus, there were struggles with balancing traditional research interests and CBR tenets.

Challenges and Opportunities for Co-constructed Partnerships

Several themes are reviewed here that represent challenges and opportunities in co-construction that other partnerships might experience in attempting to develop community-based research projects. Challenges are power dynamics and trust; opportunities include the bridge spanner role, representation structures, empowerment, and presence.

Power Dynamics

University constituents attempting to form partnerships with communities will likely encounter real or perceived power dynamics operating in the various segments of the community in contrast to what they typically expect to find. University representatives considered their emerging relationship with the Urban League to be an engagement with community, but along the way they had to rethink that assumption. In its up-close work with GCEP, those within the university discovered that the parents, teachers, classified staff, and a small number of students had formed a tight coalition, which in the context of transforming the community's school, perceived itself to be the authentic community, as opposed to a broader representation of the community.

This group, which brought itself under the umbrella of the CCC, had assumed an identity and a concentration of power that neither schools nor communities alone possess in traditional relationships with universities and school districts. The CCC provided a real-life example of the assertion made in literature that sustainable reform in low-income communities and communities of color will only take place when the people whose children attend those schools assert their interests. According to Oakes and Lipton (2002), when these parents work together with middle-class and equity-focused educators, they can produce a new cultural model for engagement. The research group found the unity among parents, teachers, and community to be an asset in building an authentic partnership.

Yet, an authentic sense of community among a subset of the partners that helped them feel powerful enough to assert themselves also destabilized a more rapid movement toward a broader partnership. Co-construction among all stakeholders including other groups that considered themselves to be authentic representatives of the community, such as the Urban League, was necessary for it slowed down the process and shifted power. The dissertation team found that the CCC perceived the LAUL to be a service provider, not a representative of the community itself, and felt concerned about the Urban League's ability to work as a partner without asserting power in the partnership. As a result of a perceived fear of being marginalized in the relationship, members of the

CCC decided their interests and perspective were more important than those of the other partners and constantly challenged other partners' authenticity or actions. The new authentic community of parents and teachers represented one of those troubling paradoxes that occur in attempting co-construction: They need to develop this level of power, but it has the potential for becoming just as much of a problem as power from the top down.

Just how assertive a community coalition needs to be is part of the challenge (Carroll et al., 2001). Through this experience, the dissertation group found that the community can be as much of a barrier to building partnerships as the institutions that are perceived to hold power. As uncomfortable as this tension may be, it is necessary to create the kind of balance in power required to transform urban schools that represent and respect the culture, knowledge, and assets of the community while also respecting the assets and knowledge of the people from the university. Further research on partnerships that are striving to operate in a co-construction mode is needed to gain insights for future attempts for partnership.

Trust

The research literature proposes that dialogue characterized by trust can help dissolve power distinctions and facilitate true collaboration (Kent & Taylor, 2001). The dissertation researchers learned from Rousseau that board meetings should not be the only venue for building trust; instead, trust should be built on visible demonstrations of the involved parties' commitment to the common task (Bridges & Husbands, 1996; Kezar, 2007; Lockwood, 1996). The parents and teachers in the CCC needed opportunities to move beyond discussion and protest and to engage in action. In this environment of a search for authentic community, power struggles, and lack of trust, several key facets emerged for reaching the goal of co-construction and overcoming these common obstacles.

The Bridge Spanner Role

The research team found the role of a critical bridge person (Bridges & Husbands, 1996; Kezer, 2007; Lockwood, 1996) to be essential in creating the conditions for partners to build trust and thus engage in the dialogue required for co-construction. Kezar (2007) defines *bridge person* as someone who understands the culture of multiple communities and is able to speak their languages and "take responsibility for monitoring the collaboration, maintaining communication, building positive group dynamics, resolving conflicts, ensuring barriers are overcome, and creating facilitators for moving the partnership forward" (p. 35).

The effective critical bridge person is respected by the group, whose members see themselves and are seen as powerless (Ostrander, 2004) and perhaps comes from among them (Freire 1970). This person has the capacity to create space (Shields, 2005) in which dialogic relationships (Freire 1970; Miller & Hafner, 2008, Shields, 2005) can be co-constructed.

Sylvia Rousseau was an ideal bridge person. Not only was she a long-time resident of the community, but also her husband had been a respected pastor there. She had been a principal in a highly diverse high school and superintendent of one of the Los Angeles Unified School District's local district-serving communities similar to the Neighborhoods@Work target area. At the time GCEP was formed, she had been a clinical professor at Rossier's for two years. Upon the request of people with the Urban League and the Tom and Ethel Bradley Foundation, the dean of Rossier consented to her spending time at the school site. The teachers and parents also accepted her role to work directly with the school in meeting the urgent goals set by No Child Left Behind, the state, and the school district. She began by working with the school and GCEP board to create a set of transition goals to present to the Los Angeles school board.

Representation Structures

The IED assisted the school in organizing a process for all stakeholders to elect representatives to a school transition team that expanded opportunities for participation beyond GCEP's elected board members. The transition team established committees whose membership was open to anyone who wanted to join. This transition team and its meetings became a parallel process for decision making beyond the official GCEP board meetings.

As a result of their work in the transition teams, parents and teachers felt more empowered to participate as partners in the board meetings. Over time, discussions about school reform efforts at GCEP board meetings became more dialogic. The partners gained respect for the capacity of CCC's parents, teachers, and students to contribute to the partnership. The research team captured the parents' and teachers' comments in meetings where they became comfortable using the term *co-construction* in defining their participation in the partnership. The conversations at GCEP board meetings, although continuing to manifest disagreement, frustration, and doubt, were nonetheless marked by growing trust, focus, and acceptance of the need for one another.

Empowerment and Presence

Rousseau spent her first month listening to what the school and community wanted to accomplish for transforming their school. It became apparent that these people had ideas for change, but because action had been undertaken toward the school without involving anyone from the school in carrying them out, they felt paralyzed and helpless. She helped the school take its own first steps by following through on the administration's desire to reorganize the school into small learning communities. Teachers, administrators, parents, and students played multiple roles in completing this task. They saw the learning communities as a means for personalizing students' experience with the school and for building collaborative relationships among faculty to improve teaching and learning. In her role of representing the University of Southern California, Rousseau advised, helped the high school shape roles, and worked with the coalition of parents and teachers to stay on task on a daily basis. She brokered discussions between the school and the other partners to ensure they all had significant roles in advancing the process. The LAUL and the Bradley Foundation sent representatives to work with the team in constructing the small learning communities, and they infused resources to advance the work. The small learning communities were planned, organized, and implemented within six months of intensive collaborative work and were a testimony to the work they could do when they collaborated and incorporated one another's resources and ideas.

The student research study identified key emerging strengths in the partnership that the research literature emphasizes as essential to sustaining effectiveness: dialogue, bridge building, leadership, governance process, and empowerment processes. These are indicators that a co-constructed model with reduced hierarchical structures is possible. Also on the positive side, GCEP met some of its early transitional goals. The number of ninth graders on track to graduate in four years increased from 44% to 63% and for 10th graders, from 28% to 37%. The four-year graduation rate climbed from 27% to 43%. The final visit by the Western Association of Schools and Colleges produced a positive report with restoration of full accreditation for three years, with a one-day visit at the end of the first year of accreditation. Enrollment increased, teachers began to create a culture that required greater accountability to one another for effective teaching, and a principal with a strong reputation for leading schools was appointed. In spite of these outcomes, the model of a co-constructed partnership with reductions in hierarchical power relationships remains tenuous and fragile. This model contradicts the traditional and historically defined roles of universities, schools, and communities; therefore, it is constantly facing challenges.

Conclusions, Insights, and Recommendations

This chapter helps provide a guiding vision for a new type of CBR that is multidimensional, interdisciplinary, strategic, co-constructed, and focused on impact. We documented how such a unique model unfolded and the various successes and challenges that emerged, particularly around the element of co-construction, which was the focus of the thematic dissertation group studying the partnership. Here we summarize some key lessons faculty conducting CBR and administrators who want to support such work might learn from this ambitious project.

As faculty, we learned the importance of a university presence in the community for effectively creating partnerships and meaningful projects with students. Presence is a critical factor in facilitating the collaborative work of partnerships, especially in urban schools that have a history of underperformance likely marked by an absence of systems and structures for transforming into high-functioning schools. Therefore, immersion in the day-to-day action taking place among stakeholders is indispensable for higher education faculty to understand the subtle and obvious ways people act in the context of school. Faculty have to be close to the places where they conduct research to connect students to the CBR sites; this is valuable for developing rich assignments and fostering meaningful discussion among students.

Another important lesson from the study is the value of having students participate as researchers, to witness up close the complexities of school reform to link theory and practice and to form theories from the ground up. Students often complain that the theories they encounter in their education become meaningless in the face of real-world challenges. Here, under the guidance of university faculty, students had an opportunity to witness real-world strategies for mitigating challenges and to match them to theories they had learned about in class. For instance, students commented on how the issue of whether the community has too much voice was not present in theories but became a reality in conducting research from the ground up. No theory would have anticipated this challenge.

CBR projects also help universities examine their curricula for their ability to prepare leaders in any field. For the Rossier School of Education, the project helped demonstrate the need to change curriculum that has been created to prepare teachers and leaders for the urban setting. The school is now looking at ways to incorporate action research methodologies into the curriculum so that teacher and leaders can leave with skills to conduct their own studies in the future. In addition, faculty members are evaluating their syllabi to ensure that classes represent an interdisciplinary perspective that is needed for addressing complex problems in communities and schools.

The CBR project also reinforced the need for university faculty to exercise restraint when offering existing services and resources to the local public school. It is difficult helping university faculty to be patient while waiting for the partnership to create trust, voice, empowerment, and a sense of authentic community before offering their expertise and services. By delaying their services until the school had developed a readiness, some of the university faculty became disillusioned with the partnership and lost interest. The bridge spanner can play a role in trying to keep faculty interested, but it may not be enough. It might be better to let impatient faculty drop out than jeopardize the overall partnership and community building needed. Individual expertise loss is less important than the overall collective effort, and as this chapter has highlighted, building trust, community, and authentic dialogue is difficult.

We also learned the challenges of implementing CBR in the face of conservative university ideals about appropriate research. While we followed the principles of CBR quite closely as the project began, toward the end, we worried if other faculty would see student findings as legitimate if the doctoral candidates conducting the research made changes based on community input; thus, the final product does not include the community feedback and involvement that is typical of CBR. In the end, power dynamics among faculty and administrators who did not embrace community input prevented a fuller usage of CBR. This process helped us understand some of the sticking points with other faculty and the type of conversations we need to have early with other faculty so that we can ensure we can incorporate all the principles of CBR.

The challenges are there. However, seeing university faculty, community members, government officials, and leaders of nonprofits feel emboldened by taking an active role in co-constructing solutions to complex problems in the community makes it well worth the effort.

Note

1. Although the study did not focus directly on community impacts, valuable outcomes appear to have resulted and are noted later. Nonetheless, the process-oriented research illustrates an approach to CBR within a framework that values long-term impact and is a collaborative, collective, and co-constructed model between students and community.

References

Bridges, D., & Husbands, C. (1996). *Consorting and collaborating in the education marketplace*. London, UK: Falmer.

Bringle, R. G., & Hatcher, J. A. (2002). Campus-community partnerships: The terms of engagement. *Journal of Social Issues, 58*(3), 503–516.

Carroll, G., LaPoint, V., & Tyler, K. (2001). Co-construction: A facilitator for school reform in school, community and university partnerships. *Journal of Negro Education*, *70*(1/2), 38–58.

Dewey, J., & Dewey, E. (1915). *Schools of to-morrow*. New York: E. P. Dutton.

Eisten, A. (1994). Survey of neighborhood-based, comprehensive, community empowerment initiatives. *Health Education and Behavior Quarterly*, *21*, 235–252.

Epstein, J. (2001). *School, family, and community partnerships: Preparing educators and improving schools*. Boulder, CO: Westview Press.

Freire, P. (1970). *Pedagogy of the oppressed*. New York, NY: Continuum.

Harlem Children's Zone. (2002). *Growth plan FY 2001–FY 2009*. Retrieved from www.bridgespan.org/getattachment/7c9ffa2f-6a3b-480e-9da2-901fcb34956c/ Harlem-Children-s-Zone-Business-Plan.aspx

Kent, M. L., & Taylor, M. (2001). Toward a dialogic theory of public relations. *Public Relations Review*, *28*(1), 21–37.

Kezar, A. (2007). A tale of two cultures: Schools and universities in partnership for school reform and student success. *Metropolitan Universities*, *18*(4), 28–47.

Lockwood, A. T. (1996). School-Community Collaboration. *New Leaders for Tomorrow*, *2*, 35.

Mayfield, L., & Lucas, E. P. (2000). Mutual awareness, mutual respect: The community and the university interact. *Cityscape*, *5*, 173–184.

Miller, P. M., & Hafner, M. M. (2008). Moving toward dialogical collaboration: A critical examination of a university-school-community partnership. *Educational Administration Quarterly*, *44*(1), 66–110. doi:10.1177/0013161X07309469

Nicols, M. (2005). *The state of Blacks in Los Angeles: Full report*. Los Angeles, CA: Los Angeles Urban League and United Way of Greater Los Angeles.

Oakes, J., & Lipton, M. (2002). Struggling for educational equity in diverse communities: School reform as social movement. *Journal of Educational Change*, *3*(3/4), 383–406.

Ostrander, S. (2004). Democracy, civic participation, and the university: A comparative study of civic engagement on five campuses. *Nonprofit and Voluntary Sector Quarterly*, *33*(1), 74–93.

Shields, C. M. (2005). Liberating discourses: Spirituality and educational leadership. *Journal of School Leadership*, *15*(6), 608–623.

Suarez-Balcazar, Y., Harper, G. W., & Lewis, R. (2005). An interactive and contextual model of community-university collaborations for research and action. *Health Education & Behavior*, *32*(1), 84–101.

Wilson, D. (2004). *Key features of successful university-community partnerships*. Retrieved from http://www.pewpartnership.org/resources/newdirections.html

17

COMMUNITY-BASED RESEARCH AND DEVELOPMENT IN HAITI

Leveraging Multiple Resources for Maximum Impact

Anthony Vinciguerra

As shown in previous chapters, community-based research (CBR) is a growing field in higher education, as it can enhance academic learning and support community-led change.[1] International CBR collaborations have become a particular area of interest for faculty and institutions committed to addressing global issues and developing a sense of "global citizenship" in their students (Bringle, Hatcher, & Jones, 2011, p. 3).

Faculty interested in international CBR collaboration, however, can easily become overwhelmed by the challenges they face. Funding for expensive travel, translation needs, navigating cross-cultural dynamics, and the investment of time necessary for creating long-term impact can all present obstacles for those involved. Therefore, the question becomes: How can faculty with limited resources develop international CBR projects that not only produce meaningful research and student learning outcomes but also contribute to long-term, sustainable impact in the developing world?

This chapter describes one such model for addressing these challenges: the St. Thomas University/Port-de-Paix, Haiti, Global Solidarity Partnership (STU GSP). An overview of the historical development, pedagogical model, and community impact of the STU GSP illustrates how CBR can play a unique role when integrated into a broader, interdisciplinary, multilevel international collaboration. Although the partnership is still young, results to date suggest that such a model can effectively use CBR to enhance both student learning and long-term community impact, even in one of the poorest regions of the poorest country in the Western Hemisphere.

Background and Partnership Framework

St. Thomas University is a small, urban, Archdiocesan Roman Catholic university located in Miami Gardens, Florida. The Diocese of Port-de-Paix (geographically equivalent to the Northwest Department of Haiti) is the sister diocese of the Archdiocese of Miami and is one of the poorest and most isolated regions in Haiti (Mugisha, 2011). Since 2006, St. Thomas has worked with partners in the Diocese of Port-de-Paix to develop the STU GSP, a collaboration aimed at providing concrete faculty research and student-learning opportunities in the developing world, while supporting long-term, Haitian-led sustainable development projects in the region.

Because of the limited resources of the university and the difficulties of working in rural Haiti, a model had to be developed that would focus the university's limited means on specific projects that had the greatest potential for making a long-term sustainable impact. A geographically centered, project-focused model of collaboration was chosen that includes multiple levels of engaged scholarship opportunities at the university. The hope was to offer a wide array of research and learning options to faculty and students while also bringing a broad spectrum of academic resources to bear on the needs of the projects as defined by the Haitian partners. CBR would play a unique role in this partnership, responding to concrete research needs as they arose, while internships, community-based learning courses, courses with partial community-based learning options, and volunteer opportunities would meet other needs of the collaboration. This chapter examines the institutional context and historical development of this partnership; the model of collaboration that was developed; and the unique outputs, outcomes, and impacts of CBR in the process.

Historical Context and Project Inception

In response to waves of Haitian immigrants arriving on the shores of south Florida, the Archbishop of Miami, Edward McCarthy, traveled to Haiti in 1980 in the hope of better understanding the reality these individuals were risking their lives to escape. Leaders from the Haitian episcopal conference sent Archbishop McCarthy to the Diocese of Port-de-Paix, an impoverished, extremely remote region in the northwest of Haiti that many of the refugees were leaving. Upon witnessing the desperate economic, political, and ecological situation of Haiti's northwest, McCarthy immediately established a sister-diocese relationship between the Archdiocese of Miami and the Diocese of Port-de-Paix. His hope was that people of the Archdiocese of Miami would build strong relationships of solidarity with the people of Port-de-Paix, dedicate themselves to bettering the social conditions of the area, and in doing so ameliorate the root causes of this dangerous migration (Love in Action, 1980).

Amor en Acción, a lay-led missionary group based in Miami, was given responsibility for the sister-diocese relationship, and its members spent the following 30 years supporting schools, providing emergency relief, and serving as some of the only consistent aid to this very remote region (Delamaza, 2011a). Over the next 30 years, however, Port-de-Paix remained one of the poorest regions in Haiti.

With a population of more than 600,000, Port-de-Paix's dry and deforested terrain exacerbated the extreme poverty. Although the area is accessible by road from Port-au-Prince, travel can take between six to nine hours because of poor, unpaved roads and the lack of bridges over several rivers. The diocese is centered in a mountainous area with no public water, few roads, and little-to-no electric power. The population suffers from numerous diseases such as malaria, tuberculosis, and typhoid fever. More than 74% of the children in the diocese are malnourished and have parasites. Although the area has consistent health crises, medical attention is rare: There are only 10 doctors for the 100,000 people in the township of Port-de-Paix. Because of the almost complete lack of infrastructure, aid from international relief and development agencies has remained rare in this remote northwest region (Delamaza, 2011b; Mugisha, 2011).

In 2006 St. Thomas University was undergoing a restructuring and as part of this transition, reviewed its institutional mission and its international engagement programs. As a Roman Catholic university, St. Thomas had a particular calling to address issues of economic inequality in the developing world (John Paul II, 1990). Integrated into its mission and programs were the principles of Catholic social thought, a body of teaching intended to guide just relationships between an individual, institutions, and society. Among these principles are a "commitment to the common good," a "preferential option for the poor and vulnerable," and a "commitment to global solidarity" (Mitch, 2011, pp. 7–8). The university had established a Center for Justice and Peace with the explicit purpose of integrating these values throughout the curriculum and activities of the university. Furthermore, as a specifically archdiocesan-sponsored university (as opposed to a Catholic institution founded by a religious order such as the Jesuits or Franciscans),

St. Thomas had the unique institutional commitment to be of, and serve, its locality (Iannone, 2010, p. 1).

Despite this institutional commitment to social justice, global solidarity, economic development, and serving its region, St. Thomas in 2006 had no institutional relationship with its own sister diocese of Port-de-Paix. The university had small programs in Spain, China, and Costa Rica but had never sent a delegation to Haiti's northwest. In response to this unfulfilled calling, the university's Center for Justice and Peace initiated a process aimed at focusing the university's international engagement specifically on its sister diocese. To begin this process, the center recruited faculty interested in international CBR to become part of a team that would explore the possibility of a fruitful collaboration between the university and its sister diocese.

Listening Process and Establishment of Collaborative Project Criteria

The exploratory team's first step was to schedule meetings with Amor en Acción's leaders to learn from their extensive work in building the sister-diocesan partnership over the prior 30 years. These early meetings laid the groundwork for what would become key elements in the future St. Thomas/Port-de-Paix partnership. To begin with, Amor en Acción staff described the deep distrust that existed in Haiti's northwest toward outside organizations coming to "help." For years, members of international nongovernmental organizations (NGOs) had arrived in the region with promises of assistance, only to pull out once difficulties were encountered or project funding ended. Amor en Acción staff made it clear that working in northwest Haiti would not be easy, and that if the university was serious about developing an authentic relationship with the people of the region, there must be a long-term commitment to the process. Furthermore, those who had worked in the northwest for years underlined the need for an attitude of listening and accompaniment, rather than project creation. The only lasting projects in Haiti's northwest were those rooted in long-term, deep relationships. They also suggested that long sessions of listening, discernment, discussion, and debate with Haitian partners would have to take place well before any specific project plans could be made.

With these guiding thoughts, the faculty and staff team made a number of visits to Port-de-Paix during 2006 and 2007 to explore possible areas of collaboration. Meetings were held with local church officials, community leaders, and grassroots organizations throughout Haiti's northwest. After two years of travel between the regions, a small group of Haitian leaders (representing community leaders, church leaders, and local Haitian organizations) coalesced as key partners for the collaboration. Amor en Acción's warning about reticence toward outside organizations was well merited, and the Haitian partners made clear to the faculty team that any collaborative projects between the university and the region would have to abide by three criteria.

Criterion 1: Building and Empowering Civil Society

From the perspective of the partners in Haiti's northwest, Haiti's history was a history of outsiders imposing their ideas on the country's development. From colonial powers, to dictators, to today's foreign NGOs, Haitians had experienced outside powers as completely uninterested in local Haitian-led programs of development. If this continued, they explained, Haitians themselves would never be able to build a sustainable society that can identify its own problems and implement its own solutions.

In light of this, it was agreed that any projects undertaken must not only create economic development but also empower local community initiatives with the hope of supporting the development of an indigenous civil society in the region. (For a fruitful discussion of civil society and its role in economic development, see Putnam, 1992.) As a symbol of this commitment to an empowering relationship, the collaboration was officially named St. Thomas University/Port-de-Paix, Haiti, Global Solidarity Partnership, drawing on the term *solidarity* as a central tenet of the Catholic social tradition that calls for models of mutual, empowering, collaborative development (Pontifical Council for Justice and Peace, 2005).

Criterion 2: Long-Term Development

In further conversations, Haitian leaders expressed their dismay that foreign institutions were quick to offer emergency aid in times of crisis but unwilling to commit to long-term projects in the region. In their own words, they wanted partners who would focus on "auto-sufficiency" for their community. There was widespread sentiment that many international partners were involved in these collaborations simply to garner further external funding rather than to really assist long-term Haitian development (Klarreich & Polman, 2012; Schwartz, 2010). In light of these critiques, and because building the long-term sustainability of the community was part of the university's goal as well, it was agreed that the university's work would be focused on long-term social and economic projects aimed at building the self-sufficiency of the region.

Criterion 3: Relationships of Mutuality

Finally, the Haitian partners expressed their sentiment that while extreme poverty existed in Haiti's northwest, there was also much to offer the university as a context for learning. Haiti in many ways is a microcosm that reflects the structural challenges facing other developing nations, and the local community voice about these challenges (and the solutions they have developed over the years) was presented as an opportunity to educate and develop globally aware, civic-minded students. As mentioned earlier, the growing literature on international CBR likewise supports this perspective (Bringle et al., 2011; Ibrahim, 2012).

At the same time, because St. Thomas is a small university, it did not have the resources needed for all forms of potential collaboration. Thus, the partnership added a final criterion that any potential projects must be a good match between the community's self-identified needs and the university's current academic programs.

Introducing the Projects

After two years of meetings and discussions at the university and in Haiti, the small faculty-and-staff team worked with their Haitian partners to identify the following three projects they felt had the greatest potential for partnership.

The Café COCANO Fair/Direct Trade Coffee Project

One of the first possibilities identified by the Haitian partners was a collaboration to export and market coffee from Haiti to the United States. Northwest Haiti has some of the oldest coffee-growing traditions in the Americas. Coffee was introduced to the area by the French in the early 1700s and quickly became one of the first major export commodities from the Caribbean. By the late eighteenth-century Haiti was the world's single largest producer of coffee, and it remained Haiti's largest export commodity for the next 200 years (Dunnington, 2001). By the mid-twentieth century, however, the lack of infrastructure in Haiti's northwest, coupled with overproduction of coffee in Latin America and Asia, resulted in plummeting coffee prices on the world market. Prices fell so low that farmers began to uproot their coffee trees and instead planted corn, beans, and root vegetables to feed their families. Unlike coffee, however, these crops did little to maintain soil on the hillsides, which exacerbated deforestation and contributed to mudslides during the rainy season. Mud would then pool along the coastline, killing reefs and destroying the fishing economy of many seaside villages. This collective process only worsened the extreme poverty of the region and led to the abandonment of much of the northwest's coffee fields (Inter-American Development Bank, 2006). Contemporary farmers of the region knew that their coffee was organic and a very high-quality, heirloom variety. They also knew that farmers would save their coffee trees, and in fact plant more, if they could get a better price for their coffee beans. The challenge, however, was the lack of a mechanism for getting the coffee to foreign markets in a way that ensured Haitian farmers a fair price.

St. Thomas University had no programs in agriculture or agronomy, yet a professor of business and a professor of communications believed that the university's management, accounting, and communications resources might be of use in building the collaboration. They became two key members of the exploratory team. Soon it was agreed that the university's team would join the newly formed *Cafeiere et Cacouyere du Nord'Ouest* (COCANO) coffee cooperative to research the possibility of a direct, fair trade partnership. Their goal would be to develop an infrastructure that could support the farmers in getting the coffee directly to foreign markets while ensuring them a price at or above international fair trade standards.

The Atelye Thevenet Fair Trade Artisan Project

In addition to the coffee collaboration, another Haitian-led project was proposed by communities in areas so deforested they could no longer produce coffee. Haiti has a rich and varied artisan production tradition, and northwest Haiti was no exception. A network of Haitian women had come together with the assistance of a local religious community to develop an artisan workshop that would provide job training, be collaboratively run, and offer economic independence to Haitian women of the region. A partnership was soon developed between the university team and the Atelye Thevenet artisan cooperative in the small northwest town of Jean-Rabel. As with the COCANO partnership, the business and communications team worked with the artisan cooperative to research areas of potential market growth and develop a system for the import, marketing, and sale of the artisan items to foreign buyers.

St. Thomas/Port-de-Paix Solar Energy Initiative

Finally, as noted earlier, access to reliable electricity is an ongoing barrier to development in northwest Haiti. There is only limited public electricity in the region's capital of Port-de-Paix, and none outside that area. Lighting is most often achieved with candles or oil lamps, and food is most often cooked over charcoal, another significant contributor to the deforestation of the land. St. Thomas University's electrical engineering and solar physics faculty joined in the emerging partnership to work with local leaders to develop sustainable energy projects for the area; train community members in the implementation, use, and maintenance of solar energy systems; and provide concrete research and learning opportunities for St. Thomas faculty and students.

Finding an Effective Model of Engagement

The university's exploratory team soon became known as the STU GSP Committee and took on the role of remaining in contact with the Haitian partners and providing broad oversight to the projects as they developed. However, committee members still faced additional challenges on campus. While the team had worked with its Haitian partners to develop criteria and identify projects, the problem remained of how to organize the university's involvement to best use its limited resources. As noted earlier, St. Thomas is a small, inner-city university with a very limited financial base. The faculty on the team had full teaching loads, the university's Center for Justice and Peace had only one staff member to support the work, and no institutional funding was available to support the collaboration.

Another on-campus challenge was student engagement. More than 55% of St. Thomas students come from disadvantaged economic backgrounds and are of African and/or Hispanic descent, reflecting the large Latin American, African American, and Afro-Caribbean communities in South Florida. Many of these students enter the university with weak high school preparation and often work second jobs while studying (STU Office of Institutional Research, 2011). The committee had to determine how to best use limited faculty and staff resources, engage an extremely diverse student body (many of whose families had left impoverished countries themselves), and translate this into impact in the poorest region of Haiti.

To face these challenges, it was decided that the partnership should be integrated into the research and teaching activities of the university. While the pedagogical benefits of engaged research and learning have already been well documented in the literature (Eyler & Giles, 1999, 2000; Fitzgerald, Burack, & Seifer, 2010), this decision was also the most pragmatic choice. Quite simply, the team felt it was unrealistic to expect faculty, already overloaded with teaching and research, or students, often working second jobs, to commit significant time to projects outside their academic commitments.

It also became clear to the STU GSP Committee that these academic initiatives would have to meet a variety of project needs. Some needs would be research oriented; for example, the need to research and develop a coffee import and distribution model. Other needs might be more suited to student internships, such as providing ongoing accounting for coffee imports and sales. Still other needs might be more appropriate projects for students in a community-based learning course, such as the development of a website for the coffee project.

The committee developed a scaffolding framework of five engagement levels to involve various constituents at the university, as well as meet the various needs of the projects as they arose. These engagement levels were identified as (a) faculty/student CBR projects, (b) for-credit internships, (c) full community-based learning (CBL) courses, (d) courses with a partial CBL/engaged learning component, and (e) volunteer opportunities. While the types of community engagement were distinct, they had the common thread of using the research and teaching resources at the university to meet the needs of the Haitian projects.

The STU GSP collaboration is still in development, and not every level of engagement has been used for every project. That being said, CBR has proven to be critical in each of the projects, particularly in the initial planning stages. We now turn to one concrete example of how CBR was used in the collaboration's development and how the results were tied to other forms of engaged learning to maximize the collaboration's long-term impact.

CBR as an Integrated Element of the Wider STU GSP Partnership

As mentioned earlier, one of the first needs of the coffee and artisan projects was the development of a business model that would (a) identify the cooperatives' strengths vis-à-vis global markets and (b) develop an export/import model that was realistic (given the lack of infrastructure in Haiti) and could guarantee the producers a price at or above international fair trade standards. Here we focus primarily on CBR and its role in the Café COCANO fair/direct trade coffee partnership, although the results for the artisan project largely followed the same path.

As mentioned earlier, a key member of the exploratory STU GSP Committee was a professor of business who also happened to be the director of the university's nascent Institute for Global Entrepreneurship. He immediately saw the potential impact of a well-designed CBR project that could identify the strengths of the coffee cooperative and help develop an effective business model. This faculty member began work with a graduate student and Center for Justice and Peace staff to research the history of coffee cooperatives in Haiti, explore export/import models, research coffee varietals and processing methods unique to Haiti, and look for niche opportunities in the specialty coffee market.

The coffee team's research showed that cooperatives in Haiti had historically failed when they were overly dependent on one export chain and source of support (Inter-American Development Bank, 2006). A number of relationships were built so that the coffee partnership would not be overly dependent on the university for all the resources it might need. A partnership was developed with Pascucci Torrefazione, an Italian coffee roaster interested in developing the cooperative and exporting the coffee to the European market. A partnership was also developed with Panther Coffee Roasters, a specialty coffee roaster in Miami that had a long history of supporting small-scale producers. Simultaneously, the university team acquired technical assistance from groups such as Catholic Relief Services, Singing Rooster, and the Just Trade Center to assist the cooperative in its organization and production planning.

The team's research also showed that the coffee produced by COCANO had the potential of being a unique product on the specialty coffee market. Because coffee was introduced early in northwest Haiti, the varietal was an heirloom arabica type, similar to the original Arabica Typica from Ethiopia, the birthplace of coffee. Because of the lack of infrastructure in Haiti and northwest Haiti's isolation from the rest of the country, coffee trees in the northwest had never been hybridized or treated with petrochemicals. Furthermore, the sun-drying processing technique used by the farmers, as compared to the large-scale wet processing used for most arabicas in the Americas, resulted in a unique flavor profile in demand by specialty coffee roasters. The team subsequently decided with their Haitian partners to build on these strengths—an heirloom, sun-dried organic arabica coffee, produced in a fair/direct trade model—to compete in the U.S. and European specialty coffee markets.

At the same time, an import and distribution process had to be developed that would guarantee maximum profit for the farmers. Historically, as many as nine middlemen were involved in Haiti's coffee export process, including speculators, regional buyers, exporters, importers, roasters, and so on, which resulted in prices paid to the farmers as low as 10 Haitian gouds (25 cents) per pound. It was clear that if profits were to be increased for farmers, these people in the middle would have to be cut out of the process, and a direct trade relationship would have to be developed between the university and the cooperative.

The coffee team began to work with Center for Justice and Peace staff to research best practices in fair/direct trade partnerships. It then worked to integrate these findings with student-run business models and best practices in service-learning and engaged scholarship curriculum development. Soon a multitiered engaged learning model was created in which St. Thomas business and marketing students would apply their learning as they imported, marketed, and sold the coffee in the United States. The levels of engagement for the coffee project corresponded to the five levels of engagement mentioned earlier, and the roles each level served in supporting the coffee partnership are briefly described next.

Faculty/Student CBR Projects

It was clear that at various times, specific research questions in the coffee project would need to be addressed. As mentioned previously, the first research question that needed attention focused on developing a structure for the project and sales processes as a whole. An attractive logo and comprehensive marketing plan would need to be researched and developed by university business students. Furthermore, the committee knew that other issues would arise. For example, the coffee bean borer beetle (*hypothenemus hampei*, referred to in Haiti as the *skolit*) had destroyed thousands of dollars in crops throughout Haiti's northwest. The search for locally sustainable, organic treatment methods of the beetle would be an excellent research project for students studying plant and insect biology. In the end, it was agreed that as specific research needs were identified, the team would recruit faculty and student teams from appropriate disciplines to address these issues in collaboration with the coffee farmers through a participatory, engaged CBR process.

Internships

Although CBR engagement could serve as a resource for specific needs of the coffee project, the initiative also needed staff to run its day-to-day operations. The STU GSP team began to work with faculty in the School of Business and Department of Communications to develop for-credit internships in sales and marketing, accounting, and public relations where students would import, market, manage inventory, and sell the coffee. This would provide intensive, hands-on learning for the students in their area of study while also involving new faculty in the process.

Full Course Integration

Similarly, it became apparent that specific project needs could be addressed by students in full semester courses. The STU GSP team proposed an upper-division, interdisciplinary social entrepreneurship class in which students would study business models that included a double bottom line of profit and social responsibility, examine entrepreneurial business issues in light of the Catholic social tradition, and apply their learning to the needs of the projects. The students took on specific tasks, such as website creation, restaurant outreach, and coffee grading, and traveled to Haiti to complete project tasks that might require site-based work.

Partial Course Engagement

The STU GSP team saw there would also be needs that did not require a full semester of research or student work but could still serve as a basic level of engagement and student learning. For example, sales events needed informed staff, outreach efforts required a group of committed members, and partner meetings required translators. In light of this, the team contacted faculty from a number of disciplines who wanted to use the coffee project as a context for a brief unit of engaged learning in their introductory-level courses.

For example, the team approached a philosophy professor teaching Introduction to Business Ethics. As part of this professor's regular course, he introduced his students to ethical issues in international commodity trade. The coffee team worked with this professor to redevelop his course with a new unit focused on coffee trade as an example of global commodity supply chains. Students in the class would now study coffee as one of the world's most-traded global commodities and then apply their learning through interactions (via Skype) with partners in the Café COCANO project. These students were also offered the opportunity to work with the project at local coffee sales and promotional events.

Volunteer Opportunities

For all other needs of the project, volunteers were recruited by interns and steering committee members to serve at one-time events, take part in outreach efforts, and so on. Although this only met a small number of the overall needs of the project, it provided a flexible labor source to be used when needed and also introduced new participants to the work who could then be encouraged to become involved in other levels of the collaboration.

The final product of the coffee team's research was a plan for marketing a high-quality, organic, naturally processed, fair/direct trade coffee internationally. It offered an integrated, multilevel import and distribution model that combined fair/direct trade social-entrepreneurial business models with best practices in engaged scholarship curriculum development.

While not perfect by any means, this model of integrating CBR research with various other levels of university engagement led to sustained and significant results using minimal resources in a minimal amount of time. Let us now consider some of the community changes that have taken place to date.

Community Matters: Output, Outcomes, and Impact

In Chapter 2, Beckman and Wood introduce a framework for achieving community impact that includes the following four critical components:

1. A well-designed group with a commitment to a long-term collaborative endeavor,

2. goal setting and other planning by the group toward the attainment of the goal,
3. diverse participation within the group that is appropriate to the goal, and
4. regular monitoring and revision of action and direction by the group. (p. 38, this volume)

Although the STU GSP collaborations were not designed with this framework in mind, in many ways the projects' development reflected these same components: (a) There was a clear coalition of partners in Haiti and the United States that understood and were committed to the long-term nature of the effort; (b) the projects were developed with the clear goal of economic self-sufficiency in northwest Haiti and the specific objective of developing fair/direct trade import processes; (c) the project included the multiple voices of faculty, students, technical assistants, and, most essentially, the Haitian partners themselves; and (d) the STU GSP Committee kept the long-term goals in mind, clarifying research needs as they became apparent and constantly evaluating and revising the initiative's direction in consultation with the project's Haitian partners. In retrospect, it seems likely that these components were key in the project's success to date.

Beckman and Wood also make clear the importance of differentiating three stages in the CBR/community change process: (a) outputs, referring to the initial results of the CBR effort; (b) outcomes, referring to the effects of the application of the CBR results; and (c) impacts, referring to the long-term contributions of this collaboration over time. Although these categories were not used in the initial planning of the projects, they prove useful in describing some of the planned, and unforeseen, community changes that have resulted from the university's collaboration. While these levels of change can also be seen in the artisan and solar collaborations, we focus here specifically on the Café COCANO initiative.

Café COCANO Fair/Direct Trade Coffee Project: Outputs, Outcomes, and Impacts

Outputs

- A CBR project led by business faculty and students identified a specific international market opportunity for Café COCANO's unique Haitian coffee varietal.
- The same CBR project led to development of the Café COCANO business model, an engaged-learning process that uses five levels of faculty and student engagement opportunities to meet the ongoing sales and marketing needs of the project.

- A faculty/student communications CBR team developed a full-length documentary of the project, *Blooming Hope* (Moyano, 2011). Produced using a participatory action and production model, *Blooming Hope* has been used to promote cooperative participation in Haiti as well as promote product sales.
- Most recently, after nine months of working collaboratively with COCANO farmers on the effort, a team of St. Thomas University science faculty and students are preparing to publish results on the effectiveness of various organic treatment methods for the coffee borer beetle in northwest Haiti's unique environment.

Outcomes

- Through the Café COCANO partnership model, coffee farmers in northwest Haiti are now exporting coffee in a fair/direct trade partnership for the first time in history (see www.cafecocano.com).
- More than 160,000 pounds of coffee have been exported by the cooperative since its inception.
- The cooperative earns $4.16/pound on exports to the United States, more than twice the current international fair trade standards of $1.85/pound (Fairtrade International, 2015). About 20 delegations from the university have traveled to Haiti to work on site, and about 40 students per year continue to be involved in for-credit activities connected to next steps on the projects.
- *Blooming Hope* has been presented at numerous regional film festivals, winning best student-produced documentary at the 2010 Miami International Film Festival and contributing to thousands of dollars in increased coffee and artisan sales.
- COCANO coffee farmers have begun to use effective combinations of ethanol and methanol to attract the coffee bean borer beetle to inexpensive traps codesigned by the COCANO farmers and St. Thomas students, thus increasing the quality and quantity of the farmers' harvest.

Impacts

- More than 300 families (and about 2,000 individuals) in six parishes of the Diocese of Port-de-Paix have been employed by the COCANO cooperative.
- The cooperative provided employment to those displaced to northwest Haiti following the 2010 earthquake in Port-au-Prince,

thus supporting decentralization of the Haitian economy (Moyano, 2010).

- In response to the 2010–2012 cholera epidemic, the cooperative saved hundreds of lives by organizing relief efforts in areas not served by foreign NGOs (CafeCocano, 2011; Ministère de la Santé Publique et de la Population & the World Health Organization, 2011).
- The cooperative has begun coffee nursery programs, planting thousands of coffee seedlings throughout northwest Haiti in what is essentially an economically incentivized reforestation program.
- The COCANO cooperative has begun to act as a conduit between coffee farmers and the Haitian government, thus supporting the development of social capital for its members and strengthening its role as a unit of civil society (Froehle, 2013).
- A deep institutionalization of the coffee project has taken place throughout St. Thomas's campus, with faculty from a number of disciplines involved in a variety of ways. This suggests that the initial goal of building a strong relationship of mutuality between the Archdiocesan university and its sister diocese is well under way.

Although these changes refer specifically to the coffee project, similar results have proven true for the artisan and solar projects as well. From the perspective of the STU GSP steering team, however, the deep institutional commitment between the university and its sister diocese, along with the Haitian community's capacity to define its own problems and implement its own solutions, best illustrate the project's long-term impact on both the Haitian partner community and the university itself.

Lessons Learned and Areas for Growth

In view of the positive experience of the STU GSP collaboration to date, the following three main lessons can be learned from the university's partnership in Haiti:

1. For institutional partnerships: A community-led, project-focused collaboration can help maximize benefits for both partners as local leadership is empowered, university resources are focused, long-term relationships developed, and the impact (community and university) synergized. A commitment to the needs of one community can productively galvanize the entire range of academic resources in a smaller university.

2. For models of engagement: An interdisciplinary scaffolding of multiple engagement levels encourages wide participation at the university while

also bringing a variety of resources to bear on the multiple needs of a single project.

3. For faculty CBR engagement: Using CBR as one integrated element of a broader university-community initiative can ensure that research findings are incorporated into long-term community impact, that travel logistics are streamlined into existing processes, and that funding needs are minimized when a collaboration's overhead is shared by a larger university-wide partnership.

Although there has been significant success, the following areas for growth have also been identified by the project partners:

1. Expand resource networks: One university may not have all the answers. In the collaboration, a number of research issues related to agronomic production have been raised, but St. Thomas does not have extensive faculty resources in this area. This suggests the possibility for expanding collaboration among a network of universities with the aim of incorporating wider resources into the projects' needs.

2. Standardize planning: Use of standardized logic models that visually map required resources (inputs), activities to take place (processes), assessable outputs, and desired outcomes is quickly becoming a best practice in university-community engagement planning. Although logic models had not been historically used by the STU GSP teams, in 2014 the STU GSP began using such models to map ideal (a) community impact outcomes, (b) academic learning outcomes, and (c) civic learning outcomes for each of the five levels of project engagement (Finley, 2013; Howard, 2001).

3. Effectively assess: Standardized assessment of each of the three principle outcome areas (community impact, academic learning, and civic learning) is another goal as the projects aim to take their efforts to an even higher level of accountability and efficacy.

Although the full results of these changes remain to be seen, the hope is that broader collaboration, more structured planning, and improved assessment processes will enhance the long-term impact of the collaborations for the university as well as the community.

Conclusion

As programs of engaged scholarship become more widespread, faculty and university administrators will continue to consider how they can use their limited community-engagement resources to maximize community impact. The STU GSP was born out of just such an effort to leverage the minimal resources of a small, urban, Catholic university into long-term development in one of the Western Hemisphere's poorest regions. Although the partnership is still young, the experience so far suggests that significant impact can be attained by adopting a model that is community led, project focused, interdisciplinary, and that uses CBR within a wider collection of engaged scholarship activities, all focused on meeting the varied needs of a single, long-term university-community initiative.

Voice of the Faculty: Business/Social Entrepreneurship

As a business faculty member, I was not the usual candidate for a community engagement effort. In 2006, however, I was invited to be part of an exploratory team for a partnership in rural Haiti, and, as a Jamaican native, I know the real impact entrepreneurial business ventures can have on Caribbean development.

When the Haitian partners identified coffee as a possible area for collaboration, it seemed a natural fit. I had an interest in social entrepreneurship, and this presented an opportunity to deepen my work in the area, engage students in the effort, and develop a model for importing the Haitian coffee. Using a CBR methodology, we investigated the profitability of such a venture as well as models that might make the project sustainable in the long term.

It has been a transformative experience. We developed a model that involves faculty and students at a variety of levels, from research projects to internships to courses. At each level, students apply their learning in business research, strategy development, business plan creation, strategic marketing, and financial management to move the projects ahead. Students realize these are not simply academic projects but important activities that will make an enormous difference in the lives of our partners. By integrating my work with the overall efforts of the university's Haiti team, we've been able to accomplish things none of us would have been able to do alone. The project is changing hundreds of lives, not only in Haiti but also on the university campus.

Justin Peart, PhD
Associate Professor of Business and Marketing
Director of Institute for Global Entrepreneurship

Voice of the Faculty: Communications/Documentary Development

As a professor of communications, I know the incredibly transformative power of the media. As a new faculty member, however, leading a community collaboration by myself would have been difficult as I tried to balance an already heavy research and teaching load.

When staff from the Center for Justice and Peace introduced me to the university's partnership in Haiti, it was a perfect fit. I not only learned about the challenges facing citizens in one of the poorest regions of the Western Hemisphere but also saw community leaders who had practical solutions to those challenges, and I saw a way I could integrate my research and teaching to make a difference.

Working with student interns and our Haitian partners, we developed a participatory action-based learning model to create a full-length documentary about the projects. Titled *Blooming Hope: Harvesting Smiles in Port-de-Paix*, the film used the lens of the camera to highlight the Haiti projects, capture social developments, promote product sales, build cooperative participation, and, most important, offer a vision of hope for Haiti's future.

It has been an incredible success. As an educator, I believe that true academic achievement is best measured by the transformation that occurs in the learning process. Through *Blooming Hope*, faculty and students have been part of a social movement in support of the most vulnerable communities of the Western Hemisphere. They have experienced the true meaning of social justice by integrating their research and teaching into community change through an effective communications and media product.

Marcela Moyano, EdD
Assistant Professor of Communications
Institute for Communications, Entertainment and Media

Note

1. Portions of this chapter were previously published as Vinciguerra, A. (2014). Haiti: Sustaining partnerships in sustainable development. *Journal of Community Engagement and Scholarship*, 7(2), 4–18. Reproduced with permission.

References

Bringle, R., Hatcher, J., & Jones, S. (2011). *International service learning: Conceptual frameworks and research*. Sterling, VA: Stylus.

CafeCocano (2012, February 21). *Cocano president on cholera response by the cooperative in northwest Haiti* [Video File]. Retrieved from www.youtube.com/watch?v=jr1jHEOz1a8

Delamaza, T. (2011a). *Amor en Acción: History and theology*. Retrieved from http://amorenaccion.com/e_html/history/history.html

Delamaza, T. (2011b). *Amor en Acción: Our Work—Haiti*. Retrieved from http://amorenaccion.com/e_html/work/ourwork_haiti.html

Dunnington, L. (2001). *A case study in brand creation with small holders: Haitian bleu*. Washington, DC: Development Alternatives.

Eyler, J., & Giles, D. (1999). *Where's the learning in service-learning*. San Francisco, CA: Jossey-Bass.

Eyler, J., & Giles, D. (2000). *At a glance: What we know about the effects of service-learning*. Retrieved from https://www.mnsu.edu/cetl/academicservicelearning/Service-Learning.pdf

Fairtrade International. (2015). *Fair trade minimum price and premium table*. Retrieved from www.fairtrade.net/price-and-premium-info.html

Finley, A. (2013, June). *Assessing together: Practical strategies for measuring civic learning*. Paper presented at the National Association of Student Personnel Administrators Civic Learning and Democratic Engagement Conference, Philadelphia, PA.

Fitzgerald, H., Burack, C., & Seifer, S. (2010). *Engaged scholarship: Contemporary landscapes, future directions*. East Lansing: Michigan State University Press.

Froehle, B. (2013). *Meeting of COCANO president, Haitian Ministry of Agriculture, Haitian consulate, and St. Thomas University* [video]. Miami Gardens, FL: St. Thomas University Center for Community Engagement.

Haiti earthquake: Population movements out of Port-au-Prince. (2010). Retrieved from reliefweb.int/node/15791

Howard, J. (2001). *Service-learning course design workbook*. Ann Arbor: University of Michigan Office of Community Service Learning.

Iannone, J. (2010) *Toward a creative partnership between the Archdiocese of Miami and Saint Thomas University*. Unpublished manuscript, School of Theology and Ministry, St. Thomas University, Miami Gardens, FL.

Ibrahim, B. L. (2012). International service-learning as a path to global citizenship. In J. A. Hatcher and R. G. Bringle (Eds.), *Understanding service-learning and community engagement: Crossing boundaries through research* (pp. 11–24). Charlotte, NC: Information Age Publishing.

Inter-American Development Bank. (2006). *Restoring the competitiveness of the coffee sector in Haiti*. Washington, DC. Retrieved from http://idbdocs.iadb.org/wsdocs/getdocument.aspx?docnum=728955

John Paul II. (1990). *Apostolic Constitution on Catholic Universities—Ex Corde Ecclesiae*. Retrieved from w2.vatican.va/content/john-paul-ii/en/apost_constitutions/documents/hf_jp-ii_apc_15081990_ex-corde-ecclesiae.html

Klarreich, K., & Polman, L. (2012, November 19). The NGO Republic of Haiti: How the international relief effort after the 2010 earthquake excluded Haitians from their own recovery. *The Nation*. Retrieved from www.thenation.com/article/170929/ngo-republic-haiti#ixzz2Xp3imnPT

Love in Action: Archbishop tours sister diocese, poorest in hemisphere. (1980, December 5). *The Voice*. Retrieved from library.stu.edu/ulma/va/3005/1980/12-05-1980.pdf

Ministère de la Santé Publique et de la Population & the World Health Organization. (2011). *Health cluster bulletin: Cholera and post-earthquake response in Haiti*. Retrieved from www.who.int/hac/crises/hti/sitreps/haiti_health_cluster_bulletin_25july2011.pdf

Mitch, M. (2011). *The challenge and spirituality of Catholic social teaching*. Maryknoll, NY: Orbis Books.

Moyano, M. (2010, October 15). *Semilforte St. Hubert talks about the earthquake in Haiti and COCANO* [Video File]. Retrieved from www.youtube.com/watch?v=9tz1LdrKbXo

Moyano, M. (2011). *Documentaries for social change: An examination of blooming hope*. Available from ProQuest Dissertations and Theses database. (UMI No. 3452863)

Mugisha, V. (2011). *Livelihoods in northern Haiti: Summary of a participatory assessment*. Baltimore, MD: Catholic Relief Services.

Pontifical Council for Justice and Peace. (2005). *Compendium of the social doctrine of the Church*. Washington, DC: USCCB Communications.

Putnam, R. (1992). *Making democracy work: Civic traditions in modern Italy*. Princeton, NJ: Princeton University Press.

Schwartz, T. (2010). *Travesty in Haiti: A true account of Christian missions, orphanages, food aid, fraud and drug trafficking*. Charleston, SC: BookSurge.

St. Thomas University, Office of Institutional Research. (2011). *2009–2010 data sets and 2010–2011 factbook*. Retrieved from web.stu.edu/Portals/0/FB2011.pdf

Vinciguerra, A. (2014). Haiti: Sustaining partnerships in sustainable development. *Journal of Community Engagement and Scholarship, 7*(2), 4–18.

18

PROGRESSIVE PROJECTS ON PARENT INVOLVEMENT

Joyce F. Long

Our community, along with other urban school districts across the nation, faces many serious challenges that hinder children from receiving an excellent education (Kilbride, 2014). When issues with poor student learning remain unresolved, children are not the only ones who suffer the consequences. Elected officials become hampered in their efforts to redevelop a city and reestablish a thriving economy, businesses are frustrated by the lack of qualified employees who possess requisite knowledge and skills, and higher education personnel must work harder to recruit desired faculty members because high-quality schooling for their children is often a precondition for relocating to a new campus.

A group of like-minded individuals from the University of Notre Dame who viewed unsatisfactory student outcomes as a reflection of inequitable and unjust learning opportunities were committed to helping reverse those trends using community-based research (CBR). In August of 2006 seven faculty members and personnel from campus met at my home for dinner with an equal number from local administrators of struggling public schools with majority numbers from at-risk, high-poverty students. Everyone was familiar with the local statistics, frustrated with the status quo, tired of feeling helpless, and eager to change those seemingly entrenched, negative student outcomes so that all children in the city could receive a stellar education.

We elected to name ourselves the Educational Collaborative Group (ECG) and continued to meet regularly over dinner at rotating schools and homes for the next three years. Because I had been teaching in Notre Dame's education, schooling, and society (ESS) minor program, I was asked to oversee the group and received a small stipend alternately provided by Notre Dame's community-based education institute, the Center for Social

Concerns (CSC); the Dean's Office of the College of Arts and Letters; and the Robinson Community Learning Center, an off-campus educational initiative of the university. My primary responsibility was to build trusting relationships between the university and community educators and create an environment where research partnerships could flourish.

Campus representatives respected the local school administrators and considered their frontline knowledge essential in moving forward. They attentively listened to each principal convey his or her own story of repeatedly trying new strategies that had failed to attain success. In response, the campus group offered its critical thinking skills and empirical modes of collecting and analyzing data as complementary diagnostic tools for accurately assessing problems and constructing solutions.

When the campus group asked administrators to suggest specific issues that could be researched, the first issue mentioned was low parent involvement. One primary school principal, Darice Austin-Phillips, stated it was a major problem in her school. All the remaining administrators nodded their heads in agreement and admitted they did not know how to remedy the situation.

Federal legislation such as No Child Left Behind (NCLB) has mandated that schools provide "parents with the tools they need to support their children's learning in the home, communicate regularly with families about children's academic progress, provide opportunities for family workshops, and offer parents chances to engage in parent leadership activities at the local site" (Caspe, Lopez, & Wolos, 2006/2007, p. 1). In implementing these directives, however, administrators and teachers of high poverty schools are often unsure how to promote involvement if meaningful contact with families is rare. Even when school personnel are "deeply convinced that schools must respect and respond to family culture and family circumstances in order to access the full power of parental support for student learning" (Hoover-Dempsey et al., 2005, p. 116), achieving involvement can be difficult.

So exactly how could administrators of high poverty schools increase parent involvement? For the past seven years, we have been pursuing solutions to that problem through the six CBR projects I describe in this chapter. I conclude with lessons learned about increasing parent involvement and facilitating change through CBR.

First CBR Project: Mangeney's Qualitative Study

When Austin-Phillips introduced the problem of low parent involvement, Stuart Greene, who at the time codirected ESS and taught the Educational Research capstone course required of all seniors in the education minor, suggested one of his students might be interested in working on the issue. Each student in the course is responsible for designing and implementing his or her own independent research project based on an issue of personal interest. One of Greene's students, Joanna Mangeney, chose to work with Austin-Phillips for her senior research project.

She designed a qualitative study based on data Austin-Phillips and a staff member had already collected, which suggested the school had three groups of parents: those "who just plain didn't really care about their child's education . . . parents who care, but don't know what to do . . . and parents who are getting it done"(Mangeney, 2006, p. 5). To address the principal's goal of gaining greater understanding about the middle group, Mangeney tested the relevance of two theoretical parent involvement models (Hoover-Dempsey & Sandler, 1995; Walker, Wilkins, Dallaire, Sandler, & Hoover-Dempsey, 2005). She found parents lacked general opportunities and invitations for involvement, already had heavy demands on their time and energy, and did not perceive themselves as having the necessary skills and knowledge to be involved in academic activities. Parents also were unaware of what involvement entailed, did not feel welcome, and thought they were unqualified to challenge teachers. In addition, any references to parents defining themselves as valuable partners with the school were glaringly absent from the focus groups' transcripts.

Second CBR Project: No Parent Left Behind

Informed by these new data, Austin-Phillips was more insistent on tackling the great divide that separated parents and teachers in her building. Although she was very familiar with typical descriptions of low-income parents as being negligent or incapable of fulfilling traditional norms of involvement, she was convinced that teachers and previously marginalized parents could learn to value each other and work together if appropriate remediation efforts were designed for both groups. Since her school was struggling to improve student achievement levels, and she wanted to boost the number of students who passed standardized tests, her first priority was to create an intervention for parents that could provide them with training on how to support student learning. She decided to focus on parents of second and third grade students who had recently failed standardized tests in language arts and mathematics.

Greene and I agreed to work with her on this more complex project, which included a mixed-methods study of teachers and parents as well as designing and implementing a curriculum for 12 parent workshops. All three of us collaborated on the CBR project design. I regularly met with Austin-Phillips to create the curriculum for the parent workshops, which we began coteaching in January of 2007. We also prepared meals for the 11 families who participated in the workshops, and while parents learned, ESS students engaged the children in different academic enrichment activities. Austin-Phillips kept her staff informed about the development of the project, which they named No Parent Left Behind (NPLB). Finances for the effort came from a one-semester grant from the local school district provided to Austin-Phillips.

For the CBR portion of this undertaking, Greene and I collected data on each group's conceptualizations, attitudes, and behaviors relative to involvement and parent-teacher connections. We individually interviewed every parent attendee and any teacher of students with parents participating in the workshops. On the first and last night of the workshops, parents completed pre- and postsurveys and participated in pre- and postfocus groups. All teachers in the building were also asked to complete a teacher version of the survey.

Preresults indicated that many of the teachers tended to distrust parents, but parents blindly believed that teachers were successfully teaching their children (Greene & Long, 2011). Parents neither recognized that their children needed additional help nor understood the school was struggling to achieve adequate yearly progress. After attending workshops, postsurveys and focus groups showed parents gained understanding and experience relative to their children's learning needs and realized the importance of their roles in supporting academic achievement. Triangulated data sources further indicated that parents had begun to reconceptualize themselves as successful in performing academic tasks (the majority of them were school dropouts), developing skills in facilitating academic learning at home, and becoming more visible at school. Although this evidence pointed to the program's effectiveness in promoting parents' increased academic engagement, parents' and teachers' responses agreed that meaningful dialogue between both groups was missing. This confirmed more work was needed to form collegial parent-school working partnerships, but funding for the project had just ended.

Eventually our CBR trio submitted a grant proposal to Memorial Hospital's Community Health Enhancement (CHE) department, which allocates 10% of the hospital's net annual income toward area initiatives that can help increase the community's health, broadly defined. As CHE requires all grant recipients to have a multiyear plan for building a program's infrastructure and capacity to achieve more permanent influence in the community, the application process forced us to enlarge our vision and commitment to parent involvement beyond a one-semester project design. We used our previous CBR findings to sculpt four goals that seemed attainable over the next two years: train 75 low-income parents to give their children academic support, assess the program's effectiveness, build a parent community, and guide parents toward using local community enrichment resources (e.g., library, art museums, and theater).

After receiving the CHE funding, in-kind donations from Notre Dame, and a smaller private gift, Greene and I co-led workshops at three sites where community partners invited us to work with them. From 2008 through 2010, we initially returned to Austin-Phillips' school, and then moved to a second school with an ECG administrator and an additional community site, the South Bend Center for the Homeless. To facilitate the expansion, we created an advanced curriculum for parent graduates and trained a larger team of ESS students to oversee a more structured academic enrichment and tutoring program for pre–K to eighth grade children of parents attending NPLB workshops. Although Austin-Phillips was involved in union contract negotiations at the time and unable to actively participate in this next stage of the work, we consistently conversed about the project and incorporated her input into its adaptations.

CBR results from these three sites continued to confirm that parents were becoming more engaged at home and at school. Parent communities were naturally emerging at each site as individuals talked together, sat together at school events, and relied on one another for advice and inspiration. An additional outcome occurred when NPLB graduates were asked to share their experiences in a number of public forums across the city (e.g., at Ivy Tech Community College). Their stories often generated tearful responses from other parents, who were dissatisfied with schools but unaware of how to bring change and help their children.

As an organization, NPLB was likewise forming more working relationships with other nonprofit groups in the city that helped children and parents (e.g., 100 Black Men, United Way). Our work was increasingly influencing a community-wide audience, and with every new partnership, the likelihood of more parental engagement seemed to be increasing. By 2009, one of ECG's principals had become the new local school superintendent. I was also moving from a full-time faculty position to a part-time adjunct position at the University of Notre Dame and a community position as director of NPLB. When the school district received a two-year, multimillion-dollar federal stimulus grant to build parent involvement in Title 1 schools, I was invited to train 11 new personnel to replicate NPLB's workshops and research program in multiple schools. This represented a significant expansion of parent involvement in struggling schools.

Third CBR Project: Why Drop Out of School?

As the facilitator of the ECG, I was given the opportunity to teach undergraduate research courses exclusively focused on educational problems in the community. Our partner in spring 2009, the school district's research director, submitted a list of 15 potential topics we could pursue. Ultimately, my students voted to focus most of their efforts on investigating why local high school students choose to drop out of school. This topic was especially interesting to me, as 60% of NPLB parents were dropouts.

We individually interviewed and surveyed dropouts and compared their stories with students in alternative school settings and a juvenile justice center. Findings revealed that all the participants experienced two powerful voids that negatively influenced their ability to succeed in traditional settings. First, they failed to develop academically because of insufficient understanding of course content and unproductive learning strategies, and this condition often became brutally apparent soon after entering intermediate school (grades five through eight). Second, they also lacked any supportive relationships in the school environment. They either felt uncomfortable asking teachers for additional help or believed teachers did not care enough to offer assistance. By the time they left traditional school settings, they often believed they were unable to learn.

After sharing these results with our community partners, my students distributed the report to other local organizations keenly interested in the issue. They also presented results in a CHE documentary film on dropouts that is still being distributed across the city. A year later, we presented the report at the annual American Educational Research Association conference in Denver (Long, Lemberger, Marsh, & Witt, 2010).

These findings were especially useful for our work with NPLB parents because the majority of them were dropouts. After learning when and how the trajectory of poor academic performance began and was perpetuated, we intentionally designed simple and natural lessons to help restore and rebuild parents' depleted levels of academic self-confidence. Each time they successfully completed an enjoyable reading or math activity in a workshop and practiced it again at home with their children, parents were accumulating new evidence that they could truly learn academic content and facilitate academic learning in their children (Long, 2011).

Fourth CBR Project: Parent Involvement in an Intermediate School

In fall 2009 my students and I collaborated with a newly appointed principal who wanted to explore options for improving parent involvement in an intermediate school. As we studied the existing parent involvement literature, we discovered findings on the importance of a teacher's trust in parents and students and how it significantly influences student learning (Goddard, Tschannen-Moran, & Hoy, 2001). This prompted us to add several survey items on trust to NPLB's existing parent and teacher measures.

Survey results from 57 parents suggested they were aware of their children's academic struggles but had limited contact with the school. Mean scores were high relative to activities at home, such as checking homework, practicing skills with children prior to a test, reading school notices, and talking about school with their children. Parents also reported trusting teachers and the school but wanted more positive communication with teachers. In comparison, teachers assessed parents as unable to help students in academic content, and trust in parents was rated low. Thus it appeared that the same disconnect between parents and teachers we had found at Austin-Phillips' primary school was also present in this intermediate school.

After analyzing the data, we presented our team's findings and recommendations to teachers, who were required by the principal to attend one of the four sessions we offered over a two-day period. At each session, we were stunned with the teachers' openly hostile responses to the data and our presentation. Most teachers denied parents' claims of supporting student learning at home, and almost everyone had a negative story to share about some past experience with a parent. Because of those painful experiences, distrust and resentment of parents was palpably evident in every session.

In spite of their critical remarks, however, a handful of teachers responded positively to our encouragement to build working relationships with parents and hosted a one-night Parent University the following semester. At the event, teachers offered rotating sessions on a variety of topics that parents wanted to learn to help their children. The school provided dinner and ESS students entertained children in the gym. The evening was very well attended and replicated the following year.

Fifth CBR Project: Teacher Trust

Our community partner for the next project (spring 2010) was a team of 11 parent support specialists (PSS), who had been hired by the local school district under their new federally funded involvement initiative. Each PSS was assigned to a different Title 1 school to conduct NPLB parent workshops and supervise 10 to 15 low-income parents as part-time helpers in their building. In most of the 11 buildings, however, teachers refused having parents work in their classrooms. Because of the teachers' actions, parents could only be hired as cafeteria, playground, or hall monitors. As a result, there were more applicants than positions for parents, even though funding was available to hire additional parents. Our community partners were stymied by the impasse and wondered how they could help teachers become interested in working with parents.

After discussing the previous intermediate school project's findings on teacher mistrust of parents with my new group of students, we decided to begin this CBR project by asking each PSS to rate the level of teacher trust in parents at his or her school using characteristics associated with trust: benevolence, reliability, competence, honesty, and openness (Tschannen-Moran & Hoy, 1999). We then requested the PSS team coordinator to rate each of the 11 schools on the same characteristics and found his scores were exactly the same as the PSS team's ratings. These tallies also showed that only two locations were categorized as high trust, and one of them was Austin-Phillips's school.

With this information, my students turned to the literature for guidance on how to develop teacher trust. Eventually, they created their own theoretical model and tested it by interviewing and observing two to three teachers at each of the 11 sites. In schools rated high trust by the PSS team, we found that teachers respected and understood parents, actively communicated with them, valued parents' supportive roles, and referred to parents as part of their team. In low-trust schools, teachers held low expectations for parents, and their responses tended to contain complaints about what parents were not doing.

Unfortunately, previous research strongly suggests that these levels of teacher mistrust across the majority of our community's Title 1 schools can be directly connected to the underachievement of students who have consistently struggled to learn. A study among 452 teachers from 47 urban elementary schools using achievement data from 2,536 fourth grade students showed that teacher trust in parents was comparable to teacher trust in students, and the latter was more likely to predict fourth grade reading and mathematics scores than socioeconomic status. The authors further noted that a teacher's trust in students and parents can "outweigh the effects of poverty" and "foster a context that supports student achievement, even in the face of poverty" (Goddard, Tschannen-Moran, & Hoy, 2001, p. 14).

Sixth CBR Project: Program Evaluation

Despite consistent encouragement to the district to formulate interim goals and options for moving ahead when the grant cycle expired, the two-year initiative abruptly ended in 2011 without plans to capitalize on its noteworthy results and momentum. NPLB was awarded a $6,000 Ganey Mini-Grant in 2012 from Notre Dame's Center for Social Concerns to assess its program effectiveness by analyzing the extensive qualitative data collected from 2009 to 2011 when the workshops were implemented in 11 schools. Our research team consisted of Notre Dame faculty members in sociology and romance languages; undergraduate students from ESS, the poverty studies minor, and an advanced Spanish class; a professor and undergraduate students in the school of education from another local higher education campus, Holy Cross College; three parents; and myself. For 18 months, we coded, tabulated, and drew conclusions from 33 focus-group transcripts and open-ended survey responses from 277 parents relative to changes attributable to participation in the program. Spanish students coded and evaluated responses from Spanish-speaking attendees (see Chapter 6 for a discussion of the effort with Spanish speakers).

Results showed all parents, regardless of race or ethnicity, gained knowledge about what involvement was and how to actively support their children's academic learning and development. These gains in knowledge and understanding were consistently linked to socioemotional and behavioral improvements in how they related to their children. They reported initiating learning activities and enjoying interactions with children as well as being more patient and confident in helping with homework. In regard to their children's learning outcomes, parents cited numerous examples of improved student attitudes about learning and increases in achievement. For example, one parent said, referring to her daughter, "Although she struggled a lot last year, now her report card was nothing but As and Bs. The information we got here was very helpful, and it made a big difference." In contrast to such positive themes, when parents expressed unsolicited comments about their children's schools, they tended to be more negative. For example, one parent said the following about a teacher's behavior: "I requested my son's missing assignments, but she didn't send them."

Lessons Learned About Parent Involvement

When the school district withdrew its extra financial support for building parent involvement in 2011, the responsibility for maintaining momentum and expanding parent involvement shifted to the shoulders of a few community organizations, like the Latino Task Force for Education, NPLB, and a small new initiative called Go-To Parents. To prepare for this additional responsibility, NPLB joined an innovative nonprofit organization, Fellow Irish Social Hub, which nurtures Notre Dame students, faculty, alumni, and local community members as social entrepreneurs. After receiving professional guidance and financial resources from their extensive network of experts, members of NPLB were able to create a business plan, file for federal tax-exempt 501(c)(3) status, enter a campus business competition, and begin marketing and selling its curriculum and training. Even these substantive efforts in one organization were not enough to maintain or improve levels of parent involvement throughout Title 1 schools in South Bend.

Nonetheless, the six CBR projects described in this chapter have provided invaluable insight on how to strategically move ahead in building parent involvement. Those findings were especially instrumental in reshaping our understanding in regard to the definition of *involvement* and the need for developing a culture of trust between parents and teachers.

Redefining the Concept of Parent Involvement

When NPLB first began developing its research materials, Greene and I were quickly frustrated with the existing surveys we found. Most of the survey items were informally sanctioned middle-class forms of involvement associated with being physically present in the building (e.g., attending school performances). We discovered this produced guilt and shame in some parents when we heard a father comment to his wife, "I thought I was a good parent until I took this survey."

To rectify this problem, we began substituting language from the qualitative data that was more reflective of parents' vocabulary and understanding. Rather than limiting examples of involvement to documenting how many times a parent participates in a list of narrowly defined activities linked with homework help or school-based activities, we created a broader and more inclusive concept of engagement that captured parents' personal interests in helping students, their knowledge of how to structure student enrichment activities, contacts with other parents, trusting interactions with school personnel, efficacious assessments of their own abilities, and opportunities to engage interactively with their children to support learning at home and in the community (e.g., trips to the library, museums).

This broader conceptualization of involvement inevitably yielded a richer and more complex portrait that more accurately reflected parents' challenges, values, and goals. Ultimately, the new measure we developed included more culturally appropriate terms using a uniform scale and open-ended items that could capture respondents' initial and final thoughts more effectively. This work has been presented in several national education conferences (e.g., Long et al., 2012), thus contributing to research in the field of parent involvement.

Creating a Culture That Supports Parent-Teacher Relationships

Our cumulative research results have shown that lack of parent involvement appears to exist when there is a lack of trusting parent-teacher working relationships. In our community's Title 1 schools, constructing these productive partnerships requires a three-prong solution. First, low-income parents need learning opportunities to rebuild awareness, knowledge, and skills in their ability to learn and forge new roles as supporters of academic learning. This is especially true for parents who struggled in school themselves. Second, strong levels of teacher distrust in parents must be dismantled. Third, productive parent-teacher partnerships require an environment that is proactively supporting the growth of trust between teachers and parents, which will then lead to higher student learning.

Such an environment will be saturated with a deep and extensive system of "beliefs, ideas, tastes and dispositions" (Langer de Ramirez, 2006, p. 2), more commonly referred to as a *culture*, that intentionally and persistently values the long-term development of productive parent-teacher partnerships. Because a culture is a grid through which an individual creates meaning, stereotypical conclusions about parents or teachers are reflective of a culture that tends to misread the other group's "aptitudes, intent, or abilities" (Delpit, 1992, p. 238). Creating a new culture is possible (Holland & Farmer-Hinton, 2009), but how does a community develop a culture that values and invests in parent-teacher relationships and involvement over the long haul?

Based on 15 years of experience in building a creative culture in one Kentucky community, Adam Russell (2013) concluded that developing a culture is not achieved through implementing a new program. Instead, programs are likely to fail unless they emerge from a supportive culture, because cultures are self-renewing and rooted in values and desires. This explains why most of the teachers in the intermediate school where my students and I conducted the CBR project were hostile to our research findings. Their existing culture opposed prioritizing parent engagement.

Although serendipity may factor into transformative change (Primavera & Martinez, 2013), foundational theories of leadership (Kotter, 1996) portray change as the result of orderly movement through specific stages. Russell's (2013) informal theory of building a culture similarly consists of six sequential steps that are analogous to developing a productive garden:

1. Clear the land.
2. Amend the soil.
3. Know when it is time to plant.
4. Water when needed.
5. Cultivate.
6. Celebrate the harvest.

This simple model helped me more thoroughly understand how Austin-Phillips used our CBR work to begin building a culture of support for productive parent-teacher partnerships throughout her building. She asked campus partners for help in assessing the terrain and identifying the types of barriers that existed and where they were located. After Mangeney's (2006) initial project helped identify some of those problems, she began addressing them. She began painstakingly and patiently removing the barren and negative mind-sets of teachers by addressing their fears of and objections to parents being more present in their building. When she heard teachers assessing parents' ability to support student academic development as being inadequate and beyond hope for change, she seized those opportunities to amend the soil by interjecting a different perspective.

At the right time, she moved ahead with her desire to plant and nurture a crop of involved parents. In addition to the numerous research design and curriculum meetings she participated in, Austin-Phillips also cotaught the first series with me. She personally visited the homes of every parent we had randomly selected to invite them to attend the first NPLB workshops. This enabled her to begin forming a deeper relationship with each parent attendee. When those parents dropped off or picked up their children, she used the moments to lavishly distribute encouragement. She also generously watered staff members who expressed an interest in the project and invited them to coteach a couple of sessions. As parents' engagement became more established, and they increased their verbal exchanges with teachers, she cultivated those developing connections and helped teachers or parents pull out weeds of misunderstanding before they choked out future relational growth.

A month after the first series of workshops ended at her school, Greene reported our research findings to Austin-Phillips' staff, while I observed their reactions. The pro-parent minority remained silent, while the hostile majority intensely made claims that parents had lied about their interactions on providing homework support or academic help. When I asked if any teachers would agree to meet with parents to discuss their issues, one teacher defiantly stated, "That's a great idea, but count me out." Rather than being discouraged, Austin-Phillips asked Greene to help her prepare six of the program graduates to talk with the entire staff about what the program meant to them and how their support had changed because of participation in the program.

There was a very noticeable change in the room's atmosphere during that subsequent meeting, primarily because parents spontaneously opened the dialogue by addressing each of their children's teachers by name and thanking them for their work in facilitating student learning. By the end of the presentation, many teachers lingered to talk graciously with parents, and their exchanges were mutually respectful. This meeting was the first indicator that the formerly barren field called parent involvement in Austin-Phillips' school might still yield a tasty crop worth celebrating.

Thus it was not an accident that the CBR study on teacher trust found that Austin-Phillips' school had become an environment of high teacher trust in parents. Her work indicated that it is possible to create a pro-parent culture even in a school with an initially hostile environment. This level of transformation, however, required a personal vision and enduring commitment to reach the long-term goal despite significant challenges.

Lessons Learned About CBR's Role in Facilitating Change

By using CBR to help develop parent involvement, we have learned that repeated CBR work performs two functions in facilitating change. First, it does an exceptional job in helping to unearth hidden truths and important clues regarding challenges that have plagued communities for extended periods of time. Prior to our work in CBR, when we witnessed a lack of eye contact or abrasive comments between parents and school personnel, we concluded that the individuals who had displayed those behaviors lacked common courtesy. After our research exposed the strong levels of animosity teachers expressed toward parents, we could classify those negative emotions as indicators of trust-reducing behaviors that were sabotaging posted policies on school websites or parent materials. Thus CBR provided us with broader and deeper insights into the hidden obstacles that lay below the surface with well-established and sizable roots. Once we were able to comprehensively grasp the full extent of these problems, we were able to revise our original ideas and construct a more realistic theory for increasing parent involvement.

Second, our CBR work provided us with unique opportunities for investing years in building enduringly strong and trusting working relationships across a community and its campuses. For example, after spending years collaborating with Austin-Phillips, we developed the type of productive and respectful partnership that continues to bear good fruit. We made a presentation together at a national conference in New York (Long & Austin-Phillips, 2007) and still consider ourselves colleagues. This same camaraderie is also evident among the members of the original ECG, although it had disbanded. Quite frankly, all of these partnerships very definitely reflect "benevolent, reliable, competent, honest and open" (Tschannen-Moran & Hoy, 1999, p. 189) responses associated with trust, whether they were with students, faculty, or community personnel.

When campus members are willing to work in partnerships at this level of vulnerability, it makes it much easier for the community to name other areas of need where faculty could provide assistance and guidance. For example, most nonprofit directors I know and work with are often immersed in a vicious cycle typical of a hand-to-mouth existence. Their organizations' livelihood and the people they serve are often totally dependent on the director's ability to generate new revenue for the organization, because grants rarely fund the maintenance of existing programming. Organizations with no regular stream of income to maintain day-to-day operations, by necessity, are more likely to focus their labor on short-term immediate goals rather than long-term change. They value and need the input and assistance from others outside their organizations who can help coordinate the type of large-scale strategic efforts described throughout the chapters in Part Three of this book that achieve community change. Forming partnerships through CBR not only highlights more effective solutions but also facilitates building working relationships that can jointly produce long-term solutions.

Conclusion

Because research is designed to identify viable solutions to problems, productive CBR partnerships enhance those typical results by forging another link in the safety net of relational support that surrounds the structure of any community. By its very nature, CBR helps shape a community's identity, direction, and purpose. Administrators who regard themselves and their campuses as part of the community see their resources as useful to the community and choose to use their extensive resources in creating authentically beneficial research partnerships with and for the community, and will undoubtedly build more powerful capacities for diminishing and eliminating the serious challenges many communities face on a daily basis.

In an atmosphere where community-campus communication about parent involvement had been virtually nonexistent before ECG began, the CBR findings described here continue to subtly influence our community. For example, we have new task forces and an adaptation of NPLB's curriculum is currently being used with preschool parents. Even though sustained support for a culture of parent involvement is still developing across our community, the undergraduate learning experience was rich and rewarding for every single student engaged in these projects. CBR thus made it possible to facilitate excellent instruction in campus classrooms and harness that valuable and rewarding instructional experience to work toward achieving positive change in a community.

References

Caspe, M., Lopez, M., & Wolos, C. (2006/2007). *Family involvement in elementary school children's education.* Cambridge, MA: Harvard Family Research Project.

Delpit, L. D. (1992). Education in a multicultural society: Our future's greatest challenge. *Journal of Negro Education, 61*(3), 237–249.

Goddard, R., Tschannen-Moran, M., & Hoy, W. (2001). A multilevel examination of the distribution and effects of teacher trust in students and parents in urban elementary schools. *Elementary School Journal, 102*(1), 3–17.

Greene, S., & Long, J. F. (2011). Flipping the script: Honoring and supporting parental involvement in an urban primary school. In C. Compton-Lilly & S. Greene (Eds.), *Bedtime stories and book reports* (pp. 15–26). New York, NY: Teachers College Press.

Holland, N. E., & Farmer-Hinton, R. L. (2009). Leave no schools behind: The importance of a college culture in urban public high schools. *High School Journal, 92*(3), 24–43.

Hoover-Dempsey, K., & Sandler, H. (1995). Parental involvement in children's education: Why does it make a difference? *Teachers College Record, 97*(2), 310–331.

Hoover-Dempsey, K. V., Walker, J. M. T., Sandler, H. M., Whetsel, D., Green, C. L., Wilkins, A. S., & Closson, K. E. (2005). Why do parents become involved? Research findings and implications. *Elementary School Journal, 106*(2), 105–130.

Kilbride, K. (2014, January 16). School district grades released. *South Bend Tribune,* A1–A2.

Kotter, J. P. (1996). *Leading change.* Boston, MA: Harvard Business School Press.

Langer de Ramirez, L. (2006). *Voices of diversity: Stories, activities, and resources for the multicultural classroom.* Upper Saddle River, NJ: Pearson.

Long, J. F. (2011). Transformative change: Parent involvement as a process of becoming. In C. Compton-Lilly & S. Greene (Eds.), *Bedtime stories and book reports* (pp. 40–50). New York, NY: Teachers College Press.

Long, J., & Austin-Phillips, D. (2007, November). No parents left behind: Honoring and supporting parental involvement in an urban primary school. In S. Greene (Chair), *Reframing parents' involvement in school: A model of community-based research.* Symposium conducted at the annual meeting of the National Council of Teachers of English, New York, NY.

Long, J. F., Lemberger, K., Caminiti, J., London, R. L., Weber, K., Reich, S., & Kenney, H. (2012, April). Developing teacher trust in parents. In A. M. Ochoa (Chair), *Promoting family, school, and community partnerships.* Roundtable conducted at the annual meeting of the American Educational Research Association, Vancouver, British Columbia, Canada.

Long, J. F., Lemberger, K., Marsh, M., & Witt, A. (2010, April). *Supporting academic development among dropouts.* Poster session presented at the annual meeting of the American Educational Research Association, Denver, CO.

Mangeney, J. (2006). *Understanding under-involvement: The involvement decisions of motivated low-SES parents.* Unpublished manuscript, University of Notre Dame, South Bend, IN.

Primavera, J., & Martinez, A. (2013). When university and community partner: Community engagement and transformative systems-level change. In H. E.

Fitzgerald & J. Primavera (Eds.), *Going public: Civic and community engagement* (pp. 309–322). East Lansing: Michigan State University Press.

Russell, A. (2013, October). *Developing a creative culture.* Paper presented at MorningStar Creative Arts Conference, Charlotte, NC.

Tschannen-Moran, M., & Hoy, W. (1999). Five faces of trust: An empirical confirmation in urban elementary schools. *Journal of School Leadership, 9*(3), 184–208.

Walker, J., Wilkins, A., Dallaire, J., Sandler, H., & Hoover-Dempsey, K. (2005). Parental involvement: Model revision through scale development. *Elementary School Journal, 106*(2), 85–104.

CONCLUSION

Themes, Challenges, and Thoughts About the Future

Mary Beckman

Thus book has the following central aims: (a) to offer examples, strategies, tools, and insights for incorporating community-based research (CBR) into one's teaching, advising, mentoring, and making curricular decisions, and (b) to show ways this can be done to enhance the possibility that the research results will lead to outcomes and even long-term impact in the communities where the work takes place. The following attempts to capture the major themes and challenges that are addressed in the process of fulfilling these aims. Finally, we suggest how such work can be deepened and strengthened even beyond what is described here.

CBR and the Disciplines

As a faculty member or other instructor, it makes sense to consider how CBR, conducted by undergraduates in your courses or even as your own scholarly work, is received in your primary discipline. The methods of inquiry used in one's discipline will likely be effective in a CBR initiative. As Frabutt and Graves explain in Chapter 1, methods from any discipline can be used in CBR. Many of the chapters in this book are written by faculty members whose students are indeed using the research methods of their teachers' fields. Mathematician Ethan Berkove and psychologist Jody Nicholson provide two examples, in Chapter 9 and Chapter 14.

It is also the case that some disciplines' methods already incorporate general features of CBR. In recounting the historical roots of CBR and its umbrella categories, Chapter 1 authors Frabutt and Graves inform readers about this possibility. The most obvious examples perhaps, are action research (AR) used by some in education and participatory action research (PAR), which some sociologists use; for these disciplines, the AR and PAR might be used interchangeably with CBR. Holter and Frabutt discuss this possibility in Chapter 10, where they focus on teaching graduate students. In any case, CBR emerged from AR and PAR and other discipline-based research methods (Strand, Cutforth, Stoecker, Marullo, & Donohue, 2003). Recognizing such links with one's disciplinary methods might encourage one to move forward with the use of CBR.

It might be, however, that the question to be investigated in a CBR project requires venturing beyond one's discipline-based research tools, as the methods in CBR should be the ones best suited for addressing the specific situation. A quantitatively oriented economist, for instance, might find that the information needed in a particular study is best obtained through focus groups, which he or she may know very little about. Parroquin describes this kind of occurrence in Chapter 6, where she notes that she did not have the qualitative tools needed for her project. She was able to turn to her community partner who had those skills. One of the pluses of the collaborative nature of CBR is that expertise beyond that of the academic researcher can likely be found on the community side as well as with academic colleagues if collaboration across disciplines is desired.

When exploring connections between one's own discipline and the requirements of a CBR initiative, it is also a good idea to consider how those in a particular field value CBR and engage scholarship generally. Some disciplines are more amenable to them than others, even sponsoring journals that devote space explicitly to such work; sociology and education are two such fields. In other cases, CBR is less well received. Even then, however, there are journals that accept such work, such as the *Journal of Higher Education Outreach and Engagement.* Also, some journals accept undergraduate research.

Furthermore, national organizations are developing standards for the evaluation of CBR and establishing review panels to critique work in association with a tenure or promotion file. More efforts of this nature are emerging all the time (Calleson, Kauper-Brown, & Seifer, 2005; "Community-Engaged Scholarship Toolkit," 2010; Driscoll & Lynton, 1999; *Evaluation Criteria for the Scholarship of Engagement,* 2002; Glassik, Huber, & Maeroff, 1997). In fact, there are quite a number of national organizations where kindred spirits can be found, such as the Engaged Scholarship Consortium (formerly known as the National Outreach Scholarship Conference), Community Campus Partnerships for Health, and, in particular for academics in the humanities, Imagining America. It is also worth noting that a number of schools have changed their tenure guidelines to be friendlier to this kind of scholarship, such as Portland State and Michigan State University.

Incorporating CBR Into Teaching and Learning

The chapters in Part Two of this book provide far-ranging examples of the incorporation of CBR into teaching. We suggest that anyone interested in designing or revising a course to include CBR follow guiding principles such as those presented by Pigza in Chapter 5. She suggests that thinking carefully in the planning stage about each of the elements of forming partnerships, objectives, the work process itself, evaluation, and reflection, can help ensure that CBR is incorporated well into any learning opportunity. Parroquin in Chapter 6 and Ruebeck in Chapter 7 explicitly demonstrate how this can be done.

Some courses, however, might parade as using CBR but do not follow through on all defined elements. As Quaranto and Stanley comment in Chapter 3: "Both of us have witnessed community-based research (CBR) done well and CBR that went so terribly wrong it should not have been called CBR" (p. 50). Owens-Manley in Chapter 12 offers some insight into the types of challenges that can hinder student course experiences from adhering to the basic principles of CBR. The instructor must decide when integrating CBR into a course how true he or she wants to be to the core defined elements described by Strand and colleagues (2003).

A related question not directly addressed in any of these chapters but worth considering is, What should be categorized as student research? For example, does a literature review suffice? In many cases, students can be extremely helpful to community organizations simply by providing them with a literature review of best practices, but not all departments or colleges in an institution would consider this sufficient to be labeled research. Although we tend to take a broad view of what can be counted as CBR for undergraduates, others may not. It is important to investigate how your own institutional culture or your program, department, school, or college defines undergraduate research (Beckman & Hensel, 2009) and then align CBR with this definition.

It is also worth remembering that students can be involved in CBR through multiple vehicles. As Bartel and Nigro describe in Chapter 8, students can engage in independent CBR if the culture of a campus supports it. Senior theses, directed readings, independent studies, even extracurricular work, can all feature CBR.

Students can also conduct CBR abroad, but this of course carries its own set of challenges, as described by Tryon and Steinhaus in Chapter 11. Many of those challenges are similar to the ones faced by students in any course taken outside their home country. For instance, currency differences or travel delays may occur on the logistical end; more substantive issues may likewise arise, such as acquiring an understanding of cultural norms sufficient to conduct CBR respectfully and effectively. Other challenges of using CBR away from one's home nation are more specific to CBR itself, such as dealing with unfamiliar institutional review board rules.

Depending on the degree to which engaged scholarship becomes prevalent in higher education, curricula may begin to incorporate it, as in the case at Cabrini College, described by Persichetti, Sturman, and Gingerich in Chapter 13. A review of their chapter might provide ideas for integrating CBR when your institution is revising its curriculum.

Time

Perhaps the foremost challenge in conducting CBR is time, and this challenge emerges at multiple levels. As Quaranto and Stanley point out in Chapter 3, faculty members' as well as community partners' time is at a premium. Faculty who are attempting to develop a course for the first time that involves CBR should allocate enough time to pace the CBR process appropriately. Parroquin discusses this issue in Chapter 6. In the course itself, the time element must be thought through so that students can collaborate with the community partner, complete the assigned research, deal with contingencies that generally occur in research, and engage in reflection. In Chapter 11, Tryon and Steinhaus also discuss time challenges when one is involving students in CBR in international academic initiatives. They address minor and major crises that can occur in international settings that can delay or even stop a project; if the effort is well planned, these factors will be less detrimental.

Overall, perhaps the most important allocation should be toward developing the type of trusting relationships that are fundamental for good CBR. Quaranto and Stanley talk about this challenge in Chapter 3, as does Long in Chapter 18. Quaranto and Stanley write about the value of developing synergy in partnerships to promote strong, sustained CBR efforts. Their chapter gives valuable guidance on how to find or develop this crucial element. It takes bonding experiences over time to create viable working partnerships that lead to sustained efforts. Long describes the Education Collaborative Group's regular meetings over meals as one example of how bonding can occur. Tryon and Steinhaus discuss the element of trust in Chapter 11. They emphasize the amount of time it takes for a faculty member to be sure that students' relationships in foreign countries will be sufficiently built on trust as well as on shared knowledge. This includes developing an understanding of and respect for different cultural norms and historical influences, flexibility, and the ability to identify common ground, commitments, and goals; these are all needed to create trust, and they do not happen overnight.

How Important Is a CBR Center?

Several of the contributors discuss directly, or more implicitly address, the value a center can have in assisting with the design and implementation of effective CBR. After reading these chapters, one might even argue that such a center is crucial for CBR to fulfill its ultimate potential in improving the community.

Perhaps Owens-Manley's work in Chapter 12 leaves the reader with the strongest sense that a CBR-type center is invaluable in this work. As the director of CBR at her college, she played a strong if not essential role in the CBR projects that most closely fit the ideal understanding of CBR and that attained the greatest effects in communities over time. Though not as explicit, the work described by Vinciguerra in Chapter 17 was largely guided by the primary staff person in a CBR-type center at his institution. Center funding supported the work done by Parroquin as discussed in Chapter 6, and guidance from a center played a significant role in the projects described by Bartel and Nigro in Chapter 8, Dailey and Dax in Chapter 15, and in two stages of Long's projects described in Chapter 18.

However, in other examples, a CBR center is absent, such as in marketing professor Ruebeck's and mathematician Berkove's experiences discussed in Chapter 7 and Chapter 9. In these two cases, CBR is part of individual courses. Persichetti, Sturman, and Gingerich in Chapter 13; Holter and Frabutt in Chapter 10; and Kezar and Rousseau in Chapter 16 likewise describe work that is unaffiliated with a CBR center or its equivalent. In these cases, however, CBR projects were integral parts of a well-structured sequence of curricular options.

It perhaps goes without saying that a college or university center that has resources, including staff time, to contribute to planning and conducting CBR can go a long way in assisting CBR to flourish over time. At the same time, departmental, programmatic, and curricular efforts can certainly provide sufficient support for engaging in CBR.

Going for Outcomes

Clearly an important theme throughout this book is that results from any CBR project should be used in communities, rather than put on a shelf or to provide information about student learning exclusively. One way to ensure that this purpose is achieved is to plan for it explicitly from the start of any CBR initiative. Even one-shot and short-term CBR can produce valuable information, as shown in the brief case study in Chapter 2. Blouin knew from the beginning that the results of his students' research would be used by a food co-op to make improvements in such things as pricing and selection of products, and indeed this is what occurred.

At the same time, it is important to think of the research as potentially having long-term effects. Research that is designed with an end in mind and in appropriate collaboration between academic and community partners can be used over time to make improvements in an organization whether or not faculty members or students continue to collaborate with the community partner. Also, it is worth it to follow up with the community partner to see what has resulted from students' efforts, even if the CBR was a single initiative. In doing this, faculty may find they can or want to assist the organization again at later points in time. Seeing that the work has had some effect is also likely to be a pleasurable and even inspiring and motivating experience.

Graduate students who take on CBR will find it beneficial to think in these terms as well. Departments and advisers may resist a graduate student's request to use a local CBR project as the basis for a thesis or dissertation, but arguing that the local project might be a pilot for a larger future study or that the results might be applied beyond the local area could be persuasive. Nicholson's experience with her dissertation study of children exposed to lead, described in Chapter 14, provides a case in point. Another example, although not based on material in this book, is the research of an engineering professor at the University of Notre Dame, James Schmiedeler, who collaborated with therapists at South Bend's Memorial Hospital in creating a new system to help people who have experienced brain injury to regain balance. The results of this collaborative work have positively affected more than 60 individuals locally, but the results of the research on this new system will assist people far beyond South Bend. We have numerous examples of collaborations in our area whose benefits extend far geographically.

Although it is time consuming, we are also urging those engaged in CBR to attempt to document how research results are used and if possible continue this documentation over time to show the value of the research. This helps any future professors or scholars who are interested in the same subject to see what has already been done and thus know where and how to effectively plug in to extend previous efforts.

Notre Dame's Colleges of Engineering and Science have joined the Center for Social Concerns to hire a person to assist their faculty in applying for National Science Foundation (NSF) grants that require evidence of what is referred to as *broader impact*. To obtain certain NSF grants, proposals must include ways the efforts will result in positive effects—termed broader impact—in communities. Because engineers and scientists are not necessarily trained in establishing the kind of partnerships with schools and other community organizations that will further such outcomes, this new position helps in the formation of such partnerships and assists with documenting results of work accomplished. Such evidence is expected to help faculty obtain similar grants in the future, as applicants will be able to show that Notre Dame has a track record of ensuring that impact is achieved. This is an example of how documenting and tracking of outcomes can be particularly useful.

On to Community Impact

Part Three of this book provides examples of collaborations that focus on social challenges in multiple ways. The chapters describe the efforts of faculty members and others to integrate CBR into their own and their students' work to contribute to the large-scale and long-term positive community change intended by these collaborations.

All efforts described in this last section involve community-wide initiatives in terms of geography. Some of the efforts described are broad; this means that work addresses multiple issues across a geographic area. Other endeavors are better characterized perhaps as deep in that they focus on single issues relevant across a community. All reflect movement away from the isolated impact approach, critiqued by Kania and Kramer (2011) and discussed in Chapter 2.

CBR and System Change

We have not addressed explicitly in this book an approach toward community impact that is of great interest to us as our own work evolves, which is using CBR explicitly toward system change (Foster-Fishman, Nowell, & Yang, 2007).

When we think of a system, we think of interacting parts. For example, from a systemic vantage point, housing and labor markets, the transportation system, and available health and child care services all intersect and interact. In an ideal world, all these factors would be considered simultaneously when trying to improve the system of public education. A system approach involves considering the interactions of the parts when determining how to support change. Since it is generally not possible to address all the interrelated factors at one time, some choices must be made about the best possible points for allocating effort. CBR can assist with such a determination.

To explain further, let's consider the work of the poverty commission in Virginia described by Dailey and Dax in Chapter 15. The poverty commission was a community-wide effort that produced initiatives to address transportation, housing, and other issues, with the hoped-for result of mitigating poverty.

If a systemic approach were taken, the poverty commission would have strategically and explicitly determined key issues to address to reduce poverty and then found ways to focus resources on those key issues. This is not exactly what happened. Dailey and Dax devote a section of their chapter to describing planned initiatives versus those that arise organically. As key facilitators of the effort, they chose to foster a number of initiatives that arose organically from poverty commission discussions. They urged action where energy and motivation appeared high, where the kind of synergy Quaranto and Stanley describe in Chapter 3 seemed to exist, rather than attempting to impose an agenda that many with an interest in the poverty commission may not have supported.

While the approach of the Poverty Commission is generally how we approach this work ourselves, we are suggesting here that to arrive at a system change, some collective body would have to determine which of the many issues involved in perpetuating the social challenge that is being addressed is the most important to focus resources on. And then resources would have been directed, for a time, toward that area.

In this situation, the role of CBR would be the same as described throughout this book, with one addition. CBR would be used to help the collective body determine the issues with the most potential for attaining the long-term goal. Thus, in addition to, or even instead of, assisting individual efforts or projects, such as the transportation initiative, Dailey's Washington and Lee students would have helped the poverty commission strategically determine the best focus for action on poverty.

City governments are clearly well suited to take this kind of systemic approach. Our local United Way has been attempting this, and the Urban League in Los Angeles, as discussed by Kezar and Rousseau in Chapter 16, seems to have done so as well.

Whoever the players are, the same community impact framework laid out in Chapter 2 could be used to assist the effort. That is, the guiding group would set a long-term goal and objectives. This oversight group, or a designated subgroup, would then check in regularly to ensure that actions aimed toward the goal were effective and that participation was robust enough to gain the kind of input and expertise needed to achieve success.

The Global Solidarity Partnership described by Vinciguerra in Chapter 17 seems to be in a good position to do what we are suggesting here. It is a long-standing body that already uses CBR and other engaged work to address multiple issues in Haiti, including coffee and craft production. Our question to that partnership would be: As your members decide what issues to work on next, is it possible for your students to help you identify one or two key efforts that will best enable the chosen geographic area to attain community development or, perhaps put more practically, to reduce poverty? Maybe greater resources would then be applied toward coffee production as the best activity for poverty reduction, or perhaps there would be a new focus for the efforts of the partnership. This shift in approach need not be dramatic; it would still be possible to support artisans and energy production, as is currently being done through the partnership. However, it would give explicit attention to the overall system in which a variety of social challenges contribute and interact.

Remembering the Old Saying About Learning to Fish

We have just asserted that the same research projects could be of value whether or not a system approach is taken. If the Global Solidarity Partnership determined that coffee was the best issue for research and action to further the group's goal, this would not necessarily preclude CBR undertakings on artisan work and energy production. A situation could arise, however, where a conflict occurs between certain types of research investment and furthering the kind of system change that would be ideal for reaching the goal. This would be a case where certain CBR projects would be putting research resources toward a giving-someone-a-fish approach when the system analysis called for a learning-to-fish approach.

The following example is hypothetical, intended to make the basic point. Let's say a coalition aims to reduce food insecurity in a geographic area. To assist the coalition, CBR is undertaken to help area food banks determine if they are effectively reaching hungry people with their food. Also, let's assume the coalition as a whole has involved students in conducting research to determine the most effective way to address the food security challenge in the area, and the coalition concludes that the focus should be on local food production. In such a case, it is conceivable that continuing to put scarce research resources toward assisting food banks would reduce the ability of the group to improve local food production. In this situation, it might be that resources should be shifted toward figuring out ways to support local food production, similar to the learning-to-fish approach, and away from distribution of food, the giving-someone-a-fish charity model.

Given the state of social challenges in our communities in the United States, it is perhaps unlikely that many scenarios exist where those involved in CBR would need to shift research attention away from one area to direct it to an area that would support a larger system change. Nonetheless, we believe it is important to be mindful of possible contradictions, especially if a partnership aims to address concerns from a system level. It is possible that in addressing the immediate need, such as hunger, the deep causes are invisible or ignored; these deeper issues would become apparent if the system were the object of attention.

We are clearly urging, however, that coalitions and other groups working toward community impact consider how they might use CBR to assist in getting information that will help them further important system change. As we evolve in our own work of using CBR to foster community impact, we will be considering this approach further. We hope that readers of this book will be joining us in this exploration.

References

Beckman, M., & Hensel, N. (2009). Making explicit the implicit: Defining undergraduate research. *CUR Quarterly, 29*(4), 40–44.

Calleson, D., Kauper-Brown, J., & Seifer, S. D. (2005). *Community-engaged scholarship toolkit.* Retrieved from depts.washington.edu/ccph/toolkit-intro.html

Community engaged scholarship toolkit. (2010). Retrieved from ccph.memberclicks .net/ces-toolkit

Driscoll, A., & Lynton, E. A. (1999). *Making outreach visible: A guide to documenting professional service and outreach.* Washington, DC: American Association of Higher Education.

Evaluation criteria for the scholarship of engagement. (2002). Retrieved from www .scholarshipofengagement.org/evaluation/evaluation_criteria.html

Foster-Fishman, P., Nowell, B., & Yang, H. (2007). Putting the system back into systems change: A framework for understanding and changing organizational and community systems. *American Journal of Community Psychology, 39*(3/4), 197–215. doi:10.1007/s10464-007-9109-0

Glassick, C., Huber, M., & Maeroff, G. (1997). *Scholarship assessed: Evaluation of the professoriate.* San Francisco, CA: Jossey-Bass.

Kania, J., & Kramer, M. (2011). Collective impact. *Stanford Social Innovation Review, 9*(1), 36–41.

Strand, K. J., Cutforth, N., Stoecker, R., Marullo, S., & Donohue, P. (2003). *Community-based research and higher education: Principles and practices.* San Francisco, CA: Jossey-Bass.

EDITORS AND CONTRIBUTORS

Editors

Mary Beckman is associate director for academic affairs and research at the University of Notre Dame Center for Social Concerns. An economist and faculty member, she codeveloped Notre Dame's poverty studies interdisciplinary minor and has codirected and taught in the program. She developed and directs a program in community-based research that offers grants to teams of faculty, community partners, and students to conduct research on issues of local concern. Beckman was a faculty member at Lafayette College in Easton, Pennsylvania, for many years where, in addition to her teaching, scholarship, and other administrative work, she directed a first-year seminar writing program and created with a colleague the college's writing-across-the-curriculum program. Her teaching experience is extensive, focusing in economics and undergraduate writing as well as on multidisciplinary content. Her publications can be found in journals including *Journal on Excellence in College Teaching, Journal of Higher Education Outreach and Engagement, Review of Radical Political Economics*, and *Women's Studies Quarterly* and in a number of books including *Handbook of Engaged Scholarship: The Contemporary Landscape* (Vol. 2; Michigan State University Press, 2010) and *Teaching the "isms": Feminist Pedagogy Across the Disciplines* (Towson University Institute for Teaching and Research on Women, 2010). The focus of her research and writing currently is on the impact of academic community engagement in communities.

Joyce F. Long is a research analyst in Memorial Hospital-South Bend's Community Health Enhancement Department. She is part of a team that strengthens the impact of local initiatives (e.g., Healthy Diabetics, Aging in Place, Unity Gardens) on the long-term health of the community, broadly defined. As a former faculty member at the University of Notre Dame in the education, schooling, and society minor, she cofounded No Parent Left Behind, a locally implemented program that helps empower parents with skills and knowledge to academically support their children. In 2013 she adapted the methodology and content for parents of preschool children in Roma communities across Eastern Europe. She currently teaches those workshops in

Slovakia and to Hispanic families in South Bend through her work with the Latino Task Force for Education. Her research interests include how interest develops, creativity, community-based research, and learning processes. Long's publications include journal articles and book chapters on motivation and parent engagement (e.g., *Bedtime Stories and Book Reports: Connecting Parent Involvement and Family Literacy* [Teachers College Press, 2011]). She earned her PhD in social and cultural foundations with a specialization in educational psychology and curriculum at The Ohio State University.

Contributors

Anna Sims Bartel is the associate director of the Center for Engaged Learning + Research at Cornell University. She has taught and built programs for campus-community partnerships and community-based teaching and research at several higher education campuses, including Cornell University, Wartburg College, and Bates College. Prior to her move to Cornell, she was associate director of the Harward Center for Community Partnerships at Bates College, where she founded the Community-Based Research Fellows Program, and served as vice chair of the board of Community Concepts, a three-county community action agency in central and western Maine. She also led a number of projects in public humanities and civil discourse for the Maine Humanities Council. Her PhD is in comparative literature from Cornell University.

Ethan Berkove is a professor of mathematics at Lafayette College. His formal training is in pure mathematics, but he developed an interest in mathematical applications while a postdoctoral Davies Fellow at the U.S. Military Academy at West Point, New York. He enjoys teaching mathematical modeling and continues to look for interesting applications of mathematics, particularly those with a community-based component. Berkove has been coprincipal investigator on a National Science Foundation Research Experience for Undergraduates grant at Lafayette College. He received his PhD in mathematics from the University of Wisconsin–Madison.

Don E. Dailey is the principal consultant for Dailey Research Consulting, where he brings extensive experience and expertise in community research and program evaluation to support educational and social initiatives. He previously served as assistant director of the Pace Center for Civic Engagement at Princeton University and as visiting associate professor of education and community-based research at Washington and Lee University. His interests cover a wide range of issues in K–12 reform and higher education as well as building capacity for community research and program evaluation across other public issues. He played a leadership role in forming the Commission on Poverty in Rockbridge County, Virginia, and in designing and launching the National High School Center in Washington, DC. He currently resides in the greater Philadelphia area where he has consulted with Research for Better Schools and other agencies and colleges. He volunteers with the Coalition to Shelter and Support the Homeless in Bucks County, Pennsylvania, and enjoys playing the fiddle. Dailey received his PhD in policy development and program evaluation with a concentration in education policy from Vanderbilt University.

David Dax is the retired executive director of the United Way of Rockbridge in Lexington, Virginia. Since retiring, he has been involved in several community-based volunteer and consulting activities. Prior to serving at the United Way, Dax was the executive director of the Franklin Township Food Bank in Somerset County, New Jersey. He has also served as the interim executive director for an affordable housing foundation in New York City and has provided consulting services in the areas of strategic planning and implementation to faith-based organizations, including the Newark (NJ) Presbytery. He also served as project director for the Presbyterian Center at Newark. Dax spent 25 years working in the fields of regional planning, housing, and community development in New York City and Albany, New York. He was one of the founders and the first president of the Capital District Habitat for Humanity affiliate in Albany. He has a master's degree in urban planning from the New York University Wagner School of Public Service.

Timothy K. Eatman is associate professor of higher education in the school of education at Syracuse University. He also currently serves as faculty codirector of Imagining America: Artists and Scholars in Public Life, the national consortium of more than 100 colleges, universities, and community-based organizations working at the nexus of publicly engaged scholarship and the cultural disciplines (humanities, arts, and design fields). Eatman describes himself as an educational sociologist, survey researcher, and overall student of higher education, who advances publicly engaged scholarship that centers on equity issues in higher education. He earned an MEd from Howard University, PhD from the University of Illinois at Urbana-Champaign and completed a postdoctoral fellowship at the University of Michigan's Center for the Study of Higher and Postsecondary Education. The recipient of the 2010 Early Career Research Award for the International Association for Research on Service Learning and Community Engagement, Eatman often consults for higher education associations, foundations, networks, and institutions conducting collaborative research to address pressing public problems. He is a nationally recognized higher education leader regularly invited to offer keynotes, workshops, and consultancies. He served as a member of the 2015 Advisory Panel for the Carnegie Engagement Classification for Community Engagement. Eatman has published work in the *Journal of Educational Finance, Readings on Equal Education, Diversity & Democracy, Liberal Education, Huffington Post* and has written several other book chapters and reports.

James M. Frabutt is the director of inclusive education and a faculty member in the Remick Leadership Program in the Alliance for Catholic Education at the University of Notre Dame. He also serves as the director of academic community engagement in the Office of the Provost. His research and engagement interests have spanned the areas of teacher action research, children's mental health, community safety, and Catholic education. He has a doctoral degree in human development and family studies from the University of North Carolina at Greensboro.

Emily Geiger-Medina graduated from the University of Notre Dame in 2015, where she studied sociology and psychology. She has been involved in a variety of service organizations, including the Boys & Girls Club of St. Joseph County, Indiana. She also spent eight weeks during the summer of 2014 at Open Arms Home for Children in Komga, South Africa, as an international summer service-learning student through Notre Dame's Center for Social Concerns. Her research and course work focused primarily on the education of minority groups. She is currently working as a survey associate at Mathematica Policy Research.

Jeff Gingerich is the provost and vice provost for academic affairs at Cabrini College, in Pennsylvania, where he is also a faculty member in the sociology and criminology department. Prior to joining Cabrini, Gingerich was associate professor of sociology at Bluffton University, in Ohio. Much of his life's work prior to entering higher education was shaped by six years as a voluntary service worker in New Orleans, Louisiana, where he coordinated conflict resolution services at the Twomey Center for Peace Through Justice at Loyola University. He received his doctoral degree in sociology at the University of Pennsylvania.

Kelly N. Graves is the executive director of the Center for Behavioral Health and Wellness at North Carolina A&T State University and an associate professor in the Department of Human Development and Services. She has more than 15 years of experience working with community-based programs to bridge the gap between research and practice by developing systems using community-based research approaches. She is the author of *Responding to Family Violence: A Research-Based Guide for Therapists* (Routledge, 2012). She also is a consultant with the U.S. Department of Justice, Office for Training and Technical Assistance, in the areas of trauma, trauma-informed care, and crime victim services. Graves received her PhD in clinical psychology, completed her clinical internship at Emory University School of Medicine, and is a licensed clinical psychologist in the state of North Carolina.

Anthony C. Holter is the executive director of the Fulcrum Foundation in Seattle, Washington, founded to encourage support for Catholic schools in the archdiocese of Seattle. Prior to his appointment at Fulcrum, Holter was a faculty member of the Mary Ann Remick Leadership Program in the Alliance for Catholic Education at the University of Notre Dame. While there, he was also director of program evaluation and research, and focused his own research on how Catholic school principals use sound inquiry and reliable data to make important decisions in their school communities. Holter earned his PhD in educational psychology from the University of Wisconsin–Madison.

Adrianna Kezar is a professor of higher education at the University of Southern California and codirector of the Pullias Center for Higher Education. Kezar is a national expert on non-tenure-track faculty, change, governance, and leadership in higher education. Her books include: *Embracing Non-Tenure Track Faculty* (Routledge, 2012) and *Understanding the New Majority of Non-Tenure Track Faculty* (Jossey-Bass, 2010). Kezar holds a PhD in higher education administration from the University of Michigan.

Brooke Kiener is an assistant professor in the Whitworth University Theatre Department. She works extensively in the field of community-based performance and has cowritten and directed productions in collaboration with community activist groups on such topics as socioeconomic discrimination, injustice in the justice system, and sustenance and sustainability. She has published several articles that examine the complexities of community-based performance in the context of higher education. She also serves as the chair of the board of directors for Spokane Arts. Kiener holds an MFA in interdisciplinary art from Goddard College.

Jody Nicholson is an assistant professor in the Department of Psychology at the University of North Florida. Her teaching and research philosophies are largely influenced by community-based practices. Her primary line of research examines how parents fit into models of health behavior change relevant to their children's physical development in early childhood. She earned her PhD in developmental psychology from the University of Notre Dame and completed a postdoctoral fellowship in pediatric psychology at St. Jude Children's Research Hospital.

Georgia Nigro is professor of psychology at Bates College. She joined the Bates faculty in 1983, after earning a PhD from Cornell University. At Cornell, she worked with the Consortium for Longitudinal Studies, which carried out some of the early evaluations of preschool programs that led to widespread support for Head Start. These early lessons in bridging the domains of research, practice, and policy serve her well today. She is a member of Imagining America's workgroup on Assessing the Practices of Public Scholarship, which focuses on community impact.

Judith Owens-Manley is the director for the Center for Community Engagement & Learning at the University of Alaska Anchorage and clinical associate professor in the School of Social Work. She moved to Alaska in 2010 from upstate New York where she served in a similar position at Hamilton College. She is interested in welcoming communities for refugee resettlement and coauthored *Bosnian Refugees in the U.S.: New Communities, New Cultures* (Springer, 2006). In addition to working in higher education, Owens-Manley was a social worker in community organizations and in a psychotherapy private practice for more than 20 years. She trains faculty at the university in the pedagogy of community engagement and supports students in becoming active and engaged citizens through a Civic Engagement Certificate program. Owens-Manley received her PhD in social welfare from the University at Albany, State University of New York.

Rachel Parroquin is the director of Spanish Community-Based Learning at the University of Notre Dame. She holds a joint appointment with the university's Department of Romance Languages and the Center for Social Concerns. Her varied teaching experience includes first grade through university-level students in English as a second language and Spanish. Conference presentations with community partners include "Reflective Teaching and Learning That Become Service" at Ohio State University's service-learning conference (October 2012, Columbus, OH). Her interests include reflection as a pedagogical tool, the use of portfolios in assessment, and integrated curriculum. She received her EdD from Loyola University Chicago.

Amy Lee Persichetti is an assistant professor in the English department of Cabrini College, in Pennsylvania. In 2005 she piloted community-based research in Cabrini's core curriculum. For the past five years, she has been instrumental in the development of Cabrini's signature curriculum, Engagements With the Common Good. Her partnership with Laurel House has served as a campuswide model for sustainable community engagement. Now in its eighth year, the partnership has helped to sustain a three-year grant from the Office of Juvenile Justice and Delinquency Prevention for domestic violence education from 2010 to 2013. She earned her EdD at Widener University.

Jennifer M. Pigza is the director of the Catholic Institute for Lasallian Social Action, the center for academic and cocurricular service-learning at Saint Mary's College of California. She is also a faculty member in the leadership graduate studies programs. After several years in the nonprofit industry, Jennifer has worked in higher education for more than 20 years. She is interested in critical pedagogy, student learning and critical reflection, Catholic social teaching's influence on engaged pedagogy, nurturing campus-community partnerships, strategic planning for mission alignment, and institutionalizing community engagement. Her publications include "Navigating Leadership Complexity Through Critical, Creative, and Practical Thinking," in *Innovative Practices for Leadership Learning* (Jossey-Bass, 2015). She received her doctorate in the social foundations of education at the University of Maryland.

Jessica Quaranto is currently pursuing a master's in counseling psychology at the Chicago School of Professional Psychology in Washington, DC. Most recently, she served as the program development manager at the Columbia Heights/Shaw Family Support Collaborative in the District of Columbia. In addition to direct program evaluation and research experience in youth violence prevention, Quaranto has worked in higher education and community settings to facilitate and develop community-based research projects. She currently advises several nonprofits in the Washington, DC region as a board member and volunteer. She holds a BS in applied mathematics from the University of Notre Dame.

Sylvia Rousseau has been a professor of clinical education and an urban scholar for the University of Southern California Rossier School of Education since 2006, where she teaches in the EdD program, focusing on instructional leadership, diversity, and organization in the K–12 concentration. Her research interests include reforming systems and structures to organize urban schools for learning, the relationship between culture and cognition in promoting learning for all students, deepening understandings of literacy acquisition in urban schools, and exploring university and K–12 partnerships. Rousseau was a local district superintendent and a former high school principal. During her tenure as superintendent, she formed partnerships with universities, school boards, and communities to create systemic change in the urban schools. Her EdD degree is from Pepperdine University.

Christopher S. Ruebeck is an associate professor in the Department of Economics at Lafayette College in Easton, Pennsylvania. His experience with community-based research began with a project organized by the Lehigh Valley Research Consortium (LVRC) in 2009. He has been on the LVRC Executive Committee since 2010 and also recently joined the steering committee for Lafayette College's new Center for Community Engagement. Ruebeck has published in the economics fields of industrial organization and labor, with papers on theory, empirical studies, and computational work. His research and curricular initiatives have received funding from the National Science Foundation, the Princeton Corporation for National and Community Service, the Mellon Foundation, and other sources. Ruebeck received his PhD in economics from Johns Hopkins University.

Paul Schadewald is the associate director of the Civic Engagement Center in the Institute for Global Citizenship at Macalester College. He develops curricular civic engagement, community-based research, and public scholarship projects, and facilitates faculty development programs on civic and urban engagement. He has research interests in urban studies, public history, and religious studies. He serves on the National Advisory Board for the Imagining America consortium and is co-coordinator of Imagining America's Research Group on Engaged Undergraduate Education. Schadewald received his PhD in history from Indiana University, Bloomington.

Debra Stanley is founder and executive director of Imani Unidad, a community-based not-for-profit organization and serves as a community-based learning coordinator through the University of Notre Dame's Center for Social Concerns. Her research interests relate to the influence of community needs and norms on learning and behavioral health outcomes. She is also concerned with data collection to identify gaps and ways to improve service delivery.

Norbert Steinhaus has been a board member of Wissenschaftsladen Bonn (Bonn Science Shop) since 1990. For the past 15 years he cooperated in international projects on training and mentoring Science Shops, citizen participation in science and technology, and responsible research and innovation. He coordinated the European projects Exploring the Ground: Fostering Scientific Understanding in Primary Schools, an educational project for primary schools and kindergartens, and Soufflearning, a project for the transfer of innovation in training staff of small and medium entrepreneurs. He is involved in three European Commission–funded projects: RRI-Tools (building a better relationship between science and society), Enhancing Responsible Research and Innovation Through Curricula in Higher Education (improving student and staff capacity in higher education), and Smart Grid Protection Against Cyber Attacks (awareness raising and engagement across 29 countries). Since the end of 2007, he has been the coordinator and international contact point for Living Knowledge (building partnerships for public access to research), the international Science Shop network, and the organization of national and international workshops and conferences. In 2014 he was a member of the steering committee for the Science Innovation and Society—Achieving Responsible Research and Innovation conference, which was organized by the National Research Council of Italy and held in Rome during the 2014 Italian presidency of the European Union.

Beth Sturman has been the executive director of Laurel House in the Philadelphia area of Pennsylvania since 2005. Prior to moving to Pennsylvania, Sturman worked in the San Francisco Bay area in a variety of human services positions, including serving as the executive director for the San Leandro Shelter for Women and Children where she was instrumental in helping the organization develop into a multiservice agency for low-income and battered women and their families. Most of Sturman's professional work has been with families and often with single female heads of households. She is committed to helping women develop the confidence and self-sufficiency as well as the connections and opportunities to succeed at home and in the workplace. Sturman completed her master's degree in public administration from California State University at Hayward (now known as California State University, East Bay).

Elizabeth Tryon is assistant director for community-based learning at the Morgridge Center for Public Service, University of Wisconsin–Madison, working with community partners and faculty and academic staff across all disciplines to develop community-based learning and research. She directs the Community-University Exchange, a Science Shop model for coordinating and streamlining academic-community projects, and is cofounder of the Midwest Knowledge Mobilization Network. She teaches a course on community-based learning/community-based research pedagogy, speaks at and conducts faculty-staff and graduate student development workshops in North America and Europe, and serves on numerous planning and review committees for national and international groups. Among other publications, she is coeditor with Randy Stoecker of *The Unheard Voices: Community Organizations and Service-Learning* (Temple University Press, 2009). She earned an MA in education from Edgewood College.

Anthony Vinciguerra is director of the Center for Community Engagement (formerly known as the Center for Justice and Peace) at St. Thomas University, in Miami Gardens, Florida, where he facilitates the university's community-based learning and research activities. These initiatives apply university resources to social concerns locally in North Miami-Dade County, regionally in central Florida with the immigrant farmworker community, and internationally through the university's involvement in three long-term development projects in the Catholic Diocese of Port-de-Paix, Haiti. A graduate of the College of the Holy Cross and the Graduate Theological Union, the majority of Vinciguerra's work has focused on addressing issues of religion, poverty, and sustainable development in a Christian and interfaith context. He has worked with Jesuits in eastern Europe, taught theology and social ethics in the United States, and lived and worked at a halfway house for Central American refugees. His studies have also taken him from Italy to Morocco, Cuba, and Cambodia.

Danielle Wood is the assistant director of community-based research and impact at the Center for Social Concerns at the University of Notre Dame. She facilitates connections between community partners and faculty/academic staff for community-based research and development of collective impact. Prior to her doctoral work, Wood worked in consulting and the non-profit sector. Her research has included examining community quality-of-life indicator programs and their effectiveness for facilitating social change. Wood received her PhD in urban and regional planning from the University of Wisconsin-Madison. She is interested in the evaluation of complex initiatives, as well as asset-based community development, participatory democracy, resilience, and sustainability and the relationships among them.

INDEX

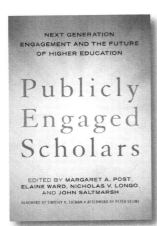

Publicly Engaged Scholars

Next Generation Engagement and the Future of Higher Education

Edited by Margaret A. Post, Elaine Ward, Nicholas V. Longo and John A. Saltmarsh

Foreword by Timothy K. Eatman

Afterword by Peter Levine

"*Publicly Engaged Scholars* is both unflinching in its presentation of the challenges—personal, professional, political—facing those who seek to transform higher education for the greater good and hopeful in its demonstration of the persistence and adaptability of engaged scholarship. Anyone concerned about higher education's contribution to democracy should read it."—*Andrew J. Seligsohn, President, Campus Compact*

Sty/us

22883 Quicksilver Drive
Sterling, VA 20166-2102

Subscribe to our e-mail alerts: www.Styluspub.com

Also available from Stylus

Engaging Higher Education
Purpose, Platforms and Programs for Community Engagement
Marshall Welch
Foreword by John A. Saltmarsh

"Rarely in a maturing scholarly field does a volume provide both breadth and depth of scholarship on community engagement, but Marshall Welch's volume accomplishes this feat masterfully. Welch provides an overview of the community engagement field in its current state, rooted in research and scholarly analysis. From its historical origins as a movement to the evolution of community engagement as a field, this volume extends an evidence-based synthesis of how higher education systems structure and implement community engagement, as well as a 'how-to' for higher education institutions. It will serve multiple purposes for higher education administrators, faculty, community engagement center directors, and graduate students in education."—**Patrick M. Green**, Founding Director, Center for Experiential Learning, Loyola University Chicago; Past Board Chair, International Association for Research on Service-Learning and Community Engagement

Engaged Research and Practice
Higher Education and the Pursuit of the Public Good
Betty Overton-Adkins, Penny A. Pasque and John C. Burkhardt
Foreword by Tony Chambers

"READ this book! The essential messages among the pages are not the first or final words regarding higher education's special relationship with the society that created and supports it. Sit with it. Put it down and pick it up again later. It shifts perspective kaleidoscopically; what you see depends on where you stand at any given moment. The messages encourage reflections, as all good work should do. Argue with the perspectives outlined in the following pages. Curse and correct the messages. But don't leave the messages and their reflections be. . . . Doing so begins the end of engagement and signals the irrelevance of scholarship. Engaged scholarship begs for engagement. Not necessarily agreement or blind fidelity . . . but stringent and earnest engagement.

"If nothing else, this collection calls higher education to question, again, its claim to relevance at a time in American society when neoliberal and commercial objectives of higher education are winning out over the broader life sustaining objectives of justice, knowledge, compassion, and community"—*from the Foreword by* **Tony Chambers**

(Continues on previous page)